ABORIGINAL CHILD WELFARE, SELF-GOVERNMENT AND THE RIGHTS OF INDIGENOUS CHILDREN

For Tim

Aboriginal Child Welfare, Self-Government and the Rights of Indigenous Children

Protecting the Vulnerable Under International Law

SONIA HARRIS-SHORT
University of Birmingham, UK

Routledge
Taylor & Francis Group
LONDON AND NEW YORK

First published 2012 by Ashgate Publishing

2 Park Square, Milton Park, Abingdon, Oxon OX14 4RN
711 Third Avenue, New York, NY 10017, USA

Routledge is an imprint of the Taylor & Francis Group, an informa business

First issued in paperback 2016

British Library Cataloguing in Publication Data
Harris-Short, Sonia.
Aboriginal child welfare, self-government and the rights of indigenous children : protecting the vulnerable under international law.
1. Indigenous children--Legal status, laws, etc.--Australia. 2. Indigenous children--Legal status, laws, etc.--Canada. 3. Child welfare--Australia. 4. Child welfare--Canada. 5. Aboriginal Australians--Politics and government. 6. Indigenous peoples--Canada--Politics and government. 7. Indigenous peoples--Canada--Government relations. 8. Self-determination, National--Canada. 9. Children (International law) 10. Indigenous peoples (International law)
I. Title
341.4'852-dc22

Library of Congress Cataloging-in-Publication Data
Harris-Short, Sonia.
Aboriginal child welfare, self-government and the rights of indigenous children : protecting the vulnerable under international law / by Sonia Harris-Short.
p. cm.
Includes bibliographical references and index.
ISBN 978-1-4094-1954-9 (hardback)
1. Indigenous children--Legal status, laws, etc.--Canada.
2. Indigenous children--Legal status, laws, etc.--Australia. I. Title.
K3248.C55H37 2011
344.03'27089--dc23

2011027175

ISBN 978-1-4094-1954-9 (hbk)
ISBN 978-1-138-26108-2 (pbk)

Contents

Table of Cases

Australia

C v T (1985) 10 Fam LR 458
Cubillo v Commonwealth [1999] FCA 518
Davis & Spring [2007] FamCA 1149
In the Marriage of Goudge [1984] FLC 91: 313
Inquest into the death of Deborah Leanne Melville-Lothian [2010] NTMC 7
Inquest into the death of Kunmanara Forbes [2009] NTMC 24
Jones v Darragh; Department of Community Services (Interveners) (1992) 15 Fam LR 757
Jones v Minister, Community Services [2001] NSWADT 192
Mabo v The State of Queensland (No. 2) [1991–1992] 175 C.L.R. 1
Minister for Health & Community Services v NB, KPP, HPP [2007] NTMC 69
Re AAA [2006] QCST 1
Re GAA [2007] QCST 14
Re Timothy [2010] NSWSC 524
RJ v Department of Communities (Child Safety Services) [2010] QCAT 619
Sheldon v Weir (No. 3) [2010] FamCA 1138
Torrens v Fleming & Anor (1980) FLC 75: 305
Trevorrow v State of South Australia (No 5) [2007] SASC 285
UI & UJ v Minister for Community Services [2006] NSWADT 16

Canada

A.L. & J.L. v D.K. & M.W. (2000) BCSC 480
Alberta (Director of Child Welfare) v Y [2002] 1 C.N.L.R. 11
Alberta (Director of Child, Youth and Family Enhancement) v T.S. and E.D. (2009) ABQB 246
Beckman v Little Salmon/Carmacks First Nation (2010) SCC 53
Brown v Canada (Attorney General) (2010) ONSC 3095
Campbell v British Columbia (Attorney General) [2000] 4 C.N.L.R. 1
C.D.R1. and C.D.R2. v Native Child and Family Services of Toronto (2007) CFSRB 20
Children's Aid Society of Owen Sound and County of Grey v M.B. [1985] O.J. No. 737 (QL)
C.J.K. v Children's Aid Society of Metropolitan Toronto [1989] 4 C.N.L.R. 75
Delgamuukw v British Columbia [1997] 3 S.C.R. 1010

Denton v Department of Community Resources and S.P. and R.L. and C.M.P. (2008) SKCA 48
Dilico Anishinabek Family Care v M.T., A.C. and M'Chigeeng First Nation (2010) ONCJ 105
Director of Child, Family and Community Service v L.S.N. (2008) BCPC 0402
Director of Youth Protection v A, B, C, and Band Council A (2007) QCCQ 13341
FNCFCS et al v Attorney General of Canada [2011] CHRT 4
Haida Nation v British Columbia (Minister of Forests) [2004] 3 S.C.R. 511
H.D. v M.H. (1997) 156 D.L.R. (4th) 548 and [1999] 1 S.C.R. 328
Jane Doe v Awasis Agency of N. Manitoba (1989) 72 D.L.R. (4th) 739
J.F.T. v C.A.S. [1993] B.C.J. No. 864 (QL)
John v Superintendent of Child Welfare (1979) [1982] 1 C.N.L.R. 40
Kenora-Patricia Child and Family Services v D.O. [2001] 4 C.N.L.R. 103
Kenora-Patricia Child and Family Services v L.P. and S.P. [2001] 4 C.N.L.R. 114
Kenora-Patricia Child and Family Services v Rose F. [1988] O.J. No. 2624 (QL)
K.J.S. v M.T. [2001] 4 C.N.L.R. 96
L.O. and S.O. v Superintendent of Child Welfare [1984] N.W.T.R. 295
Mi'Kmaw Family and Children Services of Nova Scotia v J.P. and I.M. (2007) NSFC 19
Ministry of Social Services v LB (2009) SKQB 46
Mississaugas of Scugog Island First Nation v National Automobile, Aerospace, Transportation and General Workers Union of Canada (2007) ONCA 814
Mitchell v M.N.R. [2001] 1 S.C.R. 911
Mooswa v Minister of Social Services for Saskatchewan (1976) 30 R.F.L. 101
Natural Parents v Superintendent of Child Welfare [1976] 2 S.C.R. 751
N.H. and D.H. v H.M., M.H. and the Director of Child, Family and Community Services (1998) 156 D.L.R. (4th) 548
NIL/TU,O Child and Family Services Society v B.C. Government and Service Employees' Union [2010] 2 S.C.R. 696
Northwest Child and Family Services Agency v S.J.T. (1990) 70 D.L.R. (4th) 418
Nova Scotia (Minister of Community Services) v F. (R.L.) [2002] 1 C.N.L.R. 221
N.P.P. v Regional Children's Guardian (1988) 14 R.F.L. (3d) 55
Nukon v Nukon et. al. (2005) YKSC 55
Nunavut (Director of Child and Family Services) v K.(H.) (2008) NUCJ 19
R v Badger [1996] 1 S.C.R. 771
R v Francis 2007 CanLII 8009 (ON S.C.)
R v Gladstone [1996] 2 S.C.R. 723
R v Kapp [2008] 2 S.C.R. 483
R v Marshall [1999] 3 S.C.R. 593
R v Pamajewon [1996] 2 S.C.R. 821
R v Sappier; R v Gray [2006] 2 S.C.R. 686
R v Sparrow [1990] 1 S.C.R. 1075
R v Van der Peet [1996] 2 S.C.R. 507
Racine v Woods [1983] 2 S.C.R. 173

Re A.B. (1989) 100 A.R. 150
Re Adolescent [2001] 4 C.N.L.R. 1
Re A.G. [2000] 2 C.N.L.R. 1
Re Child Welfare Act (Alta Q.B.) [1986] A.J. No. 539 (QL)
Re Child Welfare Act (Chipeway) [1986] A.J. No. 67 (QL)
Re D.F.P. [2001] 2 C.N.L.R. 51
Re D.L.C [1986] 4 C.N.L.R. 68
Re K.R. and K.M. (2009) SKQB 507
Re P.R.S. and K.P.S. (2010) SKQB 99
Re R.T., M.T., M.A.T., A.L., and K.A. (2004) SKQB 503
Re T.J.B. and others (2008) SKQB 419
Re V.J.C. and others (2009) SKQB 395
Re W (C.K.) [2002] 3 C.N.L.R. 268
Reference Re Secession of Quebec (Supreme Court of Canada) (1998) 37 I.L.M.1340
S (S.M.) v A (J.P.) (1992) 64 B.C.L.R. (2d) 344
Sagkeeng Child and Family Services v M.D.G. (2010) MBQB 234
Sawatzky v Campbell [2001] 4 C.N.L.R. 300
Southeast Child and Family Services v A.A.M.L. and J.A.L. (2010) MBQB 126
Taku River Tlingit First Nation v British Columbia [2004] 3 S.C.R. 550
The Children's Aid Society of the Districts of Sudbury and Manitoulin v D.D. (2009) CanLII 70505
The Grand Council of the Crees (Eeyou Istchee) and The Cree Regional Authority v Director of Youth Protection for A and others (2009) QCCA 1583
Tom v The Children's Aid Society of Winnipeg [1982] 1 C.N.L.R. 170
Tsilhqot'in Nation v British Columbia (2007) BCSC 1700
Winnipeg Child and Family Services v M.A. and G.R. (2002) MBQB 209

International

Ivan Kitok v. Sweden, Communication No. 197/1985, CCPR/C/33/D/197/1985 (1988)
Legal Consequences for States of the Continued Presence of South Africa in Namibia (South West Africa) Notwithstanding Security Council Resolution 276 (1970), ICJ Reports 1971, 16
Lubicon Lake Band v. Canada, Communication No. 167/1984, (A/45/40) (1990)
Sandra Lovelace v. Canada, Communication No. R.6/24, (A/36/40) (1981), 166
Western Sahara, Advisory Opinion, ICJ Reports 1975, 12

Table of Statutes

Australia

Adoption Act 1988 (SA)
Adoption Act 1988 (Tas)
Adoption Act 1993 (ACT)
Adoption Act 1994 (WA)
Adoption Act 2000 (NSW)
Adoption Act 2009 (QLD)
Adoption of Children Act 1995 (NT)
Care and Protection of Children Act 2007 (NT)
Child Protection Act 1999 (QLD)
Children and Community Services Act 2004 (WA)
Children and Young People Act 2008 (ACT)
Children and Young Persons (Care and Protection) Act 1998 (NSW)
Children, Young Persons and their Families Act (1997) (Tas)
Children, Youth and Families Act 2005 (Vic)
Children's Protection Act 1993 (SA)
Community Welfare Act (NT)
Family Law Act 1975 (Cth)

Canada

Child and Family Services Act C.C.S.M. 1985 C.80
Child and Family Services Act S.N.W.T. 1997 C.13
Child and Family Services Act S.S. 1989–1990 c. C-7.2
Child and Family Services Act R.S.O. 1990 C-11
Child and Family Services Authorities Act C.C.S.M. 2002 c. C 90
Child and Family Services Authorities Act R.S.A. 2000 C-11
Child, Family and Community Service Act [RSBC 1996] Chpt. 46
Child Protection Act R.S.P.E.I. 1988 c. C-5.1
Child, Youth and Family Enhancement Act R.S.A. 2000 c. C-12
Child, Youth and Family Services Act S.N.L. 1998 C-12.1
Children and Family Services Act S.N.S. 1990 C-5
Children's Act R.S.Y. 2002 C-22
Constitution Act, 1982, being Schedule B to the Canada Act 1982 (U.K.), 1982 c. 11

Cree Naskapi (of Quebec) Act 1984
Family Services Act S.N.B. 1980 C. F-2.2
Indian Act 1868
Indian Act 1876
James Bay and Northern Quebec Agreement and the Cree Naskapi (of Quebec) Act 1984
Sechelt Self-Government Act 1986
Youth Protection Act P. 34.1. (Quebec)

Table of International Documents

Treaties and Conventions

C107 Convention concerning the Protection and Integration of Indigenous and Other Tribal and Semi-Tribal Populations in Independent Countries, 1957

C169 Convention concerning Indigenous and Tribal Peoples in Independent Countries, 1989

International Covenant on Civil and Political Rights 1966, adopted and opened for signature, ratification and accession by General Assembly resolution 2200A (XXI) of 16 December 1966, entered into force 23 March 1976

International Covenant on Economic, Social and Cultural Rights, adopted and opened for signature, ratification and accession by General Assembly resolution 2200A (XXI) of 16 December 1966, entered into force 3 January 1976

United Nations Convention on the Rights of the Child, adopted and opened for signature, ratification and accession by General Assembly resolution 44/25 of 20 November 1989, entered into force 2 September 1990

General Assembly Resolutions

GA Resolution 1514 (XV). *Declaration on the granting of independence to colonial countries and peoples*, 1960

GA Resolution 1541 (XV). *Principles which should guide members in determining whether or not an obligation exists to transmit the information called for under article 73(e) of the Charter*, 1960

GA Resolution 2625 (XXV). *Declaration on Principles of International Law concerning Friendly Relations and Co-operation among States in accordance with the Charter of the United Nations*, 1970

GA Resolution 61/295. *United Nations Declaration on the Rights of Indigenous Peoples*, 2007

Preface

This book is about Aboriginal children and the need for fundamental changes in the design, management and delivery of child welfare services within Aboriginal communities in Canada and Australia. However, the effective implementation of those changes requires a journey well beyond the single issue of child welfare to the heart of the debate over self-government, self-determination and sovereignty in both national and international law.

In September 2007 the United Nations adopted the UN Declaration on the Rights of Indigenous Peoples. It is hoped the Declaration will mark a new dawn in the often troubled relationship between indigenous peoples and international law. It represents the culmination of a number of important changes to some of the more problematic assumptions which have underpinned international law and which, for many years, have undermined State relations with indigenous peoples. International law continues to have serious limitations as a site for the successful decolonization of indigenous peoples. However, the last 60 years have seen a considerable weakening in the once exclusive state-centric foundations of international law, a corresponding willingness to afford greater legal recognition to the rights and interests of sub-state groups and growing recognition of the importance of protecting and supporting a wide range of diverse cultures and traditions. With the UN Declaration on Indigenous Peoples enshrining long overdue recognition of indigenous peoples as colonized peoples, these developments hold out enormous promise for indigenous peoples, vindicating their strong commitment to international law as the most appropriate forum in which to address the many complex problems facing their communities.

This book is concerned with one such problem: Aboriginal child welfare. The past and present policies and practices of the state/provincial child welfare systems in Canada and Australia have been roundly condemned for their legal and cultural chauvinism and the resulting disproportionate removal of Aboriginal children from their families and communities. There is a strong consensus amongst commentators that the successful decolonization of Aboriginal child welfare can only be achieved through the implementation of Aboriginal self-government, integral to which is autonomous control of their own child welfare systems, free from the ethnocentric laws, standards and scrutiny of the Canadian and Australian governments. However, such are the socio-economic, political and cultural problems within many Aboriginal communities, that self-government over child welfare will not be a panacea and, indeed, may pose quite substantial risks to the rights of vulnerable women and children within those communities. The implementation of Aboriginal self-government over child welfare thus brings into sharp relief a familiar dilemma. How may the rights of the group be reconciled with the potentially conflicting rights of the group's individual members? More particularly, how may the right of indigenous peoples to self-government be reconciled with the rights of potentially vulnerable Aboriginal children living within those communities?

One particular aim of this book has been to broaden the current debate over Aboriginal child welfare and self-government to address the potential of international law to provide more nuanced solutions to this dilemma. The Canadian government's flawed attempts to develop a constitutional framework for the implementation of self-government that remains true to the principles of self-determination and meets the legitimate aspirations of Aboriginal communities for decolonization whilst protecting the most fundamental rights of Aboriginal women and children are telling. In light of these failings it is important to ask whether the normative framework provided by international law can provide a more constructive way forward. Clearly a number of important challenges remain to be faced if international law is to chart a better way forward for indigenous peoples. A fresh perspective is needed on the debate over the scope and meaning of indigenous peoples' right to self-determination and its implications for related issues such as the right to self-government and the protection of individual Aboriginal rights. The various mechanisms for the protection of individual rights in international law, most notably the UN Convention on the Rights of the Child, must respond more effectively to the diverse cultures and traditions of indigenous peoples if international law is to avoid the cultural limitations of many domestic human rights provisions. Yet, despite these challenges, the conclusions are encouraging. In the post-colonial world a novel and distinctive approach to the relationship between the state, indigenous peoples, indigenous cultures and the indigenous individual is emerging in international law – a distinctive approach that ensures a comprehensive culturally inclusive framework of protection for indigenous children's rights whilst holding true to the fundamental tenets of self-determination as a process of decolonization.

Acknowledgements

Aboriginal self-government over child welfare in Canada and Australia may seem a surprising topic for an English family lawyer. This is, however, an issue on which I have been working for many years, the seeds for this project having been sown whilst I was a graduate student at the University of British Columbia in the 1990s. It brings together my research interests in children's rights, child protection, indigenous peoples and the accommodation of cultural diversity in international human rights law. As such it draws on and expands a body of work that has developed and grown over the years from the strong interest first sparked in these issues during my time spent as a student in Canada. At the end of my studies, I left Canada convinced that the challenging problems facing Aboriginal children, families and communities are a legacy of the destructive forces of colonial rule to which several generations of Aboriginal people have now been subjected. I remain convinced that decolonization secured through recognition of the right of Aboriginal peoples to self-determination is the only answer to creating a better future for Aboriginal children. I hope that the arguments advanced within this book have remained true to those convictions.

This project has at times been challenging. There are many people to whom I owe enormous thanks for helping me to bring it to completion. Research for the book was carried out during visiting appointments at the University of Victoria, Canada and the University of New South Wales, Australia. I am very grateful to the British Academy and their small research grant scheme for providing financial support for those visits. I would also like to express my thanks to the Law Faculties of the University of Victoria and the University of New South Wales for making me feel so welcome during my time there. The many discussions I enjoyed with members of those faculties have proved invaluable in helping me to form and shape my ideas. During the course of the project I have also been privileged to meet with many Aboriginal individuals committed to improving the provision of Aboriginal child welfare services within their communities. I am particularly grateful to the employees of Aboriginal controlled child welfare agencies who gave so generously of their time to talk to me about their work. A number of people have read and provided valuable feedback on earlier drafts of this book. Special thanks are owed to Sally McCausland, not only for her help and advice during the very earliest stages of the project, but for her generosity and support whilst I was visiting in Australia. I would also like to thank Alison Kirk and her colleagues at Ashgate Publishing for their enthusiasm for the project and the anonymous referees who provided such helpful feedback and advice on the proposal. I am indebted to all these people. There are, however, two colleagues to whom I would like to give particular thanks. Professor Colin Warbrick and Professor John Borrows have patiently read and commented on numerous drafts of this manuscript. I am extremely grateful to them both for the time they have given and for their support and encouragement over the years.

Finally, as my friends and colleagues know well, this project has only been possible because of the dedicated support of my husband Tim. During the course of writing this book, Isaac and Olivia have arrived in our lives, bringing incredible joy but also new pressures. The difficulties of juggling the increasing demands of two academic careers with family life will be known to many. Over the last 18 months, Tim has selflessly absorbed those pressures to allow me to finish this project. I am immensely grateful for everything he does, as husband and father. This book is dedicated to him.

Sonia Harris-Short
30 September 2011

List of Abbreviations

AFN	Assembly of First Nations
AICCA	Aboriginal and Torres Strait Islander Child Care Agencies
AIHW	Australian Institute of Health and Welfare
AJI-CWI	Aboriginal Justice Inquiry – Child Welfare Initiative
AJIM	Aboriginal Justice Inquiry of Manitoba
ALRC	Australian Law Reform Commission
CERD	Committee on the Elimination of Racial Discrimination
CESCR	Committee on Economic, Social and Cultural Rights
CROC	Committee on the Rights of the Child
DCRE	Saskatchewan Department of Community Resources and Employment
DOCFS	Dakota Ojibway Child and Family Services
DoCS	Department of Community Services
FACS	Department of Family and Community Services
HRC Working Group	Commission on Human Rights Working Group
HREOC	Human Rights and Equal Opportunity Commission
ICCPR	International Covenant on Civil and Political Rights
ILO	International Labour Organisation
MOU	Memorandum of Understanding
NWAC	Native Women's Association of Canada
OCME	Office of the Chief Medical Examiner
RCADC	Royal Commission on Aboriginal Deaths in Custody
RCAP	Royal Commission on Aboriginal Peoples
UNCRC	United Nations Convention on the Rights of the Child
WGIP	Working Group on Indigenous Peoples

PART I
Introduction

Chapter 1
Introduction

Australia

James' Story[1]

James' grandmother, Helen, was four years old when she was removed from her family and placed in a white institution. Throughout her time at the institution she was denied all contact with her parents. At the age of 17 she left to work as a cook in the city. Without family support she was totally lost in the city. She had no idea who she was or where she had come from. She became pregnant at a very young age. Her partner was alcoholic and violent. They had severe financial problems. Helen became very depressed and began to drink. Her traumatic removal from her parents as a child had rendered her incapable of forming and maintaining any long-term loving familial relationships. She did not know how to love and to trust. She did not know how to parent her own children. Her marriage broke down and the children were neglected. Eventually, her children were all removed and placed into care by 'the welfare'.

James' mother, Jenny, had a chaotic childhood. Her life with Helen was characterized by alcohol and violence and she was sexually abused by her father. She was three-and-a-half when she was first removed from her parents and placed into foster care. Over the next few years she moved in and out of care, being returned on occasion to Helen before being removed again. Like her mother, Jenny was thus deprived of the stability and security of a loving family home and found herself similarly scarred. As an adult she struggled to come to terms with her childhood experiences of alcoholism, violence and sexual abuse. Daily life became a battle. She was depressed, unable to hold down a job and turned to alcohol for comfort. Her relationships with men were typically marked by alcoholism, violence and abuse. Desperate for a sense of family and to feel needed and loved she had one child after another despite struggling to cope. Although the children's basic needs were met, their lives were chaotic. Unable to manage alone, Jenny clearly needed help and support but, terrified that her children would be removed from her as she had been from her own mother, she avoided all contact with 'the welfare'. Deeply affected by the myriad of problems facing his mother, James developed his own severe emotional and behavioural problems.

---

1 Account taken from, Human Rights and Equal Opportunity Commission (1997). *Report of the National Inquiry into the Separation of Aboriginal and Torres Strait Islander Children from their Families*. Commonwealth of Australia, 229–31.

James now has his own son, Stephen. Stephen is a very intelligent, healthy boy albeit somewhat overweight. He is, however, failing at school and is socially isolated, having no friends of his own. His behaviour is erratic including sexually acting out. He frequently places himself in physical danger. It is feared that he is being sexually abused but this cannot be substantiated. Due to his aggressive, erratic behaviour he has been suspended from a number of schools. His mother cannot cope with his behaviour and he has thus been sent to live with his grandmother. His future looks bleak. Separated from his mother and siblings and excluded from school, his chances of securing stable employment as an adult and forming and sustaining healthy adult relationships are diminishing. He is at serious risk of ending up as a 'street kid'. Stephen has talked of feeling severely depressed and that his life is not worth living. He has in fact attempted to kill himself by cutting his wrists. Stephen is seven years old.

The tragic cycle of abuse and despair that has devastated James' family began four generations ago with the forced removal of his grandmother from her family and her community by the British colonial powers in Australia. It continues today in the complex problems of her seven-year-old great grandson, Stephen. The story of James' family is a living testament to the devastating consequences of Australia's colonial past. It is a shameful legacy. On 2 August 1995, Michael Lavarch, Attorney-General of Australia, requested that Australia's Human Rights and Equal Opportunity Commission (HREOC) inquire into and report on issues relating to past policies concerning the forced removal of Aboriginal children from their families and communities.[2] The resulting report (*Bringing Them Home*) concludes that between one in three and one in ten Aboriginal children were

2 In the Australian context the term 'Aboriginal' will be used collectively to refer to children of Aboriginal and/or Torres Strait Islander descent. 'Aboriginal' means a child who is a member of the Aboriginal race of Australia ('Aboriginal' meaning people who inhabited the land at the time of European settlement) or is a descendent of a person of Aboriginal descent, who identifies himself as such, and who is recognized by the Aboriginal community as an Aboriginal. For detailed discussion of the meaning of 'Aboriginal' and the problems of correctly identifying a child as an Aboriginal child, see *Sheldon v Weir (No. 3)* [2010] FamCA 1138, [461]–[486]. It is estimated from the 2006 Australian census that there are currently about 517,000 Aboriginal and/or Torres Strait Islander people living in Australia, constituting 2.5 per cent of the total population. At the time of settlement there were over 500 different clan groups or nations, speaking about 250 different languages. Indigenous social surveys indicate that just over half of the Aboriginal population continue to identify with a particular clan, tribal or language group, with about 145 languages still spoken. However, in the 2006 census only 12 per cent of Aboriginal people reported speaking an Aboriginal language at home. See: www.hreoc.gov.au/social_justice/statistics/index.html and K. Obata and J. Lee (2010). 'Languages of Aboriginal and Torres Strait Islander Peoples – A Uniquely Australian Heritage', *Year Book of Australia 2009–10*, Australian Bureau of Statistics. Note that the term 'Indigenous' is used interchangeably with the term 'Aboriginal' in some materials.

forcibly removed from their families and communities between 1910 and 1970.[3] It was a brutal policy:

> I was at the post office with my Mum and Auntie [and cousin]. They put us in the police Ute and said they were taking us to Broome. They put the mums in there as well. But when we'd gone [about 10 miles] they stopped, and threw the mothers out of the car. We jumped on our mothers' backs, crying, trying not to be left behind. But the policemen pulled us off and threw us back in the car. They pushed the mothers away and drove off, while our mothers were chasing the car, running and crying after us. We were screaming in the back of that car. When we got to Broome they put me and my cousin in the Broome lock-up. We were only ten years old. We were in the lock-up for two days waiting for the boat to Perth.[4]

The forced removal of Aboriginal children whether by 'compulsion, duress or undue influence'[5] formed just one part of a much larger pattern of dispossession, economic marginalization, systemic discrimination and genocidal practices suffered by Aboriginal people at the hands of Australia's colonial governments. However, the widespread removal of Aboriginal children was particularly devastating, causing a multitude of complex personal and inter-societal problems within Aboriginal communities, the crippling effects of which continue to overwhelm many Aboriginal communities today. As the *Bringing Them Home* report notes,

> It is difficult to capture the complexity of the effects for each individual … For the majority of witnesses to the Inquiry, the effects have been multiple and profoundly disabling. An evaluation of the following material should take into account the ongoing impacts and their compounding effects causing a cycle of damage from which it is difficult to escape unaided. Psychological and emotional damage renders many people less able to learn social skills and survival skills. Their ability to operate successfully in the world is impaired causing low educational achievement, unemployment and consequent poverty. These in turn cause their own emotional distress leading some to perpetrate violence, self-harm, substance abuse or anti-social behavior.[6]

The devastating impact of this level of individual trauma on the health of whole communities already struggling against the ravages of colonial governments hungry for land and power is now widely acknowledged.[7]

---

3 *Supra* note 1, 37.

4 Ibid., 6.

5 Ibid., 5–10.

6 Ibid., 178.

7 Ibid., Part 3, chs 10–12. See also: Inquiry into Response by Government Agencies to Complaints of Family Violence and Child Abuse in Aboriginal Communities (2002).

The forced removal of Aboriginal children from their families and communities is not, however, an historical relic to be acknowledged by Australian society but essentially consigned to Australia's past. Not only does the *Bringing Them Home* report highlight how the 'actions of the past' continue to affect the general health of Aboriginal communities today,[8] it raises strong concerns about the continuing removal of Aboriginal children by the Australian authorities, as evidenced by the disproportionate number of Aboriginal children in public state care. Although figures vary between the different states and territories, *Bringing Them Home* reports that on average indigenous children are seven times more likely to be in substitute care than non-native children, with indigenous children across Australia, who constitute just 2.7 per cent of the total population, making up 20 per cent of the number of children in care.[9] An important aspect of the Inquiry's work was thus to: 'examine current laws, practices and policies with respect to the placement and care of Aboriginal and Torres Strait Islander children and advise on any changes required taking into account the principle of self-determination by Aboriginal and Torres Strait Islander peoples'.[10] Although past practices of removal give rise to important legal questions such as the right of Aboriginal individuals and communities to recover some form of compensation for the damage they have suffered,[11] it is with this latter aspect of the Inquiry's work – the future of Aboriginal child welfare in Australia – that this book is principally concerned.

With respect to the crucial question of how best to address the continuing disproportionate removal of Aboriginal children from their families, the Inquiry reaches a deceptively simple conclusion: the answer lies in self-determination. As expressed in the report, the 'principal finding is that self-determination for Indigenous peoples provides the key to reversing the over-representation of Indigenous children in the child welfare and juvenile justice systems of the States and Territories and to eliminating unjustified removals of Indigenous children from their families and communities'.[12] Self-determination, which is defined in the report as the right to exercise control over matters directly affecting Aboriginal children, is thus regarded as the essential starting point for moving forward.[13] The

Putting the Picture Together. State Law Publisher, WA, 57–9; Victorian Indigenous Family Violence Task Force (2003). *Final Report*, 132–44; Aboriginal Child Sexual Assault Taskforce (2006). *Breaking the Silence: Creating the Future – Addressing Child Sexual Assault in Aboriginal Communities in NSW*. Attorney General's Department, NSW, 61–3; and Northern Territory Government (2007). *Board of Inquiry into the Protection of Aboriginal Children from Sexual Abuse*. Darwin, NT: Government Printer, 50.

8 HREOC, *supra* note 1, 3.

9 Ibid., 430. For more recent statistics see pp. 88–9.

10 Ibid., Terms of Reference.

11 As to the challenges of securing compensation for the loss and suffering experienced as a result of removal see *Cubillo v Commonwealth* [1999] FCA 518. For a more recent, successful action see *Trevorrow v State of South Australia (No 5)* [2007] SASC 285.

12 *Supra* note 1, 17.

13 Ibid., 560 and 565.

report goes on to outline a number of more specific recommendations concerning how this right to self-determination is to be realized within the context of Aboriginal child welfare. Central to the Inquiry's conclusions is the recommendation that national framework legislation is introduced to facilitate the negotiation of Aboriginal autonomy and, if desired, the transfer of legal responsibility for Aboriginal children from the state and territories to local communities; legislation that will, in other words, set the framework for Aboriginal self-government over child welfare including child protection, adoption and juvenile justice.[14] The national framework legislation would also establish a number of core principles and minimum national standards to be implemented across Australia whether or not a community decides to assume self-government over its own child welfare or agrees to continued service delivery by state authorities. Those standards would include the protection of indigenous children's fundamental human rights and guarantees that in any judicial or administrative decision affecting the care and protection, adoption, or residence of an indigenous child, the child's welfare would be the paramount consideration. In determining the child's best interests, the decision-maker would be required to take into account: (i) the need of the child to maintain contact with his or her indigenous family, community and culture; (ii) the significance of the child's indigenous heritage for his or her future well-being; (iii) the views of the child and his or her family; and (iv) the advice of the appropriate accredited indigenous organization.[15] Further recommendations deal with the need to establish an accreditation framework for indigenous organizations,[16] the requirement to consult with indigenous organizations in all care and protection matters,[17] the right of the child to be separately represented in court proceedings,[18] statutory recognition of the Indigenous Child Placement Principle,[19] and for the strengthening of the Family Law Act 1975 (Cth) to include explicit recognition of the importance of an Aboriginal child maintaining a meaningful connection with his/her Aboriginal culture and heritage.[20]

The recommendations in *Bringing Them Home* clearly address not only the right of Aboriginal communities to self-government over child welfare but the continuing need for the existing legal framework and those currently delivering child welfare and protection services to be more sensitive and responsive to the cultural needs of Aboriginal families and communities. In the wake of the report, many states have moved to address this objective, initiating legislative reforms

14 It is argued that national framework legislation would come within the commonwealth's external affairs and race powers. Child welfare, including Aboriginal child welfare, otherwise comes within the jurisdiction of the state and territory. The Constitution (63 & 64 Victoria, Chapter 12), ss 51 and 107. HREOC, ibid., Recommendation 43a and 43c.

15 HREOC, ibid., Recommendations 46a, 46b and 47.

16 Ibid., Recommendation 45b.

17 Ibid., Recommendation 49.

18 Ibid., Recommendation 50.

19 Ibid., Recommendation 51a. See further discussion at pp. 72–5.

20 Ibid., Recommendation 54.

aimed at affording greater recognition to the importance of an Aboriginal child's cultural identity and place within an Aboriginal community. However, it is self-government which sits at the heart of the report with a clear and unequivocal commitment to the long-term objective of achieving the transfer of control over Aboriginal child welfare to local Aboriginal communities. Disappointingly, with respect to this core objective, the response of the Australian authorities has been poor with all states and territories remaining a long way from implementing any kind of meaningful self-government over Aboriginal child welfare. An Implementation Progress Report prepared by HREOC in September 1998 records that none of the Inquiry's recommendations regarding national framework legislation for facilitating self-government and setting minimum national standards have been implemented, with the commonwealth government and the governments of Queensland and Victoria actively rejecting the need for any such legislation.[21] This picture of complacency was confirmed in 2007 by the Northern Territory Board of Enquiry into the Protection of Aboriginal Children from Sexual Abuse ('NT Board of Enquiry'), the Enquiry confirming that very little had changed in the ethos, design and delivery of child protection and welfare services in Aboriginal communities since the *Bringing Them Home* report.[22]

Canada

Richard's Story[23]

On 26 June 1984, Richard Cardinal, a 17-year-old Métis child was found hanging in the garden of his latest foster home. Richard's short life had been spent in the care of Alberta Social Services. Between the ages of four and 17, Richard experienced 28 different placements in Alberta: 16 of those were foster homes, 12 were group homes or a form of secure facility. The longest Richard spent in any one home was four years. By the age of 13 he was experiencing psychological problems manifested by bed-wetting, getting into trouble with the law, and failing at school. At the age of 16 he was arrested for shoplifting and placed on probation. By this stage in his life he had already attempted suicide twice. Richard spent the last two years of his life in various youth homes and shelters before his final placement where, after one failed attempt at suicide, he finally hung himself from a tree in the back garden. The judicial inquiry into Richard's death, presided over by Mr Justice White of the Alberta Provincial Court, revealed 'serious inadequacies in

---

21 Human Rights and Equal Opportunity Commission (1998). *Bringing Them Home: Implementation Progress Report*, 70.

22 See generally, Northern Territory Government (2007), *supra* note 7, esp. Part 1, ch. 8.

23 The following account of Richard's story is taken from, *Richard Cardinal – Cry from the Diary of a Métis Child*, Canadian Film Board, 1986.

the provincial child welfare system'.[24] His suicide provides a shocking example of the Canadian non-native child welfare system failing an Aboriginal child.

Canada's colonial legacy and, in particular, its treatment of Aboriginal children shares striking similarities with that of Australia.[25] As in Australia, the suffering and inter-generational damage which has been caused to Canada's Aboriginal communities by the forced removal of Aboriginal children into state/church administered residential schools has been widely recognized.[26] Again that damage did not end with the demise of the residential school system but was perpetuated by the deeply flawed policies and practices of the provincial child welfare system.[27] Within Canada, particularly amongst the academic community, there has been almost unanimous condemnation of the treatment of Aboriginal children by the Canadian authorities.[28] That condemnation has been voiced with

24 Ibid.

25 In the Canadian context the term 'Aboriginal' will be used collectively to denote a child who is of First Nations, Métis or Inuit descent. These three Aboriginal groups are recognized under the Canadian Constitution. Unless otherwise indicated, the term 'First Nations' is used to refer to all children of 'Indian' descent whether or not qualifying as 'registered status Indians' for the purposes of the Indian Act 1876. Métis refers to children of mixed European and First Nations ancestry who share a distinct language and culture. Inuit refers to children descended from the original inhabitants of Arctic Canada (Nunavut, North West Territories, Nunavik and Labrador). In the 2006 Canadian census more than one million people identified as Aboriginal, amounting to 4 per cent of Canada's total population. Of Canada's one million Aboriginal peoples, 53 per cent are 'Status Indians', 11 per cent 'Non-status Indians', 30 per cent Métis, and 4 per cent Inuit. There are 615 First Nations consisting of 50 Nations or cultural groups speaking 50 different languages; 390,000 Métis; and 45,000 Inuit people living in 53 communities across Northern Canada. Just over half of all Canada's Aboriginal peoples live in urban areas. For further information see the website of Indian and Northern Affairs Canada (INAC) at: www.ainc-inac.gc.ca/ai/index-eng.asp.

26 See, for example, Royal Commission on Aboriginal Peoples (1996). *Report of the Royal Commission on Aboriginal Peoples. Gathering Strength.* Part One, Vol. 3. Ottawa: Minister of Supply and Services, Canada, 34–6. On the history of the Canadian residential school system, see: J. S. Milloy (1999). *'A National Crime' – The Canadian Government and the Residential School System, 1879 to 1986.* Winnipeg: The University of Manitoba Press and J. R. Miller (1996). *Shingwauk's Vision – A History of Native Residential Schools.* Toronto: University of Toronto Press.

27 See generally, A. McGillivray (1997). 'Therapies of Freedom: The Colonization of Aboriginal Childhood', in A. McGillivray (ed.) *Governing Childhood.* Aldershot: Dartmouth, 135.

28 See generally: L. White and E. Jacobs (1992). *Liberating Our Children Liberating Our Nations, Report of the Aboriginal Committee, Community Panel Child Protection Legislation Review in British Columbia.* British Columbia: Queen's Printer; M. Kline (1992). 'Child Welfare Law, "Best Interests of the Child" Ideology and First Nations', *Osgoode Hall Law Journal*, 30: 375; M. Kline (1995), 'Complicating the Ideology of Motherhood: Child Welfare Law and First Nations Women', in M. Fineman and I. Karpin (eds) *Mothers in Law: Feminist Theory and the Legal Regulation of Motherhood.* New

particular force with respect to the residential school system. Perhaps even more striking, however, is that not only are these Canadian voices united in criticism, they are also united in the solution. In agreement with the conclusions reached by Australia's HREOC in *Bringing Them Home*, it is consistently argued in the academic literature that the successful decolonization of Aboriginal child welfare can only be achieved through the implementation of Aboriginal self-government, integral to which is autonomous control of their own child welfare systems, free from the ethnocentric laws, standards and scrutiny of the provincial or federal governments.[29] This argument is strongly reinforced by the limited success of recent initiatives introduced by the Canadian provincial governments to try and 'sensitize' the provincial child welfare systems to the cultural needs of Aboriginal children, families and communities, including trying to restore some measure of community control over the delivery of child welfare services by the creation of Aboriginal-controlled child welfare agencies. Manitoba was the first province to take this important step, the federal and provincial governments entering into a tripartite agreement with the Manitoba Indian Brotherhood and First Nations Confederacy in 1982 to establish a number of Aboriginal agencies with the authority to deliver a full range of child protection services to First Nations living on reserve.[30] Pursuant to the agreement the agencies are funded by the federal government but remain under the control of the Manitoba Director of Child and Family Services.[31] Although this model of delegated authority remains a long way from self-government, the creation of Aboriginal-controlled child welfare agencies has allowed a growing degree of autonomy to be exercised by Aboriginal communities over the welfare and protection of their own children. The Manitoba Justice Inquiry, reporting in 1991, recorded that over 450,000 First Nations people on reserve and over 28,000 First Nations people off reserve were now served by native controlled child welfare agencies.[32] In the last 20 years that number has continued to grow. In British Columbia ('BC'), for example, there are now 22

York: Columbia University Press, 118; P. Monture (1989). 'A Vicious Circle: Child Welfare and the First Nations', *Canadian Journal of Women and the Law*, 3: 1; S. Bull (1989). 'The Special Case of the Native Indian Child', *Advocate*, 47: 523; E. Carasco (1986). 'Canadian Native Children: Have Child Welfare Laws Broken the Circle?', *Canadian Journal of Family Law*, 5: 111; J. MacDonald (1985). 'Child Welfare and the Native Indian Peoples of Canada', *Windsor Yearbook of Access to Justice*, 5: 284.

29 See: White and Jacobs ibid.; Kline (1992) ibid.; Monture ibid.; and B. Morse (1980). 'Indian and Innuit Family Law and the Canadian Legal System', *American Indian Law Review*, 8: 199, 200. As to the way forward in Australia, see P. Lynch (2001). 'Keeping them Home: The Best Interests of Indigenous Children and Communities in Canada and Australia', *Sydney Law Review*, 23: 501, 505.

30 *Supra* note 27, 163.

31 Ibid.

32 Aboriginal Justice Inquiry of Manitoba (1991). *Report of the Aboriginal Justice Inquiry of Manitoba: The Justice System and Aboriginal People*, vol. 1. Winnipeg: Manitoba, 530–1.

Aboriginal-controlled child welfare agencies, nine of which exercise delegated provincial powers and deliver a full range of child protection, guardianship and family support services.[33] Of the 198 First Nation bands in British Columbia, 148 are now served by an Aboriginal agency.

These developments are of considerable importance not least for the part they play in building capacity within Aboriginal communities. However, undermined by jurisdictional wrangling, political interference and chronic under-funding, Aboriginal-controlled child welfare agencies have not been an unqualified success.[34] Certainly Aboriginal child welfare in Canada has not been transformed as a result of the delegation model, exemplifying the difficulties and frustrations for Aboriginal people trying to work within an essentially alien legal framework still imbued with the norms and concepts of the colonizing and now dominant society.[35] The combination of the existing power disparity between indigenous and non-indigenous groups and the strength with which the basic cultural concepts, understandings and beliefs of non-native society are embedded within the core foundations of the existing legal system and governmental institutions, strongly suggests that there may be only limited capacity for bringing about a fundamental change in their basic underlying philosophy and approach.[36] For bringing about such fundamental change, Aboriginal self-government is the only answer.

The right of an Aboriginal community to exercise self-government over child welfare is of course underpinned by the more general right of Aboriginal peoples to self-government over their internal affairs – a right which when properly grounded in the principles of self-determination and decolonization means an inherent right to 'sovereign'[37] jurisdiction over their people, their culture and their lands. Although the exact scope and meaning of the inherent right of Aboriginal

---

33 Of the remaining agencies, one is in the early start-up phase, three deliver family support services, and 11 provide both family support and guardianship services to children in care. For the latest developments see the Ministry for Children and Families Development website at: www.mcf.gov.bc.ca/about_us/aboriginal/delegated/index.htm. For the latest list of delegated agencies see: www.mcf.gov.bc.ca/about_us/Aboriginal/delegated/pdf/agency_list.pdf. Similar developments have occurred in other Canadian provinces which will be discussed in detail in Chapter 3.

34 For an excellent critique of the 'devolution' model see, J. Rae (2009). 'Program Delivery Devolution: A Stepping Stone or Quagmire for First Nations?', *Indigenous Law Journal*, 7: 1. See also McGillivray, *supra* note 27, 163–9.

35 For an instructive critique of recent reforms in Manitoba see, C. Bourassa (2010). *Summary Review of the Manitoba Child Welfare System for the Saskatchewan Child Welfare Review Report*.

36 See Kline (1992), *supra* note 28, 419–23 and Kline (1995), *supra* note 28, 137. For an excellent analysis of the limits of trying to work for meaningful change within the existing legal system see P. Monture-Angus (1999). *Journeying Forward. Dreaming of First Nations Independence*. Halifax, NS: Fernwood Publishing.

37 The term 'sovereign' will be used throughout this book to mean that when operating within their sphere of jurisdiction Aboriginal governments are not subject to the overriding authority of the Canadian federal or provincial governments. They may, however, still

peoples to self-government remains fiercely contested within Canadian law and politics, there is, perhaps somewhat surprisingly, a significant level of support for Aboriginal self-government over child welfare (albeit self-government which is heavily qualified) at the level of government. Indeed community control over child welfare is often identified as a clear example of the kind of power which would be 'core' or central to a self-governing Aboriginal community.[38] This level of political support has enabled much greater progress to be made towards some measure of Aboriginal self-government over child welfare in Canada than has been possible in Australia.

One community to have taken such steps is the Nisga'a Nation located in the Nass Valley, Northern British Columbia. On 17 May 1997, the Nisga'a Tribal Council and the British Columbia Ministry for Children and Families announced that the Nisga'a Nation were to begin the process of retaking control over their community's child welfare.[39] The statement explains that, in recognition of the inherent right of the Nisga'a people to jurisdiction over child welfare, they would initiate the first of a number of phases, the ultimate aim of which would be the introduction of Nisga'a legislation providing the mandate for a fully autonomous Nisga'a-controlled child welfare agency.[40] These developments have occurred within the context of the Nisga'a Nation's lengthy but ultimately successful negotiation of a modern treaty with the federal and BC provincial governments in settlement of their various land, resource and governance claims. This process culminated in the Nisga'a Final Agreement which contains detailed provisions on self-government, including self-government over child welfare and adoption.[41] The Nisga'a Agreement thus stands as a beacon of hope for the growing number of Aboriginal communities seeking to prevent tragic deaths like that of Richard Cardinal by removing child protection from the jurisdiction of the province within the context of comprehensive self-government negotiations.

Canada can now claim some 30 years of experience in seeking effective solutions to the acute needs of Aboriginal children both inside and outside of the existing provincial child welfare systems. It therefore provides a potentially important model for jurisdictions such as Australia which remain very much in the

---

be subject to some form of external control, being forced to comply with international standards such as those found in the international law of human rights.

38 Canada, Department of Indian Affairs and Northern Development (1995). *Federal Policy Guide for Aboriginal Self-Government. The Government of Canada's Approach to Implementation of the Inherent Right and the Negotiation of Aboriginal Self-Government.* Ottawa: Supply and Services.

39 British Columbia, Ministry for Children and Families Area Office, *News Release* 97:042, 'Nisga'a Tribal Council to Assume Responsibility for Child and Family Services' (13 May 1997).

40 The Nisga'a Lisims Government now provides an almost full range of child and family services (guardianship and family support services) to the Nisga'a people but have yet to enact their own child welfare legislation. See www.nisgaalisims.ca.

41 The Nisga'a Final Agreement came into effect on 11 May 2000.

infancy of these developments.[42] Indeed, Canada is often held out as an exemplar of good practice on Aboriginal issues, a reputation which prompted the focus of this particular study on the 'progressive' approach of the Canadian government to Aboriginal child welfare and the implementation of self-government over child welfare in particular. Recent developments in Canada were warmly praised by HREOC, the report observing that the Canadian government had 'shown their willingness to depart from the culture of control which had characterized relationships between Indigenous peoples and colonial societies' and had successfully recognized Aboriginal control over areas such as child welfare through the pursuit of 'creative and inclusive federalism'.[43] HREOC compares this progress within the Canadian context to the much more limited and conservative model of 'self-governance' prevailing within Australia which it critically describes as 'established within paternalistic legislative frameworks in which limited powers are delegated and functions are performed with inadequate resources, often in adverse circumstances'.[44]

Undoubtedly there is much of a positive nature which can be learned from the progress which has been made within Canada towards affording greater control over Aboriginal child welfare to Aboriginal communities, particularly as Canada moves towards a constitutionally protected model of self-government. However, developments in Canada also hold lessons of a less positive nature – lessons which point to the important limitations of seeking solutions to these difficult issues within the institutional framework of the colonizing power. If the decolonization of Aboriginal communities is to be the key to achieving real improvements for Aboriginal children, Canada's experiences reveal that both Canada and Australia will need to adopt a much more radical approach.

There is, moreover, a further important lesson to be taken from Canada's experiences with delegated Aboriginal child welfare agencies. Self-government, as well as promising much, brings important risks and challenges for Aboriginal communities and their children. These risks need to be taken seriously.

---

42 In addition to their shared British colonial past, the two jurisdictions share the same legal (common law) and political heritage making a comparative study particularly instructive. Australia is now a federal state headed by the Australian commonwealth government and consisting of eight states and territories. Under the Constitution, child welfare/child protection falls within the jurisdiction of the individual states and territories. Canada is also a federal state consisting of 13 provinces/territories. Under the Constitution, child welfare generally falls within the jurisdiction of the individual provinces but the picture is complicated in the case of Aboriginal children by the fact that the federal government retains exclusive jurisdiction over 'Indians and lands reserved for Indians' (The British North America Act 1867, s 91(24)). As will be discussed in Chapter 2, this has created highly damaging jurisdictional disputes over Aboriginal child welfare in Canada.

43 *Supra* note 1, 575.

44 Ibid.

Lester's Story[45]

On 6 March 1988, Lester Desjarlais shot himself at the home of his latest foster parents. He was 15 years old. Lester was a member of the Sandy Bay reserve community in Manitoba. His life had been destroyed by horrific physical and sexual abuse at the hands of his family and those in places of trust within the community. By the time of his death, Lester was drinking heavily, sniffing solvents, and shoplifting. At the time of his suicide Lester was a ward of the Dakota Ojibway Child and Family Services, an Aboriginal-controlled child welfare agency operating under provincial mandate. Lester had been their client from 1982 when the Dakota Ojibway Tribal Council assumed responsibility for the community's child welfare. At the Inquiry into his death, Mr Justice Giesbrecht was absolutely damning of Dakota Ojibway, declaring:

> It was negligence and incompetence pure and simple … The agency that was supposed to be protecting the boy was compounding his agony. The inmates were running the asylum.[46]

The death of Lester Desjarlais provides a shocking example of an Aboriginal-controlled child welfare agency failing an Aboriginal child. In his final report on Lester's death, Justice Giesbrecht presented a disturbing picture of a child welfare agency that was headed by unqualified, incompetent staff; an agency that was rendered useless by political interference and manipulation by powerful families on the reserve; an agency trying to serve a community in total denial of rampant violence and sexual abuse, denial that existed even within its own staff; and an agency that was abandoned by the provincial government at the earliest opportunity. Clearly, self-government over child welfare is not always the panacea it is often held out to be, with the reality of life on the ground making restoration of community control over child welfare a difficult and complex challenge.

As Aboriginal communities in Canada have gradually assumed control of key areas such as child welfare, the consequences of enduring centuries of colonial rule have begun to manifest themselves. Political corruption, the undermining of local services by dominant families, and a cynical manipulation of culture and tradition to serve those ends, are just some of the difficulties that have been experienced by Aboriginal communities moving towards self-government. Inevitably it is the more vulnerable groups or individuals within those communities who suffer the consequences of what has come to be termed the phenomena of

45 See generally, Office of the Chief Medical Examiner (1992). *The Fatalities Inquiries Act – Respecting the Death of Lester Norman Desjarlais*. Brandon: Ministry of Social Services and Housing.

46 Ibid., 35–6.

'internal colonialism'.[47] Although it is important to recognize that the recent social and political problems experienced by Aboriginal communities are by no means unique, it is fair to observe that the legacy of colonialism has intensified these difficulties for Aboriginal communities as they have moved towards self-government. The risks of self-government for potentially vulnerable children living within self-governing communities must therefore be addressed – risks which given the even greater intensity and magnitude of problems within some Aboriginal communities in Australia cannot be ignored if self-government over child welfare is to be advanced as the only long-term solution to the crisis now facing many communities.[48]

In any moves towards the implementation of self-government, the rights of Aboriginal children to a safe and secure upbringing need to be protected. This was clearly recognized by HREOC in its recommendation that there should be national legislation governing all Aboriginal child welfare services which would establish minimum national standards including the protection of indigenous children's fundamental human rights.[49] The problem is how to achieve such protection without compromising the right of indigenous peoples to self-determination.

Taking Self-Government over Aboriginal Child Welfare Forward: Balancing Rights

Behind HREOC's recommendations on self-government lies a fundamentally important question. The continuing effects of colonial rule on Aboriginal communities brings into sharp relief the difficult problem of how best to ensure the rights and interests of individual Aboriginal children are protected, whilst also according proper respect to the sovereign jurisdiction of Aboriginal governments over their people, their culture and their lands. It is a familiar conflict between, on the one hand, the right of a group to self-determination and, on the other, the individual rights of its members. This dilemma is compounded where, as in the case of Aboriginal peoples, questions of cultural difference are also engaged. With respect to child welfare, whilst native and non-native societies would agree on much, there remain many important areas of dispute where the culturally rooted norms and traditions of Aboriginal communities clash with the values and beliefs

47 For an excellent discussion of the problems and challenges raised by 'internal colonialism' see M. Boldt (1993). *Surviving as Indians. The Challenge of Self-Government.* Toronto: University of Toronto Press, 117–66.

48 As to the extent of these problems in Australia see: Inquiry into Response by Government Agencies to Complaints of Family Violence and Child Abuse in Aboriginal Communities (2002), *supra* note 7, Section 2; Victorian Indigenous Family Violence Task Force (2003), *supra* note 7, Section 3; Aboriginal Child Sexual Assault Taskforce (2006), *supra* note 7, ch. 2; and Northern Territory Government (2007), *supra* note 7, esp. at 5–6 and chs 18–20.

49 *Supra* note 1, Recommendations 43b and 44.

of the dominant society. From the perspective of non-native society, this clash of values can, in the most serious cases, give rise to concern that the rights of Aboriginal children are being unlawfully undermined. Many Aboriginal leaders would, however, reject non-native society's commitment to individual rights as the most effective mechanism for protecting vulnerable members of Aboriginal communities, arguing that rights-based discourse is culturally inappropriate and risks further undermining the normative framework of Aboriginal societies, in particular, their traditional communal base.[50]

The principal aim of this book is thus to explore whether, with reference to the particular issue of Aboriginal child welfare and self-government, these conflicting rights and interests can be successfully reconciled. Can a clear and rational legal framework for the implementation of self-government over child welfare be found that respects, on the one hand, the cultural and political sovereignty of Aboriginal peoples, whilst, on the other hand, respecting the rights and interests of potentially vulnerable children living within those communities? In seeking to answer this question, important lessons can again be learned from the Canadian experience, with the current approach towards the implementation of self-government in Canada revealing much about the potential for resolving these issues within the domestic law of settled colonial states. In many ways, there is much that augers well for Aboriginal peoples within Canadian constitutional law, with s 35 of the Constitution promising entrenched protection of the right of Aboriginal peoples to self-government. However, as Aboriginal communities have moved towards self-government, the Canadian federal government, clearly alive to the potential vulnerability of the rights and interests of individual Aboriginal children, has sought to impose a number of non-negotiable standards and conditions on Aboriginal governments, including the imposition of the Canadian Charter of Rights and Freedoms. The federal government's purported solution to the 'clash of rights' dilemma has thus been to reassert its unquestionable sovereignty and overriding authority over Aboriginal peoples, thereby perpetuating the continuing imposition of non-native values on Aboriginal communities and undermining the central tenets of self-government as a process of decolonization. It amounts, in other words, to inappropriate cultural and political imperialism which ultimately betrays the right of Aboriginal peoples to self-determination. Moreover, the unquestionable assumption of Canadian sovereignty which continues to justify the subordination of Aboriginal communities to the will of the Canadian authorities

50 See especially: M. E. Turpel (1989–1990). 'Aboriginal Peoples and the Canadian Charter: Interpretative Monopolies, Cultural Differences', *Canadian Human Rights Yearbook*, 6: 3; M. E. Turpel (1992). 'Aboriginal Peoples and the Canadian Charter of Rights and Freedoms: Contradictions and Challenges', in J. Banfield (ed.) *Readings in Law and Society*. Concord: Captus Press; P. Monture-Angus, *supra* note 33, 135–50; and M. Boldt and A. Long (1992). 'Tribal Philosophies and the Canadian Charter of Rights and Freedoms', in J. Banfield (ed.) *Readings in Law and Society*. Concord: Captus Press.

again exemplifies the inherent limitations of trying to reconcile these conflicting demands within the entrenched institutional framework of a former colonial power.

The problems identified with the Canadian approach to self-government make it a less than satisfactory model for the implementation of self-government over child welfare in Australia. The final chapters of this book will therefore turn to consider whether a more satisfactory solution may be found to the 'clash of rights' dilemma by removing these issues from the legal and political constraints of municipal states and into the realm of international law.[51] A cautious but positive conclusion is reached. As with domestic law, the ethnocentric roots and assimilationist tendencies of international law raise very real doubts as to its capacity to constitute a successful site of decolonization for Aboriginal peoples.[52] However, a weakening of positivism's grip over international law has served to make international law a much more promising forum for advancing the cause of indigenous peoples than their past experiences at the hands of the international legal system may suggest. In particular, although breaking down the limitations of a legal system dominated by the self-interest of states can be difficult and frustrating, recent attempts at norm creation in the field of indigenous rights have brought together a rich variety of perspectives and ideas on the right to self-determination that can now be constructively employed to forward the domestic debate. Indeed, with the recent adoption of the United Nations Declaration on the Rights of Indigenous Peoples ('the UN Declaration') there are tentative signs of an emerging consensus between states and indigenous peoples on this particularly complex and difficult issue. Despite the difficult historical relationship between international law and indigenous peoples, international law now promises to deliver a re-structuring of state, group and individual relations that remains much more faithful to the fundamental link between the right to self-determination and decolonization.[53]

Moreover, progress towards the creation of international legal standards on the collective rights of indigenous peoples does not mean the equally important question of ensuring adequate protection for the fundamental rights and interests of indigenous individuals is ignored. International law is well-versed in accommodating the complex and interrelated needs of both the individual and the group, whether the group in question is the state or some smaller sub-state

51 The term 'indigenous peoples' is most commonly used in international law. Although the correct legal definition of indigenous peoples is contested, it undoubtedly includes the Aboriginal peoples of Canada and Australia. See B. Kingsbury (1998). '"Indigenous Peoples" in International Law: A Constructivist Approach to the Asian Controversy', *American Journal of International Law*, 92: 414.

52 See generally, S. Wright (2001). *International Human Rights, Decolonisation and Globalisation: Becoming Human*. London: Routledge.

53 The UN Declaration on the Rights of Indigenous Peoples was adopted by the General Assembly on 13 September 2007. Four states originally voted against the Convention including Canada and Australia. Australia subsequently formally endorsed the Declaration in April 2009. Canada followed suit in November 2010.

entity. Self-determination under international law does not constitute an either/or choice between the collective and the individual. In accordance with the normative standards of the international law of human rights, no political community can now claim to enjoy absolute sovereignty over its internal affairs. In the same way, indigenous peoples exercising a right to self-determination will be subject to the same internationally recognized human rights standards and restraints. Whether those standards and restraints can be reconciled to the cultural worldview of indigenous peoples remains an issue of deep concern. However, it is, to put it no higher than this, clearly encouraging that within the particular sphere of children's rights, the United Nations Convention on the Rights of the Child, 1989 ('UNCRC'), signals a clear commitment by the UN to finding a more culturally sensitive and inclusive approach to the creation, interpretation and implementation of international human rights law. Consequently, whilst there is still considerable work to be done before it can be said with confidence that international law has finally left behind its imperialist, Euro-centric roots, it not only provides an important source of normative standards and ideas on self-determination and Aboriginal governance, but provides a more culturally appropriate starting point for moving forward, in dialogue with indigenous peoples, on securing effective protection for all Aboriginal children.

Conclusion

This book is about Aboriginal children and the need for fundamental changes in the design, management and delivery of child welfare and protection services within Aboriginal communities. However, getting those changes right requires a journey well beyond the single issue of child welfare, taking us to the heart of the debate over self-government, self-determination and sovereignty in both national and international law. Whilst to some this discussion may seem far removed from the very pressing needs of Aboriginal children in Aboriginal communities today, in moving forward with self-government it is vitally important to get the legal framework right. Failure to do so may well result in another generation of Aboriginal children being lost to their communities. The mistakes of the past must be avoided. It is time to find a new way forward.

PART II
Aboriginal Child Welfare in Australia and Canada

Chapter 2
The Colonization of Aboriginal Children and Families

> The road to hell was paved with good intentions and the child welfare system was the paving contractor.[1]

Introduction

Alex Boraine, the Deputy Chairperson of the South Africa Truth and Reconciliation Commission is reported to have commented with respect to the disappointing response of the Australian commonwealth government to the *Bringing Them Home* report:

> It is wrong simply to say "Turn the page". It is right to turn the page, but first you have to read it, understand it and acknowledge it. Then you can turn the page.[2]

This book is primarily concerned with the future direction of Aboriginal child welfare in Australia and Canada. In other words, what is to be found once the page is turned. It is, however, clear that the future direction of Aboriginal child welfare cannot be addressed without first understanding why the past policies and practices of the Australian and Canadian governments were so fundamentally flawed and why they continue to have such a debilitating effect on Aboriginal communities today.

It is now common to hear the claim that the Australian government's intervention into the lives of Aboriginal families and communities amounted to 'cultural genocide' – an allegation that the Human Rights and Equal Opportunities Commission (HREOC) accepted as justified.[3] Similar allegations have been

1 E. Kimelman (1985). *Manitoba Review Committee on Indian and Métis Adoptions and Placements, No Quiet Place, The Final Report to the Hon. Muriel Smith, Minister of Community Services*. Winnipeg: Manitoba Community Services, 276.

2 Cited in A. Durbach (2001). 'Welcome Address', in *Moving Forward – Achieving Reparations for the Stolen Generations: Conference Papers, 15th – 16th August 2001, University of New South Wales, Sydney*. Sydney: Human Rights and Equal Opportunity Commission, 9.

3 HREOC cites with approval the definition of genocide adopted by the United Nations which includes the forcible transfer of children provided the other elements of the crime are established. On the evidence, the *Bringing Them Home* report concludes 'with certainty' that whilst child removal policies were often concerned to protect and 'preserve' individual children, a principal aim was to eliminate indigenous cultures as

made with respect to the Canadian government's policy on residential schools.[4] The legacy of colonial intervention into Aboriginal families and communities in Canada is strikingly similar to that found in Australia. In both jurisdictions, Aboriginal childhood stood at the centre of colonial strategies to assimilate and absorb the 'noble savage' into civilized society.[5] Forced removals in Australia and the residential school system in Canada thus played a key role in the early assimilationist policies of the Canadian and Australian governments. In short, they were the principal tools of cultural genocide. The effects of that legacy continue to be felt in Aboriginal communities today. In both countries, the removal of Aboriginal children from their families and communities is claimed to have initiated a 'circle of abuse' – a circle which is perpetuated today by the ethnocentricity of existing child welfare legislation, the policies and practices of the non-native child welfare authorities, and the continuing imperialist attitudes of key decision-makers, including the judiciary.[6] It is the colonial underpinnings of both the past and present removals of Aboriginal children from their families and communities that makes self-government seem such a necessary and self-

distinct entities. It thus goes on to conclude that 'the policy of forcible removal of children from indigenous Australians to other groups for the purpose of raising them separately from and ignorant of their culture and people could properly be labeled 'genocidal' in breach of binding international law from at least 11 December 1946'. See Human Rights and Equal Opportunity Commission (1997). *Report of the National Inquiry into the Separation of Aboriginal and Torres Strait Islander Children from their Families*. Commonwealth of Australia, 270–75.

4 L. White and E. Jacobs (1992). *Liberating Our Children Liberating Our Nations, Report of the Aboriginal Committee, Community Panel Child Protection Legislation Review in British Columbia*. British Columbia: Queen's Printer, 16.

5 A. McGillivray (1997). 'Therapies of Freedom: The Colonization of Aboriginal Childhood', in A. McGillivray (ed.) *Governing Childhood*. Aldershot: Dartmouth, 135, 137.

6 See: Inquiry into Response by Government Agencies to Complaints of Family Violence and Child Abuse in Aboriginal Communities (2002). *Putting the Picture Together*. State Law Publisher, WA, 57–9; Victorian Indigenous Family Violence Task Force (2003). *Final Report*, 132–8; Aboriginal Child Sexual Assault Taskforce (2006). *Breaking the Silence: Creating the Future – Addressing Child Sexual Assault in Aboriginal communities in NSW*. Attorney General's Department, NSW, 61–3; and Northern Territory Government (2007). *Board of Inquiry into the Protection of Aboriginal Children from Sexual Abuse*. Darwin, NT: Government Printer, 50. See also, P. Lynch (2001). 'Keeping them Home: The Best Interests of Indigenous Children and Communities in Canada and Australia', *Sydney Law Review*, 23: 501, 511. For very similar arguments in the Canadian context see: P. Monture (1989). 'A Vicious Circle: Child Welfare and the First Nations', *Canadian Journal of Women and the Law*, 3: 1; M. Kline (1992). 'Child Welfare Law, 'Best Interests of the Child' Ideology and First Nations', *Osgoode Hall Law Journal*, 30: 375; E. Carasco (1986). 'Canadian Native Children: Have Child Welfare Laws Broken the Circle?', *Canadian Journal of Family Law*, 5: 111; B. McKenzie and P. Hudson (1985). 'Native Children and the Colonization of Native People', in K. L. Levitt and B. Wharf (eds) *The Challenge of Child Welfare*. Vancouver: University of British Columbia.

evident way forward. Self-government promises decolonization: it is through self-government that Aboriginal people believe they can reclaim their children and thereby their communities. As McGillivray explains, the Aboriginal child stands at the centre of these wider struggles.[7] For Aboriginal communities, the fight to regain control over Aboriginal child welfare stands as a potent symbol of their ongoing resistance to colonial rule and the wider struggle for self-determination.

Critics of the past and present treatment of Aboriginal children at the hands of the non-native welfare authorities make one irrefutable point: the Australian and Canadian governments have fundamentally failed Aboriginal children, families and communities. The indictment of the Canadian and Australian authorities by highly respected bodies such as HREOC, the Manitoba Justice Inquiry and the Canadian Royal Commission on Aboriginal Peoples is telling. Although their conclusions have attracted some scepticism and even outright denial, particularly by right-wing commentators, their shocking and heart-wrenching findings concerning the removal and subsequent abuse of Aboriginal children have been widely recognized and accepted, including by those most directly involved.[8] It is therefore clear, given this history, that it is vital to locate any discussion of the contemporary dynamics of Aboriginal child welfare within its proper historical and colonial context.[9]

7 *Supra* note 5, 137.

8 Jane Stewart, Indian Affairs Minister, apologized on behalf of the Canadian federal government in 1998. Similar apologies have been made by the Canadian churches including the United Church (1998) and the Anglican Church of Canada (1993). In Australia, all states and territories have apologized to the 'Stolen generations', as have many of the churches involved including the Catholic Church (2001). For many years, the notable exception remained the Australian commonwealth government who under the leadership of John Howard refused to apologize. However, soon after it was elected, the Labor government under Prime Minister Kevin Rudd issued a formal apology to Australia's Aboriginal people in the Australian parliament on 12 February 2008. The full text of the apology is available at: www.abc.net.au/news/events/apology/text.htm.

9 The history of forced removals in Australia and the residential school system in Canada have both been the subject of detailed public inquiries. See: HREOC, *supra* note 3; and Royal Commission on Aboriginal Peoples (1996). *Report of the Royal Commission on Aboriginal Peoples. Looking Forward Looking Back.* Part One, Vol. 1. Ottawa: Minister of Supply and Services, Canada. The following account draws heavily on the findings of these two inquiries.

Colonizing Aboriginal Children in Australia: Missions, Dormitories and Residential Schools

The 'Protection' of Full-Blood Aboriginal Children

The forced removal of Aboriginal children from their families and communities in Australia took a variety of different forms, depending on the particular policy in place within each individual state and whether the children involved were regarded as 'full-blood' or 'half-blood' by the relevant authorities. Although the manner of the removals differed between states, the basic objective remained the same. In the case of 'full-blood' aborigines, the colonial authorities, applying crude racist theories of social Darwinism, simply believed that, if left alone, the Aboriginal peoples would slowly decline and eventually die out.[10] Although early attempts were made to convert Aboriginal peoples to an agricultural lifestyle, the devastation caused to Aboriginal communities by a combination of frontier violence, land dispossession, economic marginalization, poverty and disease, simply confirmed in the mind of the colonial authorities the Aborigines' inherently weak and inferior status.[11] A report by the first Aborigine Protection Board to be established in Victoria in 1860 observed that 'the early extinction of the race was freely predicted'.[12] Aboriginal people thus came to be regarded by the settlers as nothing more than a nuisance and an embarrassment; a temporary inconvenience in their quest for greater land and resources.[13]

Underpinned by what were clearly racist assumptions as to the backward, uncivilized nature of Aboriginal peoples, policies were introduced across Australia aimed at isolating and protecting the Aboriginal population from further violence at the hands of the settlers until their inevitable decline was complete. Pursuant to this 'protectionist policy', the Northern Territory and every state except Tasmania, introduced legislation creating 'protected' reserves, often controlled by missions, for the sole occupation of Aboriginal communities.[14] These reserves were not aimed solely at the protection of the Aboriginal people.[15] As J. W. Bleakley, Chief Protector and Director of Native Affairs in Queensland between 1913 and 1942 explained:

> Few realise the value of work done by missions. Not only do they protect the child races from the unscrupulous white, but they help to preserve the purity of

10 HREOC, ibid., 28.

11 Ibid.

12 Cited, ibid., 57.

13 Ibid., 28.

14 Ibid.

15 Ibid., 73.

> the white race from the grave social dangers that always threaten where there is a degraded race living in loose conditions at its back door.[16]

Responsibility for the protection of the Aboriginal communities living on reserves fell to the Chief Protector, the Director of Native Affairs (Queensland) or the Protection Board of the state or territory.[17] Extensive powers were conferred on the Protectors allowing them to control every aspect of an Aboriginal person's day-to-day life, including such things as the right to marry, seek employment and engage in social activities off the reserve.[18] The Chief Protector was also empowered to move Aboriginal peoples between reserves and eventually to separate children from their families as he deemed fit.[19]

In Queensland, South Australia, Western Australia and the Northern Territory, the separation of large numbers of Aboriginal children from their families was facilitated by the appointment of the Chief Protector or Director of Native Affairs as the sole legal guardian of all Aboriginal children. Legal guardianship gave him total control over the children's upbringing and, most importantly, the unfettered power to remove an Aboriginal child from the child's family should he deem such removal necessary.[20] The gradual extension of the Chief Protector's powers over Aboriginal children in South Australia was typical of these developments. A Protector for indigenous peoples was appointed in 1844. However, until 1911 the Protector only enjoyed legal guardianship over Aboriginal children whose parents were dead or unknown.[21] This meant the majority of Aboriginal children could only be removed from their families in accordance with general child protection provisions requiring a court to be satisfied that the child was 'destitute' or 'neglected'.[22] The Protector was dissatisfied with this limit on his powers and in 1911 successfully argued for his powers to be extended making him the automatic legal guardian of every Aboriginal and half-caste child. This conferred on him wide powers to move Aboriginal peoples between reserves as a disciplinary measure and to remove Aboriginal children from their families at will.[23] This followed similar moves in Western Australia in 1905[24] and the Northern Territory in 1910.[25] A similar model was eventually implemented in Queensland. The Industrial and Reformatory Schools Act 1865 (QLD) required an administrative finding of 'neglect' to be established before a child could be sent to an industrial school or

16 Ibid.
17 Ibid., 28.
18 Ibid., 29.
19 Ibid., 72.
20 Ibid., 30.
21 Ibid., 119.
22 Ibid., 120.
23 Ibid., 120–21.
24 Ibid., 103. Aborigines Act 1905 (WA).
25 Ibid., 132. Northern Territory Aboriginals Act 1910.

reformatory on a mission.[26] Although providing some protection for the family, in reality this did not constitute any great obstacle to removing the child where the Protector so desired. A combination of the marginalized socio-economic position of Aboriginal communities and a basic lack of understanding as to Aboriginal family structures and child-rearing practices, made removal by the Protection authorities on the grounds of 'neglect' a matter of routine.[27] Nevertheless, in 1939 the Director of Native Affairs was appointed guardian of all Aboriginal children under the age of 21 giving him total control over all aspects of their lives and unfettered powers of removal. These wide powers of removal under the guardianship model persisted in Queensland until 1965, the Northern Territory until 1964, in Western Australia until 1963 and in South Australia until 1962.[28]

In Victoria and NSW, the Protector's powers were less extensive but still allowed the separation of large numbers of Aboriginal children from their families. In Victoria, children were removed pursuant to the Aborigines Protection Act 1869 which until 1957 authorized the Aborigines Protection Board to make regulations dealing with 'the care, custody and education of the children of aborigines'.[29] Pursuant to these regulations, any child found to be neglected or left unprotected by its parents could be removed.[30] This was supported by the general authority to order any Aboriginal male under the age of 14 years and any unmarried Aboriginal female under the age of 18 to 'reside, and take their meals, and sleep in any building set apart for such purposes'.[31] In NSW, the Aborigines Protection Board originally relied upon 'persuasion' to remove children from their families.[32] In 1909, the NSW Board convinced the authorities to pass the Aborigines Protection Act 1909 which gave the Board the legal power, subject to independent scrutiny by the court, to remove the children on the grounds of 'neglect'. However, in 1915, unhappy that removals were being made more difficult by the requirement to seek the consent of the court, the Board persuaded the government to amend the Act giving them unfettered power to remove the children without any necessity to establish neglect or seek the courts' approval.[33]

Given the prevailing view amongst settlers that Aboriginal peoples were a dying race, the extensive use of these powers to remove Aboriginal children from their families is somewhat surprising. Yet, although convinced that 'pure' Aborigines could not survive, it was still felt desirable that Aboriginal children be

26 Ibid., 71.
27 Ibid.
28 Ibid., 78, 112, 127 and 145.
29 Ibid., 58.
30 Ibid.
31 Ibid.
32 Ibid., 40.
33 Ibid., 41.

schooled in the ways of civilized society, converted to Christianity, and shielded from Aboriginal traditions and lifestyle.[34] In the words of one missionary:

> The young require not only isolation from the outside world, but what proved still more difficult, separation from their own people. When the latter was possible a marked difference is noted in the manners, ways and point of view, as contrasted with those who were not so fortunate.[35]

In Victoria, the missions thus established schools where they attempted to 'wean the children away from tribal influences'.[36] Whilst not removed great distances from their communities, children were housed in separate dormitories on the reserve and only allowed extremely limited contact with their families.[37] By the early 1930s, there were seven missions in the Northern Territory caring for about 1,100 Aborigines, with the children housed in dormitories.[38] In Queensland, it is estimated that between 1908 and 1971, over 2,300 Aboriginal children were removed to dormitories on missions and settlements.[39]

The 'Civilization' and 'Breeding Out' of Mixed-Race Aboriginal Children

The approach taken to mixed-race Aboriginal children was much more aggressive. Although the number of 'full-blood' Aborigines was declining under the pressures of colonization, the number of mixed race children was increasing, in some places dramatically. This rise in the number of children who were of part European descent and yet continued to identify as Aboriginal was a matter of great concern for the colonial authorities. Within some states there were fears that the mixed race population would eventually outnumber the white population and thus become the dominant majority group.[40] Other concerns centred on the need for this growing population, who unlike their 'full-blood' relatives showed no signs of natural decline, to be successfully integrated into the labour force so that they did not become an impossible financial burden on the state.[41] There thus developed a plan to try and 'breed out' the Aboriginality from the mixed-race population. The idea

---

34 Ibid., 27. From the very earliest point of contact there had been attempts to establish schools with a view to 'civilizing' Aboriginal children. The first such school, the Native Institution at Parramatta, opened in New South Wales in 1814. Ibid., 101–2.

35 Cited, ibid., 74.

36 Ibid., 57.

37 Ibid., 30.

38 Ibid., 138.

39 Ibid., 75.

40 This fear was particularly strong in the Northern Territories where there were relatively few non-indigenous women. The sexual exploitation of young indigenous girls by non-indigenous men, often resulting in pregnancy, was therefore extremely common. Ibid., 132.

41 Ibid., 29.

was a simple one. It was thought that mixed-race Aboriginal children with the appropriate education and training could be integrated into mainstream society where, over time, through increased inter-racial marriage, the proportion of Aboriginal blood within each generation would decline and the mixed Aboriginal race would eventually be 'merged' with the white population.[42] The lighter the child's skin, the more successful it was felt this policy of 'absorption' would be.[43] There was also a particular focus on Aboriginal girls. In New South Wales, the majority of children removed were female.[44] In the Northern Territories, permission was required from the Chief Protector to marry, and his control over Aboriginal females was such that they remained under his control until they died unless they married a non-Aboriginal man.[45]

By 1937, the idea of absorption had evolved into that of assimilation: a policy approved on a national scale at the first Commonwealth-State Native Welfare Conference.[46] Although based on similar prejudices, the assimilation policy was concerned less with the need to 'breed out' Aboriginality than with the need to provide Aboriginal people with the necessary education, training and skills to compete on an equal footing with their European counterparts.[47] The provision of elementary education for half-caste children was regarded as of crucial importance.[48] Consequently, from the 1950s, the Southern Australian and Western Australian governments allowed Aboriginal children to attend state schools, staying in government and mission run hostels, and being permitted to go home in the summer holidays provided they had a 'suitable' home to go to.[49] However, although receiving a basic education, many children were also sent out to work at a young age as part of the retraining objective.[50]

Under both the absorption and assimilation models Aboriginal culture was treated with disdain: as an obstacle to progress. It was therefore believed to be of crucial importance in securing the success of the absorption and assimilation policies that mixed race children be isolated and protected from the culture, traditions, and generally 'corrupting' influence of their Aboriginal families. In New South Wales, Western Australia and the Northern Territory it was therefore resolved that light-skinned, mixed-race children should from a very young age be

42 Ibid., 133.

43 This view was held with particular force by Neville, the Chief Protector of Western Australia. He believed that once half-castes were sufficiently white in colour they would be accepted by the non-indigenous community as white people. In contrast, he believed the older generations and 'full blood' Aborigines would die out and the reserves closed. Ibid., 30 and 108.

44 See, for example, 1921 figures. Ibid., 43.

45 Ibid., 133.

46 Ibid., 32.

47 Ibid.

48 Ibid., 140.

49 Ibid., 111 and 127.

50 Ibid., 75 and 164.

removed to 'training institutions' and kept totally separated from their families and communities in order to ensure their smooth transition into civilized European society.[51] The first such 'industrial school' was established in the Northern Territory in 1899.[52] The rationale behind these schools was clearly expressed in the debates leading up to the passing of the Aborigines Act 1905 in Western Australia:

> [A] half-caste, who possesses few of the virtues and nearly all of the vices of whites, grows up to be a mischievous and very immoral subject ... it may appear to be a cruel thing to tear an Aborigine child from its mother, but it is necessary in some cases to be cruel to be kind.[53]

Removing 'half-caste' Aboriginal children from their families and communities was perceived as the 'key' to the problem:

> Children are removed from the evil influence of the Aboriginal camp with its lack of moral training and its risk of serious organic infectious disease. They are properly fed, clothed and educated as white children, they are subjected to constant medical supervision and in receipt of domestic and vocational training.[54]

During this early period of removals, half-caste Aboriginal children were typically removed from their families pursuant to the general protectionist and guardianship legislation in force in the state.[55] As noted above, this typically gave the authorities the unfettered power to remove an Aboriginal child without subjecting their actions to the independent scrutiny of a court.[56] Debate centred on the most appropriate age to remove a child. In South Australia views differed, with the Secretary of State Children's Council arguing children should be removed at birth: '[i]f they are in the wurley for a week it is bad for them, but it is fatal for them to remain there for a year'.[57] Others argued that children should be removed at a slighter later age when they required less care but were still 'young enough to be attractive'.[58] Little thought or consideration was given to the effects of these separations on either the children or their parents. In the words of one of the Protectors in Western Australia:

> The half-caste is intellectually above the aborigine, and it is the duty of the State that they be given a chance to lead a better life than their mothers. I would not

51 Ibid., 31, 103 and 139.
52 Ibid., 132.
53 Ibid., 103.
54 Chief Protector Cook, cited ibid., 137.
55 Ibid., 30.
56 Ibid.
57 Ibid., 121.
58 Ibid., 122.

> hesitate for one moment to separate any half-caste from its Aboriginal mother, no matter how frantic her momentary grief might be at the time. They soon forget their offspring.[59]

The removals were pursued with brutal indifference:

> The assembled children were loaded into the truck very suddenly and their things thrown in hastily after them. The suddenness and the suppressed air of tension shocked the mothers and the children and they realised something was seriously wrong … Children began to cry and the mothers to wail and cut themselves … The tailgate was slammed shut and bolted and the truck screeched off with things still hanging over the back and mothers and other children running after it crying and wailing.[60]

The Experiences of Aboriginal Children Removed from their Families

The experiences of children placed in dormitories, missions, schools or training institutions away from their communities were singularly unhappy. Dormitories were overcrowded and lacking in basic provisions:

> One [dormitory], measuring 22 feet by 12 feet is used as a sleeping room for about 25 boys. It has three small barred windows and a small closet at one end. The floor is sanded, and on this the boys sleep with a bluey between each two of them. They are locked in at sundown and released at 8 o'clock in the morning. The other is somewhat larger, and has a verandah closed in with strong pickets round two sides and a closet at the end. There are six small windows, two of them opening on to the closed in verandah. The floor of this is also sanded and on it about 30 girls sleep. The hygienic state of these dungeons during the extremely hot summer nights can better be imagined than described. The sand is renewed once every two weeks, which is quite necessary.[61]

Starved of money and resources by the state and territory authorities, children living in these institutions experienced conditions of extreme poverty, leading to severe hunger, malnutrition and disease.[62] The conditions in Queensland were appalling:

> There were no cots or beds in the children's dormitories … and the protectress described how children slept on a single blanket on the ground with another

---

59 Quoted by Dr Christine Choo, cited ibid., 104.

60 Ibid., 141–2.

61 Description of the dormitories on the Hermannsburg mission in 1923, cited ibid., 139.

62 Ibid., 31 and 139–40.

> blanket for warmth. Clothing was allocated only twice a year and was too limited to keep clean. Children were underfed, and a recent scheme to provide one meal a day of soup and bread had been discontinued … Normal sanitation facilities were non-existent on the settlement … Indeed the facilities there were so bad that … [the doctor there] considered the common usage of the bush as a toilet as the safest practice.[63]

Conditions were similarly bad in the Northern Territory. As one former resident recalls:

> There's where food was scarce again. Hardly anything … night time we used to cry with hunger, y'know, lice, no food. And we used to go out there to the town dump … we had to come and scrounge at the dump y'know, eating old bread and smashing tomato sauce bottles and licking them. Half of the time our food we got from the rubbish dump. Always hungry there.[64]

The 'civilizing' agenda was strictly adhered to in the various institutions. Aboriginal people were vilified and held in open contempt:

> We were told our mother was an alcoholic and that she was a prostitute and she didn't care about us. They [foster family] used to warn us that when we got older we'd have to watch it because we'd turn into sluts and alcoholics, so we had to be very careful. If you were white you didn't have that dirtiness in you … It was in our breed, in us to be like that.[65]

Rules aimed at alienating Aboriginal children from their cultural roots were rigorously enforced. Any contact with members of the child's Aboriginal family was strictly limited and controlled.[66] Letters from the child's family were often destroyed with children being told their parents were dead or had abandoned them.[67] Aboriginal languages and the practice of Aboriginal customs and traditions were prohibited. Any infringement of the rules was severely punished:

> Y'know, I can remember we used to just talk lingo. [In the Home] they used to tell us not to talk that language, that it's devil's language. And they'd wash our mouths with soap. We sorta had to sit down with Bible language all the time. So it sorta wiped out all our language that we knew.[68]

---

63 Cited ibid., 73.
64 Ibid., 134.
65 Ibid., 157.
66 Ibid., 155.
67 Ibid., 155 and 177.
68 Confidential evidence 170, South Australia: woman taken from her parents with

The infliction of severe physical and emotional abuse was a daily occurrence. Although some children speak of individual staff with affection and fondness,[69] the treatment to which Aboriginal children were generally subjected is shocking. As the daughter of one child sent to the Cootamundra Institution in New South Wales recalls:

> Cootamundra in those days was very strict and cruel. The home was overcrowded. Girls were coming and going all the time. The girls were taught reading, writing and arithmetic. All the girls had to learn to scrub, launder and cook. Mum remembered once a girl who did not move too quick. She was tied to the old bell post and belted continuously. She died that night, still tied to the post, no girl ever knew what happened to the body or where she was buried.[70]

The infliction of severe physical abuse was a common theme of witnesses to the *Bringing Them Home* Inquiry:

> I've seen girls naked, strapped to chairs and whipped. We've all been through the locking up period, locked in dark rooms. I had a problem of fainting when I was growing up and I got belted every time I fainted and this is belted, not just on the hands or nothing. I've seen my sister dragged by the hair into those block rooms and belted because she's trying to protect me … How could this be for my own good? Please tell me.[71]

Even Neville, the Chief Protector of Western Australia, found the levels of abuse in some homes to be unacceptable, recording in 1947:

> One Superintendent I had, because he suspected him of some moral lapse, tarred and feathered a native, and he did the job thoroughly, calling the staff to see the rare bird he had captured … Another Manager I did appoint, an ex-Missionary, and a good man too, I had to dismiss for chaining girls to table legs … Indeed it was found necessary to provide by regulation for the abolition of "degrading" and injurious punishments and the practice of holding inmates up to ridicule, such as dressing them in old sacks or shaving girls' heads.[72]

---

her three sisters when the family, who worked and resided on a pastoral station, came into town to collect stores; placed at Umewarra mission. Cited ibid., 154.

69 See, e.g., ibid., 169–70.

70 Ibid., 52–3.

71 Confidential evidence 8, New South Wales: woman removed to Cootamundra Girls' Home in the 1940s. Cited ibid., 161.

72 Cited ibid.

One in five witnesses to the *Bringing Them Home* Inquiry reported having been subjected to physical abuse.[73] In a survey conducted by the Western Australia Aboriginal Legal Service that number was much higher, with 62.1 per cent of Aboriginal people forcibly removed as children stating that they had been physically abused.[74] Sexual abuse was also disturbingly common. Although not specifically asked about sexual abuse, one in 10 boys and just over one in 10 girls alleged that they were sexually abused whilst in a children's institution.[75] Witnesses described the most horrific abuses by institutional staff:

> There was tampering with the boys … the people who would come in to work with the children, they would grab the boys' penises, play around with them and kiss them and things like this. These were the things that were done … It was seen to be the white man's way of lookin' after you. It never happened with an Aboriginal.[76]

Similar allegations were made with respect to the Kinchela Training Institute in New South Wales:

> Kinchela was a place where they thought you were animals. You know it was like a place where they go around and kick us like a dog … It was just like a prison. Truthfully, there were boys having sex with boys … But these other dirty mongrels didn't care. We had a manager who was sent to prison because he was doing it to a lot of the boys, sexual abuse. Nothing was done. There was a pommie bloke that was doing it. These attendants – if the boys told them, they wouldn't even listen. It just happened … I don't like talking about it.[77]

Attempted escapes were common.

Colonizing Aboriginal Children in Canada: The Residential Schools

As in Australia, the issue of Aboriginal child welfare in Canada is dominated by the history of the state owned, church administered, residential schools.[78] Although there were important legal differences in the way in which the removals

---

73 Ibid., 162.

74 Ibid., 194.

75 Ibid., 163.

76 Confidential evidence 340, Western Australia: man removed in the 1930s to Sister Kate's Orphanage. Ibid.

77 Ibid., 167.

78 For the most recent analysis of the history and impact of the Canadian residential schools see RCAP, *supra* note 9, 333–409. See also Aboriginal Justice Inquiry of Manitoba (AJIM) (1991). *Report of the Aboriginal Justice Inquiry of Manitoba: The Justice System and Aboriginal People*, vol. 1. Winnipeg: Manitoba, 511–16 and White and Jacobs, *supra*

were effected in the two jurisdictions,[79] the policy and practice of removing and institutionalizing Aboriginal children away from their families and communities was a common feature of the colonization of both countries. The colonial authorities in Canada, through tools of language, literature, religion and education, established a ferocious civilizing mission aimed at 'eradicating the Savage Indian' from the child – a policy which was strikingly similar to the absorption/assimilation policy employed in Australia with respect to 'half-caste' children. As in Australia, underpinning this policy of civilization was the belief that Aboriginal peoples were a dying race and the only way in which they could survive was to be assimilated into 'superior' European society.[80] Duncan Campbell Scott, the Deputy Superintendent of Indian Affairs in Canada, speaking in the House of Commons in 1920, was absolutely clear as to the government's objectives:

> Our object is to continue until there is not a single Indian in Canada that has not been absorbed into the body politic and there is no Indian question and no Indian department.[81]

Children were again the prime target of this civilizing mission. It was, for example, the view of Nicholas Davin, a journalist commissioned by the government in 1879 to report on the aggressive civilization policy in the United States, that 'if anything is to be done with the Indian we must catch him young'.[82] Education was seen as key.[83]

Nicholas Davin's report strongly endorsed the use of industrial boarding schools to achieve assimilation, arguing that the removal of children away from the damaging influence of their 'uncivilized' parents was crucial to achieving their successful assimilation.[84] In the succeeding decade the residential school system took hold,[85] consisting of two major types of institution: the boarding school which was located on or near reserves and was intended to provide a basic education in reading, writing and arithmetic, as well as simple manual skills; and the large industrial school typically located in urban centres and intended to provide instruction in a trade, as well as a rudimentary English education.[86]

---

note 4, 512–13. The term 'Indian' will be used throughout this section as the residential school policy was applied only to registered Indians on reserve.

79 For example, the strong distinction drawn between 'full-blood' and 'half-caste' Aboriginal children witnessed in Australia, was not a feature of Canadian Aboriginal policy.

80 AJIM, *supra* note 78, 512–13. See also, J. S. Milloy (1999). *'A National Crime' – The Canadian Government and the Residential School System, 1879 to 1986*. Winnipeg: The University of Manitoba Press, 6.

81 Cited AJIM, ibid., 514.

82 Ibid., 513.

83 Milloy, *supra* note 80, 7.

84 Ibid., 8.

85 Four residential schools were already established in Ontario.

86 *Supra* note 80, 7.

Between 1879 and 1946 the residential school system stood at the centre of the federal government's assimilation policy. A total of 80 schools were built, with the number of Aboriginal children registered varying between 12 per cent and 37 per cent.[87] McGillivray reports that in 1936, roughly 50 years after inception, 42 per cent of status Indian children in Manitoba were in a residential school; 3 per cent in Quebec; 36 per cent in Ontario; 77 per cent in Saskatchewan; and 98 per cent in Alberta.[88]

In the post-Second World War era the federal government's policy on Indian education underwent significant change.[89] The dominant view emerged that the residential schools should be closed and Indian children integrated into the provincial school system.[90] Yet, despite this shift in official policy, it took nearly 40 years before the last of the residential schools was closed.[91] During this period, the schools increasingly came to operate as boarding homes for the numerous Indian children deemed by officials as unable to return to their homes and families because of the risk of 'neglect'.[92]

Unlike the forced removal of Aboriginal children in Australia where strong legal tools such as guardianship were routinely employed, the process of effecting the removal of Indian children in Canada relied, at least initially, on less coercive measures. Persuasion rather than force was the preferred approach. For many years the government resisted church demands to make school attendance compulsory.[93] Regulations issued by the Department of Indian Affairs in 1894 permitted the Indian agent to place a 'neglected child' in care by force if necessary.[94] However, the use of this provision was discouraged. In 1920, during the administration of Deputy Superintendent Duncan Campbell Scott, the Indian Act was amended to make school attendance for all children aged between seven and 15 years old compulsory. Non-compliance with this provision was punishable by fine or imprisonment although evidence suggests enforcement measures were rarely invoked.[95] The government's reluctance to adopt coercive measures meant the schools remained responsible for recruiting their own students. School officials would be sent out on recruitment missions, assisted in varying degrees by the Indian agents on reserve.[96] Some Aboriginal parents welcomed the schools for the perceived benefits of their children receiving a Christian education or as the

87 McGillivray, *supra* note 5, 154–5.

88 Ibid.

89 Milloy, *supra* note 80, xv.

90 Ibid., xv.

91 Ibid., xvi.

92 Ibid.

93 Ibid., 70.

94 Ibid.

95 Ibid., 67.

96 Ibid., 68–9. The Indian Agent was the federal government's chief appointed official on reserve.

fulfilment of treaty promises on education.[97] However, there was also widespread resistance to sending their children away.[98] School officials, under immense pressure to recruit, therefore employed increasingly 'bizarre and questionable practices'.[99] Orphans were targeted and bribery and kidnapping became commonplace.[100]

If the process of effecting the removal of Aboriginal children from their families differed between the two jurisdictions, their experiences of separation were strikingly similar. As in Australia, Canadian Indian children were placed in racially segregated residential facilities many miles from their reserves so as to isolate and 'protect' them from any 'contaminating influences'.[101] They were taught to be ashamed of their 'savage' history and culture, punished for speaking their native languages, whilst the 'achievements' and 'virtues' of non-native society were promoted and glorified.[102] As described by the son of one former resident, the objective of ridding Aboriginal children of their language and culture was often pursued with vicious and brutal determination:

> The elimination of language has always been a primary stage in a process of cultural genocide. This was the primary function of the residential school. My father, who attended Alberni Indian residential school for four years in the twenties was physically tortured by his teachers for speaking Tseshaht: they pushed sewing needles through his tongue, a routine punishment for language offenders … The needle tortures suffered by my father affected all the family (I have six brothers and sisters). My dad's attitude became, "why teach my children Indian if they are going to be punished for speaking it?" so he would not allow my mother to speak to us in his presence. I never learned to speak my own language. I am now therefore truly a "dumb Indian".[103]

Yet against all expectations of the architects of the system, Indian children did not graduate from the residential schools as 'well-educated' 'civilized' little citizens of white Canada.[104] Cultural identity could not be so easily erased and chronic under-funding meant that educational goals would never be met. Indeed, the education provided to the Indian students was grossly deficient. Moreover, the deplorable physical condition of the schools, lack of sanitation, clothing and food made survival a daily struggle.[105] Disease ran rampant through the schools and children were literally dying in their hundreds and thousands.[106] For many of the

97 McGillivray, *supra* note 5, 154.
98 Milloy, *supra* note 80, 67.
99 Ibid., 69.
100 Ibid., 69–70.
101 AJIM, *supra* note 78, 513.
102 White and Jacobs, *supra* note 4, 19.
103 Randy Fred, cited in AJIM, *supra* note 78, 514.
104 Milloy, *supra* note 80, 158–9.
105 See generally Milloy, ibid.
106 Ibid., 77–8.

children who survived, the residential school experience was marked by horrific physical, sexual and emotional abuse.[107] In many cases, school officials appear to have literally attempted to beat the Indian out of the child.

Initiating a Circle of Abuse: The Legacy of Removals

Understanding the continuing trauma caused to Aboriginal families and communities by the child removal policies of the past is key to understanding the complexity of the difficulties experienced by many Aboriginal families and children today. The *Bringing Them Home* report describes the long-term effects of the removals as 'multiple and profoundly disabling'.[108] It continues:

> Psychological and emotional damage renders many people less able to learn social skills and survival skills. Their ability to operate successfully in the world is impaired causing low educational achievement, unemployment and consequent poverty. These in turn cause their own emotional distress, leading some to perpetrate violence, self-harm, substance abuse or anti-social behaviour.[109]

Already struggling from the socio-economic marginalization that accompanied the dispossession of their land and resources, the removal of Aboriginal children and the resulting pressure on Aboriginal cultures exacerbated the growing despondency, high levels of mental illness,[110] and alcohol and drug abuse within many Aboriginal communities. In its evidence to the *Bringing Them Home* Inquiry, the Sydney Aboriginal Mental Health Unit identified amongst its patients, 'major depressive disorder and use of alcohol and other drugs to ease feelings of hopelessness, helplessness, marginalisation, discrimination and dispossession, leading to breakdown in relationships, domestic violence and abuse'.[111] The Unit concluded that the forcible removal policies were the 'principal cause' of these problems.[112] Similarly, the alienation of Aboriginal children from both 'white European' and Aboriginal society is argued to have contributed to the high rates of suicide amongst Aboriginal people, particularly amongst Aboriginal youth. The continuing disproportionate institutionalization of Aboriginal people in penal institutions as a result of the high levels of delinquency and more serious criminal

107 AJIM, *supra* note 78, 515 and White and Jacobs, *supra* note 4, 514.

108 HREOC, *supra* note 3, 178.

109 Ibid.

110 In a survey of Aboriginal patients at a medical practice in Victoria in the 1980s it was found that children separated from their families were twice as likely to suffer psychological distress in adulthood than the remainder of the participants. Ibid., 196.

111 Ibid., 197.

112 Ibid.

offending amongst this group is also attributed to the ongoing effects of child removals.[113] As the *Bringing Them Home* report acknowledges, the complex socio-economic difficulties experienced by Aboriginal communities as a result of colonization makes it impossible to identify the policy of forced removals as solely responsible for the current problems. However, it goes on to point out that 'childhood removal is a very significant cause both in its distinctive horror and in its capacity to break down resilience and render its victims perpetually vulnerable'.[114] It is important to appreciate that this is not just a matter of individual trauma. Individual trauma at this level of severity can profoundly affect the wider health of a community. Indeed, it is suggested that the current dysfunctional behaviour in many Aboriginal communities is grounded in the *communities'* unresolved grief associated with multiple layers of trauma suffered over many generations – trauma caused by years of living with the institutionalized violence, racism, dispossession and poverty of colonialism.[115]

One of the most damaging consequences of the removal of Aboriginal children was the effect, as indeed was intended, on the continuity of Aboriginal culture at both the individual and community level. As it was put in the *Bringing Them Home* report, '[c]ulture, language, land and identity were to be stripped from the children in the hope that the traditional law and culture would die by losing their claim on them and their sustenance of them'.[116] Aboriginal children removed from their families and subjected to the daily vilification of Aboriginal people and culture learned to despise everything so essential to their sense of identity.[117] Aboriginal children thus grew to be ashamed of their native heritage. The confusion and despair caused by this loss of cultural identity was deeply felt:

> Most of us girls were thinking white in the head but were feeling black inside. We weren't black or white. We were a very lonely, lost and sad displaced group of people. We were taught to think and act like a white person, but we didn't know how to think and act like an Aboriginal. We didn't know anything about our culture. We were completely brainwashed to think only like a white person. When they went to mix in white society, they found they were not accepted [because] they were Aboriginal. When they went and mixed with Aborigines, some found they couldn't identify with them either, because they had too much white ways in them. So that they were neither black nor white. They were simply a lost generation. I know. I was one of them.[118]

113 *Bringing Them Home* citing the work of Dr Elizabeth Sommerlad, ibid., 190.

114 Ibid., 193.

115 *Putting the Picture Together*, *supra* note 6, 57.

116 HREOC, *supra* note 3, 202.

117 Ibid., 202–5.

118 Confidential submission 617, New South Wales: woman removed at eight years with her three sisters in the 1940s: placed in Cootamundra Girls' Home, ibid., 152.

So effective were the institutions in their denigration of Aboriginal culture that many removed children came to despise and fear Aboriginal people:

> "Your family don't care about you anymore, they wouldn't have given you away. They don't love you. All they are, are just dirty drunken blacks." You heard this daily … When I come out of the home and come to Redfern here looking for the girls, you see a koori coming towards you, you cross the street, you run for your life, you're terrified.[119]

The problems caused by this cultural dislocation were perpetuated when children who had experienced the pain of removal themselves became parents. Alienated from their roots, many of this new generation of Aboriginal parents would not, or could not, pass down their culture and traditions to their own children.[120] The incapacity of an Aboriginal community to perpetuate its culture through its children thus resulted in a damaging cultural void.[121] On a more individual level, developing attachments and forming close loving relationships was difficult for removed children.[122] The institutionalization of Aboriginal children deprived them of any positive models of parenting and family life:

> We had been brought up on the surrogate mother of the institution and that whole lifestyle, which did not prepare us at all for any type of family life or life whereby in the future we would be surviving or fending for ourselves; and then the survival skills that we needed in order to survive in the mainstream community, because those survival skills are certainly not skills that you learn in a major institution. And the whole family value system wasn't there and then the practice that comes with that wasn't there and put in place.[123]

What these children did know from their experiences in the missions, training institutions and residential schools was raising children through violence and abuse:

> The boarding schools taught us violence. Violence was emphasised through physical, corporal punishment, strappings, beatings, bruising and control. We learned to understand that this was power and control.[124]

119 Confidential evidence 8, New South Wales: woman removed to Cootamundra Girls' Home in the 1940s, ibid., 156.

120 White and Jacobs, *supra* note 4, 19.

121 HREOC, *supra* note 3, 212–21.

122 Ibid., 222–5.

123 Ibid., 187.

124 Janet Ross, cited in AJIM, *supra* note 78, 515. See also, White and Jacobs, *supra* note 4.

This attack at the heart of family life affected the whole community. The violent regime of the missions, dormitories and residential schools in both Australia and Canada initiated what has been termed a 'circle of abuse' within Aboriginal communities, causing amongst other things, a community-wide breakdown in traditional methods of child-rearing and parenting, including the central role played by the extended family and kinship group:

> For many victims of the residential school system, not only were cultural values lost, but the experience of family relationships and the natural process of parenting were lost as well. In their place was substituted an example of child care characterised by authoritarianism, often to the point of physical abuse, a lack of compassion and, in many cases, sexual abuse. For those victims, the residential school system blurred natural limits on what normally would develop as mature love and sexual relationships.[125]

The high incidence of sexual abuse experienced by children removed from their families has had particularly tragic inter-generational effects. It is reported that up to two-thirds of children sexually abused as children experience difficulties parenting their own children and, when under stress, are vulnerable to becoming abusers themselves.[126] In some Aboriginal communities, rather than abuse, the problem is a lack of discipline.[127] The use of physical punishment as employed in the various institutions is rejected as unacceptable according to traditional methods of child-rearing.[128] However, with the loss of traditional knowledge and culture, there is often little on which Aboriginal parents can draw other than these institutional models. This leads to a potentially problematic 'discipline vacuum':

> I have a problem with smacking kids. I won't smack them. I won't control them. I'm just scared of everything about myself. I just don't know how to be a proper parent sometimes. I can never say no, because I think they're going to hate me. I remember hating [foster mother] so I never want the kids to hate me. I try to be perfect.[129]

The result of these inter-generational problems is a repeat pattern of removals. Many Aboriginal parents who were themselves removed as children experience difficulties with parenting and consequently face the removal of their own children, this time by social workers operating under general child welfare law. A survey by the Aboriginal Legal Service of Western Australia of Aboriginal people who had

125 White and Jacobs, ibid., 18–19. See also, AJIM, ibid., 515.

126 HREOC, *supra* note 3, 195.

127 Ibid., 224–5.

128 Ibid.

129 Ibid., 225

been forcibly removed as children revealed that a generation later more than one-third had had their own children removed.[130]

Entrenching Colonization: The Non-Native Child Welfare System

The missions, dormitories, training institutions and residential schools stand as the most potent symbol of the suffering and devastation caused to Aboriginal peoples by the imperialist policies of the Australian and Canadian governments. Whilst arguments continue over appropriate reparations for the victims,[131] official apologies for the removals and subsequent abuse suffered by Aboriginal children have now been issued by the Canadian and Australian governments and a number of the religious organizations involved.[132] It is, however, a sobering fact that whilst the residential schools and dormitories may have closed, the grossly disproportionate removal of Aboriginal children from their families and communities continued. The 'circle of abuse' initiated by the missions, dormitories, training institutions and residential schools did not end with their closure, for in their place arrived a new and seemingly more benevolent colonial force: the professional social worker applying general child welfare law.

The early experiences of Aboriginal peoples with the general child welfare system were almost entirely negative. The ethnocentricity entrenched at the heart of the system created a hostile, alien and deeply damaging environment for Aboriginal families. Charges of cultural genocide have again been made against the system.[133] Indeed, in 2009 a class action on behalf of 16,000 Aboriginal children was launched in Ontario against the federal government alleging that between the years of 1965 and 1984 Aboriginal children were subjected to a provincial child welfare system intended to 'systematically eradicate the Aboriginal culture, society, language, customs, traditions, and spirituality of the children' – in other

---

130 Ibid., 226.

131 In Australia, the struggle for compensation continues through the courts. See, *Cubillo v Commonwealth* [1999] FCA 518 and, for a recent more successful action, *Trevorrow v State of South Australia (No 5)* [2007] SASC 285. In Canada, former students of the schools, the churches, the Assembly of First Nations, other Aboriginal organizations, and the Canadian government entered into a Settlement Agreement in September 2007 to 'achieve a fair and lasting resolution of the legacy of the Indian Residential Schools'. The Settlement comprises five main elements: (1) a common experience payment for former residents; (2) an independent assessment process for victims of serious physical or sexual assault; (3) measures to support healing; (4) commemorative activities; and (5) the establishment of a Truth and Reconciliation Commission. For further detail see: www.ainc-inac.gc.ca/ai/rqpi/sa/index-eng.asp.

132 See note 8 above.

133 McGillivray, *supra* note 5, 158.

words, that they were subjected to a 'deliberate program of "identity genocide of children"'.[134]

The remainder of this chapter focuses on the failings of the non-native child welfare system between the 1950s and the early 1990s.[135] These failings are particularly instructive as to the contemporary challenges facing Aboriginal peoples. The repeat pattern of removals, as legitimized by the courts, reveals the extent to which the culturally rooted norms and practices of non-native society became embedded within the child welfare system, raising grave doubts as to its capacity for change to enable it to respond more effectively to the cultural needs of Aboriginal children and families. Despite the reform efforts of the last 15 years or so, much of the analysis within this chapter could be applied with equal force to contemporary practice within the social work profession and the courts.[136] Indeed, it will strike a deep chord with the many Aboriginal families still embroiled within the non-native child welfare system.

The Transfer of Responsibility to the Non-Native Child Welfare System

Australia

In 1940, NSW became the first jurisdiction to remove control over Aboriginal children from the Aborigine's Protection Board and transfer it to the general state child welfare authorities. In order to remove an Aboriginal child in New South Wales after 1940 the Board therefore had to show to the satisfaction of a court that the child was 'neglected', 'destitute' or 'uncontrollable' in accordance with the Child Welfare Act 1939.[137] Towards the end of the 1940s, other jurisdictions began to take similar steps, abandoning their 'protectionist' approach and bringing Aboriginal children within the scope of the general child welfare legislation. The process was not, however, complete until the late 1960s. Legal guardianship over Aboriginal children was restored to their parents in South Australia in 1962, the Northern Territories in 1964, in Western Australia in 1963, and in Queensland in 1965.[138]

In theory, bringing Aboriginal children under the protection of the state's child welfare legislation created important legal safeguards against the arbitrary

---

134 *Brown v Canada (Attorney General)* [2010] ONSC 3095, [1]–[4]. Although the Ontario Superior Court of Justice struck out the claim of 'identity genocide of children' as disclosing no reasonable cause of action, permission was granted for the claimants to amend the pleadings and pursue a claim against the Federal Crown alleging breach of fiduciary duty and negligence for its failure to act to protect the interests of Aboriginal children, particularly their Aboriginal cultural identity, as they were removed from their communities by provincial authorities and placed in non-Aboriginal homes. Ibid., [124].

135 More recent changes to the Australian and Canadian non-native child welfare systems will be explored in Chapter 3.

136 The impact of the recent reforms will be considered in Chapter 3.

137 HREOC, *supra* note 3, 46.

138 Ibid., 78, 112, 127 and 145.

removals experienced by Aboriginal communities in the first half of the twentieth century. Assimilation remained, however, the overriding policy objective and it continued to exert a strong influence over attitudes towards Aboriginal children and their care, such that, despite changes in the legal framework, the removal of Aboriginal children from their families remained the preferred approach. With Aboriginal peoples economically marginalized, subjected to intense scrutiny and judged according to culturally biased standards, the removal of Aboriginal children in hugely disproportionate numbers on the grounds of 'neglect' remained a huge problem. By 1983, Aboriginal children constituted 70 per cent of the total care population in the Northern Territories, 12 per cent in NSW, 60 per cent in Western Australia and 16 per cent in South Australia.[139]

Canada

The early experiences of Aboriginal people with the Canadian provincial child welfare system were similarly negative. The experience of Aboriginal communities with the non-native child welfare system is one of apparent contradictions. On one hand, the story is told of white professional social workers coming onto reserves and removing First Nations children in huge numbers.[140] On the other hand, the story is told of the provincial child welfare agencies refusing to provide services to First Nations on-reserve communities leaving children in situations of severe risk.[141] Since the 1950s, the delivery of child welfare services to Aboriginal communities in Canada has been severely compromised by an ongoing jurisdictional dispute between the provincial and federal governments. Child welfare generally falls within the sphere of provincial responsibility and off-reserve Aboriginal children are therefore served by provincial agencies. The position of First Nations children living on-reserve is considerably more difficult. The British North America Act 1867 confers exclusive jurisdiction on the federal government for 'Indians and lands reserved for Indians'. Pursuant to this provision, the provincial child welfare authorities took the view that they had no jurisdiction over on-reserve First Nations children, the delivery of child welfare services being a matter within the jurisdiction of the federal government as a matter pertaining to 'Indians and lands reserved for Indians'.[142] Prior to the 1950s, it was therefore rare for provincial child welfare services to be offered on First Nations reserves.[143] Children in need of protection were apprehended by the Indian agent and either placed with another

139 Australian Law Reform Commission (1986). *The Recognition of Aboriginal Customary Laws*, No. 31, Vol. 1. Canberra: Australian Government Publishing Service, [346].

140 AJIM, *supra* note 78, 519–20; British Columbia Royal Commission on Family and Children's Law (1975). *Native Families and the Law: Tenth Report of the Royal Commission on Family and Children's Law*. Vancouver: British Columbia Royal Commission on Family and Children's Law, 14.

141 BC Royal Commission, ibid.

142 Constitution Act 1867 (U.K.) 30 & 31 Vict. c.3, s 91(24).

143 J. MacDonald (1983). 'The Spallumcheen Indian By-Law and Its Potential

family on the reserve or sent to a residential school.[144] This position changed when the Indian Act was amended in 1951 to extend general provincial jurisdiction to First Nations reserves. Section 88 of the Indian Act now provides:

> Subject to the terms of any treaty and other act of the Parliament of Canada, all laws of general application from time to time in force in any province are applicable to and in respect of Indians in the province, except to the extent that such laws are inconsistent with this Act.

This provided the legislative basis for the extension of provincial child welfare services to the First Nation reserves.[145] The provinces nevertheless remained reluctant to assume these new extensive responsibilities without some form of financial compensation from the federal government – financial compensation the federal government was generally unwilling to provide.[146] In 1966 the federal government entered into cost-sharing agreements with the provincial governments for the provision of child welfare services on reserve.[147] However, funding difficulties remained and services were 'patchy'.[148] The truth would therefore seem to be that as a result of this jurisdictional and financial wrangling there was, and still is, great disparity in the level and quality of services offered to Aboriginal communities living on reserves.[149] It led to a situation in which, most

---

Impact on Native Indian Child Welfare Policy in British Columbia', *Canadian Journal of Family Law*, 1: 75, 77.

144 Ibid.

145 Confirmed by the Canadian Supreme Court in *Natural Parents v Superintendent of Child Welfare* [1976] 2 S.C.R. 751.

146 M. Sinclair, D. Philips and N. Bala (1991). 'Aboriginal Child Welfare in Canada', in N. Bala, J. Hornick and R. Vogl (eds) *Canadian Child Welfare – Children, Families and the State*. Toronto: Thompson Educational Publications, 183–6; Carasco, *supra* note 6, 115–18; Monture, *supra* note 6, 8–11; Kline, *supra* note 6, 382–8; S. Bull (1989). 'The Special Case of the Native Indian Child', *Advocate*, 47: 523, 523–4; MacDonald, *supra* note 143, 78; and AJIM, *supra* note 78, 517.

147 McGillivray, *supra* note 5, 160.

148 Ibid.

149 E. N. Hughes (2006). *BC Children and Youth Review: An Independent Review of BC's Child Protection System*, 50 and 58. The chronic under-funding of First Nations on-reserve child welfare services which has resulted from ongoing financial wrangling between the federal and provincial governments continues to impact on the quality of the services provided to First Nations children. However, a recent legal challenge to the problematic funding of First Nations child welfare services was unsuccessful. In March 2011, the Canadian Human Rights Tribunal dismissed a complaint brought by the First Nations Child and Family Caring Society (FNCFCS) and the Assembly of First Nations (AFN) against the federal government in which FNCFCS and AFN alleged that the disparity in funding provided by the federal government for on-reserve child welfare services as compared with that provided by the provincial government to off-reserve Aboriginal and non-Aboriginal children, constituted discrimination against First Nations children contrary to s 5(b) of the

significantly, apprehension, rather than the provision of expensive prevention and family support services, became the standard operating procedure.[150] McGillivray effectively summarizes the position as one in which 'protective apprehension of Indian children was essentially a smash-and-grab operation, strongly resisted'.[151] The result: a hugely disproportionate number of Aboriginal children in non-native child welfare institutions.

The figures for the proportion of Aboriginal children in care across Canada in 1981–1982 tell a similar tale to that told in Australia. In Saskatchewan, 63 per cent of the total number of children in care were Aboriginal; in Manitoba, the figure stood at 32 per cent; Prince Edward Island, 10.7 per cent; Alberta, 41 per cent, and British Columbia, 40 per cent.[152] In fact, the only province in which the number of Aboriginal children in care was not clearly disproportionate to the total number of Aboriginal people in the province was the North West Territories.[153]

The experiences of Aboriginal children in state care

This second period of forced removals in Canada and Australia, what Patrick Johnston tellingly termed in Canada 'the sixties scoop', had similarly devastating consequences for the children and communities involved. For many years, Aboriginal children removed from their families in Australia continued to be institutionalized. In NSW, for example, if an Aboriginal child was successfully removed from their community, the child became a ward of the Aborigines' Protection Board who had the power to establish homes for their 'reception, maintenance and training'.[154] This remained the position until 1969 when the Aborigines' Welfare Board was established and complete responsibility for Aboriginal children passed to the Department for Child Welfare and Social Welfare.[155] Children were therefore removed to the

---

Canadian Human Rights Act. The Tribunal dismissed the complaint on the basis that in order to establish discrimination for the purposes of the legislation, it was not permissible to compare the service provided to First Nations children by the federal government with the service provided by a different service provider (the provincial government) to non-Aboriginal children. See *FNCFCS et al. v Attorney General of Canada* [2011] CHRT 4. For further information on the background to this challenge see C. Blackstock (2007). 'Residential Schools: Did They Really Close or Just Morph into Child Welfare?', *Indigenous Law Journal*, 6: 71.

150 D. Durst (1999). 'The Wellness of Aboriginal Children: Seeking Solutions through Self-government', in J. Hylton (ed.) *Aboriginal Self-Government in Canada: Current Trends and Issues*. Saskatoon: Purich Pub, 193.

151 McGillivray, *supra* note 5, 160.

152 Royal Commission on Aboriginal Peoples (1996). *Report of the Royal Commission on Aboriginal Peoples. Gathering Strength*. Part One, Vol. 3. Ottawa: Minister of Supply and Services, Canada, 25.

153 Ibid.

154 HREOC, *supra* note 3, 46–7.

155 Ibid., 49.

very same 'civilizing' institutions to which their parents had been removed a generation before. With the goal of assimilation remaining deeply entrenched, children removed under the general law and made wards of the Board were again prohibited from maintaining any contact with their Aboriginal families. Indeed, it was an offence for an Aboriginal person to try and make contact with an Aboriginal child placed within a home.

In the 1950s and 1960s, change to the routine institutionalization of Aboriginal children was forced upon the authorities. Such was the increase in the number of children coming into state care that the authorities simply found themselves struggling to cope.[156] Institutions became hopelessly overcrowded and conditions worsened. In line with changing professional attitudes towards the institutionalization of children, the authorities therefore began to employ a new and they hoped more effective tool of assimilation: the placement of Aboriginal children, particularly lighter skinned children, in non-native homes to be fostered or adopted by non-native parents.[157] In 1950, the Aborigines' Welfare Board in NSW advertised for foster parents to come forward. By 1960, over 300 Aboriginal children were in foster homes across the state.[158] A similar approach was adopted in Queensland, South Australia and the Northern Territories, with the majority of Aboriginal children being fostered or adopted into non-native homes. By 1971, 97 per cent of children in foster care in the Northern Territory were Aboriginal.[159]

The adoption of Aboriginal children into non-native homes similarly came to be regarded as the 'ideal fix' in Canada.[160] Against the backdrop of significant social changes which saw a significant decline in the number of adoptable 'white' babies, interest in transracial adoption grew strongly, providing an apparently 'perfect' solution to the 'problem' of Aboriginal children in state care.[161] As McGillivray explains, throughout the 1970s and 1980s transracial adoption was aggressively promoted throughout the Western Canadian provinces, resulting in large numbers of apprehended Aboriginal children being adopted by non-native parents, many of which lived outside the province at a considerable distance from the reserve.[162] Indeed, a significant proportion of First Nations children were sent for adoption in the United States.[163]

---

156 Ibid., 34.

157 Ibid.

158 Ibid., 48.

159 Ibid., 146.

160 McGillivray, *supra* note 5, 161–2.

161 Ibid.

162 Ibid. McGillivray reports that between 1971 and 1981, 3,400 Aboriginal children were adopted in Manitoba, 70–80 per cent of whom were status Indians. Durst records that in 1980 there were approximately 81 adoptions per 1,000 live Aboriginal births.

163 Ibid. McGillivray reports that 38 per cent of the status Indian children and 17 per cent of the Métis children placed for adoption in Manitoba in 1981 were sent to the United States.

Unfortunately, being fostered or adopted into a non-native home did not necessarily guarantee a less painful experience for removed Aboriginal children. Many foster parents held strongly prejudicial views about Aboriginal people and were as disparaging of Aboriginal traditions and culture as the staff at residential schools, missions and training institutions:

> I grew up sadly not knowing one Aboriginal person and the view that was given to me was one of fear towards [my] people. I was told not to have anything to do with them as they were dirty, lived in shabby conditions and, of course, drank to excess. Not once was I told that I was of Aboriginal descent. I was told that with my features I was from some Island and they [foster family] knew nothing of my family or the circumstances.[164]

Abuse was also a recurring problem, with the levels of sexual abuse within foster homes reportedly higher than it had been at the state institutions. The *Bringing Them Home* report records that one in ten boys and one in three girls alleged that they had been sexually abused in an Australian non-native foster home.[165] Unsurprisingly, Aboriginal children did not thrive in this 'hostile' environment.[166] Alienated from their cultural roots, deprived of their family and community, frequently abused and struggling to meet the assimilationist expectations of their non-native families, Aboriginal children often suffered considerable distress and confusion even when placed within the most loving and well-intentioned of families.[167] As with their parents, low self-esteem, low self-confidence and a painful loss of identity commonly manifested itself in substance abuse, juvenile delinquency, violence, suicide and incarceration.[168] For the children, the intervention of non-native child welfare agencies had itself become a form of abuse. For the communities who once again found themselves deprived of large numbers of their children, it meant another generation to whom the traditions, laws and cultural values of their society would be lost – it meant continuing social disintegration at the level of the individual, family and community. The self-perpetuating 'circle of abuse' initiated by the residential schools had become entrenched.

---

164 HREOC, *supra* note 3, 156.

165 Ibid., 163.

166 Durst, *supra* note 150, 196.

167 White and Jacobs, *supra* note 4, 19–22.

168 Kimelman, *supra* note 1, 147 and 158; Monture, *supra* note 6, 3–7; White and Jacobs, ibid., 22; and Royal Commission on Aboriginal Peoples (1996). *Report of the Royal Commission on Aboriginal Peoples. Perspectives and Realities*. Part One, Vol. 4. Ottawa: Minister of Supply and Services, Canada, 149–61.

Continuing Colonization or Legitimate Concern?

The socio-economic and cultural context

The large-scale apprehension of Aboriginal children between the 1960s and 1980s in Australia and Canada does not necessarily justify labelling the policies and practices of the non-native child welfare agencies as 'colonialist', 'imperialist' or 'genocidal'. After all, once general child welfare law was being applied to Aboriginal communities, formal equality with non-native society was secured. The same threshold grounds for intervention had to be established by the child welfare agency before the children could be removed and it could certainly be argued that, when compared against the standards of non-native society, social workers would have legitimate grounds for concern.

During the 1960s in Canada, a period in which large numbers of Aboriginal peoples were moving into urban centres for the first time, there was a growing awareness amongst non-native society of the grave social and economic conditions in which many Aboriginal peoples lived.[169] In both urban and rural areas, the First Nations, having been dispossessed of their lands and their traditional economic base, formed a marginalized, severely disadvantaged group.[170] Housing was well below accepted standards, usually overcrowded,[171] and many homes did not have running water.[172] Many communities were suffering from the effects of high unemployment,[173] welfare dependency,[174] poverty and a variety of related social problems, particularly alcoholism, domestic violence and sexual abuse.[175]

169 AJIM, *supra* note 78, 517.

170 M. Jackson (1988). *Locking Up Natives in Canada: Report to the Canadian Bar Association Committee on Imprisonment and Release*. Ottawa: Canadian Bar Association, 6–7. See also RCAP, *supra* note 9, 137–200 and 411–523; and M. Boldt (1993). *Surviving as Indians. The Challenge of Self-Government*. Toronto: University of Toronto Press, 170–6 and 223–6.

171 MacDonald, *supra* note 143, 81–2. It should, however, be noted that the presence of several generations of the family in the same dwelling house is not simply the result of poverty but has cultural roots in the extended family tradition. See, e.g. Kimelman, *supra* note 1, 133.

172 White and Jacobs, *supra* note 4, 19.

173 According to the 1981 census only half of the adult native population under 65 years of age were employed, compared to two-thirds of non-native society. Where First Nations people were employed they were more likely to be engaged in short-term seasonal work. J. MacDonald (1985). 'Child Welfare and the Native Indian Peoples of Canada', *Windsor Yearbook of Access to Justice*, 5: 284, 287.

174 In 1985 it was found that almost 50 per cent of Indians living on reserves in Canada were in receipt of social assistance. Ibid., 287.

175 Ibid., 287–8; Office of the Chief Medical Examiner (1992). *The Fatalities Inquiries Act – Respecting the Death of Lester Norman Desjarlais*. Brandon: Ministry of Social Services and Housing, 233–58; Mackenzie Valley Pipeline Inquiry (1977). *Northern Frontier, Northern Homeland. The Report of the Mackenzie Valley Pipeline Inquiry*. Toronto: James Lorimer; Ottawa: Supply and Services Canada, 152.

Aboriginal communities in Australia were suffering from similar difficulties. Having been dispossessed of their land and deprived of their traditional economic base, high unemployment led to a crippling 'lack of self-confidence, a sense of permanent and inescapable marginalisation, [and] a feeling of powerlessness'.[176] Welfare dependency became a key feature of Aboriginal lives.[177] At the same time as economic difficulties were intensifying, the pressures on Aboriginal cultural and social norms intensified such that traditional forms of social control began to break down leading to increased delinquency and levels of anti-social behaviour.[178] The Australian government's policy of dispersing Aboriginal peoples into mainstream society through the closure of reserves, missions and outstations led to increased migration to urban centres and again the grave socio-economic problems facing Aboriginal peoples became more visible to non-native society. Indeed, families who migrated towards the urban centres found themselves under increasing levels of state surveillance and particularly vulnerable to the unwanted attentions of the welfare authorities.[179]

The disproportionate number of Aboriginal children in care could be accounted for by factors such as these.[180] It has long been argued that there is a close association between poverty, social dysfunction and child neglect.[181] The Gove Inquiry in British Columbia refers with approval to a report by the Canadian Institute of Child Health which argues that children from economically marginalized families run a higher risk of suffering from low birth weight, chronic health problems and fatal injuries, are twice as likely to suffer from a psychiatric disorder and are three times more likely to drop out of school early.[182] Thus if the state is to apply the same standards across both native and non-native society you

176 Royal Commission into Aboriginal Deaths in Custody (1991). *National Report*, Vol. 2. Canberra: Australian Govt. Pub. Service, [17.1.24].

177 It is estimated that 53 per cent of Aboriginal income derives from social security payments in comparison to 11 per cent of the average Australian household. RCADC, ibid., [17.2.3].

178 Royal Commission into Aboriginal Deaths in Custody (1991). *National Report*, Vol. 4. Canberra: Australian Govt. Pub. Service, 2.

179 HREOC, *supra* note 3, 112. In Queensland, for example, liaison officers were employed to monitor the hygiene practices and social habits of Aboriginal families by inspecting their homes. Ibid., 80.

180 See, for example, the arguments raised by Timpson cited in RCAP, *supra* note 152, 26–7.

181 See, for example, the research cited by the Northern Territory Government (2007), *supra* note 6, 224 and Hughes, *supra* note 149, 52. See also, *Putting the Picture Together*, *supra* note 6, 57–9; Victorian Indigenous Family Violence Task Force, *supra* note 6, 132–44; *Breaking the Silence*, *supra* note 6, 61–3.

182 Gove Inquiry into Child Protection (1995). *Report of the Gove Inquiry into Child Protection in British Columbia: Matthew's Legacy, Volume 1*. Vancouver, British Columbia: The Inquiry.

would perhaps expect to find that in areas of high unemployment and poverty there will be more apprehensions as a result of child welfare concerns.

However, whilst socio-economic factors are clearly important, the responsibility of the Canadian and Australian governments for the crippling poverty of many Aboriginal families should not be forgotten. As concluded by the Gove Inquiry, 'poverty is a child welfare issue and when government allows children to live in poverty, they are, in effect, committing systemic child neglect'.[183] Moreover, socio-economic problems in Aboriginal communities provide only a partial explanation of what was happening. The emphasis placed on 'blaming' these community dynamics has the tendency to encourage the argument that the non-native child welfare system was a wholly innocent party simply responding to the 'pathological problems' of Aboriginal communities and individual Aboriginal parents, particularly Aboriginal mothers.[184] Its own complicity and the complicity of the law in justifying the removal of such high numbers of Aboriginal children from their families and communities, is ignored.[185] However, as Marlee Kline argues in her seminal articles on Canada, the disproportionate number of Aboriginal children in care lies not only with the problem of poverty but with the ethnocentricity at the heart of the non-native child welfare system.[186] Kline argues that by applying apparently neutral, universal and objective legal standards such as 'neglect', 'harm' and 'best interests' to Aboriginal children and families, the inherent colonialism within the system and the assumption of cultural superiority which lies behind it, became legitimized and entrenched.[187] Thus, behind this façade of neutrality, she argues, Aboriginal values, laws and practices were degraded and excluded,[188] the importance of cultural identity to Aboriginal children ignored, the interests of the child's community marginalized,[189] and a 'culturally biased perception of Aboriginal families and communities as impoverished, primitive, socially disorganized, and as generally unsuitable environments for children'[190] allowed to take hold within the mindset of the decision-makers.[191] In the words

183 Ibid., 24–5. See also C. Blackstock (2007). 'Residential Schools: Did They Really Close or Just Morph into Child Welfare?', *Indigenous Law Journal*, 6: 71, 75–6.

184 Kline, *supra* note 6, 378, fn 8 and M. Kline (1995). 'Complicating the ideology of Motherhood: Child Welfare Law and First Nations Women', in M. Fineman and I. Karpin (eds) *Mothers in Law: Feminist Theory and the Legal Regulation of Motherhood*. New York: Columbia University Press, 118, 123–9.

185 McKenzie and Hudson, *supra* note 6, 129 and 132 and Kline, *supra* note 6, 388–9 and 415.

186 See generally, Kline (1992), *supra* note 6 and Kline (1995), *supra* note 184. See also, Monture, *supra* note 6, 12–15.

187 Kline (1992), ibid., 388–9 and 415.

188 Kline, *supra* note 184, 131–5.

189 Kline, *supra* note 6, 410–14; Carasco, *supra* note 6, 127–9; and Monture, *supra* note 6, 6.

190 McKenzie and Hudson, *supra* note 6, 132.

191 Kline, *supra* note 184, 123–9.

of Kline, the Canadian non-native child welfare system amounted to nothing more than a new, more nuanced, but equally devastating 'modality of colonialist regulation'. Her arguments hold equal resonance and force when applied to the Australian context.

The cultural blindness of the non-native child welfare agencies

Critics argue that the colonial underpinnings of the child welfare system are revealed from the very first moment of intervention by the non-native authorities. It is argued that a significant cause of the large number of Aboriginal children removed from their families was the cultural prejudice and misunderstanding of Aboriginal cultures by non-native child welfare workers. As Morse argues, the scope for cultural insensitivity by non-native child welfare workers was made possible by the use of such broad, indeterminate concepts as 'harm' and 'neglect' – terms which are inherently vulnerable to culturally biased interpretation according to the worker's own particular cultural values and standards.[192] Traditional Aboriginal child-rearing practices were thus consistently misinterpreted through the culturally biased eyes of non-native social workers as 'neglect'.[193]

Although there are important cultural differences between the many diverse Aboriginal groups in Canada and Australia, it is possible to identify a number of common themes in their approach to the upbringing of children that differ quite markedly from Western ideas and practices and have thus been the subject of strong disapproval by the dominant society. The care of an Aboriginal child is often described in somewhat idealized terms:

> Life for a child on a Reserve or in a native community is described as one of safety, love, adventure and freedom. A child feels, and is, welcome in any home and may join any family for a meal. A mother is not concerned if a child does not return home for a meal or even to sleep. The mother knows that some family is willingly providing for the child.[194]

Given the cultural dislocation and severe socio-economic problems being experienced by many communities, the reality for Aboriginal children can often be far from one of 'safety, love, adventure and freedom'. However, despite the pressure to which Aboriginal cultures have been subjected, they have survived. Fundamentally important cultural differences between Aboriginal and non-

---

192 B. Morse (1980). 'Indian and Innuit Family Law and the Canadian Legal System', *American Indian Law Review*, 8: 199, 202.

193 For a discussion of traditional Aboriginal child-rearing practices and the misunderstanding of non-native social workers, see especially: AJIM, *supra* note 78, 524–5; White and Jacobs, *supra* note 4, 5–10; Kimelman, *supra* note 1, Part V; Sinclair et al., *supra* note 146, 175–9; Bull, *supra* note 146, 114; and McKenzie and Hudson, *supra* note 6, 70.

194 Sinclair et al., ibid., 175 (citing Kimelman, *supra* note 1, 163).

Aboriginal societies remain, including differences with respect to the care and upbringing of children. The response of the non-native child welfare system to these differences has been one of its key failings.

Aboriginal parents in Canada are often said to adhere to a norm of non-interference: that is, they generally allow the child much greater freedom to develop in his or her own way.[195] Children are therefore given a much wider scope to discover things for themselves. Independence and self-sufficiency is emphasized, with children expected to take much greater responsibility for their actions from a very young age.[196] This can be contrasted to the much more authoritarian, interventionist methods of parenting which predominate in non-native society and which were particularly strongly entrenched in the 1950s and 1960s. The difference can be presented in stark terms:

> Indian parents pay high respect to the individuality of their children, allowing them great freedom to grow and develop in natural ways. Parents instruct their children about right and wrong, but allow them the decision. Non-Indian parents tend to believe that it is the parents' responsibility to direct and control children until they have internalized the values of the parents, and have been prepared for their superior role in the scheme of things.[197]

It is suggested that the freedom afforded to Aboriginal children was, and often still is, misinterpreted as indifference or neglect by non-native social workers who take as their cultural frame of reference the much more authoritarian model of parenting preferred by non-native parents.

The same cultural clash is evident in Australia where Aboriginal communities adopt a very similar 'hands-off' approach to parenting.[198] The *Bringing Them Home* report suggests that close supervision of very young children and high levels of autonomy amongst older children constitute core features of Aboriginal child-rearing common to communities across Australia.[199] In a study of child-rearing practices amongst the Anbarra of Arnhem Land, it was observed how adult–child relations were characterized by the almost 'absolute indulgence of small children' and by the way in which children were made to take responsibility both for themselves and others within the kinship group:

> Adults make no systematic attempts to train children, either in social behaviour or in any other area. Instead, they expect the children naturally to learn what they

195 Bull, *supra* note 146, 527 and Sinclair et al., ibid., 176.

196 C. Stuart (1982/1983). 'Cross-cultural Treatment for Native Children: A Point from which to Begin', *Journal of Child Law*, 1; AJIM, *supra* note 78, 513; Kimelman, *supra* note 1, 162.

197 Bull, *supra* note 146, 528.

198 Northern Territory Government, *supra* note 181, 72.

199 HREOC, *supra* note 3, 451–2.

> need to know and they expect that the child will be normally co-operative and friendly and reasonable, not naughty and self-willed and anti-social.[200]

A common theme of studies into Aboriginal child-rearing is the emphasis placed by adults on the need to display independent and assertive behaviour from an early age. A study in NSW observed how the development of a 'cheeky assertiveness' is rewarded by Aboriginal adults who refer approvingly to the child as 'a cheeky black kid'. Similarly, a study of Yolgnu children in the Northern Territory revealed that from the age of three, children begin to transfer their physical and emotional dependence from their mother to their camp group and between the ages of five and 15 enjoy considerable independence.[201] As in Canada, the promotion of such strong cultural values in Aboriginal children was not understood or valued by non-native society. As the Royal Commission on Aboriginal Deaths in Custody observed:

> The overall picture is one in which Aboriginal ways of operating as a family unit and child rearing practices (for instance the encouragement of self-direction and independent action) have been undermined by assumptions of a European welfare model. The emerging situation for Aboriginal children in many communities is therefore an experience of loss of role, of place and of family in their community.[202]

The less-interventionist approach of Aboriginal peoples to parenting is often accompanied by a different approach to discipline. Physical punishment is viewed by many Aboriginal groups in Canada as abhorrent. With respect to the early contact between the French and the Huron First Nation, the Aboriginal Justice Inquiry of Manitoba observed:

> In view of current ideas about child rearing, it is interesting to reflect that no aspect of behaviour shocked the French more than their refusal to use physical punishment to discipline their children. On general principles, the Huron considered it wrong to coerce or humiliate an individual publicly. To their own way of thinking a child was an amorphous that must be moulded into shape.[203]

A study of discipline in the Numbulwar community in Australia revealed a similar dislike of the use of physical punishment, at least until a child reaches physical maturity.[204] Rather than resort to physical punishment, some Aboriginal communities employ a disciplinary model that uses shame and humour to

200 Cited in RCADC, *supra* note 176, [11.9.11].
201 HREOC, *supra* note 3, 452.
202 RCADC, *supra* note 176, 73.
203 AJIM, *supra* note 78, 512–13.
204 Cited in RCADC, *supra* note 176, [11.9.14].

encourage the child to behave: a method of child-rearing that was viewed by some non-native social workers as amounting to psychological abuse.[205] The socialization of Aboriginal children is also quite different from the approach taken by non-native parents. Bala, Hornick and Vogl note that Aboriginal children in Canada are often taught not to express emotions in public except at appropriate times. However, when presented with a quiet, submissive child displaying great emotional control, non-native social workers often misinterpreted the child's behaviour as symptomatic of abuse and neglect.[206]

Perhaps, however, the most important difference between the child-rearing methods employed in Aboriginal and non-Aboriginal communities, is the role played within Aboriginal communities by members of the extended family. As it is put by one commentator, children are regarded within Aboriginal communities as 'communal resources rather than as the private property of their parents'.[207] Within many Aboriginal communities in Australia, the extended family is situated at the core of a complex system of family relations and kinship ties.[208] The kinship system defines a person's place within the community, determining roles and responsibilities and structures for the provision of financial and moral support.[209] A key feature of the kinship system is the shared responsibility for raising and educating children.[210] As explained by one Aboriginal leader in Australia:

> All people with the same skin grouping as my mothers … They have the right, the same as my mother, to watch over me, to control what I'm doing, to make sure that I do the right thing. It's an extended family thing … It's a wonderful secure system.[211]

Aboriginal children in Canada are similarly allowed to wander more freely within the community, with parents relying upon the tradition of the community's collective responsibility for children to ensure that children remain properly cared for and safe.[212] If for any reason the parents are unable to fulfil their responsibilities to the child, it is expected that the extended family will provide the appropriate support for the family and, if necessary, assume primary responsibility for the child's care:

---

205 Sinclair et al., *supra* note 146, 177. RCADC, ibid., [11.9.19].

206 Bull, *supra* note 146, 527.

207 Ibid.

208 Australian Museum Online (2004). *Indigenous Australia: Family.*

209 Ibid.

210 Ibid.

211 Wadjularbinna Doomadgee, Gungalidda leader. Ibid.

212 Kimelman, *supra* note 1, 161 and 163. See also Sinclair et al., *supra* note 146, 177.

> Traditionally the care of a child is the overall responsibility of an extended family, with members of that extended family playing various roles. In the event that any member of the family might be disabled or absent, there are many more people to take on their responsibilities. More importantly, it was never necessary to surrender children to the care of strangers. There were always people to whom the child was bonded and amongst whom he or she felt secure.[213]

Again, Aboriginal concepts of the collective responsibility of the extended family for safeguarding a child's welfare stand in sharp contrast to the Western notion of a nuclear family and the common perception of non-native children as the 'property' of their parents.[214] Justice Kimelman, reporting in 1985 on the practice of Aboriginal and Métis adoptions into non-native homes in Canada, provides one example of how this misunderstanding over cultural values could seriously disadvantage Aboriginal parents:

> It is a frequent demand that a child care agency will make of a mother of native descent that, in order to regain custody of her child, she establish her own independent domicile. This demand goes against the native patterns of child care. In the Native tradition the need of a young mother to be mothered herself is recognised. The grandparents and aunts and uncles expect the demands and the rewards of raising the new member of the family. To insist that the mother remove herself from the supports of her family when she needs them most is unrealistic and cruel.[215]

The same imposition of non-native, ethnocentric standards of childcare extended more broadly to the socio-economic conditions in which many Aboriginal children lived. The response of non-native social workers to the reality of poverty in many Aboriginal communities was to insist upon adherence to the standards of non-native, middle-class society; standards which Aboriginal families were rarely able to meet. Poverty, as manifested in poor housing and inadequate means of support, was routinely treated by non-native social workers as synonymous with neglect.[216] Similarly, traditional Aboriginal practices such as the need to travel long distances or for long periods of time to attend cultural events or to seek seasonal employment were regarded as unsuitable lifestyles for children.[217] The underlying cultural or economic reasons for the lifestyle of these Aboriginal families were simply ignored.

Non-native social workers, whether due to a genuine lack of cultural understanding or a more paternalistic desire to 'rescue' Aboriginal children from

---

213 White and Jacobs, *supra* note 4, 10.

214 Ibid., 13–14.

215 Kimelman, *supra* note 1, 132–3.

216 HREOC, *supra* note 3, 47.

217 Ibid.

these 'unenlightened' practices, therefore became the vehicle for the imposition of culturally alien and inappropriate European middle-class standards of childcare on Aboriginal communities. Unfortunately, this cultural insensitivity to the traditional practices and economic realities of Aboriginal communities impacted not just on Aboriginal parents facing the removal of a child, but on the making of placement decisions once the child was in care. Until the more recent legislative reforms introducing an Aboriginal placement principle,[218] it was relatively unusual for an Aboriginal child to be placed within their extended family or community.[219] Members of the extended family offering to care for a child in care were assessed according to the same criteria and standards as any other applicant. These standards generally focused on material wealth, stability, employment status and educational opportunities – not the cultural security the home would offer the child. The emphasis placed by non-native agencies on material factors immediately raised problems for many low-income Aboriginal families who could have offered the child a home but were living in poor, overcrowded accommodation with limited access to schools and health facilities.[220] Even those child welfare agencies who recognized the need to place Aboriginal children within Aboriginal families and communities encountered difficulties in finding suitable homes. The observations of O'Sullivan J in the Canadian case of *Tom v The Children's Aid Society of Winnipeg*[221] regarding the opposition of the Winnipeg Children's Aid Society (a non-native child welfare agency) to the policy of the neighbouring Fort Frances Children's Society of trying to place First Nations children within the extended family on their reserve, is telling:

> The Winnipeg Society does not approve of the practice of the Fort Frances society of allowing children to be nurtured by an extended family on an Indian reserve. The Winnipeg society appears to prefer that a child be placed either in a foster home or in adopting home *with two caring parents who meet the Winnipeg Society's standards as to housing, maturity and parenting capacity.* The Winnipeg Society is not adverse to placing children in Indian reserves, but only if there is on the reserve a couple who is willing and able to meet the Winnipeg Society's standards (emphasis added).[222]

Many non-native child welfare workers interpreted problems in the recruitment of Aboriginal foster and adoptive parents as further evidence of the indifference of Aboriginal communities towards the well-being of their children.[223] However,

218 See discussion in Chapter 3.

219 Morse, *supra* note 192, 204.

220 BC Royal Commission, *supra* note 140, 20–2.

221 [1982] 1 C.N.L.R. 170. (Manitoba CA).

222 Ibid., 171.

223 E. Sommerlad (1977). 'Aboriginal Children in the Aboriginal Community: Changing Practices in Adoption', *Australian Journal of Social Issues*, 12, 169.

a more likely explanation than community indifference was the reluctance of Aboriginal families to submit themselves to the scrutiny and judgment of non-native agencies applying alien and quite often inappropriate criteria. It is not at all surprising that Aboriginal families were unwilling to cooperate with agencies who, because of their standard practice of removing Aboriginal children, were feared and resented within many communities.[224]

Aboriginal Child Welfare in the Canadian Courts: Marlee Kline's Critique

Significant responsibility for the crisis that developed in Aboriginal child welfare can therefore be laid at the door of the non-native child welfare agencies. The cultural chauvinism inherent in their standards and judgments, and the refusal of some non-native social workers to acknowledge the potential value of Aboriginal culture and traditions, caused considerable unnecessary suffering for many Aboriginal families. However, non-native child welfare agencies were not the only imperialist force at work within Aboriginal communities. The courts were deeply complicit in 'legitimizing' the unwarranted removal of Aboriginal children from their homes and communities. Indeed, the damaging application of ethnocentric standards to Aboriginal families by non-native social workers was compounded and entrenched by the cultural bias and insensitivity of the Australian and Canadian judiciary.[225] Little attempt was made by the courts to try and mitigate the harsh effects of non-native child welfare legislation with its pre-existing cultural bias. Moreover, the judiciary leant strong support to the cultural chauvinism of non-native social workers, their own decision-making being strongly informed, whether consciously or not, by a deep-seated belief in the superiority of their own culturally rooted mores and practices.

Criticism of the Canadian judiciary has focused in particular on their culture-blind application of the best interests principle. Marlee Kline, in her persuasive critique of the Canadian case law, argues that the best interests principle was employed by decision-makers to portray the apprehension and placement of Aboriginal children away from their families and communities as 'natural, necessary and legitimate, rather than coercive and destructive'.[226] In particular, she claims it legitimated the judiciary's refusal to give recognition to what Carasco first termed the 'indigenous factor'.[227] The 'indigenous factor' encapsulates the idea that a child's Aboriginal heritage, culture and identity, as experienced through family and community, are central to the child's sense of security, well-being and happiness. However, Kline

224 Morse, *supra* note 192, 205; BC Royal Commission, *supra* note 140, 20–2; Sommerlad, ibid., 170. For a discussion of the similar difficulties experienced in the recruitment of Aboriginal foster carers in Australia, see HREOC, *supra* note 3, 450.

225 See, in particular: Carasco, Monture and Kline, all *supra* note 6.

226 Kline (1992), *supra* note 6, 389 and 394. See also Kline (1995), *supra* note 184.

227 Kline (1992), ibid., 393 and 396.

argues that when the courts applied the best interests principle to an Aboriginal child, they treated the child as a de-contextualized individual, removing the child from any place within family, community or culture. This allowed the courts to render the child's cultural identity and membership within a particular Aboriginal community of marginal importance when determining the child's welfare. This in turn made the child's ultimate removal from his or her particular cultural context seem relatively unproblematic.

Natural Parents v Superintendent of Child Welfare[228] provides a classic example of this approach, with the Supreme Court holding that when determining the best interests of the child, the child has to be considered 'as an individual not as part of a race or culture'.[229] The Supreme Court took exactly the same approach in *Racine v Woods*.[230] *Racine v Woods* remains the leading authority on the weight to be afforded to the 'indigenous factor' when considering the best interests of an indigenous child. Although the Supreme Court did not altogether reject its relevance, it is clear that it thought the indigenous factor should be given little weight. The case concerned an application for the adoption of a seven-year-old status Indian child by Métis foster parents against the wishes of the natural mother who wished to raise the child within her own particular Aboriginal traditions and culture. In a crucial section of the judgment, Wilson J concludes:

> In my view when the test to be met is the best interests of the child, the significance of cultural background and heritage as opposed to bonding abates over time. The closer the bond that develops with the prospective adoptive parents the less important the racial element becomes.[231]

Monture argues that this approach is simply wrong, pointing out that there is in fact strong evidence that the importance of cultural background and heritage does not abate over time but remains extremely important to the child's sense of security and identity, especially during adolescence.[232] She suggests that the reason behind Wilson J's negation of this evidence is her unspoken belief in the benefits of the assimilation of Aboriginal children into non-native society, such that Aboriginal children in non-native homes will come to identify with their non-native parents and cultural identity will cease to be an issue.[233] Underlying this approach is a belief in the transient and interchangeable nature of cultural identity. Thus any loss of the child's Aboriginal heritage can be more than compensated for by the cultural benefits provided by non-native society. The construction of one's identity is however a much more complex process than this would suggest. The assumption

228 [1976] 2 S.C.R. 751.
229 Ibid., 768. For commentary see Kline, *supra* note 6, 397.
230 [1983] 2 S.C.R. 173.
231 Ibid., 247.
232 Monture, *supra* note 6, 13.
233 Ibid.

that a child's Aboriginal identity will cease to be of importance as the child grows older is not supported by the substantial body of evidence dealing with the identity 'crisis' experienced by many adopted children as they reach adolescence; problems which are clearly intensified in a transracial placement.[234] As Carasco points out, even the best intentioned, most capable of foster parents often seem incapable of preventing 'the high incidence of unhappiness, rebellion and anti-social behaviour exhibited by native children in their care'.[235] The significance of these problems is, however, minimized by Wilson J:

> I believe that interracial adoption, like interracial marriage is now an accepted phenomenon in our pluralist society. The implications of it might have been overly dramatised by the respondent in this case.[236]

Despite the concerns surrounding the Supreme Court's decision in *Racine*, Wilson J's approach was consistently applied by the Canadian courts to justify downgrading the importance of a child's cultural identity.[237] Although in subsequent years the courts undoubtedly showed an increasing willingness to have regard to the 'indigenous factor', Kline argues that it was rarely accorded the status of an overriding or even substantially weighty factor, with other considerations, such as the apparent stability and security of the alternative home and the bond which has developed between the alternative care giver and the child, being afforded a higher priority in determining the child's best interests.[238] Indeed, in many cases these other factors proved determinative of the decision. In the case of *J.F.T. v C.A.S.*,[239] the British Columbia Court of Appeal overturned the judgment of the BC Supreme Court which had placed strong emphasis on the child's Aboriginal heritage, deciding the case instead on the basis of the child's attachment to the prospective adoptive parents. *Racine* was cited as authority for the proposition that the importance of cultural identity would have to give way to the status quo where strong bonds had developed between the child and the alternative carer. The same reasoning was applied in *Re Child Welfare Act (Chipeway)*,[240] a decision of the Alberta Court of Queen's Bench. The court acknowledged that 'an important consideration in this case is the native background' but then went on to dismiss

234 Carasco, *supra* note 6, 114–15. See also A. McGillivray (1985). 'Transracial Adoption and the Status Indian Child', *Canadian Journal of Family Law*, 4: 437, 437–67; McKenzie and Hudson, *supra* note 6, 71; Sommerlad, *supra* note 223, 173; Bull, *supra* note 146, 525; Sinclair et al., *supra* note 146, 177; BC Royal Commission, *supra* note 140, 28–30 and 33–4; Kimelman, *supra* note 1; AJIM, *supra* note 78, 523–4; White and Jacobs, *supra* note 4, 20.

235 Carasco, ibid., 115.

236 [1983] 2 S.C.R. 173, 188.

237 See generally, Sinclair et al., *supra* note 146, 178–9.

238 Kline, *supra* note 6, 399–406.

239 [1993] B.C.J. No. 864 (QL).

240 [1986] A.J. No. 67 (QL).

its significance on the facts because of the strong psychological bond that had developed between the foster parents and the child.[241]

The distress and potential harm caused to a child by removing the child from a carer with whom he or she has formed a secure attachment (particularly if the alternative carer has been the child's primary carer since birth) is of course an important consideration. However, the concern of scholars such as Kline and Carasco is that these decisions fail to give due consideration to the longer-term interests of the child in which cultural identity plays an increasingly significant part.[242] As Kline argues, the courts' legitimate concern with the stability and security of the child's environment was mistakenly separated from the maintenance of the child's Aboriginal identity and heritage.[243]

A further problem encountered by Aboriginal parents was that where the courts were willing to accept, in principle, the relevance of a child's cultural identity, they would insist that the importance of maintaining links with the child's Aboriginal heritage be proved for that individual child in that particular case.[244] General observations about the importance of cultural identity and the traumatic effects of losing that identity by being placed in non-native homes did not suffice; the potential for harm had to be proved in relation to every individual child.[245] If such harm could not be established, it was simply assumed that non-native culture would meet the child's needs. As it was put by Perry L.J. in *John v Superintendent of Child Welfare*,[246] the proposition 'that an Indian child has a better chance in life by living among his relatives and among others of his race' could not be accepted unless it was 'possible to demonstrate that this [was] so, by way of some cogent evidence, with particular reference to this child'.[247] The BC Supreme Court accordingly attached little weight to evidence demonstrating in general terms the experience of identity crisis and dislocation faced by Aboriginal children when raised in non-native homes.[248]

The necessity to prove the importance of maintaining cultural links for each individual child posed particular difficulties for Aboriginal parents living within urban centres. Aboriginal people who migrate to cities and towns may well have weaker links with 'traditional' Aboriginal communities and have only limited involvement with traditional cultural activities. This problem was evident in the case of *Children's Aid Society of Owen Sound and County of Grey v M.B.*,[249] where the Ontario Provincial Court held not only that the importance of Aboriginal culture

---

241 The case was concerned with an application for permanent wardship to facilitate the adoption of the child. The child had been in the care of the foster parents for five years.

242 Carasco, *supra* note 6, 124 and Kline, *supra* note 6, 403.

243 Kline, ibid., 403.

244 Ibid., 398–9.

245 Ibid.

246 (1979) [1982] 1 C.N.L.R. 40.

247 Ibid., 47. For commentary see Kline, *supra* note 6, 398.

248 Kline, ibid., 398.

249 [1985] O.J. No. 737 (QL).

to the child must be proved in every case, but that the exposure to Aboriginal culture must be 'quality' exposure:

> There is no hard empirical evidence before the courts on the benefits of culture. The court does not think it is enough to say there is exposure therefore it is good. If we accept that it is important for an Indian child to be exposed to the Indian culture, as does the new Act, that there is a uniqueness of Indian and native cultural heritage and tradition, and there is a need to preserve the child's cultural identity, it seems to me that that exposure must still have the potential of being quality exposure.[250]

On the facts, the court held that the mother had spent her life crossing between the white culture and her native culture ('even living with a white man') and had 'not really been able to expose the child to the Indian culture in a very meaningful way'. The clear implication to be drawn from the judgment is that the mother, and consequently her children, were not 'real Indians' if they flirted with white society in this way.[251]

A further problem raised by Kline is that even when the courts attributed significant weight to the indigenous factor, they wrongly assumed that exposure to *any* Aboriginal culture would be adequate to protect the child's developing sense of cultural identity.[252] This was so even if that exposure was facilitated by non-native foster parents. Consequently, the courts commonly found that provided the alternative carers undertook to expose the child to some form of Aboriginal culture and heritage, they were satisfactorily meeting the demands of the 'indigenous factor'. For example, in the case of *Children's Aid Society of Owen Sound and County of Grey v M.B.*,[253] the court seemed satisfied that the non-native foster parents' exposure to Aboriginal culture and their willingness to facilitate similar exposure for the child was sufficient to meet the child's cultural needs:

> The proposed adoptive white parents are prepared to expose the child to native culture such as would be secured by reading, attending exhibitions, libraries, cultural displays, museums and pow wows. Both have worked in Indian communities in the James Bay area, the mother as a teacher for a year and the father as a builder of schools. They have fostered Indian children and are the adoptive parents of two Indian boys.

---

250 Ibid.

251 This reasoning has strong parallels to that found in *R v Van der Peet* (1996) 2 S.C.R. 507 and the 'integral to a distinctive culture' test which was established by the Supreme Court. See also *Re Child Welfare Act (Alta Q.B.)* [1986] A.J. No. 539 (QL) and *C.J.K. v Children's Aid Society of Metropolitan Toronto* [1989] 4 C.N.L.R. 75 (Ont. Prov. Ct. Fam. Div.).

252 Kline, *supra* note 6, 401–2.

253 [1985] O.J. No. 737 (QL).

Similarly, in the case of *Re A.B.*,[254] Landerkin J. of the Alberta Provincial Court assumed that because the foster parents of the Aboriginal child lived 'contiguous to a large Indian reserve ... it would be a fair inference that this physical location would allow this part of their heritage to be explored'.[255] Whether or not the child was actually a member of that reserve community or even the same Aboriginal group was regarded as irrelevant by the court.[256] As Kline argues, the courts were able to adopt this attitude because once the child had been constructed as an individual abstracted out of his or her particular culture, there appeared to be no particular need to maintain the child's link with any specific cultural community.[257]

The culture blind application of the best interests principle is not the only problem Kline identifies with the way in which it was interpreted and applied by the courts in relation to Aboriginal children. In line with the pattern established by non-native social workers, Kline argues that the courts also imposed culturally biased standards as to cleanliness, organization and good parenting when determining whether or not a child was neglected and in need of protection.[258] She contends that the imposition of these culturally biased standards worked to the particular disadvantage of Aboriginal women unable to live up to the courts' 'ideological constructions of good motherhood'.[259] Thus, an Aboriginal mother was presumed to be a 'bad mother' if she lived a nomadic life and the home she provided appeared disorganized and untidy.[260] These factors, which are often rooted in the disproportionate poverty suffered by Aboriginal women, were taken as indicative of the quality of the mother's care and could lead to a child's removal, even if there was no evidence of actual neglect.[261] In *L.O. and S.O. v Superintendent of Child Welfare*[262] a 19-month-old Inuit girl suffering from serious skin rashes was removed from her caregivers, despite their high standing within the community, because, in the opinion of the court, the house 'was just not tidy enough for such a tender skinned little girl'.[263]

Moving beyond the welfare principle itself, the individualistic foundations of the non-native legal system also caused difficulties in accommodating a role for the extended family and wider Aboriginal community in securing the welfare of Aboriginal children.[264] The communal ethos of many Aboriginal communities, particularly the notion of a collective responsibility for the upbringing and care of

254 (1989) 100 A.R. 150 (Alta. Prov. Ct.). For commentary see Kline, *supra* note 6, 401.

255 (1989) 100 A.R. 150 (Alta. Prov. Ct.), 154; Kline, ibid., 401.

256 Kline, ibid.

257 Ibid.

258 Kline, *supra* note 184, 123 and 126. See also Carasco, *supra* note 6, 130–2.

259 Kline, ibid., 128.

260 Ibid.

261 Ibid.

262 [1984] N.W.T.R. 295.

263 Cited in Kline, *supra* note 184, 128.

264 See especially, Kline, *supra* note 6, 410–14; Carasco, *supra* note 6, 127–9.

children, fits uneasily within the dominant legal framework. The courts therefore struggled to accept the potential role played in the care of Aboriginal children by the extended family and other community members. In *N.P.P. & M.E.P. v Regional Children's Guardian*,[265] the Regional Children's Guardian of Alberta had his decision to remove a nine-year-old Cree child from his/her non-native foster parents and placed with an aunt on the mother's reserve quashed in an action for judicial review. The court found that the guardian had made an error of law in interpreting the word 'family' in the relevant legislation as including members of a Band who share a common ancestry. According to the court, the term 'family' referred only to the nuclear family as understood in non-native society.[266] This approach to the 'family' meant that the involvement and commitment of extended family members when the parents were unable to fulfil their responsibilities, was given little recognition and weight by the courts.[267] In particular, concerns about the mother's individual capacity to cope were not viewed within the context of the care which could be provided by the extended family as a whole.[268] In *Mooswa v Minister of Social Services for Saskatchewan*[269] the court was called on to determine if an apprehended child should be returned to her mother who had recently overcome an alcohol dependency.[270] Even though the mother had moved in with her own mother and was perfectly adequately caring for a newborn child, the court was not prepared to take into account that the grandmother would be heavily involved in the child's care.[271]

Embedded within the courts' approach was a strong belief that children are better cared for by one or two primary carers. To confuse this picture with a number of indeterminate caregivers was perceived as potentially harmful to a child's interests. The courts would therefore not countenance any attempt by a First Nations Band to be granted custody of a child. This argument was firmly rejected by the British Columbia Court of Appeal in *S (S.M.) v A (J.P.)*:

> The second reason why the Akhiok tribe's request for custody could not be granted is that the tribe is not a person eligible to apply for or be granted child custody under the Family Relations Act. Custody is a personal relationship between an adult individual with duties and responsibilities and a child to whom the duties and responsibilities are owing. The entire thrust of the custody provisions of the Act is towards that person to person relationship … Regardless of the nature of the tie that binds the members together, the notion that such a group can be regarded as an individual for purposes of child custody is entirely

265 (1988) 14 R.F.L. (3d) 55. For commentary, see Kline, ibid., 413.

266 (1988) 14 R.F.L. (3d) 55, 67–70. Kline, ibid.

267 Kline, *supra* note 184, 132.

268 Ibid.

269 (1976) 30 R.F.L. 101.

270 Kline, *supra* note 184, 132.

271 Ibid. See also *Re D.L.C.* [1986] 4 C.N.L.R. 68.

> foreign to the concept of custody, and to the individual duties and responsibilities implicit in the concept.[272]

Collective notions of parenthood simply do not conform to the judiciary's culturally rooted perception of the normative model of family life.

The courts were similarly hostile to the argument that the collective interests of the group were capable, in certain circumstances, of overriding the best interests of an individual Aboriginal child. As far as the courts were concerned, the child must be regarded as an individual, not as a member of a community, and consequently the needs and interests of the community in relation to the child were given little consideration. Yet, from an Aboriginal perspective, keeping children within their families and communities is of vital importance in helping them to rebuild their communities in the wake of the devastation caused by colonial rule. Looking at the child as a member of that community and with an interest in seeing that community survive, and indeed flourish, some Aboriginal communities may thus take the view that the child's best interests may well be best served, at least in the longer term, by allowing the child to remain within the community. This community-orientated approach is consistent with the worldview of many Aboriginal cultures.[273] It is, however, antithetical to the highly individualistic ethos behind the concept of the child's best interests in Canadian child welfare law which tends to assume a conflicted relationship between the community's collective interests and the individual interests of the child. This is of course not necessarily the case. Protecting the collective interests of the group in preserving their distinctive culture and traditions, thereby helping to foster community viability, is very much in the interests of individual Aboriginal children. The courts have, however, been extremely wary of any suggestion that the community's collective interests should be prioritized over the individual interests of the child. Arguments about the impact of the child welfare system upon Aboriginal communities have thus tended to be dismissed as entirely irrelevant.[274] This reluctance to consider the collective interests of the group is exemplified in the cases of *S (S.M.) v A (J.P.)*[275] and *Jane Doe v Awasis Agency of N. Manitoba*.[276] In both these cases the court condemned the community's actions of putting what the court believed to be their collective political goals before the individual interests and welfare of the child.

These tensions were undoubtedly exacerbated by the lack of involvement in the non-native child welfare system by Aboriginal communities. In particular, Aboriginal communities experienced great difficulty in securing their active involvement in child welfare decisions before the courts.[277] In *Kenora-Patricia*

---

272 (1992) 64 B.C.L.R. (2d) 344, 354.

273 Kline, *supra* note 6, 410. See also Monture, *supra* note 6, 6.

274 Kline, ibid., 412.

275 (1992) 64 B.C.L.R. (2d) 344.

276 (1989) 72 D.L.R. (4th) (Man. C.A.).

277 Kline, *supra* note 6, 412.

Child and Family Services v Rose F.,[278] Justice Littel sent a strong warning to Aboriginal communities seeking to intervene in family proceedings, observing that they had better have strong substantive arguments, backed by appropriate supporting evidence, to put before the court or the courts would not hesitate to 'punish' their interference. On the facts of this particular case, the child's Band had raised a general argument concerning the damaging effects of removing the child from his or her community and had therefore proposed that the child be placed with a member of the extended family or a member of the Band. Littel J ordered costs against the Band because of the generalized nature of its arguments and its failure to make specific reference to the child. The courts also sought to limit the intervention of Aboriginal communities in proceedings even when there was an arguable basis for their participation in statute. In *Northwest Child and Family Services Agency v S.J.T.*,[279] Anishnaabe Child and Family Services was refused leave to intervene in an application for guardianship of an Anishnaabe child who resided off the reserve, the court holding that the community, through Anishnaabe, could only intervene in cases of children residing on the reserve; it had no extended jurisdiction with respect to off-reserve children.

Aboriginal child welfare in the Australian courts

It would not be surprising to find that Kline's arguments regarding the ethnocentricity embedded within the Canadian courts' interpretation of the welfare principle can be applied with equal force and persuasiveness to much of the early Australian case law.[280] There is, however, a dearth in reported decisions concerning Aboriginal children involved in public law child protection proceedings in Australia, rendering it almost impossible to evaluate the response of the Australian judiciary to the 'indigenous factor' and Aboriginal child-rearing practices within these particularly difficult cases. The comments of the Australian Law Reform Commission suggest the picture in Australia was very similar to that found in the Canadian case law:

> The fact remains that deliberate policies of assimilation in the past, together with the emphasis which sometimes tends to be placed on material comfort in determining child placements, have resulted in large numbers of Aboriginal children being removed from their families and placed within non-Aboriginal families and in institutions. In some cases such decisions are not taken publicly by judges who, after argument from both sides, are required to spell out their reasons for decision, but by an administrative official in private. In such

278 [1988] O.J. No. 2624 (QL) (Ont. Prov. Ct.).

279 (1990) 70 D.L.R. (4th) 418 (Man. Q.B.).

280 See, e.g. *C v T* (1985) 10 Fam LR 458; *Torrens v Fleming & Anor* (1980) FLC 75: 305; and *Jones v Darragh; Department of Community Services (Interveners)* (1992) 15 Fam LR 757.

> situations the lack of specific guidance provided by the "welfare principle" can mean that the original decision is virtually unreviewable.[281]

The disproportionate number of Aboriginal children in care across Australia in the 1980s would suggest Kline's critique of the Canadian case law holds considerable force in the Australian context.[282] Certainly, the lack of accessibility to and thus transparency of cases concerning the removal and placement of Aboriginal children into state and territory care during this period is a matter of enormous concern. Quite simply, without transparency there can be no accountability.

Research carried out into the attitudes of front-line social workers gives further grounds for concern. In a study of Aboriginal children's welfare files carried out in Victoria in 1990 it was found that there was still a lack of understanding amongst social workers about the role and responsibilities of the extended family, with the functioning of the extended family often being characterized in departmental files as 'pathological or dysfunctional'.[283] This negative perception of the extended family is clearly reflected in the file note of one worker:

> Concerns were expressed around the number of people who may attend the home while the children are present [for Christmas]. Mrs A agreed to request that all extended family members other than her mother, will be asked to leave while the children are there.[284]

Evidence of the racist stereotyping of Aboriginal people was also present with workers identifying Aboriginality as a cause of delinquency and problems:

> Potential foster mother can already sense that she may already have Aboriginal tendencies, as she can be happily playing in the school ground with the other children and all of a sudden cut off and "go walkabout". I think failure as human beings may be an issue which will come up as that is a common experience with Aboriginal people.[285]

Whilst some of the files reviewed did identify the child's Aboriginality as the most important factor to be considered in determining the child's future, others ignored it.[286] The researchers thus conclude that there was a continuing failure to 'contextualise the child's needs … address racism in the education system, housing

281 ALRC, *supra* note 139, [351].
282 For the most recent statistics see below at pp. 88–9.
283 Thomas cited in HREOC, *supra* note 3, 452.
284 Ibid.
285 Ibid.
286 Ibid., 453.

problems, lack of family relations … poverty and structural factors resulting in interventions'.[287]

Conclusion

As will be explored in Chapter 3, recent years have seen significant efforts in both Canada and Australia to try and increase the sensitivity of the non-native child welfare system to the needs of Aboriginal communities. However, in trying to find ways to effectively decolonize Aboriginal child welfare, the insights of Kline and others into the strong cultural bias and basic ethnocentrism entrenched within the non-native system need to be borne in mind. It is clearly important not to ignore the complexity of the colonial relationship between native and non-native society by creating false boundaries and dichotomies between native and non-native cultures.[288] As Kline recognizes, indigenous peoples are not just passive victims of colonial power; there is always scope for 'resistance' by marginalized groups trying to work within the hegemonic framework.[289] However, the combination of the existing power disparity between non-native Australians and Canadians on the one hand and Aboriginal peoples on the other, and the strength with which the basic cultural concepts, understandings and beliefs of non-native society are embedded within the core foundations and normative legal framework of the existing child welfare system suggests there may be only limited capacity for bringing about a fundamental change in its basic underlying philosophy and approach.[290] Certainly, there is no more sobering reminder of the serious limitations of the current legal and administrative framework for protecting Aboriginal children than the extent to which Aboriginal children continue to be grossly over-represented in state care across both Canada and Australia.

---

287 Ibid.

288 For a good introduction to post-colonial theory see B. Ashcroft, G. Griffiths and H. Tiffin (eds) (1995). *The Post-Colonial Studies Reader*. London: Routledge.

289 See, e.g., J. Borrows (1994). 'Constitutional Law from a First Nation Perspective', *UBC Law Review*, 28: 1.

290 Kline, *supra* note 6, 419–23 and Kline, *supra* note 184, 137. For an excellent analysis of the limits of trying to work for meaningful change within the existing legal system see P. Monture-Angus (1999). *Journeying Forward. Dreaming of First Nations Independence*. Halifax, NS: Fernwood Publishing.

Chapter 3
Reforming the Australian and Canadian Child Welfare Systems: Sensitization and Accommodation

Introduction

Recent years have witnessed concerted efforts in both Canada and Australia to address the past failings of the non-native child welfare system and provide a more sensitive and effective service to Aboriginal communities. Growing judicial sensitivity to the issues surrounding Aboriginal child welfare has been underpinned by significant legislative reform aimed at entrenching the centrality of the 'indigenous factor' in all decisions concerning an Aboriginal child. The importance of protecting an Aboriginal child's cultural identity and, wherever possible, keeping Aboriginal children within their families and communities is now afforded strong recognition throughout the Canadian and Australian legislation. The desirability of accommodating Aboriginal child-rearing norms and practices within the non-native system and securing greater community involvement in decision-making and service delivery are also common themes of the reforms. In Canada, the creation of Aboriginal-controlled child welfare agencies exercising delegated provincial powers provides a promising model for increasing Aboriginal community involvement in the administration and delivery of Aboriginal child welfare to the communities. These developments are now being supported by a more comprehensive programme of administrative re-structuring in Manitoba aimed at transferring the management of all Aboriginal child welfare services to devolved Aboriginal Authorities. Reforms such as these could be usefully adapted to the Australian context.

However, whilst reform initiatives aimed at sensitizing the non-native system to the cultural needs of Aboriginal children are important, Kline's analysis suggests caution. Such is the strength with which the philosophy, norms and practices of the non-Aboriginal population are entrenched within the governing, legal and administrative framework of the non-native system, there are strong grounds for concern that reforms such as these may only ever enjoy qualified success. Indeed, those concerns are borne out by the limited impact of the recent reforms in Canada and Australia,[1] providing considerable fuel for the argument that the only

1 For a good critique of the policy of devolving Aboriginal child welfare services to Aboriginal-controlled agencies in Canada see, J. Rae (2009). 'Program Delivery

effective long-term solution for Aboriginal children and families is the autonomy and freedom promised by self-government.

Australian Reforms to the Non-Native Child Welfare System

Legislative Reforms

The current approach to Aboriginal child welfare in Australia is firmly entrenched within the rhetoric of self-determination. The *Bringing Them Home* report notes that in their evidence to the Inquiry the states and territories placed great emphasis on the need for Aboriginal communities to exercise greater control over their own child welfare. As it was put by the government of Queensland:

> The essence of self-determination in this context is an understanding that only Aboriginal people can find solutions to the problems which confront them, and that Aboriginal people have the right to make decisions concerning their own lives and their own communities and the right to retain their culture and develop it.[2]

Whilst avoiding the more powerful language of self-determination, the Northern Territory Board of Inquiry premised its report on similar key principles, emphasizing the need for 'decolonising attitudes',[3] 'empowerment'[4] and 'genuine consultation'[5] with Aboriginal communities. The need for 'community ownership' of solutions to child abuse problems is a recurring theme:

> The thrust of our recommendations, which are designed to advise the Northern Territory Government on how it can help support communities to effectively prevent and tackle child sexual abuse, is for there to be consultation with, and ownership by the communities, of those solutions. The underlying

---

Devolution: A Stepping Stone or Quagmire for First Nations?', *Indigenous Law Journal*, 7: 1. For reviews of the more recent administrative reforms in Manitoba see: C. Bourassa (2010). *Summary Review of the Manitoba Child Welfare System for the Saskatchewan Child Welfare Report*. Available at: http://saskchildwelfarereview.ca/Review-Manitoba-Child-Welfare-System-CBourassa.pdf; and P. Hudson and B. McKenzie (2003). 'Extending Aboriginal Control Over Child Welfare Services – The Manitoba Child Welfare Initiative', *Canadian Review of Social Policy*, 51: 49.

2 Cited in Human Rights and Equal Opportunity Commission (HREOC) (1997). *Report of the National Inquiry into the Separation of Aboriginal and Torres Strait Islander Children from their Families*. Commonwealth of Australia, 436.

3 Northern Territory Government (2007). *Board of Inquiry into the Protection of Aboriginal Children from Sexual Abuse*. Darwin, NT: Government Printer, 53.

4 Ibid., 13.

5 Ibid., 22.

> dysfunctionality where child sexual abuse flourishes needs to be attacked, and the strength returned to Aboriginal people.[6]

The language of self-determination has also found its way into state and territorial legislation, with New South Wales, Western Australia, Victoria and the Northern Territories all placing their specific provisions on Aboriginal children within the context of Aboriginal self-determination. The Children and Young Persons (Care and Protection) Act 1998 (NSW), for example, enshrines the principle that Aboriginal communities should be able to participate in the care and protection of Aboriginal children in accordance with self-determination:

> (1) It is a principle to be applied in the administration of this Act that Aboriginal and Torres Strait Islander people are to participate in the care and protection of their children and young persons with as much self-determination as is possible.
>
> (2) To assist in the implementation of the principle in subsection (1), the Minister may negotiate and agree with Aboriginal and Torres Strait Islander people to the implementation of programs and strategies that promote self-determination.[7]

Similar provisions apply in Western Australia, Victoria and the Northern Territories.[8]

Unfortunately, although clear efforts have been made to 'sensitize' existing child welfare agencies to Aboriginal needs and cultural differences, the reality of Aboriginal child welfare in Australia is far removed from the principles of 'self-determination' and 'community ownership' that the rhetoric of governments would suggest. Recent legislative changes aimed at making the child welfare system more responsive to the needs of Aboriginal communities have been concerned with three major objectives: (1) ensuring greater recognition is accorded to the 'indigenous factor' and the particular cultural needs of Aboriginal children by the introduction of targeted provisions such as the Aboriginal placement principle; (2) improving the participation of Aboriginal people in the mainstream child protection system through more effective consultation procedures and, where deemed appropriate, the delegation of certain child welfare services to Aboriginal workers and agencies; and (3) ensuring greater sensitivity to Aboriginal child-rearing practices and traditions. All of the Australian states and territories now make specific legislative provision for Aboriginal children in accordance with these broad objectives.

---

6 Ibid., 21.

7 Children and Young Persons (Care and Protection) Act 1998 (NSW), s 11. See also Adoption Act 2000 (NSW), s 35(1).

8 Care and Protection of Children Act 2007 (NT), Part 1.3, s 12(1). See also, Children and Community Services Act 2004 (WA), s 13 and Children, Youth and Families Act 2005 (Vic), s 12(1).

Recognition of the 'indigenous factor' and the Aboriginal placement principle

The states and territories have taken clear steps to ensure that their much-maligned failure to ensure proper weight and consideration is given to the 'indigenous factor' when making child welfare decisions is effectively remedied. Most state and territorial legislation now makes explicit provision for the protection of a child's cultural identity either as one of the Act's guiding principles or as an integral part of determining the best interests of the child. The Children's Protection Act 1993 (SA), for example, provides that in determining the child's best interests consideration must be given to: 'the need to encourage, preserve and enhance the child's sense of racial, ethnic, religious, spiritual and cultural identity and to respect traditions and values of the community into which the child was born'.[9] The Care and Protection of Children Act 2007 (NT) similarly provides that in determining the best interests of the child, consideration should be given to the child's cultural, ethnic and religious background.[10] The Act's guiding principles also provide that the child's family 'should be able to bring up the child in any language or tradition and foster in the child any cultural, ethnic or religious values'. It goes on to state that decisions involving a child 'should be made in a way that is consistent with the cultural, ethnic and religious values and traditions relevant to a child'.[11]

These now standard provisions protecting a child's ethnic, religious and cultural identity, whilst of general application, are of importance in drawing attention to the significance of culture for Aboriginal children. However, to reinforce the particular and 'unique' significance of Aboriginal identity, most states and territories have also included more targeted provisions aimed at addressing the specific cultural needs of Aboriginal children. Thus, in determining the best interests of a child, the Children, Youth and Families Act 2005 (Vic) provides that consideration must be given to: 'the need, in relation to an Aboriginal child, to protect and promote his or her Aboriginal cultural and spiritual identity and development by, wherever possible, maintaining and building their connections to their Aboriginal family and community'.[12] The Act goes on to provide that 'a cultural plan' must be prepared for every Aboriginal child in out-of-home care, setting out how the child is to remain connected to his or her Aboriginal community and Aboriginal culture.[13] Compliance with the plan by the child's carers must be monitored.[14] A similar emphasis on the cultural needs of Aboriginal children is enshrined within the statutory guidance on the application of the best interests principle in Queensland,

9 Children's Protection Act 1993 (SA), s 4(4)(c). See also: Children, Youth and Families Act 2005 (Vic), s 10(3)(l) and (m); Children, Young Persons and their Families Act (1997) (Tas), s 8(2)(b)(v); and Children and Young People Act 2008, s 9(1)(a).

10 Care and Protection of Children Act 2007 (NT), Part 1.3.

11 Ibid. See also, Children and Community Services Act 2004 (WA), s 9(i) and Child Protection Act 1999 (QLD), s 5B(m).

12 Children, Youth and Families Act 2005 (Vic), s 10(3)(c).

13 Ibid., s 176(1)–(2). See also Children and Young People Act 2008 (ACT), s 513.

14 Children, Youth and Families Act 2005 (Vic), s 176(4).

the Child Protection Act 1999 (QLD) providing: 'the child should be allowed to develop and maintain a connection with the child's family, culture, traditions, language and community'; and 'the long-term effect of a decision on the child's identity and connection with their family and community should be taken into account'.[15]

The most prominent of these targeted provisions is what has come to be termed the Aboriginal placement principle. The gradual legislative endorsement of the Aboriginal placement principle with a view to preventing the unnecessary removal of Aboriginal children from their families and communities constitutes an important change in Australian policy and practice.[16] All Australian jurisdictions now recognize in legislative form that when Aboriginal children require out-of-home care they should be placed, whenever possible, within their own cultural community and that placement with a non-Aboriginal family should only be considered as a very last resort.[17] The precise wording of the principle differs between jurisdictions, but the formulation as contained in the Children and Young Persons (Care and Protection) Act 1998 (NSW) is fairly typical:

> (1) … [A]n Aboriginal or Torres Strait Islander child or young person who needs to be placed in out-of-home care is to be placed with:
>
> (a) a member of the child's or young person's extended family or kinship group, as recognised by the Aboriginal or Torres Strait Islander community to which the child or young person belongs, or
>
> (b) if it is not practicable for the child or young person to be placed in accordance with paragraph (a) or it would not be in the best interests of the child or young person to be so placed-a member of the Aboriginal or Torres Strait Islander community to which the child or young person belongs, or
>
> (c) if it is not practicable for the child or young person to be placed in accordance with paragraph (a) or (b) or it would not be in the best interests of the child or young person to be so placed-a member of some other Aboriginal or Torres Strait Islander family residing in the vicinity of the child's or young person's usual place of residence, or
>
> (d) if it is not practicable for the child or young person to be placed in accordance with paragraph (a), (b) or (c) or it would be detrimental to the safety, welfare

15 Child Protection Act 1999 (QLD), s 5C. See also: Children and Community Services Act 2004 (WA), s 8(1)(j); and Children and Young People Act 2008 (ACT), s 10(a).

16 HREOC, *supra* note 2, 437.

17 Ibid., 439.

> and well-being of the child or young person to be so placed-a suitable person approved by the Director-General after consultation with:
>
> (i) members of the child's or young person's extended family or kinship group, as recognised by the Aboriginal or Torres Strait Islander community to which the child or young person belongs, and
>
> (ii) such Aboriginal or Torres Strait Islander organisations as are appropriate to the child or young person.[18]

The legislation thus envisages progression from a preferred placement within the child's extended family or kinship group (as determined by community practice and tradition), to a 'last resort' position of placement with a non-Aboriginal carer. A placement with a non-Aboriginal carer is only permitted if placement with an Aboriginal carer would positively endanger the child's safety, welfare and well-being (a different and more exacting standard than placement with a non-Aboriginal carer simply being deemed to be in the best interests of the child). Before such a placement can be approved, the child's extended family and an appropriate Aboriginal organization must also be consulted. If a placement with a non-Aboriginal carer is deemed necessary, further statutory duties apply with a view to safeguarding the child's relationship with his or her family, community and culture. Thus, reunification with the child's Aboriginal family remains the overriding objective. Continuing contact must also be ensured between the child and his or her Aboriginal family, community and culture.[19]

The New South Wales and Victoria legislation are distinctive in providing specifically for mixed-race Aboriginal children. In other jurisdictions, the application of the Aboriginal placement principle to mixed-race children simply depends on whether or not the child is regarded as 'Aboriginal' for the purposes of the Act; the term 'Aboriginal' being fairly broadly and inclusively defined.[20]

---

18 Children and Young Persons (Care and Protection) Act 1998 (NSW), s 13(1).

19 Ibid., s 13(6). This detailed exposition of the Aboriginal placement principle is replicated in similar terms in the legislation of Queensland (Child Protection Act 1999 (QLD), s 83), the Northern Territories (Care and Protection of Children Act 2007 (NT), Part 1.3), Western Australia (Children and Community Services Act 2004 (WA), s 12(2)), Victoria (Children, Youth and Families Act 2005 (Vic), s 13), and the ACT (Children and Young People Act 2008 (ACT), s 513). A much more vague commitment to keeping Aboriginal children within Aboriginal communities is included in the legislation of South Australia (Children's Protection Act 1993 (SA), s 5(2)(c)) and Tasmania (Children, Young Persons and their Families Act (1997) (Tas), s 9(2)(c)).

20 For example, the Children's Protection Act (1993) (SA), s 6(1), provides that an Aboriginal child means: 'a child who is a descendant of the indigenous inhabitants of Australia and who regards himself or herself as an Aboriginal or, if he or she is a young child, is regarded as an Aboriginal by at least one of his or her parents'. The definition of 'Aboriginal' in the Children and Young People Act 1999 (ACT) is almost identical. See also

However, NSW and Victoria treat mixed-race children differently, providing that in the case of a mixed-race child whilst the Aboriginal placement principle *may* be applied, the child is to be placed simply in accordance with his or her best interests.[21] The NSW legislation goes on to provide that regardless of placement, contact with the child's family, community and culture, both Aboriginal and non-Aboriginal, must be secured.[22] The Victoria legislation restricts this protection to contact with the child's Aboriginal community.[23]

The decision of the NSW and Victoria legislature not to make compliance with the Aboriginal placement principle mandatory in such circumstances is somewhat disappointing given the particular problems faced by mixed-race Aboriginal children.[24] When placed within the wider context of a welfare test, the need for mixed-race Aboriginal children to be placed within an Aboriginal family can be easily displaced by other 'more weighty' considerations. This weakness is clearly illustrated by the decision of the NSW Administrative Appeals Tribunal in *Jones v Minister, Community Services*.[25] In overturning the decision of the Minister to remove a mixed race Aboriginal child from her non-Aboriginal carer, about whom the Department had serious concerns given her apparent denial of the child's Aboriginality, the Tribunal emphasized that placement with an Aboriginal family was not an overriding principle to be applied despite all other considerations: it was just one relevant factor, albeit an extremely important one, to be placed in the balance with all other relevant considerations, including the child's psychological bond with the alternative carer. In this case that bond proved to be determinative.[26] However, whilst the NSW legislation may be disappointing in this respect, it is alone in placing a clear and specific obligation on the relevant authorities to take reasonable steps to determine whether or not a particular child is an Aboriginal or Torres Strait Islander child and thus should be dealt with in accordance with the legislation's specific protection for Aboriginal children.[27]

Consultation and participation in decision-making processes

The second major legislative change to occur in recent years has been the move to ensure improved participation by the child's Aboriginal community in the decision-

---

the broad definitions of 'Aboriginal' in the Community and Services Act 2004 (WA), s 3; Adoption of Children Act 1995 (NT), s 3; Adoption Act 1993 (ACT), s 4(1); and Adoption Act 1988 (SA), s 4(2).

21 Children and Young Persons (Care and Protection) Act 1998 (NSW), s 13(4). Children, Youth and Families Act 2005 (Vic), s 14(4).

22 Children and Young Persons (Care and Protection) Act 1998 (NSW), s 13(5).

23 Children, Youth and Families Act 2005 (Vic), s 14(5).

24 See the more sensitive approach taken in other areas of Australian family law, esp. Evatt CJ's dissent in *In the Marriage of Goudge* [1984] FLC 91: 313.

25 [2001] NSWADT 192.

26 Ibid., [93]–[94].

27 Children and Young Persons (Care and Protection) Act 1998 (NSW), s 32.

making process. Although often dressed in the guise of self-determination,[28] what is intended by these legislative changes is not Aboriginal self-government or even self-management over child welfare but the much more limited vision of ensuring greater Aboriginal involvement in the decisions of the non-native child welfare authorities. Initiatives aimed at ensuring the participation of extended family members and members of the clan, tribe or group are now common. In Queensland, members of the extended family and representatives of the wider community are entitled to participate in the care planning process through their involvement in family group meetings.[29] In New South Wales, the Department of Justice, Attorney-General's Department and the Department of Community Services (DoCS) have developed a joint 'care circle' initiative aimed at securing the involvement of community elders before final orders are made.[30] Many of the states and territories have also attempted to facilitate greater Aboriginal community involvement by affording a more formal role to Aboriginal childcare agencies including the delegation of some service provision.

It was thought that the creation of Aboriginal and Torres Strait Islander Child Care Agencies (AICCAs) would be the key to ensuring greater Aboriginal involvement in the child welfare system. First established in the 1970s, all AICCAs adhere to three basic principles: (1) Aboriginal children are best cared for within their own communities; (2) that the placement of Aboriginal children in non-native families must end; and (3) that Aboriginal families should be preserved and supported to achieve that end.[31] According to the *Bringing Them Home* report, it was hoped that AICCAs, as community organizations, would be able to help bridge the gulf that existed between the state and territorial child welfare agencies by building on existing resources within the community and developing service delivery models that were sensitive to and reflective of the needs of Aboriginal children and families.[32] There are now over 100 AICCAs across Australia performing a multitude of functions including the provision of preventative services, assisting with the care of children under care and protection orders and providing a range of adoption and fostering services.[33] The input of Aboriginal communities into the general child welfare system through the medium of Aboriginal childcare agencies has, however, remained limited. The key problem remains the location of power

---

28 See, in particular, Children and Young Persons (Care and Protection Act) 1998 (NSW), s 11; Care and Protection of Children Act 2007 (NT), Part 1.3; Children and Community Services Act 2004 (WA), s 13; and Children, Youth and Families Act 2005 (Vic), s 12.

29 Child Protection Act 1999 (QLD), ss 51E and 51H.

30 The 'care circle' has been given a statutory footing as a form of alternative dispute resolution provided for under s 37 of the Children and Young Persons (Care and Protection) Act 1998 (NSW). For more detail see *Re Timothy* [2010] NSWSC 524.

31 Royal Commission into Aboriginal Deaths in Custody (RCADC) (c. 1991). *National Report*, Vol. 2. Canberra: Australian Govt. Pub. Service, [11.8.2].

32 HREOC, *supra* note 2, 435.

33 Ibid.

and decision-making authority within the child welfare system as prescribed by the legislation. Although AICCAs provide a variety of services, their role is strictly limited to one of consultation and advice, with all decision-making authority from policy development and budget setting to day-to-day placement decisions, remaining in the hands of the non-native child welfare system. It is important to recognize that recent legislative reforms on consultation and participation have not changed that basic position.

Strong provisions on the need for consultation with Aboriginal communities are found in the legislation of South Australia, Queensland, the ACT and Victoria. In South Australia, s 5(1) of the Children's Protection Act 1993 (SA) provides in clear terms that: 'no decision or order may be made ... as to where or with whom an Aboriginal or Torres Strait Islander child will reside' unless a recognized Aboriginal or Torres Strait Islander organization has first been consulted.[34] Further to this basic principle, a mandatory obligation is placed on all persons, including the court, to have regard to the submissions made by a recognized Aboriginal or Torres Strait Islander organization when making *any* decision with respect to an Aboriginal or Torres Strait Islander child under the Act.[35] If no organization has been consulted then the decision-maker is directed to have regard to: 'Aboriginal or Torres Strait Islander traditions and cultural values (including kinship rules) as generally expressed by the Aboriginal or Torres Strait Islander community' and 'to the general principle that an Aboriginal or Torres Strait Islander child should be kept within the Aboriginal or Torres Strait Islander community'.[36] The relevant authorities under the Act are further directed when conducting any meeting involving an Aboriginal person to use 'all reasonable endeavours' to ensure the meeting is carried out in a manner that is respectful and sympathetic to Aboriginal traditions.[37] Similar provisions apply in Queensland for mandatory participation by a 'recognised Aboriginal entity' in all 'significant' decisions concerning the child and for consultation regarding all other decisions.[38] The Queensland legislation also more specifically provides that representatives from the agencies should be invited to attend family group meetings and any conferences held between the parties in the course of the child protection proceedings.[39]

34 Children's Protection Act 1993 (SA), s 5(1).

35 Ibid., s 5(2).

36 Ibid., ss 5(2)(b) and (c).

37 Ibid., ss 5(5) and 5(6). For the purposes of these provisions, a recognized Aboriginal or Torres Strait Islander organization is an organization that, following consultation with the Aboriginal or Torres Strait Islander community, is so recognized by the Minister by publication of an appropriate notice in the Gazette. Aboriginal representation thus remains subject to the approval of the Minister. See Children's Protection Act 1993 (SA), s 5(3).

38 Child Protection Act 1999 (QLD), ss 6, 7(o), and 83. See also, Children and Young People Act 2008 (ACT), ss 10(b) and 457(1)(a)(iv).

39 Child Protection Act 1999 (QLD), ss 51L and 70. A conference between the parties must be held in any proceedings where the making of a child protection order is contested before the order can be made. See Child Protection Act 1999 (QLD), s 59(1)(c). A family

The Victoria legislation has the most interesting consultation provisions in that it appears to confer on Aboriginal agencies a limited power of veto over the placement of Aboriginal children with non-Aboriginal carers. The Children, Youth and Families Act 2005 (Vic) enshrines the general principle that when making a decision or taking any action in relation to an Aboriginal child, an opportunity should be given to members of the child's Aboriginal community or other respected Aboriginal persons to contribute their views.[40] This obligation is strengthened in relation to a decision over the placement of a child or 'other significant decision' where a meeting must be convened by an Aboriginal Convener approved by an Aboriginal agency.[41] The meeting should be attended by the child, the child's parents, the child's extended family and other appropriate members of the child's community.[42] The legislation goes on to specify that in making a decision to place a child in out-of-home care an Aboriginal agency must first be consulted[43] and that the court will not be able to make a permanent care order placing an Aboriginal child with a non-Aboriginal carer unless the court has received a report from an Aboriginal agency recommending the order is made.[44] In the absence of such a recommendation it would seem that the court has no jurisdiction to make the order.[45]

Other jurisdictions also provide for consultation with Aboriginal communities but such consultation is either more limited in scope, for example to placement decisions, or is expressed in weaker, more nebulous, terms.[46]

Beyond the need for greater consultation with Aboriginal communities, a common theme in the legislation is an apparent commitment to helping Aboriginal communities develop greater capacity for their own child welfare provision. In South Australia, for example, one specified function of the Minister under the legislation is to: 'assist the Aboriginal community to establish its own programmes for preventing or reducing the incidence of abuse or neglect of children within

meeting should also be convened to give the child, members of the child's extended family, and other members of the child's clan, tribe, or group the opportunity to contribute to the care planning process. See Child Protection Act 1999 (QLD), ss 51E and 51H.

40 Children, Youth and Families Act 2005 (Vic), s 12(1)(a).

41 Ibid., s 12(1)(b).

42 Ibid.

43 Ibid., s 12(1)(c).

44 Ibid., s 323(b).

45 Ibid.

46 Children and Community Services Act 2004 (WA), s 14; Children and Young Persons (Care and Protection) Act 1998 (NSW), ss 12 and 13(1)(d). In both WA and NSW there is a mandatory duty to consult with members of the child's extended family or kinship group and appropriate Aboriginal welfare organizations before an Aboriginal child is placed. There is no mandatory duty to consult in the Northern Territories, although the principle of participation is recognized. See Care and Protection of Children Act 2007 (NT), Part 1.3.

the Aboriginal community'.[47] Key to the development of Aboriginal community services is the possibility of Aboriginal agencies assuming increasing amounts of responsibility under the legislation. This is made possible by the inclusion of general provisions allowing the Minister or his/her equivalent to delegate certain of his/her powers and functions under the Act.[48] The New South Wales legislation, for example, provides that: 'the Minister may negotiate and agree with Aboriginal and Torres Strait Islander people to the implementation of programs and strategies that promote self-determination'.[49] However, the possibility of delegating responsibility over all child welfare services to Aboriginal agencies or communities has not been properly explored in the Australian context. AICCAs currently remain strictly limited to an advisory role and the provision of out-of-home care and some preventative services. They do not provide a full range of child protection services and crucially do not hold decision-making powers. It is significant that, with only one exception, none of the states or territories have made provision for Aboriginal representation on key decision/policy-making bodies.[50]

Aboriginal child-rearing practices, traditions and values

Although there has been some progress of note in this area, the state and territorial legislatures have generally been much more cautious when it comes to the accommodation of specific Aboriginal child-rearing practices, traditions and values. Progress has therefore been patchy. To the extent that such recognition exists it tends to be limited to the role of the extended family; albeit that recognition is important. Thus, in the Care and Protection of Children Act 2007 (NT) the definition of a child's family includes the extended family as determined by any customary law, tradition, custom or practice applicable to the child.[51] The South Australia legislation similarly tries to take an inclusive approach, providing that the word 'family' means:

> [T]he child's immediate family (including all guardians) and the child's extended family (that is to say, all other persons to whom the child is related by blood or marriage) and, in relation to an Aboriginal or Torres Strait Islander

---

47 Children's Protection Act 1993 (SA), s 8. See also, Child Protection Act 1999 (QLD), s 7(f).

48 See: Care and Protection of Children Act 2007 (NT), Part 2.1; Children's Protection Act 1993 (SA), s 57; Child Protection Act 1999 (QLD), s 156; Children and Community Services Act 2004 (WA), s 24; Children, Young Persons and their Families Act (1997) (Tas), s 110; Children, Youth and Families Act 2005 (Vic), ss 17–18; Children and Young Persons (Care and Protection) Act 1998 (NSW), s 250.

49 Children and Young Persons (Care and Protection) Act 1998 (NSW), s 11(2).

50 As to the exception see, Children and Youth Services Council in ACT: Children and Young People Act 2008 (ACT), s 30(3)(b).

51 Care and Protection of Children Act 2007 (NT), Part 1.4.

> child, includes any person held to be related to the child according to Aboriginal kinship rules, or Torres Strait Islander kinship rules, as the case may require.[52]

More generally, the ACT legislation provides that in making any decision under the Act the decision-maker *must* take into account 'Aboriginal and Torres Strait Islander traditions and cultural values (including kinship rules) as identified by reference to the child's or young person's family and kinship relationships and the community with which the child or young person has the strongest affiliation'.[53]

Adoption

Many of the recent changes to the Australian child protection legislation have been consolidated by similar legislative changes to the law on adoption. With its traditional emphasis on the absolute transfer of the child from the birth family to the adoptive parents, adoption represents the strongest challenge to the child's cultural identity and need for a continuing relationship with his or her Aboriginal family and community. The risk of children being permanently alienated from their cultural heritage is particularly high in the adoption context. The states and territories, with the notable exception of Tasmania,[54] have thus responded to this challenge by the introduction of an Aboriginal placement principle, very similar to that applied when a child is taken into care, aimed at ensuring that the adoption of an Aboriginal child into a non-Aboriginal family is only used as a measure of very last resort. The need for consultation with Aboriginal communities and/or Aboriginal childcare agencies before an Aboriginal child is adopted is also very firmly entrenched.

The Northern Territory's adoption legislation contains perhaps the strongest recognition of the concerns of Aboriginal communities as to the adoption of Aboriginal children by non-native families. The need to have regard to the ethnicity and religion of the birth parents is specifically recognized when determining the best interests of the child.[55] The various matters which the authorities are to take

52 Children's Protection Act 1993 (SA), s 6. See also the definition of 'relative' in Children and Community Services Act 2004 (WA), s 3 and the general definition of 'parent' in the Child Protection Act 1999 (QLD), s 11(3). The problems of adopting a narrow interpretation of terms such as 'parent', 'guardian' and 'custody' for extended family members caring for children in accordance with Aboriginal tradition has been recognized in the courts. See *Minister for Health & Community Services v NB, KPP, HPP* [2007] NTMC 69, [9].

53 Children and Young People Act 2008 (ACT), s 10(c). See also, Children's Protection Act 1993 (SA), s 5(2)(b).

54 Adoption Act 1988 (Tas). When assessing the suitability of prospective adoptive parents and placing the child in an adoptive home, s 24(1)(b) of the Adoption Act 1988 (Tas) does provide in general terms for the relevant authority to have regard to any expressed wish of the parents and/or the child as to the cultural identity of the adoptive parents and their ability to meet the child's cultural needs.

55 Adoption of Children Act 1995 (NT), s 8(2).

into account when applying this principle are then further elaborated in Schedule 1 of the Act. In general terms, it is stated that the Minister and the court must take into account that it is 'preferable that the child should be placed with a family that has the same ethnic and cultural origins as the child's birth parents in order to facilitate an environment that will promote the child's cultural heritage and identity'.[56] However, with specific regard to Aboriginal children, the Schedule goes on to provide that consideration must be given to the fact that adoption is alien to traditional Aboriginal cultures and that Aboriginal people have legitimate concerns as to the effects of practices such as adoption on the cultural integrity of their communities:

> Where the child is an Aboriginal child, recognition is to be given to –
>
> (i) the absence of adoption in customary Aboriginal child care arrangements, arrangements for the custody and guardianship of the child being made within the child's extended family or with other Aboriginal people who have the correct relationship under customary Aboriginal law; and
>
> (ii) the desire and effort of the Aboriginal community to preserve the integrity of its culture and kinship relationships so that efforts must be made to find placements within families, kin groups or ethnic communities as appropriate.[57]

In a provision unique in Australian child welfare legislation, the needs and interests of the child's Aboriginal community are thus incorporated into the court's determination of the best interests of the individual Aboriginal child.[58] The Schedule goes on to provide for 'appropriate consultation' between the child's parents or other relatives or appropriate Aboriginal representatives in order to ascertain how best to promote the ethnic welfare and development of the child.[59]

Beyond these extended provisions on determining the best interests of an Aboriginal child, the legislation also provides in explicit terms for an Aboriginal placement principle virtually identical to that found in the child protection legislation. Strong preference is thus given to arranging appropriate custody arrangements with the child's extended family and kin before adoption outside the community can be considered. The need to act in accordance with Aboriginal customary law and to consult with the child's parents and wider Aboriginal

56 Ibid., Schedule 1(1).

57 Ibid., Schedule 1(2).

58 This comes close to the approach advocated by Philip Lynch that the best interests of the child's community must be considered as integral to the best interests of an individual Aboriginal child. See P. Lynch (2001). 'Keeping them Home: The Best Interests of Indigenous Children and Communities in Canada and Australia', *Sydney Law Review*, 23: 501, 535, 506 and 527–8.

59 Adoption of Children Act 1995 (NT), Schedule 1(3).

community (as determined by customary law) are also distinctive features of the Northern Territory's statutory recognition of the Aboriginal placement principle within this particular context.[60]

Recent reforms to adoption legislation in New South Wales have introduced similarly strong provisions. The legislation contains clear recognition of the importance of cultural identity for all children.[61] As in the legislation of the Northern Territory, strong and distinct recognition is also given to the particular concerns relating to the adoption of Aboriginal children. Strong obligations are imposed on the relevant authorities to consult with Aboriginal families and communities over the adoption and placement of an Aboriginal child. Section 33 thus makes it mandatory for the Director General to consult either an Aboriginal adoption consultative organization[62] or a person with relevant expertise nominated by the child's parents, extended family, kinship group or community, as to the placement of the child. The Act further directs that in placing an Aboriginal child for adoption, the 'Aboriginal child placement principles' will apply.[63] Indeed, s 90 of the Act provides that the court cannot make an adoption order unless it is satisfied that the Aboriginal placement principles have been adhered to. In similar terms to those found in the child protection legislation, the child is thus to be placed in order of preference: (1) with a prospective adoptive parent or parents belonging to the child's Aboriginal community; (2) a prospective adoptive parent or parents from another Aboriginal community; and (3) only if these first two options are not practicable or in the child's best interests can the child be placed with a non-Aboriginal carer.[64] Furthermore, before the child can be placed with a

60 Ibid., s 11.

61 Section 32 of the Adoption Act 2000 (NSW) provides: '(1) In placing a child (other than an Aboriginal or Torres Strait Islander child) for adoption, the decision maker must take into account the culture, any disability, language and religion of the child and the principle that the child's given name, identity, language and cultural and religious ties should, as far as possible, be preserved. (2) Without limiting matters that may be taken into account, the decision maker must take into account whether a prospective adoptive parent of a different cultural heritage to that of the child has demonstrated the following: (a) the capacity to assist the child to develop a healthy and positive cultural identity; (b) knowledge of or a willingness to learn about, and teach the child about, the child's cultural heritage; (c) a willingness to foster links with that heritage in the child's upbringing; (d) the capacity to help the child if the child encounters racism or discrimination in school or in the wider community.'

62 Section 195 of the Adoption Act 2000 (NSW) provides that the Director General may approve certain Aboriginal organizations as Aboriginal adoption consultative organizations to provide advice and assistance to Aboriginal families and kinship groups regarding the care of Aboriginal children. Amongst other functions Aboriginal adoption consultative organisations are to provide counselling to a person before he/she gives their consent to the adoption of an Aboriginal child. See Adoption Act 2000 (NSW), s 64.

63 As with the child protection legislation these placement principles do not apply to mixed race Aboriginal children. See Adoption Act 2000 (NSW), ss 35(4) and (5).

64 Ibid., s 35(2).

prospective non-Aboriginal adopter, the court must be satisfied that the prospective adoptive parent will support and encourage the child's Aboriginal identity.[65] As with the NSW child protection legislation, the Director General is placed under an obligation to make 'reasonable inquiries' as to whether a particular child is an Aboriginal child and thus should be placed in accordance with these principles.[66] Furthermore, in an approach not taken anywhere else in Australia, the legislation provides that in order to ensure these principles have been properly satisfied and the court is not faced with a fait accompli, a preliminary hearing must be held in every case concerning an Aboriginal child where it is proposed he or she should be placed with a non-Aboriginal family.[67]

Similar extensive provisions on the adoption of Aboriginal children apply in the ACT,[68] Queensland[69] and South Australia.[70]

The Success and Limitations of the Australian Legislative Reforms

Important steps have clearly been taken in recent years to try and focus the minds of decision-makers on the specific cultural needs of Aboriginal children. To varying degrees, the 'indigenous factor' is now recognized in most state and territorial legislation, with some additional accommodation of Aboriginal child-rearing practices and traditions. Without doubt, the most marked success of recent years is the clear statutory grounding now given throughout most of Australia to the Aboriginal placement principle. The clear duty imposed on decision-makers to place Aboriginal children wherever possible with Aboriginal carers in order to protect their cultural identity should help increase understanding of the particular cultural needs of Aboriginal children. That understanding was, for example, evident in the case of *UI & UJ v Minister for Community Services*,[71] one of the few reported decisions concerning the placement of an Aboriginal child.[72] In upholding the decision of the Minister for Community Services (NSW) to move three Aboriginal children from non-Aboriginal carers to an Aboriginal placement in accordance with the NSW legislation, the NSW Administrative Decisions Tribunal accepted the relevance of the evidence regarding the general damage that has been done to Aboriginal people by past policies of assimilation, as well as the more specific research evidence regarding the identity problems experienced by Aboriginal children placed in non-Aboriginal homes, particularly during

65 Ibid., s 35(3).

66 Ibid., s 34.

67 Ibid., s 80(2).

68 Adoption Act 1993 (ACT), ss 6 and 39G.

69 Adoption Act 2009 (QLD), ss 131, 163, 165(2)(c) and 172.

70 Adoption Act 1988 (SA), s 11.

71 [2006] NSWADT 16.

72 Cf. the less encouraging decision of the Tribunal in *Jones v Minister, Community Services* [2001] NSWADT 192, discussed above at p. 75.

adolescence.[73] The Tribunal also accepted the conceptualization of Aboriginal culture now securely established in other areas of Australian family law as an active lived experience requiring sustained and meaningful exposure.[74] The provision of information about Aboriginal culture was thus deemed insufficient to safeguard the children's cultural identity, the Tribunal observing: 'culture is a matter of exposure and needs to be absorbed as a daily thing'.[75] Taking a long-term view of the children's best interests, the Tribunal thus held that given the risk that a non-Aboriginal placement would 'de-culturalise' the children, it was in their best interests to be moved to an Aboriginal family.[76]

However, even positive developments such as this are not without their difficulties. The clear focus of the Australian authorities on the much more limited, and less challenging step, of giving legislative status to the Aboriginal placement principle – a principle which only comes into play once a child has been deemed to be in need of care and protection and the initial crucial decision to remove the child from his or her Aboriginal family has been taken – has arguably deflected attention from the bigger, more difficult questions about the fundamental failings of the child protection system. Crucial questions such as how the initial need for apprehension and removal can be avoided, and the extent to which Aboriginal communities should have decision-making authority over Aboriginal child welfare restored, have been sidelined in recent years.

The application of the Aboriginal placement principle has also not been consistent, with cultural identity still given little weight in the welfare balance by some members of the Australian judiciary who maintain that whilst the child has a right to be placed in culturally appropriate care and to maintain relationships with his family and community, the primary consideration must be to ensure the child's physical and psychological safety.[77] Reconciling these two considerations remains exceptionally difficult when there are so few resources to provide safe alternative care within the Aboriginal community. A common theme in the few reported Australian child protection decisions is the difficulty of complying with the Aboriginal placement principle due to a continuing lack of culturally appropriate homes.[78] There are complex reasons behind this continuing shortage in Aboriginal foster carers, including the reluctance of potential carers to subject themselves to the scrutiny of a system that is generally viewed with such strong suspicion and distrust. Those Aboriginal foster carers who do come forward are consequently being placed under intolerable pressure, with resulting concerns

73 [2006] NSWADT 16, [123]–[125].

74 See, for example, *Davis & Spring* [2007] FamCA 1149, [79] (per Young J).

75 [2006] NSWADT 16, [216].

76 Ibid., [125]–[126].

77 *Re GAA* [2007] QCST 14, [53]–[55] and [90]; *RJ v Department of Communities (Child Safety Services)* [2010] QCAT 619, [32].

78 Ibid., [28].

about the standard of care being provided.[79] At the inquest into the death of Deborah Leanne Melville-Lothian, a 12-year-old Aboriginal girl who suffered 'deplorable neglect' at the hands of her great aunt, the coroner noted that the great aunt had been pressured into taking on the care of Deborah and her four siblings by the Department of Family and Community Services (FACS) who were very anxious to secure a culturally appropriate placement despite the fact the great aunt, a single parent, already had seven children of her own in her care.[80] The ill-fated nature of this placement was then compounded by the absence of any proper monitoring of the care being provided, FACS taking the view that the ongoing assessment of kinship carers needed to be less rigorous as kinship carers would have a greater natural affinity for the children.[81] Crucially, not only was kinship care regarded as needing less rigorous monitoring, kinship carers were assumed to need less in the way of support.[82] This single parent of 12 children was thus left largely to her own devices, the placement being regarded as a 'low priority' for a grossly overstretched department.[83] The inquest found that by the time of Deborah's death her great aunt had 'almost completely abandoned her legal and moral responsibilities as a carer'.[84] Deborah had also been effectively abandoned by FACS.

As was clear from the Melville-Lothian Inquest, attitudes amongst front-line social workers remain problematic. Research conducted by Cunneen and Libesman on files held by the New South Wales Department of Community Services in the year 1996–1997 reveals that, amongst other failings, the Aboriginality of the child is often treated as of only incidental relevance and that in some cases the Aboriginal identity of the child is not recognized at all, thus undermining any 'sensitization' initiatives including consultation requirements.[85] They also note that front-line workers displayed a lack of awareness of the effects of past colonial

---

79 See, for example, *Re AAA* [2006] QCST 1, in which the Queensland Children Services Tribunal ordered the return of three Aboriginal children to the care of their Aboriginal foster parents after the Department of Child Safety had removed them following notifications concerning the foster parents' excessive use of physical punishment, inappropriate parenting techniques, and problems with cleanliness and hygiene in the home. The Tribunal found the concerns to be of little substance, particularly when balanced against the strong evidence from the community as to the positive difference the foster parents had made to Aboriginal children in their care, including the three children in question.

80 *Inquest into the death of Deborah Leanne Melville-Lothian* [2010] NTMC 7, [7] and [27]–[37].

81 Ibid., [61].

82 Ibid., [77].

83 Ibid., [77].

84 Ibid., [7].

85 C. Cunneen and T. Libesman (2002). 'Removed and Discarded: The Contemporary Legacy of the Stolen Generations', *Australia Indigenous Law Reporter*, 55; 7(4). The research was carried out on files of indigenous children found to be neglected or emotionally abused in the year 1996–1997.

experiences on contemporary Aboriginal communities and individuals, including the inter-generational effects of past removals, and that biased, Euro-centric judgments continued to be applied against Aboriginal people when assessing their suitability as carers.

Limitations and problems with the recent reforms are also clearly evident in the provisions dealing with Aboriginal consultation and participation. There are strongly differing views between the Aboriginal communities and the state and territorial governments as to the success of the various legislative provisions aimed at securing greater community involvement in the decision-making process. Where the right of consultation arises only at the stage of placing the child, i.e. at the very final stages of child protection proceedings, it clearly comes too late. However, even where consultation is, in theory, to occur throughout the child protection process, its effectiveness is undermined by a myriad of problems. Some view consultation in accordance with the legislation as amounting to nothing more than empty rhetoric. The Pitjantjatjara women of the Anangu Pitjantjatjara lands described their experience of 'consultation' with Family and Community Services to the *Bringing Them Home* Inquiry as one: 'where the department exercises blanket powers, fails to recognise AP protocols and fails to inform families when the department is visiting, why or what is likely to happen'.[86] The Chief Executive Officer of SA Family and Community Services had a rather different perception:

> [T]he challenge for us is to balance the legislative obligations we have and implementing these obligations in a way that gives Aboriginal agencies and people scope to ensure that we are meeting needs in terms that are appropriate for them, and in a way that enables Aboriginal families to make decisions about the future of their own young people, and in a way that enables Aboriginal agencies to play a significant part … it's entirely consistent with our current legislation that [in] decisions we make that involve Aboriginal families and children, we should be actively seen to have taken the advice of appropriate Aboriginal leaders and agencies.[87]

As the *Bringing Them Home* report notes, the lack of clear guidelines as to when and in what form consultation should take place means that, 'discussions typically occur too late in the decision-making process and in too cursory a manner to permit an effective contribution being made'.[88] Moreover, without the non-native authorities being prepared to surrender real power and decision-making authority over child welfare to Aboriginal communities, consultation is often accurately perceived as paying little more than lip-service to the principles of participation

86 HREOC, *supra* note 2, 456.

87 Cited, ibid.

88 Ibid., 448.

and self-determination, exacerbating the sense of 'consultation fatigue' which has now set in within many Aboriginal communities.[89]

The limited role afforded to Aboriginal childcare agencies has also done little to secure meaningful consultation with Aboriginal communities. AICCAs clearly have the potential to play a significant role at all stages of the child protection process but their efforts are currently more narrowly focused on trying to secure the placement of Aboriginal children with Aboriginal families following apprehension. Consequently, not enough work is being done with communities at the earlier stages of the child protection process to prevent the initial intervention and removal. As the *Bringing Them Home* report points out, AICCAs could engage in preventative work with the family, help the family implement the changes required to prevent apprehension and play a crucial role in recruiting, training and supporting alternative Aboriginal carers. In order to perform this much wider role effectively, however, Aboriginal agencies must be consulted and involved throughout the child protection process.[90] Moreover, as with the communities they serve, Aboriginal childcare agencies need to be given real decision-making power and authority. As things stand, with state and territorial authorities typically required to only 'have regard' to the submissions of the Aboriginal agencies, their views can be effectively ignored.[91] The current position is neatly summarized in the *Bringing Them Home* report:

> "Partnerships" between Indigenous children's agencies and government departments, where they exist, are unequal partnerships. Departments retain full executive decision making power and the power to allocate resources affecting Indigenous children's welfare. Judicial decision making occurs within non-Indigenous courts. In no jurisdiction are Indigenous child care agencies permitted to be involved in the investigation of an allegation of neglect or abuse. The difference between being allowed to participate and having the right to make decisions is evident in Indigenous communities' experiences of child welfare systems.[92]

It is striking that even the relatively conservative model of allowing Aboriginal child welfare agencies to exercise delegated decision-making authority within the framework of the existing state or territorial legislation (as has been the case in Canada for many years), has yet to gain any kind of acceptance within Australia. Furthermore, continuing progress on these issues at a state and territorial level cannot be assumed. It is sobering to note that in many ways the most recent 2007 legislation in the Northern Territory is less progressive than its predecessor, with a weaker Aboriginal placement principle, more limited recognition of Aboriginal

89 Ibid., 436–7.

90 Ibid., 448.

91 See *Re GAA* [2007] QCST 14.

92 HREOC, *supra* note 2, 449.

customary law and less robust provisions on consultation with the Aboriginal community.[93]

Despite the reforms of recent years, serious problems therefore remain. The most fundamental difficulty is that none of the initiatives of the last 20 years have really challenged the basic conceptual framework of the non-native system and its relevance and suitability as a governing structure within Aboriginal communities.[94] It is a problem not only of translating law and policy into practice, but the continuing limitations of the law itself. The limitations of the 'sensitization' and 'accommodation' reform agenda are clearly evidenced by the continuing disproportionate number of Aboriginal children represented at all stages of the child protection system. Media reports that non-native social workers are now reluctant to intervene in Aboriginal communities out of fears they will be accused of racism are not borne out by the statistics.[95] Figures from 2009–2010 show that Aboriginal children were significantly more likely to be the subject of a substantiation[96] than non-indigenous children in all states and territories.[97] In New South Wales, indigenous children were 8.7 times more likely to be the subject of a substantiation than non-indigenous children, rising to 12.7 in Western Australia, 10.1 in South Australia and 6.1 in Queensland.[98] Moreover, the rates of Aboriginal children involved in a substantiation have been steadily and quite markedly increasing year upon year. Interestingly, the distinctive pattern of justifying state intervention into the lives of Aboriginal families on the more nebulous ground of 'neglect' (as opposed to physical, sexual or emotional abuse) has continued. In Western Australia, for example, 48.8 per cent of substantiations of Aboriginal children were on the basis of neglect compared with 32.8 per cent of non-indigenous children.[99]

The disproportionate number of Aboriginal children caught up in the child protection process is repeated at the next stage of proceedings: the making of care and protection orders by the courts. A snapshot picture taken on 30 June 2010 reveals that across Australia there were 48.3 Aboriginal children per 1,000

93 Cf. Care and Protection of Children Act 2007 (NT), Part 1.3, with the Community Welfare Act (NT), ss 68–71.

94 For a discussion of similar problems with legislative initiatives in the juvenile justice sphere, see C. Cunneen (1998). 'Reforming Juvenile Justice and Creating the Space for Indigenous Self-Determination', *UNSW Law Journal*, 21(1) (Forum 4, No 3): 241.

95 See, for example, *Sydney Morning Herald* (18 July 2002). '"Hands Off Policy" Leaves Kids at Risk'.

96 A substantiated case is one in which a notification of potential abuse or neglect has been made and investigated and the child welfare agency is satisfied that that there is a risk of harm such that services should be provided to the family.

97 Australian Institute of Health and Welfare (AIHW) (2011). *Child Protection Australia 2009–10.* AIHW Cat no. CWS 39. Canberra: AIHW (Child Welfare Series No. 51), table 2.9.

98 Ibid.

99 Ibid., table A1.5.

subject to a care and protection order, compared with just 5.4 per 1,000 non-indigenous children.[100] Aboriginal children are therefore nine times more likely to be the subject of a court order than their non-indigenous counterparts.[101] The disproportionate use of care and protection orders with respect to Aboriginal children is fairly constant across the states and territories. In the ACT, indigenous children were 13 times more likely to be the subject of a care and protection order than non-indigenous children; in South Australia that figure stands at 9.2; in Western Australia 13; in New South Wales 10; and in Victoria 13.7.[102] Again it is particularly disappointing that the disproportionate use of care and protection orders with respect to Aboriginal children is continuing to worsen. Taking the figures for Australia as a whole, the greater likelihood of an Aboriginal child being subjected to a care and protection order when compared with a non-indigenous child rose from 6.6 in 2006 to 9 in 2010.[103]

Perhaps, however, the most disappointing finding to emerge from these statistics is that, despite the recent legislative changes, there has been no clear discernible reduction in the disproportionate number of Aboriginal children removed from their families and placed with alternative carers. On 30 June 2010, the rate of Aboriginal children in out-of-home care across Australia was 48.4 per 1,000 children compared with 5.0 per 1,000 non-indigenous children.[104] The disproportionate use of out-of-home care for Aboriginal children was highest in Victoria, with Aboriginal children 14.3 times more likely than non-indigenous children to be removed from their families.[105] Figures were also high for Western Australia (13.5 times more likely); New South Wales (11.3 times more likely); South Australia (10.2 times more likely) and the ACT (12.4 times more likely).[106] More encouraging are the figures concerning the nature of out-of-home care now provided for Aboriginal children. The snapshot picture taken of the placement of Aboriginal children on 30 June 2010 revealed that, with the exception of the Northern Territories and Tasmania, at least 50 per cent of Aboriginal children across Australia are now placed with an Aboriginal carer or relative, that figure being over 80 per cent in New South Wales.[107] Implementation of the Aboriginal placement principle would thus appear to have made a positive difference to the placement of apprehended Aboriginal children in need of substitute care. The overall picture is, however, disappointing.

---

100 Ibid., table 3.8.

101 Ibid.

102 Ibid.

103 Ibid., and Human Rights and Equal Opportunity Commission (HREOC) (2006). *A Statistical Overview of Aboriginal and Torres Strait Islander Peoples in Australia.*

104 AIHW, ibid., table 4.8.

105 Ibid.

106 Ibid.

107 Ibid., table A1.17.

Canadian Reforms to the Non-Native Child Welfare System

Legislative Reforms

Recognition of the 'indigenous factor'

The disappointing results of Australia's various 'sensitization' measures are echoed in the Canadian context. Many of the Canadian provincial governments responded to the stringent criticism of their past policies and practices with the introduction of similar legislative measures to those found in Australia, the main aims of which were again to secure greater recognition of the importance of a child's Aboriginal identity and to enhance Aboriginal community involvement in decision-making and service delivery. In many provinces, the reforms are much more far-reaching than those found within the Australian legislation. The failings are therefore all the more disappointing.

The premise from which many of the provinces begin is that the child protection system should afford respect to the cultural differences of Aboriginal people and respond sensitively to Aboriginal norms and practices in service provision.[108] Recognition of the importance of a child's Aboriginal identity is a central part of respecting those cultural differences and is now enshrined in most provincial legislation across Canada. The British Columbia, Child, Family and Community Service Act 1996,[109] is typical, providing within its guiding principles that: 'the cultural identity of Aboriginal children should be preserved' and 'kinship ties and a child's attachment to the extended family should be preserved if possible'.[110] It also stipulates that a child in care has the right 'to receive guidance and encouragement to maintain their cultural heritage'.[111] These general principles are reflected in several of the Act's more specific provisions. For example, the importance of an Aboriginal child's cultural identity is given explicit recognition when determining the child's best interests[112] and the legislation provides that the Director's interim plan for a child in care must include details of the steps to be taken to preserve the child's Aboriginal identity.[113] Similar protection of an Aboriginal child's cultural identity is found in Alberta, with the Child, Youth and Family Enhancement Act 2000 providing that any person coming to a decision under the Act relating to an Aboriginal child must respect 'the uniqueness of Aboriginal culture, heritage, spirituality and traditions' and take into consideration 'the importance of preserving

108 See, for example, Child and Family Services Act S.N.W.T. 1997 C.13, Preamble.

109 Child, Family and Community Service Act [RSBC 1996] Chpt. 46.

110 Ibid., ss 2(e) and (f).

111 Ibid., s 70(1)(j). Child Protection Act R.S.P.E.I. 1988, c. C-5.1, Preamble.

112 Section 4(2) of the Child, Family and Community Service Act [RSBC 1996] Chpt. 46, provides: 'If the child is an Aboriginal child, the importance of preserving the child's cultural identity must be considered in determining the child's best interests.'

113 Child, Family and Community Service Act [RSBC 1996] Chpt. 46, s 35(1)(b). See also Child, Youth and Family Enhancement Act R.S.A. 2000 C-12, s 52(1.3).

the child's cultural identity'.[114] Almost identical wording is found as part of the best interests principle in s 37(4) of the Ontario Child and Family Services Act.[115] For those provinces which do not afford special protection to Aboriginal identity, the child's cultural identity is protected in general terms.[116]

There is also clear recognition within the Canadian provincial legislation of the importance of keeping Aboriginal children who are in need of support or protection services within their family and community wherever possible. The importance of employing more culturally appropriate support mechanisms in order to realize this objective is also recognized. Thus, the British Columbia Child, Family and Community Service Act 1996 provides that in making arrangements for voluntary care, the Director may enter into an agreement with a person who has 'a cultural or traditional responsibility towards a child' and agree to provide some level of financial support for that placement.[117] A family conferencing model is also used to enable the family to develop a plan of care which can take into account the role of the child's family and community, and include provision, with the Director's consent, for the child to be placed with a relative or some other person.[118] The BC legislation also enshrines an 'Aboriginal placement principle' akin to that found within the Australian state and territorial legislation, providing:

> (3) If the child is an Aboriginal child, the Director must give priority to placing the child as follows:
>
> (a) with the child's extended family or within the child's Aboriginal cultural community;
>
> (b) with another Aboriginal family, if the child cannot be safely placed under paragraph (a);

114 Child, Youth and Family Enhancement Act R.S.A. 2000 c. C-12, s 2(p). See also, Child and Family Services Authorities Act R.S.A. 2000 C-11, Preamble.

115 Child and Family Services Act R.S.O. 1990 C-11, s 37(4). See also, Child Protection Act R.S.P.E.I. 1988, c. C-5.1, s 2(2)(j).

116 Child and Family Services Act S.S. 1989–90 c. C-7.2, s 4(c); Child and Family Services Act C.C.S.M. 1985 C.80, s 2(1)(h); Children and Family Services Act S.N.S. 1990 C-5, s 3(2)(g); Children's Act R.S.Y. 2002 C-22, s 133(k); Family Services Act S.N.B. 1980 C. F-2.2, s 1(g); Child, Youth and Family Services Act S.N.L. 1998 C-12.1, s 9(c); Child and Family Services Act S.N.W.T. 1997 C.13, ss 3 and 3(c). The Newfoundland legislation also recognizes the importance of cultural heritage as a general principle: Child, Youth and Family Services Act S.N.L. 1998 C-12.1, ss 7(f) and (g).

117 Child, Family and Community Service Act [RSBC 1996] Chpt. 46, ss 8(1)(a) and 8(2).

118 Ibid., ss 20–21.

(c) in accordance with subsection (2), if the child cannot be safely placed under paragraph (a) or (b) of this subsection.[119]

The Ontario Child and Family Services Act 1990 similarly puts the Aboriginal placement principle on a statutory footing.[120] Although the remaining Canadian provinces do not enshrine an Aboriginal placement principle as such, most recognize in general terms that when placing a child in out-of-home care, the child should be placed whenever possible with a member of the extended family or, failing that, with a member of the child's community in close geographical proximity to the child's family.[121]

Participation and consultation

The need for greater community involvement in decision-making about a child and, more generally, in the design and delivery of child protection services is also given legislative force in most of the Canadian provinces. Again, British Columbia and Ontario have some of the most progressive provisions, although most of the provinces make some provision for the involvement of the child's Aboriginal community in any formal court proceedings concerning the child, either through an Aboriginal agency or more directly through a community representative such as the Band Chief. The Child, Family and Community Service Act 1996 (BC), for example, provides that the relevant Aboriginal authority[122] must, if practicable, be given notice of the first presentation hearing after an Aboriginal child is removed from the family or deemed to be in need of supervised care.[123] Thereafter, the Aboriginal authority is entitled to be served with notice of the proceedings[124] and, if in attendance at the commencement of the proceedings, will be entitled to full party status.[125] In Ontario, a representative chosen by the child's community is entitled to participate in placement decisions and reviews;[126] to be a party to any

119 Ibid., s 71(3).

120 Child and Family Services Act R.S.O. 1990 C-11, s 57(5). See also ss 61(2)(d) and 34(10)(f).

121 Child and Family Services Act S.S. 1989–90 c. C-7.2, s 53; Children and Family Services Act S.N.S. 1990 C-5, ss 20(d), 39(8)(c), 44(3)(c) and 47(5); Children's Act R.S.Y. 2002 C-22, s 110.

122 Either a prescribed Aboriginal organization, the Nisga'a Lisims Government or a Treaty First Nation.

123 Child, Family and Community Service Act [RSBC 1996] Chpt. 46, ss 33.1(4), 34(3) and 36(2.1).

124 The relevant orders are: protection, continuing custody, permanent transfer of custody and access. Child, Family and Community Service Act [RSBC 1996] Chpt. 46, ss 38(1), 49(2), 54.1(2), 55(3), 56(2) and 57.1(2).

125 This does not include an application relating to permanent transfer of custody. Child, Family and Community Service Act [RSBC 1996] Chpt. 46, ss 39(1) and 49(3).

126 Child and Family Services Act R.S.O. 1990 C-11, s 36(4)(c).

child protection proceedings;[127] to receive a copy of a report of any assessment carried out in the course of child protection proceedings;[128] may apply for orders and receive notice of any applications with respect to contact with a child in care;[129] may apply for a review of the child's status;[130] and may appeal an order or apply for an order to be varied, extended or terminated.[131] Similarly, the Child and Family Services Act 1989–1990 in Saskatchewan provides that the Chief of the child's Band is entitled to be notified of any proceedings for a protection order, to be a party to those proceedings and make representations to the court.[132]

In addition to according party status to representatives of the child's community, the Ontario legislation provides for a broader right of consultation with Aboriginal communities about the exercise of child protection powers and the provision of services to Aboriginal children.[133] Consultation is to occur with respect to generic issues as well as with respect to individual cases.[134] Narrower obligations to consult are enshrined in Alberta and Prince Edward Island. In Prince Edward Island, the Aboriginal community has a limited right to be consulted in developing a plan of care for the child.[135] Similarly, in Alberta, where there is no specific right for the community to be a party to child protection proceedings, a representative of the child's Band has the right to be consulted in planning services to be provided to the child at all key stages of the child protection process.[136] The child's Band is also entitled to receive a copy of any supervision order, temporary guardianship order or permanent guardianship order made in the course of the proceedings.[137]

It can be argued that these specific statutory provisions on the need to consult with Aboriginal communities over child protection policies and practices are also underpinned by a broader constitutional duty on the provincial governments to consult and, where appropriate, accommodate Aboriginal interests as part of the process of fair dealing and reconciliation between Aboriginal peoples and the Crown. Although the constitutional duty to consult has yet to be explored within the specific context of Aboriginal child welfare, the Supreme Court of Canada's

127 Ibid., s 39(1)(4).

128 Ibid., s 54(3)(f).

129 Ibid., ss 58(2)(b) and 58(4).

130 Ibid., s 64(4)(d).

131 Ibid., ss 69(1)(e) and 80(4)(f).

132 Child and Family Services Act S.S. 1989–90 C. 7.2, ss 37(10), 37(11) and 37(4)(c). Almost identical provisions apply in Prince Edward Island, the North West Territories and Nunavut. See Child Protection Act R.S.P.E.I. 1988 c. C-51, ss 30(2), 32(2), 35(1)(b), 37(2), 37(4) and 39(2)(b); and Child and Family Services Act S.N.W.T. 1997 C. 13, ss 25(2), 27(2)(vi) and 29(2).

133 Child and Family Services Act R.S.O. 1990 C-11, s 213.

134 Ibid., s 213.1.

135 Child Protection Act R.S.P.E.I. 1988 c. C-51, s 37(4).

136 Child, Youth and Family Enhancement Act R.S.A. 2000 c. C-12, s 107.

137 Ibid., s 107.

decision in *Haida Nation v British Columbia (Minister of Forests)*[138] would support the argument that where the Crown has real or constructive knowledge of the potential existence of an Aboriginal right to self-government over child welfare under s 35 of the Constitution, the Crown (in this context the provincial government) has a duty to consult with Aboriginal peoples before taking any steps that might adversely affect that right.[139] The requirement to consult is not a requirement to reach agreement. What is required is a 'meaningful process of consultation in good faith', the exact scope of which will depend on the strength of the community's claim to self-government and the extent to which the Aboriginal right will be adversely affected by the Crown's intended action.[140] At one end of the scale, the duty to consult may therefore require the province to change or amend its decisions in order to accommodate Aboriginal concerns and find a satisfactory interim solution pending final resolution of the community's claim.[141] At the other end of the scale, it may give rise to a mere duty to notify the community of the province's intentions, provide information and discuss any issues arising.[142]

Where a community is actively involved in self-government negotiations which include self-government over child welfare, the Crown is clearly on notice of the existence of a claim. The fact negotiations are in progress also testifies to the prima facie strength of the community's claim.[143] Any unilateral action by the province with respect to either individual Aboriginal children or generic matters affecting the delivery of child welfare services to Aboriginal communities, will adversely affect the right of Aboriginal peoples to self-government. With the welfare of Aboriginal children at stake, the potential damage caused to Aboriginal communities by misconceived provincial child welfare policies is serious. Moreover, the damage caused to communities, particularly by the removal of Aboriginal children from their families, has serious long-term implications for the right to self-government. In these circumstances, the duty to consult may therefore demand something quite extensive by way of consultation with the community, with accommodation of the Aboriginal community's concerns the minimum required to 'maintain the honour of the Crown'. In contrast, outside the context of treaty negotiations, the difficulties experienced by Aboriginal communities in establishing a right to self-government over child welfare, would suggest that the strength of the community's claim is likely to be regarded as weak and as thus demanding little more than notification.[144]

---

138 [2004] 3 S.C.R. 511.

139 Ibid., [35].

140 Ibid., [38].

141 Ibid., [44].

142 Ibid., [43].

143 *Taku River Tlingit First Nation v British Columbia (Project Assessment Director)* [2004] 3 S.C.R. 550, [30].

144 The difficulties of establishing such a right are discussed in detail in Chapter 5.

Governance, policy development and Aboriginal child welfare agencies

Some of the most encouraging reforms in Canada have come in the way child protection services are organized and managed, with Aboriginal communities being afforded a much greater role in policy development and service design and delivery. The principle of Aboriginal involvement in service design and delivery is entrenched in British Columbia's legislation. The central principles underpinning the Act are set down in s 3 which provides that Aboriginal people should be involved in the planning and delivery of services; that services should be planned and provided in a culturally sensitive manner; and that the community should be involved, wherever possible and appropriate, in the planning and delivery of services.[145] Similarly, the Ontario Child and Family Services Act 1990 provides that one of the key purposes of the legislation is:

> To recognize that Indian and native people should be entitled to provide, wherever possible, their own child and family services, and that all services to Indian and native children and families should be provided in a manner that recognizes their culture, heritage and traditions and the concept of the extended family.[146]

Pursuant to these broad principles of 'community ownership' over the delivery of child welfare services, a number of the Canadian provinces make specific provision within the legislation for the delegation of the delivery of child protection services to Aboriginal-controlled child welfare agencies. In Manitoba, intertribal Aboriginal child welfare agencies were first mandated to exercise provincial child protection powers by virtue of a tripartite agreement entered into between the federal, provincial and Aboriginal governments in 1982.[147] The intertribal agencies established under these tripartite agreements were given a statutory basis in 1986.[148] In Ontario, Aboriginal child welfare agencies are similarly provided for by statute. Under the legislation, any approved agency providing delegated services to an Aboriginal community must have a certain number of Band or community representatives on its board of directors.[149] However, the Band or community may also choose to establish its own 'Indian and native child and family service authority' which, if successfully designated an approved children's aid society by the Minister, can perform a variety of prescribed functions, including a full

145 Child, Family and Community Service Act [RSBC 1996] Chpt. 46, s 3.

146 Child and Family Services Act R.S.O. 1990 C-11, s 1(2)5.

147 A. McGillivray (1997). 'Therapies of Freedom: The Colonization of Aboriginal Childhood', in A. McGillivray (ed.) *Governing Childhood.* Aldershot: Dartmouth, 135, 163.

148 Ibid.

149 Child and Family Services Act R.S.O. 1990 C-11, s 13(3).

range of delegated child protection services.[150] Almost identical provisions apply in British Columbia and Saskatchewan.[151]

These legislative provisions have facilitated the development of Aboriginal-controlled child welfare agencies offering a range of child protection and family support services to Aboriginal communities across Canada.[152] There are, for example, currently 22 such agencies operating within British Columbia, serving 148 of the approximately 198 Bands.[153] Nine of the agencies provide a full range of child protection services; 11 provide guardianship and family support services for children in continuing care; three can provide voluntary services and recruit and approve foster homes; and one is in the early stages of capacity building.[154] There are 20 similar such Aboriginal child welfare agencies in Alberta; 18 in Manitoba; nine in New Brunswick; 12 in Ontario; 25 in Quebec; 22 in Saskatchewan and one each in Newfoundland and Nova Scotia.[155] Although many of these agencies provide a limited range of services, employ both native and non-native staff, operate within provincial policies, legislative standards and service-delivery frameworks, and remain ultimately accountable to the provincial ministry,[156] the agencies are managed at a local level by the Aboriginal communities they serve, affording the community a greater role in determining the services to be provided and how those services can be both designed and delivered to reflect their particular cultural values and traditions.

Recent administrative re-structuring in Manitoba has taken this model of delegating child protection services to Aboriginal communities a step further with the creation of larger Aboriginal governing authorities who are intended to assume overarching responsibility from the central Ministry for service delivery to Aboriginal communities, including management of Aboriginal child welfare agencies.[157] Whilst recognizing the limitations of these reforms, Aboriginal peoples in Manitoba generally welcomed the re-structuring process, describing it as constituting 'a fundamental shift in government policy, unprecedented in

150 Ibid., s 211.

151 Child, Family and Community Service Act [RSBC 1996] Chpt. 46, s 93(1)(g)(iii) and Child and Family Services Act S.S. 1989–90 C 7.2, s 61(1). See also Youth Protection Act R.S.Q. c. P-34.1, s 37.5. Individual social workers receive designated powers to provide a full range of child protection services from the Director.

152 For a full list of Aboriginal child welfare agencies, see www.fncfcs.com/resources/agency-list.

153 For the latest figures, see: www.mcf.gov.bc.ca/about_us/Aboriginal/delegated/index.htm.

154 Ibid.

155 See: www.fncfcs.com/resources/agency-list.

156 Before such agencies can become operational they have to comply with a number of stringent requirements as set down by the Ministry. See: www.mcf.gov.bc.ca/about_us/Aboriginal/delegated/delegation_process.htm.

157 Similar reform efforts in British Columbia aimed at the creation of Regional Aboriginal Authorities were abandoned.

Manitoba and Canadian history, toward involving and empowering Aboriginal peoples throughout the system'.[158] Whilst clearly not self-government, developments such as these arguably bring Aboriginal communities an important step closer to achieving that ultimate goal.

The reform process in Manitoba was led by the work of the *Aboriginal Justice Inquiry – Child Welfare Initiative* and has resulted in two important advances on the intertribal model previously in place.[159] First Nations jurisdiction has been expanded to cover all off-reserve as well as on-reserve First Nations children. The process of administrative re-structuring has also secured the creation of a Métis Child and Family Services Authority with jurisdiction to provide child welfare services to Métis children across the province.[160] Four new administrative authorities have been created, three of which are responsible for managing service delivery to Aboriginal peoples: a Métis Child and Family Services Authority; a First Nations of Northern Manitoba Child and Family Services Authority; and a First Nations of Southern Manitoba Child and Family Services Authority. The Authorities have concurrent jurisdiction throughout Manitoba with children served by the Authority which is most culturally appropriate. The three Aboriginal Authorities exist alongside a general 'catch-all' authority which provides services to non-Aboriginal children across the province. The Board of the Métis Child and Family Services Authority is appointed by the Manitoba Métis Federation; the Board of the First Nations of Northern Manitoba Child and Family Services Authority is appointed by the Manitoba Keewatinowi Okimakanak; and the Board of the First Nations of Southern Manitoba Child and Family Services Authority by the Assembly of Manitoba Chiefs Secretariat, thus ensuring Aboriginal communities have political 'ownership' of the new Authorities.[161] A forum for 'government-to-government' discussions concerning child and family services is provided for by a Leadership Council comprised of political leaders from the First Nations, Métis and provincial governments.[162] The Council acts in an advisory capacity to the Ministry.

This new administrative structure is premised on the concept of a 'shared responsibility' between the province and Aboriginal communities for the delivery of Aboriginal child welfare services.[163] The principles governing the process of reform were established in three separate Memorandums of Understanding (MOU) entered into between the provincial government and the Manitoba Métis

158 Aboriginal Justice Inquiry – Child Welfare Initiative (AJI-CWI) (2001). *Promise of Hope: Commitment to Change*, 3.

159 For more detail on the intertribal model see McGillivray, *supra* note 147, 162–9.

160 For more detailed information as to the reform process in Manitoba see Bourassa, *supra* note 1 and P. Gough (2006). 'Manitoba's Child Welfare System', Centre of Excellence for Child Welfare.

161 Child and Family Services Authorities Act C.C.S.M. 2002 c.C90, s 6.

162 Ibid., s 29.

163 AJI-CWI, *supra* note 158, 13.

Federation, the Assembly of Manitoba Chiefs and the Manitoba Keewatinowi Okimakanak. The importance of services being culturally appropriate and community-led is clear from the MOUs. The MOU entered into with the Assembly of Manitoba Chiefs provides:

> 3. It is acknowledged that the delivery of child and family services and programs to First Nations people within Manitoba must occur in a manner which respects their unique status, as well as their cultural and linguistic heritage.
>
> 5. The parties acknowledge that the First Nations people have a right to control the delivery of child and family services and programs for their respective community members.
>
> 6. The parties acknowledge that solutions developed locally with respect to both the delivery of child and family services and programs, as well as adoption services are the most effective and practical approach towards ensuring self-determination and healthy communities.[164]

Pursuant to these principles, the Child and Family Services Authorities Act 2002 provides that each new Aboriginal authority is responsible for the management, organization and delivery of child welfare services to any First Nations or Métis person living on or off reserve within the province who is a member of, or identifies with, a community falling within their respective jurisdictions.[165] Central to the work of the new Authorities is their role with respect to the Aboriginal child welfare agencies delivering child and family services to the communities. The new Authorities have assumed responsibility for mandating and overseeing the work of the agencies; allocating funding for services in accordance with their priorities and objectives;[166] developing culturally appropriate standards for services, practices and procedures;[167] ensuring the development of appropriate placement resources for children;[168] supervising or directing the supervision of children in care; and receiving and disbursing care subsidies.[169] It is hoped that the control which Aboriginal communities now exercise over the design and delivery of child welfare services will lead to a re-orientation of the goals and objectives of the system, with efforts directed at providing a more holistic range of services, a

164 Memorandum of Understanding between the Assembly of Manitoba Chiefs and Her Majesty the Queen in Right of the Province of Manitoba (April 2000), preambular paras. 3, 5 and 6.

165 Child and Family Services Authorities Act C.C.S.M. 2002 c.C90, ss 17(1)–(3).

166 Ibid., s 19(i).

167 Ibid., s 19(c).

168 Ibid., s 19(l).

169 Ibid., s 19(n).

greater focus on preventative programming and much greater emphasis on keeping children within their families and communities.[170]

The Success and Limitations of the Canadian Legislative Reforms

To the extent that these legislative reforms have helped to 'sensitize' the existing child welfare system to the particular cultural needs of Aboriginal children, they are, of course, extremely welcome. Both Aboriginal and non-Aboriginal people have devoted a huge amount of time and energy and shown great commitment and goodwill in striving to improve the existing system for the good of Aboriginal children. Clearly, as a result of their efforts, significant improvements have been made in a number of key areas which, at least in part, address the criticisms raised by Kline and others.[171] However, the commitment and determination of those working to improve the system should not disguise the problems and limitations of the reforms which have been undertaken. At the most fundamental level, without really challenging existing sources of power and authority, the various legislative measures and attempts at administrative re-structuring discussed above, cannot be expected to bring about a fundamental change in the status quo.

The recent reforms to the provincial child welfare legislation have received a mixed response in the courts. There have been a number of positive decisions showing clear signs of growing judicial sensitivity to the issues and in which the importance of the 'indigenous factor' as now entrenched in the legislation has been fully endorsed and acted upon in determining the best outcome for the child.[172] There is clearly some remaining resistance amongst social work managers to the very principle that additional or special factors need to be taken into account when considering the future placement of Aboriginal children. It was, for example, argued by the Director of Child, Youth and Family Enhancement in the case of *Alberta (Director of Child, Youth and Family Enhancement) v T.S. and E.D.* that, despite the statutory recognition given in s 2(p) of the Child, Youth and Family Enhancement Act to the importance of preserving the child's cultural identity, it is important not to single out Aboriginal children for special consideration because of the number of Aboriginal children in care.[173] That argument was given short shrift by the court, Darlene Acton J holding that the factors specified under s 2, including the importance of preserving the child's Aboriginal identity, must inform *all* decisions made under the legislation including an application for permanent

170 AJI-CWI, *supra* note 158, 4.

171 See Chapter 2.

172 See, for example, the positive outcomes in *Director of Child, Family and Community Service v L.S.N.* (2008) BCPC 0402 and *Southeast Child and Family Services v A.A.M.L. and J.A.L.* (2010) MBQB 126.

173 *Alberta (Director of Child, Youth and Family Enhancement) v T.S. and E.D.* (2009) ABQB 246, [13].

guardianship with respect to a child already in the care of the Director.[174] Similarly, the reform efforts were given unequivocal backing by the British Columbia Court of Appeal in the case of *N.H. and D.H. v H.M., M.H. and the Director of Child, Family and Community Services*.[175] The case concerned a custody dispute between a child's adoptive (non-native) grandparents and his biological (Aboriginal) grandfather. In granting custody to the biological grandfather, Hall J referred to the 'considerable history' of failed outcomes for Aboriginal children raised in non-native homes and, noting the efforts of Indian Bands and governments to address these problems through legislative reforms such as those contained within the BC Child, Family and Community Service Act 1996, held that the 'courts ought to show deference to the legislative initiatives in this area'.[176] The Court of Appeal thus overturned the decision of the trial judge to grant custody to the adoptive grandparents, holding that the trial judge had placed insufficient emphasis on 'the ties of blood and culture' that bound the child to his biological grandfather.[177]

The child's Aboriginal identity has clearly been a factor of increasing importance in the case law. There are now a number of cases in which it has been held that the court requires no particular authority or evidence in support of the argument that culture and heritage are of profound importance in determining the child's interests.[178] Thus, although it is made clear that cultural identity is not necessarily a decisive or determining factor, it is nevertheless recognized as a weighty consideration.[179] In the case of *A.L. & J.L. v D.K. & M.W.*,[180] which concerned a custody dispute between the child's Aboriginal parents and her paternal aunt and uncle, the British Columbia Supreme Court distinguished the Supreme Court of Canada's decision in *Racine v Woods*. The court held that as the child had important existing ties with the parents and her wider Aboriginal community, as well as the alternative carers, *Racine's* maxim (that the closer the bond with the alternative carers the less important the cultural element becomes) did not apply in this case.[181] Moreover, in examining the nature of the child's existing ties, the court adopted a broad and inclusive approach, focusing not just on the child's ties with the parents and the aunt, but her ties with the wider extended family and the two distinct Aboriginal communities to which her parents belonged:

> It must be remembered that the circumstances of M. include the fact that she is a child member of an Aboriginal community, namely, the Namgis, if not

174 Ibid., [18].

175 *N.H. and D.H. v H.M., M.H. and the Director of Child, Family and Community Service* (1998) 156 D.L.R. (4th) 548.

176 Ibid., [16]–[17].

177 Ibid., [13].

178 Ibid., [18]; *Nukon v Nukon et. al.* (2005) YKSC 55, [27].

179 *A.L. & J.L. v D.K. & M.W.* (2000) BCSC 480, [63].

180 Ibid.

181 Ibid., [51].

> the neighbouring Tsawataineuk as well. Accordingly, as the evidence shows, she enjoys ties of consanguinity and culture to her extended family and other members of the two culturally distinctive communities. Hence, I find that M.'s ties to persons other than the parties favour a life in Albert Bay and Kingcome Inlet where her siblings, extended family and Aboriginal communities continue to live. These people constitute the epicenter of M's familial and cultural identity. In short, they are her roots.[182]

In an even more striking departure from the court's traditional focus on the nuclear family, when considering the child's cultural identity, the BC Supreme Court took into account not only the child's ties with the extended family and Aboriginal community, but her special relationship with the lands on which that community had traditionally lived and practised their traditions and culture. Indeed, the court described that relationship with the land as of a similar nature and importance to the child as her ties with the people around her. It was thus important, according to the court, that the child lived not just with a person of similar Aboriginal descent (the paternal aunt, although wanting to raise the child in Mexico, clearly shared the same Aboriginal ancestry as the child) but that, where possible, the child was able to live and experience her culture on the traditional territories to which she belonged:

> The circumstances of an Aboriginal child like M. are such that the child is situated within one or more culturally distinctive Aboriginal community. In the result, consideration of the need for preserving and nurturing the child's cultural identity should include a consideration of preserving and nurturing any ties similar to love and affection that exist between the child and the traditional lands of his or her community … the preservation and nurturing of M.'s cultural identity, to the extent that it entails her relationship to ancestral land, is clearly better served by a life centred in Alert Bay, Kingcome Inlet, the Nimpkish Valley and the relevant surrounding area. In this context, formative years lived primarily in Mexico and to some degree Victoria inherently would be a long way from home.[183]

In fostering her cultural identity, the court also acknowledged the importance of being educated within the community's schools where the traditional language and culture form a core part of the school's ethos, as well as the more formal taught curriculum.[184] Beyond the child's formal schooling, the court also recognized the importance of the child being able to participate in the community's traditional methods of teaching and transmitting their cultural values and practices to the next

182 Ibid., [50].
183 Ibid., [52]–[55].
184 Ibid., [57].

generation, which in this case was through the customary practice of potlaching.[185] In weighing all these factors, the court granted custody to the child's father, despite the fact the child was settled and happy in Mexico, had a strong bond with the paternal aunt and would enjoy many more material advantages living with her aunt and uncle. Although the child's cultural identity was not, in the court's words, a 'decisive criterion', it clearly dominated the court's reasoning and the eventual outcome.

Courts hearing public law child protection cases have also displayed a strong commitment to the 'indigenous factor', most notably in giving effect to the Aboriginal placement principle when determining with whom a child in care is to live. In the case of *Re AG*, for example, Bedard J in the Court of Quebec, Youth Division,[186] was highly critical of the Minokin child welfare agency for failing to recruit sufficient Aboriginal foster families, thereby necessitating the placement of Algonquin children in non-native foster homes. The court held that such placements violated the legislative imperative to place Aboriginal children in Aboriginal homes as set down in s 2.4(5)[187] of the Youth Protection Act:

> [W]here a very young child is placed for an extended period of time with a family which is not Algonquin, returning the child to his or her community becomes difficult and sometimes impossible. The evidence provided concerning the impossibility of finding an Algonquin family for the two youngest children was not convincing … The Court was not prepared to conclude on the basis of the community worker's inability to find appropriate foster parents that the Algonquin community was unable to assume its responsibilities to children in need. Recruiting foster parents is difficult, but Minokin Social Services had to establish a recruitment and evaluation strategy to give it access to Algonquin foster parents for medium and long term placements if it was to justify its existence. While placing children with non-Algonquin foster parents may have allowed Minokin to make up for its recruitment problems, this approach violated the fundamental principles of the statute and failed to respect the rights of the children and their parents.[188]

185 Ibid., [59]. On the importance of Aboriginal culture being 'lived' through 'day to day exposure' see also, *C.D.R1. and C.D.R2. v Native Child and Family Services of Toronto* (2007) CFSRB 20, [39].

186 *Re A.G.* [2000] 2 C.N.L.R. 1.

187 Section 2.4(5) of the Youth Protection Act P-34.1 provides: 'every person called upon to make decisions with respect to a child under the Act shall, in their interventions, take into account the necessity … of opting for measures, in respect of the child and the child's parents, which allow action to be taken diligently to ensure the child's protection, considering that a child's perception of time differs from that of adults, and which take into consideration the following factors: … (c) the characteristics of Native communities'.

188 *Re A.G.* [2000] 2 C.N.L.R. 1, [5]–[9] (English translation). For a further example of the sensitivity of the Quebec Youth Court to traditional Aboriginal practices, in particular

Justice Bedard's strong commitment to upholding the Aboriginal placement principle as one of the primary mechanisms for 'correcting the errors of the past' is very clear.[189]

Unfortunately, as is perhaps to be expected, not all cases have demonstrated the same degree of commitment and sensitivity to the importance of cultural identity. Decisions such as that of Bishop J in the Ontario Court of Justice in *Kenora-Patricia Child and Family Services v L.P.*[190] serve as an important reminder that many Aboriginal families are still subjected to culturally biased, ethnocentric standards when determining the best interests of the child. In the case of *L.P.*, despite the possibility of placing the children with a paternal aunt – the plan supported, in accordance with the children's wishes, by the father, the father's Band and the children's lawyer – the court nevertheless deemed the interests of the children to be better served by the 'structure, consistency, and role-modelling'[191] available in the non-native foster homes. The statutory obligation to place the children in accordance with the Aboriginal placement principle was simply dismissed as being contrary to the child's best interests, demonstrating the inherent weakness of the principle if its application is always to be subject to a straightforward welfare test.[192]

A second decision by Justice Bishop in *Kenora-Patricia Child and Family Services v D.O.*[193] shows similarly worrying trends. The court again found that, despite the possibility of placing the child with a member of the mother's Band, it was in the child's best interests, given the 'stability that he enjoys and the progress he has made', to remain with his non-native foster parents.[194] Moreover, the court fell back on a narrow understanding of the child's cultural needs, holding that the foster parents' 'genuine commitment' to 'allow the child to know his culture and know his community' was perfectly adequate to address concerns as to his cultural identity.[195] Bishop J thus shows no appreciation that a child's Aboriginal identity

---

customary adoption and the use of the extended family network to safeguard the interests of the child, see *Re D.F.P.* [2001] 2 C.N.L.R. 51.

189 *Re A.G.*, ibid., [12].

190 *Kenora-Patricia Child and Family Services v L.P. and S.P.* [2001] 4 C.N.L.R. 114.

191 Cited from the agreed statement of facts: ibid., [19].

192 Ibid., [25]. See, Child and Family Services Act R.S.O. 1990 C-11, s 57(5).

193 *Kenora-Patricia Child and Family Services v D.O.* [2001] 4 C.N.L.R. 103.

194 There are other important examples in recent case law of the courts expressing preference for the stability and structure provided by a non-native foster home over the 'passive' parenting style of an Aboriginal parent. See, for example, *Re V.J.C. and others* (2009) SKQB 395, [2], [18], [140] and [142]. The importance of this difference in parenting styles is often intensified given the current professional view that children with special emotional or educational needs require a high degree of structure in their lives.

195 *Kenora-Patricia Child and Family Services v D.O.* [2001] 4 C.N.L.R. 103, [65(6)] and [65(12)].

cannot be neatly packaged into 'videos', 'moccasins' and 'art work'[196] and cannot be routinely and satisfactorily addressed by the commitment of a non-native carer to foster and encourage that identity, no matter how well intentioned.[197] As regards s 57(5) and the Aboriginal placement principle, Bishop J was again dismissive:

> The court does not accept the proposition that subsection 57(5) of the Act overrides the overall best interests of the child. The interpretation that the Band wishes to place on subsection 57(5) is that the cultural prerogative is the utmost consideration. This simply is not the case. The four concerns raised in the home study by Ms Murray on the K placement [the Aboriginal carers] are substantial in themselves and have not been adequately addressed by the evidence of Mrs K.[198]

These decisions are not alone in giving little weight to the indigenous factor. There are many examples in the recent case law of the judiciary emphasizing that culture is just one factor to be taken into account in the welfare balance; a factor, moreover, which will be easily outweighed by other considerations.[199] As it was put by Kraus J in *Ministry of Social Services v LB*:

> The court is not mandated to merely give overriding importance to culture … While the child's connection to her aboriginal culture is unquestionably an important factor to be taken into account in determining the best interests of the

196 Ibid., [19].

197 See also *Alberta (Director of Child Welfare) v Y* [2002] 1 C.N.L.R. 11, [21]–[22]. A similar approach to the question of the importance which should be attributed to Aboriginal identity can be discerned in private law custody disputes between Aboriginal and non-Aboriginal carers. See: *K.J.S. v M.T.* [2001] 4 C.N.L.R. 96; *Sawatzky v Campbell* [2001] 4 C.N.L.R. 300; *Nova Scotia (Minister of Community Services) v F. (R.L.)* [2002] 1 C.N.L.R. 221; and *H.D. v M.H.* [1997] 156 D.L.R. (4th) 548 and [1999] 1 S.C.R. 328. This latter case, in which the British Columbia Supreme Court, later upheld by the Canadian Supreme Court, decided to grant custody of a Swan Lake First Nation child to her non-Aboriginal adoptive grandparents living in the United States, despite the fact that the child had been happily settled in the home of his Aboriginal grandfather, a member of the Sagkeeng First Nation, for three years, sparked a furious response from the Assembly of First Nations. At their annual Assembly in 1999 a resolution was passed denouncing the decision as a 'dangerous precedent' and reiterating the Assembly's opposition to the adoption of First Nations children by non-First Nation families. It also called for an end to the use of economic standards as the main test for determining adoption placements and the implementation of a federal First Nations Child Welfare Law. See Resolution No.4/99, available at: http://64.26.129.156/article.asp?id=946.

198 *Kenora-Patricia Child and Family Services v D.O.* [2001] 4 C.N.L.R. 103, [65(8)].

199 See, for example, *Mi'Kmaw Family and Children Services of Nova Scotia v J.P. and I.M.* (2007) NSFC 19, [8]; *Re P.R.S. and K.P.S.* (2010) SKQB 99, [45]; *Sagkeeng Child and Family Services v M.D.G.* (2010) MBQB 234, [91].

> child under the Act, the plain and unambiguous meaning of s 4 of the Act and the jurisprudence cited by counsel do not elevate culture to supercede all other factors which the court must take into account in determining the best interests of the child.[200]

It is concerning that in this case the foster parents were found to be satisfactorily meeting all of the child's 'emotional, physical, psychological and spiritual needs' despite the evidence that very little was being done to ensure the child's Aboriginal identity was being protected.[201] Whilst the child's cultural identity clearly cannot be the courts' only consideration when determining the child's best interests, the significance of this particular factor for Aboriginal children does demand it is given much greater weight than decisions such as this suggest. Indeed, there is a strong argument that by placing a distinct statutory obligation on the court to place a child, whenever possible, within his or her Aboriginal community, the legislature has made it clear that this factor should carry 'utmost' or 'pre-eminent' weight unless there are 'substantial' reasons against such a placement. Given the findings of the home study in *Kenora-Patricia Child and Family Services v D.O.* that the 'K.s had a good marriage, a good home, were employed and had a good support system', it is interesting to reflect on the 'substantial' reasons weighing against the Aboriginal placement:

> (1) [T]heir financial situation was not good as they had debt and spent both of their combined incomes each month;[202]
>
> (2) there were some health concerns as both experience migraines that may debilitate one or both of them as Ms. K. indicated that she had migraines once a month;
>
> (3) the K.'s had busy social lives with a lot of activity, family and friends and a young toddler particularly with special needs who required minimal [*sic*] interaction might not be a good match for this couple;[203]
>
> (4) Mr K had a criminal record dating back to 1988 with one charge of mischief.[204]

---

200 *Ministry of Social Services v LB* (2009) SKQB 46, [103].

201 Ibid., [103].

202 Economic difficulties, in particular, the lack of suitable housing, was also identified as a problem in *Kenora-Patricia Child and Family Services v L.P. and S.P.* [2001] 4 C.N.L.R. 114, [13].

203 This can be compared to the non-native home which was described by Kenora-Patricia's social worker as 'warm, welcoming and friendly with a certain amount of structure', and where '[t]here are not a lot of people coming and going'. See *Kenora-Patricia Child and Family Services v D.O.* [2001] 4 C.N.L.R. 103, [24].

204 Ibid., [40].

It is difficult to understand how this can amount to 'substantial' reasons outweighing the importance of a culturally appropriate placement.

In all three cases of *Kenora-Patricia Child and Family Services v L.P.*, *Kenora-Patricia Child and Family Services v D.O.* and *Ministry of Social Services v LB* a further important factor weighing against the Aboriginal placement was the fact that by the time of the final disposition hearing the child had been settled in the care of the non-native foster parents for some time allowing a strong bond to develop between them.[205] This highlights a very practical problem that risks seriously undermining the effectiveness of the Aboriginal placement principle. If Aboriginal children are routinely placed in non-Aboriginal homes immediately after apprehension because of a lack of approved Aboriginal carers, the court may well be faced with a fait accompli in subsequent proceedings. It is, however, a persistent theme in the case law that despite the involvement of an Aboriginal agency and/or direct consultation with the child's Band, no resource could be identified from within the child's extended family or wider Aboriginal community.[206] Clearly, if the Aboriginal placement principle is to make a real difference to Aboriginal children in care, the initial apprehension and immediate placement of the children must be carefully planned and more done to try and secure a culturally appropriate placement from the outset. As pointed out by Bode J in *Dilico Anishinabek Family Care v M.T., A.C. and M'Chigeeng First Nation*, this initial period after apprehension is crucial:

> In child protection cases, the importance of a child's Ojibway heritage is probably at its highest point during the period from the child's apprehension to the point where the agency caring for the child needs to make permanency planning decisions for the child. It is during this phase of the child protection continuum that the development of the best possible plan for the preservation of a child's native culture is most critical. It is during this phase that options like customary care agreements, placement with extended family members and placement with members of the child's aboriginal community need to be very carefully examined.

Aboriginal child welfare agencies thus have an important responsibility to increase the number of approved Aboriginal carers and to identify possible

205 This was regarded as decisive in *Ministry of Social Services v LB* (2009) SKQB 46, [97]–[98].

206 See: *Ministry of Social Services v LB* (2009) SKQB 46, [21]–[23], [81]–[82]; *Dilico Anishinabek Family Care v M.T., A.C. and M'Chigeeng First Nation* (2010) ONCJ 105, [33]; *Re K.R. and K.M.* (2009) SKQB 507, [7], [42]; *Re T.J.B. and others* (2008) SKQB 419, [35], [157]; *The Grand Council of the Crees (Eeyou Istchee) and The Cree Regional Authority v Director of Youth Protection for A and others* (2009) QCCA 1583, [16]; and *Kenora-Patricia Child and Family Services v D.O.* [2001] 4 C.N.L.R. 103, [31].

placements in the extended family or community *before or immediately after* the children are removed.[207]

There is, moreover, an ever diminishing window of time within which an appropriate Aboriginal placement must be found. The pressure on Aboriginal agencies to find culturally appropriate placements has been intensified in recent years by the increasing emphasis on the importance of permanency planning within the non-native child welfare system.[208] The current strong emphasis placed on the importance of children not being left to languish in care indefinitely has provided a further impetus towards the placement of Aboriginal children with non-native families, often with a view to adoption. The child's need for the security of a permanent placement has been found to outweigh both the parents' pleas for more time to resolve long-term, often intractable, problems and the Aboriginal community's objections to permanent placement in a non-native home whilst they continue to search for a more culturally appropriate resource.[209] With this is mind, the comments of Mr Justice Carruthers regarding the unsuccessful search of Siksika Child and Family Services for an Aboriginal placement for five Aboriginal children belonging to the Siksika Band are a matter of some concern:

> I commend Siksika Child and Family Services. I think they have taken all reasonable steps in the circumstances to try and find affiliated placements. Child and Family Services are not a search organization. I think they have to rely upon the initiative of the family to come forward and make representations.[210]

Given the importance of this issue, a more proactive approach might have been expected.

Efforts to secure greater participation by Aboriginal communities in decision-making and service delivery have also met with only limited success. There remains strong resistance to any notion that the child's best interests are inextricably linked to those of the Band.[211] Consequently, any attempts at re-conceptualizing

---

207 *Re A.G.* [2000] 2 C.N.L.R. 1 (per Bedard J).

208 In Saskatchewan, for example, the legislation provides that a temporary order should not exceed 24 months. See the analysis of Ryan-Froslie J in *Re T.J.B. and others* (2008) SKQB 419, [167]–[172].

209 See generally *Re T.J.B. and others* (2008) SKQB 419. See also, *The Children's Aid Society of the Districts of Sudbury and Manitoulin v D.D.* (2009) CanLII 70505 (ON S.C.).

210 *Alberta (Director of Child Welfare) v Y* [2002] 1 C.N.L.R. 11, [18]–[19].

211 *C.D.R1 and C.D.R2 v Native Child and Family Services of Toronto* (2007) CFSRB 20, [37]. Cf. *The Grand Council of the Crees (Eeyou Istchee) and The Cree Regional Authority v Director of Youth Protection for A and others* (2009) QCCA 1583, in which it was held that the child, as a member of the Cree community, had a direct interest in determining whether, under the terms of the James Bay and Northern Quebec Agreement, the Cree Board had exclusive jurisdiction over the adoption of Cree children within their territory and whether customary adoption was protected as a treaty right under s 35 of the

the highly individualistic focus of the best interests principle to accommodate the interests of the extended family and wider Aboriginal community within the decision-making framework tend to be firmly rejected.[212] In the words of Claude Tremblay J.C.Q., 'the best interests of the child must be considered from the standpoint of the child and not from the standpoints of his or her siblings, family (either immediate or extended), community, the First Nation as a whole, or all members of First Nations'.[213] In *Director of Youth Protection v A, B and C and Band Council A*, the Band Council was thus refused permission to intervene in adoption proceedings, the court holding that the single issue of cultural heritage on which the Band Council was (inappropriately) focused could be dealt with adequately by the child's mother and grandmother.[214] The Band Council's wish to raise issues concerning differences between Aboriginal and Quebec cultural values, the impact of adoption on the Aboriginal community, the identity problems experienced by Aboriginal children adopted into non-native homes and the Band's desire to present alternative solutions to the court, were dismissed as of general public importance but insufficiently focused on the private individual interests of the child.[215]

The perceived lack of concern by Aboriginal leaders for the particular 'unique' interests of the individual Aboriginal child is a common theme in the case law, with Bands being frequently criticized for pursuing a 'political' agenda or 'dogmatically' seeking redress for historic wrongs.[216] In *Re W. (C.K.)*,[217] the Selkirk First Nation was denied the status of a party to the proceedings on the basis that their position was a 'largely political one', based 'only on the child's citizenship and not on a legal interest in the issues before the Court'. The court went on to observe:

> The Selkirk First Nation is rightly concerned about the adverse social conditions in their community that results in a high rate of apprehensions and children in care. Those issues cannot be resolved by the Selkirk First Nation participating as a party in the protection hearing involving C.K.W. The Selkirk First Nation

Constitution thereby barring a subsequent adoption facilitated by the provincial authorities. Moreover, it was recognized that adoption of an Aboriginal child by non-Aboriginal adoptive parents raised a sensitive issue of general concern affecting the rights and interests of all Aboriginal children. It was thus held that it was in the best interests of the child for constitutional questions determining the validity of such an adoption process in the wake of the James Bay and Northern Quebec Agreement to be determined, despite the inevitable delay and uncertainty it would cause.

212 *Re V.J.C. and others* (2009) SKQB 395, [7].

213 *Director of Youth Protection v A, B, C, and Band Council A* (2007) QCCQ 13341, [27].

214 Ibid., [27]–[28].

215 Ibid., [28].

216 *Ministry of Social Services v LB* (2009) SKQB 46, [103].

217 *Re W (C.K.)* [2002] 3 C.N.L.R. 268.

> wants to have equal standing with the Director in this hearing but has not identified what it can contribute to the resolution of the legal issues facing the court … I agree that C.K.W. must remain the focus of these proceedings. This is not the proper forum for the Selkirk First Nation to raise concerns about past or future dealings with the Director. The hearing must not be sidetracked by political issues.[218]

The concern that Aboriginal communities are using Aboriginal children as a political tool has made the efforts of some provincial authorities to ensure Aboriginal communities are meaningfully involved in decisions regarding Aboriginal children extremely contentious. The placement of Aboriginal children in non-native homes has raised particular concern where it is proposed that the child is adopted. In response to the concerns of Aboriginal communities, a number of Canadian provinces, including Manitoba and Saskatchewan, introduced a moratorium on the adoption of Aboriginal children by non-native adopters unless they had the consent of the Band or the appropriate Aboriginal child welfare agency. Without that consent, Aboriginal children would remain in long-term foster care, giving Aboriginal communities an effective veto over the child's adoption. However, whilst intended to help address the historical wrong of Aboriginal children being permanently alienated from their communities through the process of adoption, the application of this policy caused considerable problems. Without sufficient numbers of approved Aboriginal carers willing to adopt, Aboriginal children were being left in a state of limbo (often in long-term foster care with non-native foster carers) because their communities were unwilling to consent to adoption by non-native adoptive parents. Starting from the premise, which many Aboriginal communities would dispute, that adoption provides the optimum solution for children in long-term care, the refusal of some Bands and Aboriginal child welfare agencies to consent to a non-native adoption therefore attracted stringent criticism from the courts.

In the case of *Winnipeg Child and Family Services v M.A. and G.R.*,[219] a case where the child was to be placed in a non-native foster home because the Band refused to consent to adoption, Beard J accused the Swan Lake community and Dakota Ojibway Child and Family Services (DOCFS) of adopting an unfair, dogmatic position that sacrificed the individual interests of the child for historical and political reasons that had nothing to do with her particular case.[220] Moreover, the court held that by vetoing the adoption, the Band were denying the child her right to a permanent, secure family and perpetuating the discrimination suffered by individual Aboriginal children at the hands of the child welfare system by

---

218 Ibid., [47]–[48]. See also, *Denton v Department of Community Resources and S.P. and R.L. and C.M.P.* (2008) SKCA 48 and *Alberta (Director of Child Welfare) v Y* [2002] 1 C.N.L.R. 11, [18].

219 *Winnipeg Child and Family Services v M.A. and G.R.* (2002) MBQB 209.

220 Ibid., [1].

depriving them of the same opportunities afforded to non-Aboriginal children.[221] However, although fiercely critical of the damaging effects on individual children of the community's blanket application of the power to veto non-native adoptions, the court had no jurisdiction to overrule the decision of Winnipeg Child and Family Services to respect the Band's decision.[222]

The issue arose again, however, in the case of *Re R.T., M.T., M.A.T., A.L., and K.A.*,[223] where a constitutional challenge was brought against a similar 'veto policy' adopted by the Saskatchewan Department of Community Resources and Employment (DCRE). Again, DCRE had adopted a policy which provided that First Nations children would not be placed for adoption without the consent of the child's Band and, if relevant, the Aboriginal child welfare agency. The Band withheld their consent to the adoption of all five children, in this case arguing that they did not want the children to lose contact with their Aboriginal community and culture. However, with no extended family or Band members able to care for them, the children were left 'destined to remain in long-term foster care'.[224] The Saskatchewan Queen's Bench upheld the argument on behalf of the children that the veto policy violated ss 7 (the right to life, liberty and security of the person) and 15(1) (equality guarantee) of the Canadian Charter.[225]

On the question of the s 7 violation, the court held that the policy had been applied 'arbitrarily and without regard to the individual circumstances or needs of the children' and that there was the 'potential for serious harm' to these children if forced to remain in long-term foster care. In these circumstances, Ryan-Froslie J held that it was clear that the children's s 7 rights to security of the person had been infringed. As to whether or not that violation infringed the principles of fundamental justice, Ryan-Froslie J again held that it did. She concluded that the detailed legislative scheme providing for a hearing process that, with proper community involvement, was responsible for determining the child's best interests was rendered meaningless for Aboriginal children if the Band were subsequently to be handed a veto power over adoption:

> The policy flies in the face of these provisions. It usurps the hearing process and renders it meaningless insofar as permanent orders for First Nations children are concerned. The effect of the policy is to abdicate the Minister's responsibility under the Act to a child's Band and/or agency, if any. A hearing is necessary

221 Ibid.

222 Ibid., [33].

223 *Re R.T., M.T., M.A.T., A.L., and K.A.* (2004) SKQB 503.

224 Ibid., [69].

225 The Band also argued that they had a constitutionally protected Aboriginal right to speak for their children under ss 25 and 35 of the Canadian Constitution. That argument was dismissed. For further discussion of this aspect of the case, see Chapter 5, pp. 163–4.

> to protect the children's rights to liberty and security of the person. Bands and agencies have the ability to participate fully in such hearings.[226]

Ryan-Froslie J went on to observe that the proper forum for the Band to be heard regarding the importance of keeping Aboriginal children within their communities and ensuring the children's cultural needs were properly addressed, was the protection hearing, not through the exercise of a veto power.[227]

As regards the s 15 equality challenge, the court acknowledged the crucial point of principle that true equality does not necessarily demand identical treatment – indeed, the opposite may be true.[228] It is therefore perfectly legitimate to apply different rules, principles and processes to Aboriginal children provided it secures equality in outcome with non-Aboriginal children. However, in determining whether the differential treatment of Aboriginal and non-Aboriginal children with regards to being placed for adoption amounted to discrimination, Ryan-Froslie J held that in light of the evidence regarding the damage caused to children caught in the 'limbo' of long-term foster care and where almost 70 per cent of children in care were Aboriginal, the Band's refusal to consent to adoption, even where there was no alternative placement available, breached the children's equality rights.[229] Ryan-Froslie J went on to dismiss the argument that this discrimination had an ameliorative purpose under s 15(2) of the Canadian Charter: that it prevented the taking of Aboriginal children from their families, communities and culture. In reaching this conclusion she observed that Aboriginal communities were already guaranteed a 'voice' in decisions regarding First Nations children; that adoption does not necessarily mean Aboriginal children will be placed in non-Aboriginal homes; that open adoption allows for children to maintain their connections to family, community and culture;[230] that there is no evidence that the adoption of Aboriginal children by non-Aboriginal families causes harm to the children involved; and that the effect of the policy is to deny Aboriginal children permanent homes and stable, long-lasting relationships – the very things necessary for children to develop a strong sense of self-identity and positive feelings of self-worth.[231] She continued:

> The policy in issue here is blind to the individual needs, capacities and merits of the children to which it is applied. As such, it harms their human dignity.

226 *Re R.T., M.T., M.A.T., A.L., and K.A.* (2004) SKQB 503, [72].

227 Ibid.

228 Ibid., [77].

229 Ibid., [81]–[84].

230 Indeed, open adoption whereby the child retains some contact with members of his/her family and community is often seen as the answer to the permanency vs. culture dilemma. See, for example, *Nunavut (Director of Child and Family Services) v K.(H.)* (2008) NUCJ 19.

231 *Re R.T., M.T., M.A.T., A.L., and K.A.* (2004) SKQB 503, [88]–[92].

> Implementing the policy has the potential of destroying the child's self-identity and self-worth, the very things it was established to protect.[232]

For the same reasons, Ryan-Froslie J dismissed the argument that the infringements of ss 7 and 15 could be justified under s 1 of the Charter.[233] The court thus declared that the policy was unconstitutional and directed DCRE to deal with Aboriginal children in a manner consistent with their best interests, including placing them for adoption where appropriate without reference to the discredited policy.[234]

The success of this constitutional challenge to a policy aimed at conferring decision-making authority on Aboriginal communities over the adoption of Aboriginal children is revealing. On one level, the decision of Ryan-Froslie J can be criticized for undermining efforts to restore real decision-making authority to Aboriginal communities. The judgment could be read to suggest that whilst perfectly happy to allow Aboriginal communities to participate in decisions over Aboriginal children, that participation is only acceptable insofar as it remains subject to the overriding decision-making authority of the province. Thus, the total 'abdication' of the Ministry's decision-making authority over the adoption of Aboriginal children to the Aboriginal communities, was deemed a step too far and one, moreover, that was unnecessary given the legislative measures securing 'adequate participation' by Aboriginal communities in the decision-making process. It could thus be argued that the real reason the policy failed was because it tried to cross that seemingly impenetrable hurdle of wresting real authority and control from the non-native authorities. However, whilst those criticisms may be fair, the decision also reveals the complexity of restoring decision-making authority to Aboriginal communities when there is a current lack of community resources for meeting the needs of Aboriginal children in care. In exercising the decision-making authority conferred on them, the community chose to adhere to a blanket policy that admitted of no exceptions. Whilst understandable when looked at within the wider historical and political context, it is difficult to avoid the conclusion that such an approach threatened to harm the long-term interests of the individual children involved. Consequently, the community could be legitimately criticized for failing to exercise their decision-making authority in a way that gave greater respect to the individual needs of what were already extremely vulnerable children.[235]

As regards efforts to secure greater participation by Aboriginal communities at the level of service delivery, the creation of Aboriginal controlled child welfare agencies exercising delegated provincial powers is clearly an important step forward – not least for the opportunity they provide to help build the community's

---

232 Ibid., [93].

233 Ibid., [104].

234 Ibid., [107].

235 This criticism of the communities involved will be discussed in greater detail in Chapter 5.

capacity for the assumption of self-governing powers. The Manitoba Justice Inquiry said of these agencies that their achievements had been little less than 'remarkable', concluding:

> We believe that Aboriginal child welfare agencies have been an outstanding success and that they warrant further support and encouragement. They are dealing with Aboriginal families with sensitivity, commitment and ability.[236]

More recent reviews have also identified a number of positive changes in the delivery of Aboriginal child welfare as a result of the work of the delegated agencies. Based on a survey of agencies in Manitoba, Bourassa argues that they are now able to offer more culturally appropriate services, in particular introducing Aboriginal ways of thinking including a holistic approach to child welfare in which prevention and support rather than apprehension is the central philosophy.[237] In contrast to non-native agencies, it is suggested that Aboriginal agencies have focused on family healing and supporting the child within the family rather than directing services exclusively at the child and have resisted removing children in an attempt to strengthen social and family cohesion.[238] Initiatives such as the use of the Opikinawasowin in Saskatchewan, a 'culturally sensitive and respectful forum' which improves family, community and elder involvement in planning for the child, have been introduced.[239] When removal is necessary, total separation from the family is seen as a very last resort with much greater use of the extended family as a potential resource.[240] Aboriginal agencies have also allowed a greater sense of community control and ownership over child welfare programmes which, in turn, has improved the effectiveness of services and the willingness of the community to engage with them.[241] Bourassa also reports that as a result of these improvements more Aboriginal children are being successfully returned to their communities.[242]

The agencies themselves have also seen important changes and improvements as they have grown in confidence and experience. Agencies are now more stable with better staffing levels and training.[243] Bourassa argues that child welfare is no

---

236 Aboriginal Justice Inquiry of Manitoba (AJIM) (1991). *Report of the Aboriginal Justice Inquiry of Manitoba: The Justice System and Aboriginal People*, vol. 1. Winnipeg: Manitoba, 532 and 530.

237 Bourassa, *supra* note 1, 39. As to the positive aspects of devolved Aboriginal agencies, see also Rae, *supra* note 1, 18–19.

238 Bourassa, ibid., 19–20.

239 See, for example, the use of the Opik in the case of *Re V.J.C.* (2009) SKQB 395.

240 Bourassa, *supra* note 1, 19–20.

241 Ibid., 39.

242 Ibid. See also C. Blackstock (2007). 'Residential Schools: Did They Really Close or Just Morph into Child Welfare?', *Indigenous Law Journal*, 6: 71, 74. Note, however, the statistics discussed below which would seem to contradict this finding.

243 Bourassa, ibid., 39.

longer such a politically driven issue with more effective leadership and systems of accountability, a situation further improved by the recent administrative restructuring in Manitoba which has created a greater 'arm's length relationship' between the Authorities, the agencies and local leaders.[244]

However, as the case law indicates, the delegated agencies have not been an unqualified success. Despite the undoubted positives, in many cases they have failed to bring about the extent of the changes that were hoped for, sometimes attracting strong judicial criticism for their perceived failings. In two of the cases considered above, the agency criticized for failing to adhere to the Aboriginal placement principle was native controlled.[245] The frustration felt by Bedard J with Minokin Social Services and the communities it serves is clear in the case of *Re AG*:

> The goal of the three Algonquin communities in taking responsibility for providing social services must have been to provide services better suited to the customs and traditions of the Algonquins ... The Court was not prepared to conclude on the basis of the community worker's inability to find appropriate foster parents that the Algonquin community was unable to assume its responsibilities to children in need. Recruiting foster parents is difficult, but Minokin Social Services had to establish a recruitment and evaluation strategy to give it access to Algonquin foster parents for medium and long-term placements if it was to justify its existence.[246]

Again a lack of community resources to care for Aboriginal children requiring out-of-home care was at the heart of the problem.

The growing number of Aboriginal-controlled child welfare agencies has also failed to make any significant impact on the disproportionate number of Aboriginal children in care. Figures published in 2007 show that Aboriginal children still represent about 50 per cent of the total number of children in care in British Columbia, whilst making up only 9.3 per cent of the total child population.[247] There has therefore been no improvement on the figures from the early 1980s.[248]

---

244 Ibid., 38–9.

245 See, *Re A.G.* [2000] 2 C.N.L.R. 1 and *Alberta (Director of Child Welfare) v Y* [2002] 1 C.N.L.R. 11.

246 *Re A.G.*, ibid., [5]–[8].

247 British Columbia Ministry of Children and Family Development (2007). *2006/07 Annual Service Plan Report*, 13.

248 The figures for 1992–1993 show only a modest reduction in the proportion of Aboriginal children in care from a high of between 6 and 6.5 per cent in the 1970s, to an average of 4 per cent. That represents just a 0.6 per cent drop since 1981–1982. See Royal Commission on Aboriginal Peoples (RCAP) (1996). *Report of the Royal Commission on Aboriginal Peoples. Gathering Strength.* Part One, Vol. 3. Ottawa: Minister of Supply and Services, Canada, 25–26, 32 and 126. As Durst reports, Aboriginal children still remain five times more likely to enter care than the national average. See D. Durst (1999). 'The

Moreover, despite the legislative changes, the number of Aboriginal children in care in British Columbia is actually increasing. In the year 2003/2004 the BC government reports that there were 4,211 Aboriginal children in care. By the year 2006/2007 that number had increased to 4,721. These disappointing statistics are repeated across the provinces. In Ontario, 17 per cent of the province's child welfare caseload concerns Aboriginal children;[249] in Saskatchewan about two-thirds of the children in care are Aboriginal;[250] in Alberta, 58 per cent of the children in care are Aboriginal;[251] and, perhaps most staggering, in Manitoba over 85 per cent of the children in care are Aboriginal whilst they constitute just 20 per cent of the total population.[252]

Statistics such as these could be explained by a number of factors, some positive, including higher Aboriginal birth rates,[253] greater openness about abuse within the communities and a greater willingness among community members to work with the staff of an Aboriginal agency.[254] Nevertheless, the continuing practice of apprehending Aboriginal children in hugely disproportionate numbers is a matter of considerable concern. There have been some improvements in the placement of Aboriginal children. In Alberta, for example, 37.6 per cent of Aboriginal children are now placed in an Aboriginal foster home or in kinship care.[255] In Manitoba, one-third of Aboriginal children in care are placed in Aboriginal homes.[256] However, these figures are lower than those achieved in Australia where the statutory grounding given to the Aboriginal placement principle appears to have been much more effective.

The limited success of Aboriginal child welfare agencies in keeping Aboriginal children out of care and, if apprehension is necessary, being able to find culturally appropriate placements, is disappointing, particularly given the length of time some agencies have now been operating. However, the inability of these agencies to find effective solutions to the problems surrounding Aboriginal child welfare in Canada is not surprising given the context within which they are forced to operate.

Wellness of Aboriginal Children: Seeking Solutions through Self-government', in J. Hylton (ed.) *Aboriginal Self-Government in Canada: Current Trends and Issues*. Saskatoon: Purich Pub, 196.

249 Ontario Ministry of Aboriginal Affairs (2005). *Ontario's New Approach to Aboriginal Affairs*. Queen's Printer for Ontario, 9.

250 Saskatchewan Department of Community Resources (2007). *2007–08, Saskatchewan Provincial Budget – Performance Plan. Saskatchewan Community Resources*, 17 and 27.

251 Alberta Children's Services (2008). *Children and Youth Services Business Plan 2008–11*, 48.

252 Manitoba Family Services and Housing (2007). *Annual Report 2006–07*, 94. See also B. Hallett (2006). *Aboriginal People in Manitoba*. Queen's Printer Canada, 42.

253 See Durst, *supra* note 248, 192.

254 AJIM, *supra* note 236, 532.

255 Alberta Children's Services, *supra* note 251, 54.

256 Manitoba Family Services and Housing, *supra* note 252.

Wholly inadequate funding remains a major obstacle to the successful operation of Aboriginal agencies. As Rae reports, in 2000 child welfare funding for Aboriginal agencies from Indian Affairs was 22 per cent less than the provincial average, leaving those agencies mandated to serve the communities with the most crippling socio-economic problems, the least well supported.[257] The federal government's funding formula for Aboriginal agencies also continues to exacerbate these problems with resources remaining focused on the maintenance of apprehended children, depriving Aboriginal families of much needed investment in the supportive and preventative services that non-native families enjoy.[258] Furthermore, as a result of this chronic under-funding, the development of culturally appropriate and effective policies and programmes has been seriously undermined with agencies caught in a vicious circle of crisis management, struggling to operate on a skeletal, poorly resourced and exhausted staff.[259] Perhaps, however, the most serious constraint on the ability of Aboriginal agencies to develop innovative and effective culturally based solutions to the problems facing their communities is the fact that, at their core, the agencies remain wholly provincial in nature.[260] Aboriginal-controlled agencies still have to operate under provincial mandate, apply provincial child welfare law, operate within the provincial governance structure and are ultimately accountable to the provincial ministry for maintaining provincial standards of care and protection. When operating within these constraints Aboriginal agencies do not have the jurisdictional space or resources to introduce the kind of holistic, community-centred approach to child welfare that many Aboriginal communities desire.[261] Bourassa's survey of Aboriginal agencies in Manitoba revealed a strong sense of frustration with the slow pace of change and the inherent limitations of the reforms.[262] Agencies and communities felt they had 'inherited a flawed

---

257 Rae, *supra* note 1, 28–9. See also Blackstock, *supra* note 242, 74.

258 Rae, ibid., 37–8. As Durst explains: 'The federal government has refused to fund supportive or supplemental services such as respite care, child care, or in-home support. Preventive and educational programs must be paid from the core funds or additional monies obtained from elsewhere. Children must be in care before they can access additional services. This system reinforces past practices of apprehension and temporary substitute care. Agencies are forced to keep the numbers of children in care up in order to ensure dependable funding.' See Durst, *supra* note 248, 198. See also E. N. Hughes (2006). *BC Children and Youth Review: An Independent Review of BC's Child Protection System*, 58–9.

259 Rae, ibid., 29. See also Bourassa, *supra* note 1, 46. The problems experienced by devolved Aboriginal agencies will be considered in greater detail in Chapter 4.

260 See the Supreme Court's analysis of the essential nature of the agencies' operations in *NIL/TU,O Child and Family Services Society v B.C. Government and Service Employees' Union* [2010] 2 S.C.R. 696, esp at [36]–[39] (per Abella J) and [80] (per McLachlin C.J. and Fish J.). See also, Rae, ibid., 6.

261 See, AJIM, *supra* note 236, 529–31; L. White and E. Jacobs (1992). *Liberating Our Children Liberating Our Nations, Report of the Aboriginal Committee, Community Panel Child Protection Legislation Review in British Columbia.* British Columbia: Queen's Printer, 5–10; Rae, *supra* note 1, 23; Blackstock, *supra* note 242, 74–5.

262 Bourassa, *supra* note 1, 48.

system' with limited scope for fundamental change.[263] Similar problems have been encountered with Aboriginal justice initiatives. As Patricia Monture-Angus remarks:

> Especially in the areas of child welfare and justice, this trend [in Aboriginal communities of solutions that mimic the manner in which white people govern themselves] is notable. Despite the many attempts to create programs which "accommodate" Aboriginal people in the Canadian criminal justice system, the overall rates of Aboriginal over-representation have not decreased and in fact have continued to rise. The essential and often overlooked step in creating a renewed relationship between Aboriginal Peoples and Canadians is an examination of the meaning of the concepts we are building our relationship with.[264]

Particularly notable by its absence in the reform efforts of recent years has been the failure to begin an even tentative examination of how Aboriginal law could be employed to help address the cultural bias of the existing legal framework within which the non-native child welfare system operates. Yet, Aboriginal law provides a potentially rich body of norms which could be drawn upon to inform existing legal concepts such as 'welfare', 'neglect' and 'consultation', as well as providing alternative legal standards and solutions to deal in culturally appropriate ways with child protection concerns within Aboriginal communities.[265]

For these same reasons, the recent administrative re-structuring in Manitoba is unlikely to prove any more successful. It is of course hoped that by transferring responsibility for the organization and delivery of existing provincial services to devolved Aboriginal Authorities, some space will be created for the development and implementation of more culturally appropriate policies, services and governance structures. Again, however, the limitations of these initiatives must be borne in mind. The central problem remains that overriding authority and control remains firmly vested in the province. The delineation of the respective powers and duties of the provincial Minister and the new Aboriginal Authorities in Manitoba is telling. For example, the duties of an Aboriginal Authority include developing objectives and priorities for providing child and family services, but only insofar as those objectives and priorities are 'consistent with provincial objectives and priorities'.[266] Similarly, whilst the Authority must ensure that culturally appropriate standards for services, practices and procedures are developed, those standards

263 Ibid.

264 P. Monture-Angus (1999). *Journeying Forward. Dreaming of First Nations Independence.* Halifax, NS: Fernwood Publishing, 33. See also, Durst, *supra* note 248, 196.

265 See generally, J. Y. Henderson (2006). 'First Nations Jurisprudence and Aboriginal Rights: Defining the Just Society'. Canada: Native Law Centre.

266 Child and Family Services Authorities Act, C.C.S.M. 2002 c.C90, s 19(b).

must again be 'consistent with provincial standards, objectives and priorities'.[267] The ultimate control and authority which remains vested in the Minister is clear from the delineation of his powers and responsibilities under s 24 of the legislation. Thus the Minister retains responsibility for setting provincial objectives and priorities; establishing policies and standards for the provision of services; monitoring and assessing how the Authorities carry out their responsibilities; and allocating funding and resources to the Authorities.[268] With the provincial minister retaining ultimate authority for determining objectives, priorities, policies and service delivery standards throughout the province, administrative re-structuring of this nature is highly unlikely to result in any significant shift in the underlying philosophy, conceptual design and therefore delivery of what will remain essentially provincial, and not Aboriginal, child welfare services.

It is clear that the limitations of the Manitoban reforms were plainly apparent to the Aboriginal communities involved. The MOU entered into between the Manitoba provincial government and the Manitoba Keewatinowi Okimakanak draws a clear distinction between the proposed process of administrative re-structuring and ongoing self-government negotiations (under the umbrella of the Manitoba Framework Agreement Initiative) aimed at restoring 'jurisdiction and authority' over Aboriginal child welfare to the First Nations.[269] The inherent jurisdiction and law-making authority of Aboriginal peoples over child and family services will not be restored by this process of administrative re-structuring. Yet, if decolonization is to be achieved, Aboriginal communities must be freed from the control of the provincial governments and guaranteed the jurisdictional space and legal and political authority to rebuild their own child-welfare systems. Reforms such as these do not give them that space.

Conclusion

The rhetoric of change is now firmly established in both Australia and Canada. Through legislation and improved judicial understanding, governments have promised improved sensitivity and responsiveness to Aboriginal cultural differences and socio-economic needs, and have acted upon the recognized need for much greater involvement of Aboriginal communities in decision-making forums and in the delivery and design of Aboriginal child welfare services. The need for effective consultation with Aboriginal communities and better participation in the decision-making process is now an almost unquestioned part of the child protection process. Yet, despite all the goodwill and effort which has

267 Ibid., ss 19(c)–(d).

268 Ibid., s 24.

269 Memorandum of Understanding between the Manitoba Keewatinowi Okimakanak and Her Majesty the Queen in Right of the Province of Manitoba. July 2000, Preambular paras. 7–8, effective para. [2.3].

gone into these reforms, the results remain disappointing. Judicial acceptance of the new legislative principles has lacked consistency, the impact of core principles such as the Aboriginal placement principle on actual outcomes in individual cases has been patchy, and Aboriginal children remain grossly over-represented in the care system. Indeed, the picture continues to worsen rather than improve. It is not surprising that Aboriginal communities remain deeply disillusioned by the non-native child welfare system, with feelings of fear, distrust, marginalization and victimization continuing to dominate. The prevailing picture in Australia was summed up in the *Bringing Them Home* report:

> Welfare legislation and the language of welfare policy have changed. However, submissions to the Inquiry from indigenous organisations working with Indigenous families indicate little change in practice. Paternalistic attitudes persist in welfare departments. Indigenous children continue to be severely over-represented within all State and Territory welfare systems. Departmental attempts to provide culturally appropriate welfare services to Indigenous communities have not overcome the weight of Indigenous peoples' historical experience of "The Welfare" or the attitudes and structures entrenched in welfare departments.[270]

Even within Canada, where reforms to the general child welfare system have generally been much more far-reaching, the overall picture remains discouraging.

One thing emerges clearly from Canadian and Australian experiences in trying to reform the child welfare system: 'sensitization initiatives' will always remain limited whilst constrained by the system itself. The system itself must therefore change – not just at the level of service delivery but at the level of governance, policy development and law. The relative failings of the legislative reforms of recent years have clearly fuelled the arguments in favour of a much more radical response to the mistakes of the past if the needs and interests of Aboriginal children are to be successfully addressed. That more radical solution lies in affording Aboriginal communities the jurisdictional space to find their own culturally grounded solutions to protecting their own children. It means restoring the political and legal decision-making authority of Aboriginal communities over Aboriginal child welfare. It means self-government. And it is therefore to the debate surrounding Aboriginal self-government over child welfare that the following two chapters turn.

---

270 HREOC, *supra* note 2, 458.

PART III
Self-Government over Aboriginal Child Welfare: Lessons from Canada

Chapter 4
The Promise and the Risks of Aboriginal Self-Government over Aboriginal Child Welfare

Introduction

The somewhat disappointing results of recent initiatives aimed at sensitizing the existing Australian and Canadian child welfare systems to the needs of Aboriginal children and families, exemplify the limitations and problems of trying to accommodate what is a fundamentally different indigenous worldview within the established normative framework of non-native society. The apparent difficulties in achieving satisfactory reform have led many commentators to reject 'accommodation' and 'sensitization' as viable ways forward, at least in the longer term. Aboriginal communities, strongly supported by many academic commentators, contend that the successful decolonization of Aboriginal child welfare can only be achieved by recognizing and respecting the inherent right of Aboriginal peoples to self-government over child welfare.[1] That has to be right. Tinkering with the edges of the non-native child welfare system is certainly not decolonization and may therefore prove, in the long term, to be an expensive and time-consuming distraction.[2] Essentially, the solutions to the problems surrounding Aboriginal child welfare will have to come from within the communities themselves and that can only be achieved by truly empowering those communities and recognizing that they have the ultimate responsibility for their own children. It means self-government.

In Canada, where moves towards self-government are far more advanced than in Australia, self-government is now recognized by the federal government as

1 L. White and E. Jacobs (1992). *Liberating Our Children Liberating Our Nations, Report of the Aboriginal Committee, Community Panel Child Protection Legislation Review in British Columbia*. British Columbia: Queen's Printer; M. Kline (1992). 'Child Welfare Law, "Best Interests of the Child" Ideology and First Nations', *Osgoode Hall Law Journal*, 30: 375, 423–5; P. Monture (1989). 'A Vicious Circle: Child Welfare and the First Nations', *Canadian Journal of Women and the Law*, 3: 1, 6–7; B. Morse (1980). 'Indian and Innuit Family Law and the Canadian Legal System', *American Indian Law Review*, 8: 199, 200; P. Lynch (2001). 'Keeping them Home: The Best Interests of Indigenous Children and Communities in Canada and Australia', *Sydney Law Review*, 23: 501, 505.

2 See J. Rae (2009). 'Program Delivery Devolution: A Stepping Stone or Quagmire for First Nations?', *Indigenous Law Journal*, 7: 1.

an inherent right or entitlement of Aboriginal peoples.[3] In principle, the right of Aboriginal communities to exercise self-government over child welfare therefore requires no further justification. However, there are a number of claimed advantages to Aboriginal self-government which if realized promise to transform the lives of Aboriginal children. These claimed advantages whilst not necessary in principle to justify Aboriginal claims to self-government, strengthen the strategic case for support. Indeed, the *potential* benefits of self-government over child welfare can be seen, albeit at times only weakly, in the success of a number of initiatives aimed at restoring a large degree of Aboriginal autonomy over a range of social welfare and justice programmes, including Aboriginal-controlled child welfare agencies. However, it is equally clear from the Canadian experience that self-government is not a panacea. And whilst the work of Aboriginal controlled child welfare agencies in Canada has illustrated some of the potential benefits of self-government, so has it highlighted some of the more serious risks – risks which, given the extreme socio-economic marginalization of Aboriginal communities in Australia, are of even greater concern within the Australian context. It is crucial that the potential risks posed by self-government to the rights and interests of vulnerable Aboriginal children stand at the forefront of any debate concerning Aboriginal self-government over child welfare.

Against the backdrop of the failings of the sensitization and accommodation strategies, the next two chapters will therefore consider the various arguments in favour of self-government over child welfare, as well as the purported 'domestic' solutions to protecting children who may be perceived to be at risk within self-governing communities. They will necessarily focus on Canada where the political and legal debate over the right of Aboriginal peoples to self-government, as well as actual moves towards implementation of that right, are considerably more advanced than in Australia. Drawing on Canada's experience of the tentative moves towards restoring Aboriginal control over a range of social welfare programmes, including child welfare, the case for self-government based on its perceived benefits and risks will first be discussed. The following chapter will then turn to examine Canada's approach to the inherent right of Aboriginal peoples to self-government as revealed through the jurisprudence of the Supreme Court and the modern treaty process. The implications of Canada's general approach to self-government for the implementation of Aboriginal self-government over child welfare in particular will then be considered, before finally examining the Canadian government's approach, within this framework of self-government, to ensuring adequate protection for the rights and interests of individual Aboriginal children. It is hoped the problems identified with Canada's approach to self-government and the protection of Aboriginal children's rights within self-governing communities will prove instructive for those currently engaged in debates concerning Aboriginal self-government over child welfare in Australia.

3 The Constitution Act 1982, being Schedule B to the Canada Act 1982 (U.K.) 1982, c. 11.

The Promise of Self-Government

Although Canada has yet to see the implementation of Aboriginal self-government on a national scale, there are numerous examples of smaller community-led projects in the fields of criminal justice, health and social welfare in which the community's sense of control and ownership over the project, as promised more generally by self-government, has proved vitally important to its success.[4] A number of communities have, for example, successfully taken control of problems such as substance and alcohol abuse and began, by their own initiative, the process of individual and community healing.[5] It is claimed that, unlike programmes imposed by non-native governments, community-driven programmes such as these can be tailored to meet specific needs, are realistic and therefore work.[6] Moreover, they can draw on the community's own rich body of traditions, values and practices to find solutions which accord with the community's philosophy and beliefs and reinforce a positive sense of cultural identity. There are similarly encouraging signs within the context of child welfare that programmes designed and delivered by Aboriginal people are more effective in attaining their objectives than programmes that are designed and delivered by non-Aboriginal people.[7] As discussed in Chapter 3, although there have clearly been limitations as to what Aboriginal-controlled child welfare agencies have been able to achieve, programmes which have been designed and delivered at the community level have been able to generate a level of community support and involvement far beyond that which could be achieved by non-Aboriginal agencies.[8] Where the community has been fully involved in the design of a programme, it is claimed

4 See especially, J. Hylton (ed.) (1994). *Aboriginal Self-government in Canada: Current Trends and Issues*. Saskatoon: Purich Publishing, 34–48, for an analysis of the importance of community control over social welfare programmes. See further, Royal Commission on Aboriginal Peoples (RCAPc) (1996). *Report of the Royal Commission on Aboriginal Peoples. Gathering Strength*. Part One, Vol. 3. Ottawa: Minister of Supply and Services, Canada, 39–42.

5 Office of the Chief Medical Examiner (OCME) (1992). *The Fatalities Inquiries Act – Respecting the Death of Lester Norman Desjarlais*. Brandon: Ministry of Social Services and Housing, 243–4. For further discussion of community healing initiatives see: RCAPc, ibid., 39–42, 83–6 and 107–347; Royal Commission on Aboriginal Peoples (RCAPd) (1996). *Report of the Royal Commission on Aboriginal Peoples. Perspectives and Realities*. Part One, Vol. 4. Ottawa: Minister of Supply and Services, Canada, 53–62; Hylton, ibid., 67–89; Aboriginal Justice Inquiry of Manitoba (AJIM) (1991). *Report of the Aboriginal Justice Inquiry of Manitoba: The Justice System and Aboriginal People*, vol. 1. Winnipeg: Manitoba, 492–8; Royal Commission on Aboriginal Peoples (RCAPe) (1996). *Report of the Royal Commission on Aboriginal Peoples. Perspectives and Realities*. Part One, Vol. 4. Ottawa: Minister of Supply and Services, Canada, 148–68.

6 Interview with Robert Kiyoshk, BC Institute Against Family Violence, *Newsletter* (Summer, 1996).

7 Hylton, *supra* note 4, 39–40.

8 AJIM, *supra* note 5, 532. See generally, J. Rae (2009), *supra* note 2 and C. Bourassa

that the sense of invasion once felt by the community is replaced by a sense of control.[9] The programme consequently enjoys much greater trust, acceptance and support from the community and people are generally more willing to cooperate.[10] The close involvement of the community in the design of the programme can also ensure a more culturally appropriate service and one that, at least to some degree, is able to incorporate the basic cultural norms of the community into its underlying philosophy and approach.[11] More generally, by involving the community in the design and delivery of child welfare programmes, the community's level of awareness and understanding about issues such as domestic violence and substance and alcohol abuse can be significantly improved.[12] With greater awareness comes greater interest in, and commitment to, addressing the problems.

Moreover, self-government over child welfare will not occur in isolation and the benefits of self-government therefore extend far beyond the improvements which have been achieved in specific programmes such as these. It is important to see self-government over child welfare within the wider context – in which it forms just one core part of a much broader picture in which Aboriginal communities should once again enjoy the space to begin rebuilding healthy, functioning, cultural, social, economic, legal and political communities.[13] Many of the problems within contemporary Aboriginal communities can be directly attributed to the destructive forces of colonialism.[14] The need for decolonization to enable Aboriginal people

(2010). *Summary Review of the Manitoba Child Welfare System for the Saskatchewan Child Welfare Review Report.*

9 Hylton, *supra* note 4, 40–1.

10 Ibid., 43; AJIM, *supra* note 5, 532.

11 AJIM, ibid., 532.

12 Hylton, *supra* note 4, 43.

13 It should, for example, be borne in mind that the problems experienced with Aboriginal controlled child welfare agencies have occurred against a backdrop of imposed colonial systems of governance that are themselves a key part of the problem. See discussion below and Royal Commission on Aboriginal Peoples (RCAPa) (1996). *Report of the Royal Commission on Aboriginal Peoples. Looking Forward Looking Back.* Part One, Vol. 1. Ottawa: Minister of Supply and Services, Canada, 274–6, 279–81 and 285–6; M. Boldt (1993). *Surviving as Indians. The Challenge of Self-Government.* Toronto: University of Toronto Press, 120–4; and Royal Commission on Aboriginal Peoples (RCAPb) (1996). *Report of the Royal Commission on Aboriginal Peoples. Restructuring the Relationship.* Part One, Vol. 2. Ottawa: Minister of Supply and Services, Canada, 115–39. As to the process of post-colonial cultural rejuvenation more generally see C. Taylor (1992). 'Multiculturalism and the "Politics of Recognition": An Essay', in A. Gutmann (ed.) *Multiculturalism.* Princeton: Princeton University Press; W. Kymlicka (1991). *Liberalism, Community and Culture.* Oxford: Clarendon Press.

14 For an excellent analysis of the destructive effects of colonialism on Aboriginal cultures and communities see especially Boldt, ibid., 167–76; RCAPe, *supra* note 5, 39–53; RCAPa, ibid., 137–99 and 247–523. As to the effects of colonialism on community social norms and standards and resulting violence within the communities, see especially M. Jackson (1988). *Locking Up Natives in Canada: Report to the Canadian Bar Association*

to rebuild their devastated communities is now widely supported by post-colonial theory.[15] Building from an appreciation of the debilitating effects of colonialism, post-colonial theorists argue that if Aboriginal communities are to begin to address the consequences of the attempted destruction of their political, economic, cultural and social identities, including overcoming the 'culture of dependency'[16] that now dominates within many communities, they must be recognized as autonomous cultural and political groups within the Canadian system.[17] They must be afforded self-government.[18] Key to self-government is ending the paternalism that has permeated every aspect of the relationship between Aboriginal peoples and the federal and provincial governments, guaranteeing Aboriginal communities the necessary jurisdictional space to rejuvenate their cultural and traditional values, and to re-establish their unique identity as distinct peoples.[19] Sustainable economic growth and political development, alongside the rejuvenation of Aboriginal legal systems, cultures and traditions, will be central to the rebuilding process.[20]

All of these wider changes will have an important impact on Aboriginal child welfare. For example, the re-emergence of prosperous, healthy communities, governed by strong cultural and political values, is likely to have a dramatic effect on the current levels of violence and abuse within Aboriginal communities. Attacking the underlying causes of the problem can help alleviate the symptoms. Children will be the direct beneficiaries of such a process. Clearly, the best interests of Aboriginal children lie within the context of strong functioning communities. If self-government can promote such communities it can therefore only be to the benefit of Aboriginal children.[21]

A move to self-government, including self-government over Aboriginal child welfare, therefore holds out enormous promise for Aboriginal peoples. The economic, social, cultural and political advantages of decolonization should be felt by the whole community, including Aboriginal children. In the specific context

---

Committee on Imprisonment and Release. Ottawa: Canadian Bar Association and H. Finkler (1992). 'Community Participation in Socio-Legal Control: The Northern Context', *Canadian Journal of Criminology*, 34: 503.

15 For an introduction to post-colonial theory and the process of decolonization, see: B. Ashcroft, G. Griffiths and H. Tiffin (eds) (1995). *The Post-Colonial Studies Reader*. London: Routledge.

16 Boldt, *supra* note 13, 170 and 172–4.

17 See especially, Taylor, *supra* note 13; Boldt, *supra* note 13, 176–80 and 200–3; Kymlicka, *supra* note 13, 135–205.

18 Hylton, *supra* note 4, 39.

19 See generally, Taylor, *supra* note 13.

20 Rae, *supra* note 2, 5. For a discussion of the social effects of the destruction of the traditional economies of Aboriginal communities and the strategies for economic rejuvenation see, Boldt, *supra* note 13, 223–63; RCAPc, *supra* note 4, 217–19; Hylton, *supra* note 4, 34–9. For a general account of economic development within First Nations communities see, RCAPb, *supra* note 13, 775–996.

21 RCAPc, *supra* note 4, 52. See also Rae, *supra* note 2, 6.

of child welfare, self-government should restore to Aboriginal communities the jurisdictional space and the political and legal authority to craft their own distinctly 'Aboriginal' child welfare systems, enabling them to deliver culturally appropriate services 'owned' and understood by the communities. However, self-government is not an easy answer. The restoration of community-control over Aboriginal child welfare is a complex and challenging process carrying significant risks as well as benefits for Aboriginal children.

The Risks of Self-Government: The Desjarlais Inquiry and Beyond

The findings of the Inquiry into the death of 15-year-old Lester Desjarlais whilst in the care of Dakota Ojibway Child and Family Services (DOCFS), an Aboriginal-controlled child welfare agency delivering child and family services to the Sandy Bay reserve community in Manitoba, stand as a shocking testament to the fact that community control over child welfare is not a panacea for the current problems.[22] The Inquiry into Lester's death, headed by Justice Giesbrecht of the Manitoba Provincial Court, revealed an intensity and depth of socio-economic and political problems within the Sandy Bay reserve community that fundamentally undermined the work of DOCFS, whilst raising very serious questions about the capacity of the community to exercise responsible government and protect its most vulnerable members. Caution is required in drawing any generalized conclusions from this one tragic case, particularly given events now occurred almost 25 years ago. However, it is clear that these problems were not peculiar to one particular time and one particular place. Although it is to be expected that things within the Sandy Bay community and DOCFS will have improved, perhaps dramatically, over the intervening years, the depth and complexity of the problems revealed by the Desjarlais Inquiry clearly present a long-term challenge to effective self-government. Similarly, the serious problems identified by the Desjarlais Inquiry are not unique to Sandy Bay. The voices of many Aboriginal women regarding the extent of intra-familial violence and abuse within their communities,[23] as well as their clear concern at the inadequate response of their political leadership to

22 OCME, *supra* note 5. For commentary on the Desjarlais Inquiry and the problems with Aboriginal controlled child welfare agencies in Manitoba during this period, see A. McGillivray (1997). 'Therapies of Freedom: The Colonization of Aboriginal Childhood', in A. McGillivray (ed.) *Governing Childhood.* Aldershot: Dartmouth, 135, 164–9.

23 For example, Nahanee describes violence against women within Aboriginal communities as reaching near 'epidemic proportions'. See T. Nahanee (1996). 'Dancing with a Gorilla: Aboriginal Women, Justice and the Charter', in *Royal Commission on Aboriginal Peoples, Round Table Discussion on Justice Issues.* Ottawa: Minister of Supply and Services, Canada, 359, 360. See generally, A. McGillivray and B. Comaskey (1999). *Black Eyes All of the Time. Intimate Violence, Aboriginal Women and the Justice System.* Toronto: University of Toronto Press.

that phenomenon,[24] provides strong support for Justice Giesbrecht's conclusion that the serious problems he had identified were common to many Aboriginal communities.[25] Whilst focusing on the death of Lester Desjarlais, the Inquiry thus provides a crucial insight into the risks of self-government for Aboriginal communities and their most vulnerable citizens across the Canadian provinces.

The Colonial Legacy

Poverty and community disintegration

Poverty and the attempted destruction of Aboriginal cultures have contributed enormously to the current problems within Aboriginal communities.[26] It is clear from the Inquiry into the death of Lester Desjarlais that many Aboriginal communities face the most appalling socio-economic problems. Poverty, amongst other things, can have a devastating effect on the levels of violence and abuse within a community.[27] To understand the full effect of poverty on Aboriginal communities, it must be seen within the wider colonial context. As was discussed in Chapter 2, the arrival of the European colonial forces led to the widespread dispossession of Aboriginal people from their land, resulting in mass relocation.[28] One of the most debilitating consequences of this process was that many Aboriginal communities lost their traditional economic base, without sharing in the benefits of the 'advance' of industrialization and development.[29] The isolation of many Aboriginal communities has compounded their economic crisis.[30] Some communities are too geographically isolated to become economically self-sufficient, whilst others are situated on land that is generally unsuitable for sustained economic development.[31] Crippling unemployment and resulting

---

24 See, for example, AJIM, *supra* note 5, 475–507; RCAPd, *supra* note 5, 62–8 and 71–83; RCAPc, *supra* note 4, 54–86; and Nahanee, ibid., 360–4 and 366.

25 OCME, *supra* note 5, 60, 61, 105, 108 and 258. See also D. Durst (1999). 'The Wellness of Aboriginal Children: Seeking Solutions through Self-government', in J. Hylton (ed.) *Aboriginal Self-Government in Canada: Current Trends and Issues*. Saskatoon: Purich Pub., 200.

26 OCME, ibid., 234–5 (citing S. Longstaffe and B. Hamilton (1987). *A New Justice for Indian Children: Final report of the Child Advocacy Project*. Winnipeg, Manitoba, Child Protection Centre, Children's Hospital, Health Sciences Centre).

27 Ibid., 233–58.

28 See especially, RCAPa, *supra* note 13, 137–200 and 411–523.

29 See especially, Boldt, *supra* note 13, 170–4 and 223–30. See also, Mackenzie Valley Pipeline Inquiry (1977). *Northern Frontier, Northern Homeland. The Report of the Mackenzie Valley Pipeline Inquiry*. Toronto: James Lorimer; Ottawa: Supply and Services Canada, 152.

30 C. LaPrairie (1988). 'The Young Offenders Act and Aboriginal Youth', in J. Hudon, J. Hornick and B. Burrows (eds), *Justice and the Young Offender in Canada*. Toronto: Wall and Thompson, 159, 161.

31 Ibid., 161.

welfare dependency on the Canadian government has been the result. Poverty and the creation of a 'dependency culture' make communities extremely vulnerable to the problems of serious abusive behaviour.[32]

A further complicating legacy of colonialism and 'modernization' has been the weakening of Aboriginal community institutions which traditionally maintained social cohesion and control.[33] The destabilizing loss of traditional social and political institutions has been exacerbated by the imposition of a foreign system of governance in the form of Band Councils under the Indian Act.[34] The consequence has been a weakening of community ties, values and societal standards of behaviour across Aboriginal communities.[35] McCaskill argues that in communities which are functioning well there exist strong social pressures to obey the values and standards of one's group.[36] These pressures are exerted through interaction with the community and the positive influence of leaders and role models.[37] A strong sense of identity, belonging and community cohesion is nurtured.[38] On the other hand, when these community ties do not exist, 'frustration, alienation, and confusion' develop.[39] Resulting disintegration is manifested in violence, sexual abuse and alcoholism, with family instability one of the most common symptoms of this disintegration in community life.

The situation is not of course this bleak in all Aboriginal communities. Different Aboriginal communities across Canada have suffered the effects of colonialism to varying degrees of severity, and many communities have begun the process of community healing and cultural regeneration, returning to their traditional values and social institutions to rebuild their devastated communities. However, as the death of Lester Desjarlais makes very clear, the effects of colonialism are not easily forgotten. To establish effective self-government under these conditions is a mammoth challenge, and the difficulties facing the communities should not be underestimated.

---

32 Ibid., 162. See also, Boldt, *supra* note 13, 176.

33 For a discussion on the disintegration in traditional institutions of social control and its effects see especially, C. LaPrairie (1992). 'Aboriginal Crime and Justice. Explaining the Present, Exploring the Future', *Canadian Journal of Criminology*, 34: 281 and Finkler, *supra* note 14.

34 Rae, *supra* note 2, 23–4. The problematic imposition of the Indian Act system of governance on First Nations communities is extensively documented. For the most recent overview see, RCAPa, *supra* note 13, 255–332.

35 S. Clark (1992). 'Crime and Community Issues and Directions in Aboriginal Justice', *Canadian Journal of Criminology*, 34: 513, 514–15.

36 D. McCaskill (1985). *Patterns of Criminality and Correction Among Native Young Offenders in Manitoba: A Longitudinal Analysis*. Ottawa: Correctional Services of Canada. See also C. LaPrairie (1995). 'Conferencing in Aboriginal Communities in Canada: Finding Middle Ground in Criminal Justice', *Criminal Law Forum*, 6: 576.

37 McCaskill, ibid.

38 Ibid.

39 Ibid.

Sexual abuse and violence: complacency and denial

The devastating consequences of a complete disintegration in community life were clearly evident in Sandy Bay where there would appear to have been a complete collapse in any kind of community norms or standards. This collapse was most clearly seen in the rampant sexual abuse to which children on the reserve were subjected.[40] Strong complacency about the sexual abuse of children was a major problem, with the levels of sexual abuse so high that for many it had simply become an accepted phenomenon in the community: an ordinary part of daily life. Other members of the Band appeared to have been in complete denial that sexual abuse even existed within the community.[41] Those who did admit there was a problem engaged their energies in trying to hide the fact from the outside world, rather than protect the children at risk and deal with the offenders.[42] The most shocking aspect of this denial was that it even affected the child protection workers at DOCFS, some of whom publicly defended known abusers.[43] Community denial and complacency over the sexual abuse of children permeated every bad decision that was made with regard to Lester.[44]

This tragic problem is not restricted to Sandy Bay. The Desjarlais Inquiry was unequivocal that the evidence 'strongly suggests that the problem of sexual abuse on reserves is simply enormous'[45] – a problem of 'epidemic proportions'.[46] Justice Giesbrecht's conclusions are more than borne out by similar reported experiences across reserve communities in Canada.[47] Nahanee claims that there is an 'almost total victimisation of women and children in Aboriginal communities', and agrees with Justice Giesbrecht that violence in Aboriginal communities has now reached 'epidemic proportions', with sexual and physical violence affecting over 80 per cent of Aboriginal children.[48] It is estimated that up to 80 per cent of Aboriginal girls and 50 per cent of Aboriginal boys in the North West Territories have been sexually abused by the age of eight.[49]

40 OCME, *supra* note 5, 14, 58, 60, 105, 234 and 236–7.

41 Ibid., 57–61 and 233–74.

42 Ibid., 58.

43 Ibid., 104.

44 Ibid., 61.

45 Ibid., 60.

46 Ibid., 105.

47 For a strong account of the problems of violence and sexual abuse across Aboriginal communities see, Nahanee, *supra* note 23 and McGillivray and Comaskey, *supra* note 23. See also RCAPc, *supra* note 4, 54–97.

48 Nahanee, ibid., 5 and 15.

49 Ibid., 15. These statistics are supported by those presented to the Manitoba Justice Inquiry by the Native Council of Canada suggesting that seven out of 10 First Nations girls are sexually abused by the age of 16. See R. Fossett (1989–1991). *Aboriginal Child Welfare in Canada: Literature Review and Selected Bibliography*. Public Inquiry into the Administration of Justice and Aboriginal People, Paper No. 15, vol. 4. Manitoba: The Inquiry, 49. See also Kuptana (1991). *No More Secrets: Acknowledging the Problem*

The phenomenon of sexual abuse and violence within Aboriginal reserve communities was again thrust into the national spotlight with a series of reports on the South Island Justice initiative in British Columbia.[50] Violence and abuse was revealed to be rampant on the South Island reserves. Exacerbating the problem was the founding of the South Island Justice Committee which made it difficult for women to seek help outside the reserve community. It was claimed that women seeking to take action against an abuser were persecuted and 'intimidated into using a council of elders and the bighouse rather than to pursue charges and reveal family secrets in the Canadian legal system'.[51] The problem of abuse was clearly extensive. It was observed that in some communities there was not one person who had not been touched by sexual abuse.[52] One former member of the Tsartlip Band claimed:

> There are 40 women on one reserve alone who could lay sexual assault charges. There is almost a pathology of enslavement. The life support system is the Band, the reserve, the family, the extended family. They are dependent for their housing, their food, their utilities even their clothing. If you break the code of silence there is a price to pay.[53]

Complacency towards violence and abuse would again appear to be a common experience within Aboriginal communities. As it was put by the Royal Commission:

> In too many Aboriginal communities, or among subgroups within Aboriginal communities, violence has become so pervasive that there is a danger of it coming to be seen as normal.[54]

It is suggested that a change of attitude towards sexual abuse has occurred within some communities, from one of abhorrence, to the acceptance of abuse and violence as a 'normal' part of daily life, even something to be proud of.[55]

---

of Child Sexual Abuse in Inuit Communities: The First Step Towards Healing. Ottawa: Pauktuuit. The shocking statistics on the sexual abuse of children are supported by those on violence against women. Nahanee claims that eight out of 10 native women have been sexually abused. A study of MicMac women revealed that 80 per cent had suffered physical abuse whilst a study conducted by Ontario's Native Women's Association found that 80 per cent of Aboriginal women had experienced violence and 57 per cent had been sexually abused. See, RCAPc, *supra* note 4, 58.

50 H. Nathan, 'Nightmare of the Shadow People', *Victoria Times – Colonist* (26 and 27 July 1992).

51 Ibid.

52 Judith Lavoie, 'Ex-Wife Differs with Band-Head on Abuse Issue', *Victoria Times – Colonist* (29 July 1992).

53 'Dorothy' – former Tsartlip Band member. Nathan, *supra* note 50.

54 RCAPc, *supra* note 4, 75.

55 Nathan, *supra* note 50.

Many communities have preferred to keep silent on the issue – a silence which has proved to be an enormous barrier to community healing.[56] The response of the South Island community leaders to the South Island reports exhibit strong signs of denial. It is reported that one local leader claimed he 'had never heard of any sexual abuse on his reserve. It is not a problem that we are aware of. It has not been reported to anyone I know'.[57] Another common response was to attack the behaviour of the women:

> Native Indian women worried about Indian self-government should go home to their communities and stop listening to white Toronto feminists. A lot of this is driven by the white women's movement. Instead of romping around with non-Indian women in Toronto, maybe they should be in their communities working with their people to make the changes they know have to be made.[58]

One explanation by another community leader for the concerns over the justice initiative and the resulting vulnerability of Aboriginal women was that women simply did not understand the true traditions of the community:

> I would feel intimidated too. That's because these women don't understand the native process.[59]

These responses denigrate the very real concerns of Aboriginal women. The refusal of some community leaders to take women's concerns over violence and abuse seriously undermines confidence in the capacity of the Aboriginal leadership to protect vulnerable women and children under self-governing political regimes. As two key inquiries have pointed out, community leaders and those with influence in the community have a critical role to play in addressing these issues.[60] There needs to be leadership from influential community members by giving a clear message to the communities that violence and abuse is unacceptable. By refusing to speak out against violence, the abuse is thereby condoned. However, the Aboriginal leadership are accused of compounding rather than helping to solve the problems:

> Although denial is rampant concerning Aboriginal male abusiveness, it is primarily men who have almost total power and control in Aboriginal communities e.g. Band Councils and Chiefs, male police, etc. These Aboriginal male leaders have protected each other and have collectively or collusively

---

56 RCAPb, *supra* note 13, 64.

57 Reported in, 'Ex-Wife Differs with Band-Head on Abuse Issue', *Victoria Times – Colonist* (29 July 1992).

58 Richard Watts, 'Whites Behind Woes', *Victoria Times – Colonist* (30 July 1992).

59 Gerald Young, 'Let Native Victims and Offenders Deal With Own Cases – Peninsula Leader', *Victoria Times – Colonist* (1 August 1992).

60 AJIM, *supra* note 5, 485, and RCAPc, *supra* note 4, 65–7.

> contributed to the violence against Aboriginal women and children through their inaction, ineptness, ineffectiveness or neglect.[61]

Problems with the current leadership are not restricted to the local level. Regional and national leaders have been equally muted on the question of sexual abuse and violence against Aboriginal children and women. As Justice Giesbrecht observed:

> The track record of the Assembly of Manitoba Chiefs on these issues is very poor and too often the response of the chiefs has been to play politics instead of addressing the problems, or to simply condemn governments for past injustices and then blame the absence of action on the problems of a "lack of resources".[62]

The Manitoba Justice Inquiry reached a similarly damning conclusion:

> The unwillingness of chiefs and council to address the plight of women and children suffering abuse at the hand of husband and father is quite alarming. We are concerned enough about it to state that we believe that the failure of Aboriginal government leaders to deal at all with the problem of domestic abuse is unconscionable. We believe that there is a heavy responsibility on Aboriginal leaders to recognise the significance of the problem within their own communities. They must begin to recognise as well, how much their silence and failure to act actually contribute to the problem.[63]

Many Aboriginal women similarly feel that the national leadership have ignored their concerns. Ovide Mercredi, the former leader of the Assembly of First Nations, has argued that the concerns of Aboriginal women will be answered when self-government is in place and the damaging colonial structures are dismantled.[64] However, he has been criticized for pressuring Aboriginal women to keep quiet.[65] This apparent opposition to women speaking out could be founded on the understandable fear of Aboriginal leaders that by raising issues of abuse and violence within the communities, the fight for self-government will be undermined. It is, however, suggested by some Aboriginal women that it finds its real basis in the fear of the male leadership that they will lose their privileged positions of power.[66]

---

61 Nahanee, *supra* note 23, 6–7.

62 OCME, *supra* note 5, 258.

63 Manitoba Justice Inquiry, cited in RCAPc, *supra* note 4, 66.

64 'Abuse Tales Prove Self-Rule Untimely', *Victoria Times – Colonist* (28 July 1992).

65 Ibid.

66 RCAPc, *supra* note 4, 78.

Band Councils and community leaders: internal colonialism

Problems surrounding the generally male dominated Aboriginal leadership have been particularly acute at the local Band level. These problems have been explained by a concept termed 'internal colonialism'.[67] It must be appreciated that many of the current difficulties surrounding the Aboriginal male leadership results from their own victimization and abuse at the hands of non-native governments.[68] These difficulties have been exacerbated by the imposition of a colonial system of government at the Band level and the indoctrination of Aboriginal men with a patriarchal understanding of dominance and power.[69] Hammersmith has argued that many Aboriginal leaders are now the paid agents of the colonial government and that instead of a sense of responsibility characteristic of traditional Indian leadership, money has become the bigger issue.[70] The colonial underpinnings of these problems do not, however, lessen the very real plight of Aboriginal women and children currently facing such high levels of violence and abuse.[71]

Local government officials on the reserves have come under particularly harsh criticism, not only for their silence on issues of abuse, but in some cases for their active participation as perpetrators of the violence and for protecting other known abusers from investigation and punishment.[72] This criticism is applied not only to the Chief and Council, but Elders who hold important positions of respect and influence within the community.[73] Nahanee argues that they too have been the perpetrators of violence and abuse:

> The role of male elders as perpetrators of violence and arbitrators needs serious examination. Aboriginal elders today abuse women and children within the community. Some Aboriginal women have been subjected to sexual, physical, emotional and psychological abuse in the form of "teaching". An Aboriginal elder is a person in a trust position with children and women, particularly when the elder is a grand-parent to the child s/he abuses, or a spiritual advisor to women within the community. If elders are to have a role in ending sexual, physical, emotional and psychological abuse within Aboriginal communities they must speak out and take a leadership role.[74]

---

67 Internal colonialism refers to a process by which an elite group of Aboriginal leaders have become 'allies' of the dominant system because of the privileges they enjoy by virtue of their cooperation with that system. See Boldt, *supra* note 13, 117–66.

68 OCME, *supra* note 5, 14.

69 B. McKenzie, reported by D. Roberts, 'Suicides Lead to Finger Pointing', *The Globe and Mail* (25 June 1992).

70 B. Hammersmith (1992). 'Aboriginal Women and Self-Government', in D. Engelstadt and J. Bird (eds) *Nation to Nation: Aboriginal Sovereignty and the Future in Canada*. Don Mills, Ontario: Anansi Press, 55–6.

71 OCME, *supra* note 5, 181.

72 Nathan, *supra* note 50.

73 Ibid.

74 Nahanee, *supra* note 23, 14.

The problem of ineffective Band Councils is often intensified by the domination of the Band Council by one or two powerful families. Victims argue that on some small isolated reserves, children and women are at the mercy of one or two powerful men, whose control is entrenched by the Indian Act's imposed system of 'elected' government.[75]

The death of Lester Desjarlais tragically exemplifies many of these concerns. One of the most debilitating problems DOCFS had to deal with was interference and manipulation by the Chief, Band Council and powerful members of the reserve.[76] As McGillivray points out, 'the structure invited nepotism'.[77] Political interference clearly prevented DOCFS from doing its job properly.[78] Throughout the time Lester was in the care of DOCFS, members of his extended family, who were powerful men on the reserve, were using their power to dictate to the agency if Lester should be apprehended, and, if taken, where he should be placed.[79] If they disagreed with a decision of DOCFS they would simply remove him by force.[80] The agency and its employees lacked the authority and the will to prevent this happening. Some of the child protection workers at the agency simply surrendered to the domination of these powerful men, becoming, in effect, allies in the efforts to prevent the sexual abuse of Lester from becoming public.[81] And Lester was not the only child affected. It is clear that throughout this period, certain children were 'off limits' to DOCFS because of the positions held by members of their extended family. The primary concern of Chief and Council was clearly not to protect the interests of the community's children, but to prevent the sexual abuse from being discovered. Their interference with the work of DOCFS even extended to ordering the destruction of individual child protection files containing allegations of sexual abuse, which, rather than being opposed by DOCFS, was defended before the Inquiry as a perfectly proper exercise of the Band Council's powers.[82]

The problems surrounding Band Councils and the male Aboriginal leadership again differ in severity from community to community and from individual to individual. In some communities women have achieved leadership roles and increasingly play an important role in Band level and national politics. Other communities have managed to retain more traditional forms of leadership.[83] Nevertheless, ineffective Band Councils would appear to be a widespread problem and pose a serious threat to the effective protection of children. These problems

75 'Ex-Wife Differs with Band-Head on Abuse Issue', *Victoria Times – Colonist* (29 July 1992); Young, *supra* note 59.

76 Issues of political interference are raised throughout the Inquiry but see especially, OCME, *supra* note 5, 210–32.

77 McGillivray, *supra* note 22, 164.

78 OCME, *supra* note 5, 210.

79 Ibid., 29–41.

80 Ibid., 35.

81 Ibid., 40.

82 Ibid., 71–80.

83 See, RCAPa, *supra* note 13, 279–80 and Boldt, *supra* note 13, 121–2.

have led some, although clearly not all, Aboriginal women to oppose moves to self-government out of fear that it will hand the abusers more power.[84] Sharon McIvor, a former spokeswoman for the Native Women's Association of Canada (NWAC), is reported as saying that the nightmare of the abused women on Vancouver Island proves Aboriginal men are not ready for self-government and that NWAC has been 'begging politicians of all colours not to abandon Canada's native women to the mercy of the men who govern band councils'.[85] Nahanee has also expressed fears over self-government, pointing out that Aboriginal women 'do not want to live under brown patriarchs who abuse power'.[86]

The place of tradition

Many Aboriginal people are of the view that the most effective way of addressing violence and sexual abuse within the communities is through a return to self-government informed by the traditional cultural values and practices of the communities.[87] Self-government is therefore seen as the answer to the problem; not a cause for concern. This places a great deal of faith in the potential of self-government and a return to 'tradition' to free Aboriginal peoples from the legacy of colonialism that has taken such a deep hold within their communities. An important part of the decolonization process has been a desire on the part of Aboriginal communities to reassert their distinctive identities free from the contaminating influence of colonial governments.[88] Tradition and a 'pure' form of pre-contact culture have consequently come to play a prominent role in providing meaning

84 For a good summary of the different positions taken by Aboriginal women on self-government, see Hylton, *supra* note 7, 187–93.

85 'Abuse Tales Prove Self-Rule Untimely', *Victoria Times – Colonist* (28 July 1992).

86 Nahanee, *supra* note 23, 19.

87 See, for example, the comments of Mary Ellen Turpel reported in: 'Reform Attacks Native Self-Rule', *The Globe and Mail* (5 October 1992). Nahanee agrees that, '[t]here needs to be a return to traditional ways, healing circles, and a sharing of power between men and women'. Nahanee, ibid., 9. Patricia Monture-Angus is a strong proponent of the need for a return to traditional values to inform contemporary Aboriginal governments. See, for example, P. Monture-Angus (1999). *Journeying Forward. Dreaming of First Nations Independence*. Halifax, NS: Fernwood Publishing. Marilyn Fontaine's submission to the RCAP on behalf of the Aboriginal Women's Unity Coalition, stated: 'We believe that true Aboriginal governments must reflect the values which our pre-contact governments were based upon.' See RCAPb, *supra* note 13, 125. Wendy Grant-John has expressed concern that NWAC's insistence on entrenching the Charter would, 'jeopardize key elements of traditional Native government, law and society'. See, Hylton, *supra* note 4, 188. For a discussion of NWAC's arguments concerning the need to return to traditional notions of Indian Motherhood, see L. E. Krosenbrink-Gelissen (1991). *Sexual Equality as an Aboriginal Right. The Native Women's Association of Canada and the Constitutional Process on Aboriginal Matters 1982 – 1987*. Nijmeegs Instituut voor Comparatieve Cultuur – en Ontwikkelingsstudies, 120–45.

88 H. Tiffin (1995). 'Post-Colonial Literature and Counter-Discourse', in B. Ashcroft, G. Griffiths and H. Tiffin (eds) *The Post-Colonial Studies Reader*. London: Routledge. See

and substance to the concept of self-government. However, the desire to inform contemporary Aboriginal governments by the practices and traditions of the past is not without difficulty.[89] Whilst some Aboriginal people place strong faith in the role of tradition, others are more sceptical, causing damaging conflict and factionalism within the communities. For some Aboriginal people, self-government creates the opportunity to address abuses in the community, not only by dismantling external colonial structures, but by pulling down the internal structures of colonialism and returning to traditional forms of government. Others, who tend to benefit from the imposed form of Indian Act government, are fighting this return to tradition. They want to build a future based on existing structures. Whilst this is a common starting point for decolonization, the real motivation behind this position may well be a concern to protect their current positions of privilege and power.

The continuing relevance of tradition to contemporary Aboriginal governments is also questioned by some Aboriginal women.[90] In particular, many Aboriginal women are concerned about a return to tradition which is imbued with colonial patriarchal prejudices that denies them equality as they understand the concept of equality today.[91] In their view, the question of whether women were equal in pre-contact Aboriginal cultures is irrelevant. The important point is the expectations of Aboriginal women for equality today.[92] By this view, Aboriginal people should be cautious about looking backwards and look forward to what is needed to meet the demands and desires of self-governing Aboriginal communities in the twenty-first century.

The contentious question of who will have the authority to define traditional practices and values is closely related to these concerns over equality and the current distribution of power within the communities. Tradition which is defined and implemented within the current colonial framework may well be vulnerable to distortion and abuse – even complete invention. Clearly, there is a risk that if those with the authority to determine 'tradition' are the very people who currently perpetuate violence within the communities, 'tradition' may simply be used to

---

also, Boldt, *supra* note 13, 195–203, for a critical account of the 'false hope' of many First Nations seeking to 'return to their past world'.

89 Boldt, ibid., 176–80 and 195–203.

90 See generally, E. Luther (2010). 'Whose "Distinctive Culture"? Aboriginal Feminism and *R. v. Van der Peet*', *Indigenous Law Journal*, 8: 27.

91 Ibid., 43. For a discussion of the fight of Aboriginal women to secure equality in contemporary Aboriginal societies, see: Krosenbrink-Gelissen, *supra* note 87; W. Moss (1990). 'Indigenous Self-government and Sexual Equality under the Indian Act', *Queen's L.J.*, 15: 279; D. Greschner (1992). 'Aboriginal Women, the Constitution, and Criminal Justice', *U.B.C. Law Rev.*, Aboriginal Justice Special Edition, 338; and J. Borrows (1994). 'Contemporary Traditional Equality: The Effect of the Charter on First Nations Politics', *University of New Brunswick Law Journal*, 43: 19.

92 Krosenbrink-Gelissen, ibid., 118. See also, Borrows, ibid.

mask oppression and justify abuse.[93] Moreover, in fighting oppression reinforced by 'tradition', victims will face an even more difficult task:

> Tradition is invoked by most politicians in defence of certain choices. Women must always ask – whose tradition? Is "tradition" beyond critique? How often is tradition cited to advance or deny our women's positions? ... Some Aboriginal men put forward the proposition that a return to traditional government would remedy the abusive and inequitable conditions of women's lives. We have no reason to put our trust in a return to "tradition", especially tradition that is defined, structured and implemented by the same men who now routinely marginalise and victimise us for political activism.[94]

The Desjarlais Inquiry provides a graphic illustration of the dangers of 'tradition' when manipulated and abused. In its evidence to the Inquiry, DOCFS tried to use 'tradition' to explain away its basic incompetence and complicity in the death of Lester. Evidence was even given to the Inquiry that protecting children from abuse was not consistent with the duties of an Aboriginal child welfare agency:

> [One child care worker] was constantly told that thoroughly investigating child abuse complaints was wrong and contrary to the "Indian way". In other words these things should simply be left alone.[95]

DOCFS also accused the Inquiry of being culturally insensitive for criticizing their decision not to remove Lester's sister from his mother's care, arguing that Aboriginal communities deal with sexual and physical abuse by methods other than removing the child from the home of the abuser.[96] However, in Justice Giesbrecht's opinion the agency was simply guilty of gross negligence and traditional practices were being misused as a shield to ward off legitimate criticism.[97] The chaos in which DOCFS' files were found was also explained by the fact that Aboriginal societies are characterized by an oral tradition. Consequently, it was argued that writing things down in files was contrary to traditional practices.[98] Again Justice Giesbrecht disagreed:

> When working on the file system of DOCFS, the Director should not let himself be diverted from his task by vague references to Aboriginal tradition being oral and not written, and other weak arguments. These are excuses only ... A child welfare agency that cannot keep proper files must not be allowed to continue

93 RCAPb, *supra* note 13, 125.
94 Ibid., 135.
95 OCME, *supra* note 5, 216.
96 Ibid., 134.
97 Ibid.
98 Ibid., 90–4.

> operating … Good file keeping is just as necessary for an Aboriginal agency as for a non-Aboriginal agency. Aboriginal workers are every bit as able to keep good notes and running records as other workers.[99]

Placing faith in tradition can also raise further difficulties for Aboriginal communities. Much of the uncertainty surrounding Aboriginal 'tradition' derives from the fact that the pressure wrought by non-native governments on Aboriginal communities was such that many traditions and cultural practices are no longer recognized or respected. To seek to re-establish traditional practices in a 'modernized', partly assimilated community, is very difficult and it cannot be too readily assumed that lost or seriously weakened traditions will be readily restored. In fact, some traditions may meet with active resistance from community members to whom such practices now seem inappropriate. It is therefore unrealistic and potentially harmful to rely on a pristine and perhaps idealized form of 'tradition' as the foundation of self-government when it bears little relation to contemporary community life.

Again, the danger of relying on traditional practices that lack a substantial foundation within the community's contemporary way of life is evidenced by the findings of the Desjarlais Inquiry. In their evidence to the Inquiry, DOCFS placed great emphasis on their policy of relying on the traditional responsibility of the extended family for raising Aboriginal children when making apprehension and placement decisions.[100] DOCFS argued that this reliance on the extended family justified their actions leading up to the death of Lester. The simple problem was that the extended family tradition had not survived the pressures of colonization in that particular community.[101] Justice Giesbrecht concluded that both the concept of extended family care and the notion of communal responsibility for children were completely absent from Sandy Bay. Thus, by relying on the extended family to care for Lester, DOCFS had effectively abandoned him.[102] At the very least, self-governing Aboriginal child welfare agencies will have to exercise considerable caution before relying on weakened traditional practices if individual children are not to be placed at risk.

The Failings of Dakota Ojibway Child and Family Services

The problems experienced by DOCFS in fulfilling its mandate to Aboriginal children, serves as an important warning of the challenges and obstacles that must be addressed by Aboriginal child welfare agencies if the safety and welfare of Aboriginal children is not to be jeopardized by the move to self-government. Internal difficulties, as well as the challenging context in which it was operating,

99 Ibid., 90–1.

100 Ibid., 24.

101 Ibid.

102 Ibid., 21 and 25.

had a profound effect on the ability of DOCFS to do its job. Its impotence in the face of these pressures provides sobering reading. In the words of Justice Giesbrecht, 'the agency that was supposed to be protecting the boy was compounding his agony. The Inmates were running the asylum'.[103]

Political interference was perhaps the biggest problem facing DOCFS. Community participation in the design and delivery of Aboriginal child welfare services can be of great benefit, but there is a fine and difficult line between the community being involved in policy formation and service delivery and inappropriate interference in the professional decisions of social workers by politicians and others. That line was very clearly crossed in Lester's case. The extent to which powerful members of the reserve were able to intervene in certain cases seriously undermined the professional independence of the staff at DOCFS and fundamentally compromised their ability to act fearlessly in the best interests of the children.

The problems with political interference at DOCFS were compounded by the obvious confusion that existed within DOCFS about the lines of authority between the agency and the community, particularly with respect to the local child welfare committee and the Band Council.[104] Neither the staff nor the community fully understood that the child welfare committee, which came to be dominated by reserve politicians, was intended only as an advisory body and did not hold any ultimate decision-making power.[105] There was equal confusion about the role of the Chief and the Council in child welfare matters, with Cecil Desjarlais, the Band Councillor holding the child welfare portfolio for the Sandy Bay reserve, believing that he had the authority to intervene in the work of DOCFS on behalf of community members and to overrule their decisions as he felt necessary.[106] The political domination of DOCFS by Band officials was exacerbated when in 1991 it was decided that the Regional Board of DOCFS would be composed of representatives from the Band Councils instead of, as originally envisaged, from the local child welfare committees.[107] When added to the problem that the Band Council were already dominating the local child welfare committee, it meant politicians and politics were 'now controlling the bottom, top and middle of the organization'.[108]

The ease with which local Band politicians were able to manipulate the child care workers at DOCFS was also symptomatic of another serious problem. One reason many of the staff were unable to withstand the political pressures being placed upon them was that they were seriously under-qualified and lacking in professional

103 Ibid., 36.

104 Again, the confusion of the community and the agency as to their respective roles and responsibilities is evident throughout the Inquiry but see especially, ibid., at 112–82.

105 Ibid., 160.

106 Ibid., 117–18.

107 Ibid., 167–9.

108 Ibid., 168.

experience.[109] The qualifications, training and experience of staff employed at DOCFS, where 'Aboriginality' and 'life experience' were deemed more important than formal qualifications, fell well below provincial levels and that which would be expected in non-Aboriginal child welfare agencies.[110] It is clearly desirable, wherever possible, for Aboriginal-controlled child welfare agencies to engage Aboriginal child care workers who are able to provide child protection services in a more culturally sensitive manner. The current lack of appropriately qualified Aboriginal social workers is therefore a difficult challenge for all child welfare agencies. However, child protection work is a difficult, highly-skilled profession for which qualifications and training are vitally important. In Lester's case, the lack of professional expertise and inexperience in child protection work amongst DOCFS staff made them vulnerable to the 'power politics' of Band members. This vulnerability was compounded by their failure to comply with sound child protection practice, such as their reliance on short-term, ad hoc placements rather than developing any kind of permanency plan for Lester.[111] Although many of the staff acted out of the very best of intentions, in following the orders of Chief and Council rather than exercising their independent professional judgments, their inexperience and, in some cases, basic incompetence in child protection work, was putting the lives of children at risk.

The Politicization of Child Welfare – Beyond the Desjarlais Inquiry

The death of Lester Desjarlais is a particularly shocking case and it is important not to indict all Aboriginal-controlled child welfare agencies and the communities they serve on the basis of this one tragedy. The majority of Aboriginal child welfare agencies do an excellent job in difficult, challenging circumstances.[112] However, concerns have arisen over the policies, procedures and practices of other Aboriginal-controlled child welfare agencies which again require careful consideration by Aboriginal communities as they move towards self-government. These concerns are closely tied to the political stance of Aboriginal communities on certain child welfare issues. The close relationship between local Aboriginal leaders and Aboriginal-controlled child welfare agencies, whilst not resulting in the extensive political interference witnessed in Sandy Bay, has led to the politicization of Aboriginal child welfare in a way that has sometimes been damaging to the interests of individual children. In some cases, rather than independently pursue their mandate to protect the interests of an individual child, agencies have been happy to adopt the community's position in which the interests of individual children have been marginalized or even completely ignored.

109 Ibid., 43–7 and 183–209.

110 Ibid., 184 and 189.

111 Ibid., 22–3.

112 AJIM, *supra* note 5, 532.

The case of *Jane Doe v Awasis Agency of Northern Manitoba*[113] provides one particularly striking example of how political concerns have been allowed to override the interests of an individual Aboriginal child. The child involved in this case was removed from her foster parents at the insistence of the Awasis Agency pursuant to their repatriation policy for all Aboriginal children who had been fostered out of the reserve. The Awasis Agency is a native-controlled child welfare agency again operating in Manitoba under provincial mandate. The child, who was then aged 13, had been living with her foster parents since birth. She was returned to the care and custody of her natural parents on an isolated reserve in Northern Manitoba even though she could not speak the native Dene language and her immediate family could not speak English. Communication was consequently extremely difficult and she was alienated within the community. On numerous occasions she was forcibly confined, sexually assaulted and raped by a number of male residents on the reserve.[114] As a result of the abuse she suffered, she contracted venereal disease and was finally removed six months later by a fly-in doctor. Whilst in hospital she was made a ward of court to prevent Awasis removing her again, and she was subsequently returned to her foster parents. What is most worrying about the case is that when the abuse was brought to the attention of the Awasis Agency, they did nothing to help her. It was their view that the interests of the child and the community were best served by keeping her on the reserve. Even when she was hospitalized, Awasis maintained the position that she should be returned to the reserve.[115] Whilst there are clearly strong reasons, both in the interests of individual Aboriginal children and the wider interests of Aboriginal communities, to keep Aboriginal children, wherever possible, on the reserve, in this instance the individual interests of the child were clearly sacrificed to the wider interests of the community in a way that is difficult to justify. The adoption of policies and practices aimed at redressing the damage caused to Aboriginal communities by the wrongful removal of their children is a perfectly legitimate function of Aboriginal child welfare agencies. However, these policies cannot be pursued at all costs. The dogmatic application of such a policy in this case, despite the substantial harm which was obviously being caused to the child, can be legitimately criticized as politicizing the issue and subordinating the welfare of an individual child in a wholly disproportionate manner to a wider political agenda.

Two more recent cases give rise to similar concerns about the dogmatic pursuit of policies and practices by Aboriginal child welfare agencies at the instigation of the communities they serve, regardless of the damage being caused to an individual child. Strong judicial criticism was levelled at DOCFS and the Swan Lake Band in *Winnipeg Child and Family Services v M.A. and G.R.*[116] for their unswerving

113 *Jane Doe v Awasis Agency of Northern Manitoba* (1989) 72 D.L.R. (4th) 739.

114 Ibid., 740.

115 A settlement was reached by which the Awasis agency paid general damages to the child of $75,000 for the physical and emotional injury that had been caused to her.

116 *Winnipeg Child and Family Services v M.A. and G.R.* (2002) MBQB 209.

adherence to a policy of withholding permission for any of the community's children to be adopted by non-Aboriginal families. In criticizing DOCFS and the Swan Lake Band for the stance they had chosen to adopt, it was clearly of importance that there was no alternative Aboriginal home available for the child. As Beard J observed, this was not therefore a case about the non-Aboriginal child welfare system preferring a non-Aboriginal family over an Aboriginal family. No Aboriginal family could be found for her. By refusing to give their consent to the adoption, DOCFS and the Swan Lake community were therefore depriving the child of a permanent, secure family in favour of the uncertainty of long-term foster care with non-Aboriginal carers – an outcome which neither fostered nor supported the child's Aboriginal identity more effectively than adoption nor served the wider interests of the community in any meaningful way. Moreover, in sticking rigidly to its policy on adoption, the court was clearly concerned at the indifference exhibited by the agency and the Band as to the impact of their position on the particular needs and interests of the child in question. As Beard J pointed out, neither DOCFS nor the community knew anything at all about the child and her individual circumstances. And although DOCFS had been notified as soon as the child was first apprehended and been given the right and opportunity to be involved in planning for her care, including helping to find a culturally appropriate placement, they had declined to do so. Similarly, the Swan Lake community committee had declined to participate in planning for the child and had been unable to make any proposals for a culturally appropriate placement. In fact, neither DOCFS nor the Swan Lake community participated at any stage of the proceedings, their only involvement being to refuse to give their consent to the adoption.[117] Again, DOCFS and the community in question can be fairly criticized for the way in which they acted in this case. When holding and exercising such significant power over the future welfare of a child, considerably more care and attention needs to be paid to the child's individual needs and circumstances at every stage of the proceedings.

A similar criticism can be levelled at the NASC Agency and the children's Band in the case of *Re R.T.*[118] Again, although the agency refused to consent to the adoption of the children by non-native families, there were no alternative Aboriginal homes available for them. Similarly, there was a certain disinterest shown in the individual fate of the children. Although the NASC Agency, as the Band's designated representative, was served with notice of the applications relating to the children, neither the agency nor the Band chose to take any part in the proceedings until the question of legal counsel for the children was raised.[119] There was of course nothing inherently unconstitutional about the policy of the Department of Community Resources and Employment (DCRE) to defer to the decision of the NASC agency and the children's Band over whether an adoption

117 Ibid., [23].

118 *Re R.T., M.T., M.A.T., A.L., and K.A.* (2004) SKQB 503.

119 Ibid., [72].

of a child by a non-Aboriginal carer should be allowed to proceed. The problem here lay with the way in which the agency and the Band were exercising that decision-making authority. If the community had exercised their powers in a more judicious fashion, had chosen to involve themselves in the court proceedings, had agreed to participate in planning for the children's care and, perhaps most importantly, had been able to produce any concrete proposals showing how they would be able to better protect the children's cultural needs if placed in long-term foster care, the Charter challenge to the DCRE's policy would have had very little substance. As it was, their dogmatic application of the policy, without regard to the individual circumstances of the child, meant it was being applied in an arbitrary and disproportionate manner, and in such a way that it was difficult to defend the criticism that the children's rights to equal treatment and to liberty and security of the person under ss 7 and 15 of the Canadian Charter were being infringed. The parties to this case can therefore again be legitimately criticized for unfairly sacrificing the individual interests of the children for largely historical and political reasons. What the case of *Re R.T.* clearly shows is that whilst the Canadian Charter may not be the most appropriate vehicle for safeguarding Aboriginal children, they can be just as vulnerable to the arbitrary, harmful and ill-judged decisions of their own communities, as they are to the decisions of the non-native authorities.

Australia: A Challenging Context for Self-Government

Australia has, as yet, no experience with Aboriginal-controlled child welfare agencies that can testify to either the risks or advantages of Aboriginal self-government. It is, however, clear that given the serious socio-economic and governance problems facing Australia's Aboriginal peoples, any attempts to restore community control over child welfare will face the same difficult challenges that have been experienced in Canada.[120] If anything, those challenges will be considerably worse. As in Canada, poverty,[121] high unemployment,[122]

120 As to community problems affecting the safety of children, see *Inquest into the death of Kunmanara Forbes* [2009] NTMC 24.

121 In 2001, the average gross household income for Aboriginal and Torres Strait Islander people in Australia was 38 per cent lower than the average income level for non-indigenous Australians. Moreover, this economic disparity is worsening. Between 1996 and 2001 the average household income for indigenous persons rose by 11 per cent compared with 13 per cent for non-indigenous Australians. See Human Rights and Equal Opportunity Commission (2006). *A Statistical Overview of Aboriginal and Torres Strait Islander Peoples in Australia.*

122 Ibid. In the 2001 census, the unemployment rate for Aboriginal people was approximately three times higher than the unemployment rate for non-indigenous Australians.

poor housing,[123] alcohol abuse, drug addiction and domestic violence continue to characterize the lives of many Aboriginal people:

> The disintegration of Aboriginal family support is reflected in domestic violence, poverty, shortened life expectancy, drinking, child neglect and fostering. What has been set in motion is a generational cycle of family breakdown. The socio-historical legacy of Aboriginal people is thus linked into the contemporary experience of a generation in which particular Aboriginal families are vulnerable.[124]

Alcohol abuse is having a particularly devastating effect on Aboriginal communities in Australia:

> Sickness and death, violence and despair, exclusion from education and meaningful employment, families and communities in disarray; we have observed all of this and have heard many Aboriginal people, those most affected, attributing this tragic state to alcohol.[125]

Again, as in Canada, the high level of alcohol and drug abuse is having a particularly devastating affect on the safety of Aboriginal children. The Northern Territory Board of Inquiry found that alcohol abuse, amongst other problems, increased the possibility that a person would sexually abuse a child; was making children, who were themselves increasingly abusing alcohol, vulnerable to abuse; led to decreased levels of supervision and protection by family members with children being neglected or 'forgotten'; and was leading, more generally, to a significant increase in physical violence, family dysfunction and cultural breakdown.[126]

Anecdotal evidence, particularly from Aboriginal women, would suggest that violence against both women and children within many Aboriginal communities

---

123 Ibid. In 2001, only 13 per cent of Aboriginal Australians owned their home outright as compared with 40 per cent of other households. Overcrowding remains a problem particularly in remote areas, as does infrastructure. In 2001, 48 per cent of indigenous communities with a population of 50 or more experienced overflows or leakages from the sewerage system.

124 Royal Commission into Aboriginal Deaths in Custody (RCADCa) (c. 1991). *National Report*, Vol. 2. Canberra: Australian Govt. Pub. Service, [11.11.19].

125 Ibid., [15.2.1]. See also, Northern Territory Government (2007). *Board of Inquiry into the Protection of Aboriginal Children from Sexual Abuse*. Darwin, NT: Government Printer, 16. It is important to note, however, that a 2001 ABS National Health Survey showed that Aboriginal people are actually less likely to consume alcohol than non-indigenous Australians: 56 per cent of Aboriginal Australians compared to 38 per cent of non-indigenous Australians reported that they did not drink alcohol. See HREOC, *supra* note 121. The difference seems to be that a higher proportion of Aboriginal people who do drink do so at harmful levels. See Northern Territory Government, ibid., 161.

126 Northern Territory Government, ibid., 161.

has now reached crisis point. Due to an absence of data it is difficult to ascertain the exact levels of violence with any kind of precision. It has, however, been estimated that in the Northern Territories in Australia, about one-third of Aboriginal women are assaulted every year.[127] The Northern Territory Board of Inquiry concluded that family violence in Aboriginal communities is 'disproportionately high', with the sexual abuse of Aboriginal children 'common, widespread and grossly under-reported'.[128] Similarly, the NSW Child Sexual Abuse Taskforce concluded that child sexual abuse was of 'epidemic' proportions in some Aboriginal communities.[129] A 2001 study carried out in NSW found that indigenous women are 6.2 times more likely than non-indigenous women to be a victim of domestic violence, 5.2 times more likely to be a victim of assault, 2.9 times more likely to be the victim of a sexual assault and 1.9 times more likely to be the victim of a murder.[130] The same study showed that Aboriginal children under the age of 15 are 1.4 times more likely to be the victim of a sexual assault.[131] A similar 2001 study in Western Australia reported that Aboriginal women were 13 times more likely to be a victim of assault and 3.3 times more likely to be a victim of sexual assault.[132]

Statistics such as these provide a stark and sobering reminder of just how difficult restoring Aboriginal control over child welfare will be without creating unacceptably high risks for the safety of Aboriginal children.

Conclusion

The Desjarlais Inquiry provides an important insight into some of the challenges, obstacles and risks that Aboriginal communities may face in moving towards self-government over child welfare. It is important not to lose sight of the benefits of self-government for Aboriginal communities, with self-government holding out the promise of healthier and more prosperous communities. Children will be the ultimate beneficiaries of this process of rejuvenation and rebuilding. However, as exemplified by the Desjarlais Inquiry, there are also problems. The complex and sometimes seemingly overwhelming problems faced by many Aboriginal communities in Australia and Canada give rise to an understandable concern that to proceed with self-government over child welfare is both reckless and irresponsible. Such concerns are, however, misplaced. The above analysis of the circumstances surrounding the tragic death of Lester Desjarlais is not intended as

127 RCADCa, *supra* note 124, [11.9.66].

128 Northern Territory Government, *supra* note 125, 16, 40 and 57.

129 Aboriginal Child Sexual Assault Taskforce (2006). *Breaking the Silence: Creating the Future – Addressing Child Sexual Assault in Aboriginal Communities in NSW*. Attorney General's Department, NSW, 49.

130 HREOC, *supra* note 121, 2006.

131 Ibid.

132 Ibid.

a basis for the argument that self-government should be resisted. Self-government is an inherent right of Aboriginal people that cannot, nor should it, be negated because its implementation carries certain risks. However, the above analysis does show that there are very serious difficulties in proceeding to self-government which should not be underestimated or ignored. If deaths such as that of Lester Desjarlais are to be avoided in the future, there is a need for self-government to proceed cautiously and with adequate safeguards for the protection of potentially vulnerable Aboriginal children in place. Achieving this delicate balance between, on the one hand, the inherent right of Aboriginal people to self-government and, on the other hand, ensuring adequate safeguards for the individual rights and interests of Aboriginal children, is not easy. In striving to find that balance, the achievements, as well as the failures and limitations of the Canadian approach, again hold a number of important lessons for both the Canadian and Australian governments.

Chapter 5
The Right to Self-Government and Protecting the Vulnerable: Balancing Rights under Canadian Constitutional Law

Introduction

The successful decolonization of Aboriginal child welfare in Canada can only be achieved by recognizing and respecting the inherent right of Aboriginal peoples to self-government. Despite the risks, self-government over child welfare must therefore remain the ultimate goal. The question is how that ultimate goal can be achieved whilst minimizing the risks to individual Aboriginal children. A balance needs to be found between affording proper respect to the right of Aboriginal peoples to self-government over child welfare on the one hand, whilst ensuring adequate safeguards for the rights of Aboriginal children on the other. In examining whether the Canadian government has got that balance right, the issue of child welfare cannot be looked at in isolation. It must be considered within the context of the wider right of Aboriginal peoples to self-government over all their internal affairs and the impact of the various limitations and restrictions that the Canadian government has sought to impose upon that right. Inevitably, the extent to which Aboriginal peoples are successful in establishing the broader right to self-government, and the manner in which that right is implemented, particularly the degree of autonomy and independence secured by Aboriginal governments, will determine the degree of control enjoyed by Aboriginal communities over child welfare and other related family law matters.

Unfortunately, the conclusions reached are not encouraging. As regards the respect afforded to the right of Aboriginal peoples to self-government, it is highly questionable whether the heavily qualified right to self-government advanced by the Canadian government and the Canadian courts can meet the aspirations of indigenous peoples for self-determination and decolonization and, therefore, whether it really provides a promising way forward for Aboriginal peoples within key areas of jurisdiction such as child welfare. The approach adopted to the equally vital question of ensuring adequate protection for the rights and interests of individual Aboriginal children is similarly disappointing. Whilst important progress has been made on Aboriginal self-government, the limitations and restrictions placed on the inherent right seriously undermine its potential to deliver effective decolonization. In particular, the Canadian government's imposed solutions for ensuring the protection of individual Aboriginal rights are not only unresponsive to the Aboriginal worldview but perpetuate a colonial mindset in which the fundamental norms and values of non-native society are further entrenched.

Self-Determination, Sovereignty and the Inherent Right to Self-Government

The moral, legal and political imperative for contemporary recognition of the inherent right to self-government can be found in the concept of self-determination. In simple terms, self-determination is the right of Aboriginal peoples to determine their own social, economic and political futures. It is closely tied to the decolonization process, providing the principal means by which historical wrongs can be put right and justice secured for colonized peoples. From the perspective of Aboriginal peoples, core to understanding the right to self-determination is the recognition contained therein of their inherent sovereignty over their people and their lands. This concept of sovereignty is important, for it means that Aboriginal peoples are subjected to no higher authority or power. In the context of child welfare it would mean the Aboriginal community could exercise unfettered authority and power over their own children.

Sovereignty is regarded by many Aboriginal people as a gift from the Creator.[1] Consequently, they believe that sovereignty cannot be shared, taken away, nor its basic terms negotiated.[2] From an Aboriginal perspective, neither the British Crown's unilateral assertion of sovereignty over Canadian territory nor subsequent attempts at extinguishment or infringement are capable of extinguishing the inherent right of Aboriginal peoples to sovereign autonomous government. The right persists despite the repeated attempts of external powers to extinguish it. As an inherent right flowing from sources within a people or nation, it has no dependence on such external legal or political sources.[3] Therefore, whilst many indigenous groups have embarked upon a long and difficult struggle to gain *recognition* of their right to self-determination, such recognition is in principle unnecessary. As it was put by Herb George of the Gitksan-Wet'suwet'en Nation in his evidence to the Royal Commission on Aboriginal Peoples:

---

1 Royal Commission on Aboriginal Peoples (RCAP) (1996). *Report of the Royal Commission on Aboriginal Peoples. Restructuring the Relationship*. Part One, Vol. 2. Ottawa: Minister of Supply and Services, Canada, 109. For Aboriginal perspectives on self-determination and sovereignty see F. Cassidy (ed.) (1991). *Aboriginal Self-Determination*. Lantzville: Oolichan Books, 33–84 and 111–23; D. Englelstad and J. Bird (eds) (1992). *Nation to Nation: Aboriginal Sovereignty and the Future of Canada*. Concord, Ontario: Anasi Press, 3–11 and 199–292; F. Cassidy and R. Bish (1991). *Indian Government: Its Meaning in Practice*. Lantzville: Oolichan Books, 32–9.

2 RCAP, ibid., 109.

3 Ibid.

> What is required here is not an inquiry of the current law or international law to determine the source of our rights. What is required here is the recognition that our rights exist in spite of what the common law says, and in spite of what have been the policies of this government to the present day. If this issue is to be dealt with in a fair way, then what is required is a strong recommendation from this Commission to government that the source of our right, the source of our lives and the source of our government is from us. That the source of our lives comes from Gitskan-Wet'suwet'en law.

The twin principles of self-determination and inherent Aboriginal sovereignty underpin contemporary arguments in favour of the inherent right to self-government. According to the view that prevailed until the 1980s, Aboriginal rights, including the right to self-government, were entirely contingent upon the goodwill of the Canadian government. The only rights that Aboriginal peoples could therefore claim were those that the federal and provincial governments were willing to grant them.[4] As Asch and Macklem explain, this had important implications for Aboriginal sovereignty and the fight of Aboriginal peoples for self-government:

> [U]nder a contingent theory of Aboriginal right, self-government is a label for a bundle of rights that attach to Native people as a result of legislative or executive action or constitutional amendment, and is not dependent upon a prior acceptance of First Nations sovereignty. In fact a contingent theory of Aboriginal right implicitly denies any assertion of First Nations sovereignty by viewing the existence or non-existence of Aboriginal rights, including rights of self-government, as dependent upon the exercise of Canadian sovereign authority.[5]

The inherent right theory proceeds from a very different premise. As Asch and Macklem explain, this approach to self-government is derived from the prior sovereignty of Aboriginal people:

> According to an inherent rights approach, First Nations sovereignty is a term used to describe the totality of powers and responsibilities necessary or integral to the maintenance and reproduction of Aboriginal identity and social organization. Under an inherent rights theory, First Nations sovereignty and Aboriginal forms of government, as the means by which Aboriginal identity and social organisation are reproduced, pre-existed the settlement of Canada and continue to exist notwithstanding the interposition of the Canadian state.[6]

---

4 M. Asch and P. Macklem (1991). 'Aboriginal Rights and Canadian Sovereignty: An Essay on *R v Sparrow*', *Constitutional Studies*, XXIX: 498, 501–2.

5 Ibid., 502.

6 Ibid., 503.

The inherent right to self-government, of which self-government over child welfare would be a central component, therefore arises from within the inherent sovereignty of Aboriginal communities. It does not rely upon grant or recognition from the governments of Canada and, as a right which is neither created by, nor devolved from, the Canadian government, the Canadian government should not, in theory, be able to dictate its meaning and scope.

Surprisingly, the Canadian legal and political establishment would seem to accept that the Aboriginal peoples of Canada have an 'inherent right to self-government' which, since 1982, has been protected under s 35 of the Canadian Constitution.[7] This position was unequivocally endorsed by the Royal Commission on Aboriginal Peoples in 1996[8] and, most significantly, has been the official policy of the Canadian federal government since 1995.[9] The Federal Policy Guide for Aboriginal Self-Government thus provides:

> The Government of Canada recognises the inherent right of self-government as an existing Aboriginal right under section 35 of the Constitution Act, 1982. It recognises as well, that the inherent right may find expression in treaties, and in the context of the Crown's relationship with treaty First Nations. Recognition of the inherent right is based on the view that the Aboriginal peoples of Canada have the right to govern themselves in relation to matters that are internal to their communities, integral to their unique cultures, identities, traditions, languages, and institutions, and with respect to their special relationship to their land and resources.[10]

The federal government's apparent acceptance that the right to self-government is an inherent right protected under the Constitution and that, pursuant to that right, Aboriginal peoples have the right to govern themselves on all matters such as child welfare which are internal to their communities, seems to promise much. However, as the substance of this promise has been subjected to the intensive scrutiny of various legal and political processes, it has become clear that the reality of what is envisaged by the Canadian authorities falls a long way short of what Aboriginal peoples demand by way of self-determination and sovereignty.

---

7 That is not to say that there does not remain strong opposition to Aboriginal self-government amongst some sectors of Canadian society. See, for example, M. Smith (1995). *Our Home or Native Land? What Government's Aboriginal Policy is doing to Canada.* Victoria BC: Crown Western and *Campbell v British Columbia (Attorney General)* [2000] 4 C.N.L.R. 1.

8 See especially, RCAP, *supra* note 1, 166–8, 186–213 and 240–4.

9 Canada, Department of Indian Affairs and Northern Development (1995). *Federal Policy Guide for Aboriginal Self-Government. The Government of Canada's Approach to Implementation of the Inherent Right and the Negotiation of Aboriginal Self-Government.* Ottawa: Supply and Services.

10 Ibid., 3.

The inherent right to self-government has the potential to be extremely expansive in scope. The inherent right approach, particularly when founded on the principles of self-determination and Aboriginal sovereignty, would support wide autonomy for Aboriginal peoples with extensive governmental powers over internal, and possibly also external, matters. It also renders uncertain the sovereign authority of the Canadian government to circumscribe those powers in accordance with its own agenda. At its most extreme, arguments supporting the inherent right could be used to justify Aboriginal peoples unilaterally asserting their independence from Canada.[11] The Canadian authorities have therefore adopted an alternative approach to self-government which seeks to distance the inherent right theory from the problematic concepts of self-determination and sovereignty. This approach, which reflects the common law position on Aboriginal rights, is closely tied to the historical process of settlement and the political and legal response of the colonial authorities to the fact that Aboriginal peoples were in prior occupation of the territory. The argument here focuses on the fact that Aboriginal peoples were living as organized socio-political entities exercising sovereign powers over their own people prior to the arrival of the Europeans. To this extent, the rights are therefore inherent; finding their source from within pre-contact Aboriginal communities themselves. However, whilst it is recognized that the facts of prior occupancy and prior sovereignty justify continuing recognition, and indeed constitutional protection, of distinct Aboriginal rights, those rights are understood to exist subject to the Crown's unilateral assertion of sovereignty over Aboriginal peoples and their territory. Aboriginal rights, including the inherent right to self-government over child welfare, must thus be exercised within the legal and political framework of Canada and are ultimately subject to the overriding authority of the Crown. The inherent right is still a subordinate right.

At the heart of the debate over Aboriginal self-government is thus a fundamental impasse between the Canadian authorities and Aboriginal communities as to the scope and meaning of the 'inherent right' policy. Clearly, the Canadian authorities have been willing to engage with the language of the inherent right. However, fearful of the potentially explosive political, legal and economic fallout, they have not been prepared to countenance any claims to Aboriginal sovereignty that may pose a challenge to the ultimate sovereignty of the Canadian government. For their part, Aboriginal leaders have been at pains to stress that they wish to remain part of the constitutional framework of Canada. However, pursuant to their right to self-determination, they wish to negotiate their way into Canadian federalism on very different terms and with a very different status from that currently enjoyed.[12] What Aboriginal peoples are demanding is recognition of their inherent sovereignty,

11 P. Macklem (1996). 'Normative Dimensions on the Right of Aboriginal Self-Government' in Royal Commission on Aboriginal Peoples, *Aboriginal Self-government. Legal and Constitutional Issues*. Ottawa: Ministry of Supply and Services, Canada, 29.

12 S. Graben (2007). 'The Nisga'a Final Agreement: Negotiating Federalism', *Indigenous Law Journal*, 6: 63, 87–8.

that they have been the victims of colonization and that the unilateral assertion of British sovereignty over their people and their lands is without legal or moral foundation. For them, the inherent right to self-government means decolonization.

Given the political impasse surrounding this 'clash of sovereignty', Aboriginal peoples have turned to the Canadian courts to help determine the scope and meaning of their inherent rights as now protected under s 35 of the Canadian Constitution. However, as the Supreme Court of Canada's jurisprudence on Aboriginal issues demonstrates, Aboriginal people have had an uneasy relationship with the Canadian legal system. Whilst enjoying some key victories, Aboriginal peoples have ultimately faced a politically astute Court unwilling to engage with the more fundamental questions of Aboriginal and Canadian sovereignty and the implications of this sovereignty debate for the inherent right of Aboriginal peoples to self-government.

Self-Government in the Courts

The Constitutional Framework

In 1982, the context of the debate over Aboriginal peoples' right to self-government changed dramatically. For the first time, Aboriginal rights were afforded constitutional protection under s 35 of the Constitution Act 1982.[13] Constitutional entrenchment of Aboriginal rights was a fundamentally important step. It meant that the distinctive rights of Canada's Aboriginal peoples were no longer wholly dependent on the will of the Canadian government, enjoying, for the first time, substantive protection from unilateral extinguishment and any further encroachment by the Canadian authorities. As regards self-government, the key question thus became whether the inherent right to self-government was 'an existing Aboriginal or treaty right' attracting constitutional protection under s 35. In 1995, the federal government finally accepted that this was indeed the correct constitutional position. However, as a constitutional right protected under s 35 of the Constitution, it ultimately falls to the Supreme Court and not the federal government to determine the substantive scope and content of the right, as well as the legitimacy of any limitations the federal government may seek to place upon it. Achieving judicial recognition of the inherent right to self-government under s 35, which would automatically include within its scope self-government over core internal matters such as child welfare, has therefore been an issue of vital importance for Aboriginal peoples.

13 Section 35 provides: 'The existing Aboriginal and treaty rights of the Aboriginal peoples of Canada are hereby recognised and affirmed.'

The Right to Self-Government and the Canadian Supreme Court

Establishing an Aboriginal right under s 35

Securing the Supreme Court's approval of the constitutional argument that the inherent right to self-government falls within the scope of s 35 of the Constitution would constitute a major breakthrough for Aboriginal people. However, the Supreme Court has a variable record on Aboriginal issues and has proved particularly disappointing on the question of self-government. In setting down the basic framework for establishing an Aboriginal right under s 35, the Supreme Court's decision in *R v Sparrow* (1990),[14] its first as to the scope and meaning of Aboriginal rights under s 35, seemed to hold out significant promise that the inherent right to self-government could be found to fall within its scope. Dickson CJ and La Forest J, giving judgment, at least appeared to begin from an inherent rights approach, holding that Aboriginal rights were not contingent on executive or legislative action but found their source from within the laws, customs and practices of Aboriginal peoples themselves.[15] In determining whether or not an Aboriginal right was still 'existing' for the purposes of attracting constitutional protection under s 35, the Court held that the term 'existing' meant simply those rights which were in existence, i.e. had not been extinguished, when the Constitution Act 1982 came into effect. This meant any Aboriginal rights that had previously been extinguished were not revived by the new Constitutional provisions.[16] However, the court went on to hold that regulation of the right, even if extensive, did not constitute extinguishment. In order for the right to be effectively extinguished there needed to be 'a clear and plain intention' to extinguish by the Sovereign.[17] Detailed regulation did not, in their view, demonstrate such a clear and plain intent. Furthermore, the Supreme Court held that existing Aboriginal rights enjoying constitutional protection under s 35 were not to be restrictively defined in accordance with the regulations then in force. To do so would, in the Supreme Court's now infamous phrase, 'incorporate into the Constitution a crazy patchwork of regulations'.[18] Moreover, the Supreme Court emphasized that existing Aboriginal rights must be interpreted in a contemporary form to allow their evolution over time.[19] In other words, Aboriginal rights were not to be 'frozen' as they were at a particular point in history; they were part of living cultures in which evolution, development and change were to be recognized and respected.

---

14 [1990] 1 S.C.R. 1075.

15 Ibid., 1094–5. Subsequent Supreme Court decisions have confirmed the inherent rights approach. See, e.g., *R v Van der Peet* [1996] 2 S.C.R. 507, [30]–[31] (per Lamer CJ); [106], [112] (per L'Heureux-Dube J); [230], [247] (per McLachlin J). For discussion see Asch and Macklem, *supra* note 4, esp. at 505–7.

16 [1990] 1 S.C.R. 1075, 1091.

17 Ibid., 1099.

18 Ibid., 1091.

19 Ibid., 1093.

All of this augured well for the argument that the inherent right to self-government was an existing Aboriginal right under s 35 of the Constitution.[20] The factual basis for establishing such a claim – Aboriginal peoples' prior occupation of the land in organized 'self-governing' societies – appeared relatively straightforward. The Supreme Court found no difficulty, for example, in concluding that the Musqueam had 'lived in the area as an organized society long before the coming of European settlers'.[21] Applying the principle from *Sparrow*, although any Aboriginal powers of self-government which had been successfully extinguished by the Canadian government prior to 1982 could not be revived, even extensive regulation of an Aboriginal community's self-governing powers would not amount to extinguishment if lacking the requisite clear and plain intent.[22] Furthermore, once established, the right to self-government could be given expression in contemporary form, allowing Aboriginal communities to respond and adapt as they deemed appropriate to the political, economic, social and cultural needs of Aboriginal peoples living in modern-day Canada: the right to self-government would not, in other words, be tethered to seventeenth-century conceptions of governance. Unfortunately, subsequent cases seeking to interpret and apply the Supreme Court's approach to establishing an Aboriginal right under s 35 have not delivered on the promise of *Sparrow*.

The majority decision of the Supreme Court in *R v Van der Peet* has played a crucial role in narrowing the range of Aboriginal rights which are likely to be successfully established under s 35.[23] *Van der Peet* focused on how Aboriginal rights were to be identified and defined for the purposes of determining whether they were 'existing' for the purposes of s 35 – a question which did not arise for direct consideration in *Sparrow*. Lamer CJ, giving judgment for the majority, began by setting out the context within which the protection afforded to Aboriginal rights under s 35 must be understood. A number of positive factors emerged from this discussion. Lamer CJ emphasized that a purposive approach must be taken to the interpretation of Aboriginal rights, with the Crown's fiduciary obligation to Aboriginal peoples dictating that a 'generous and liberal interpretation is adopted' and that any doubts or ambiguities as to whether a claimed right falls within the

20 See generally J. Borrows (2005). 'Tracking Trajectories: Aboriginal Governance as an Aboriginal Right', *UBC Law Review*, 38: 285. The more problematic aspects of the *Sparrow* decision will be considered below. Note some commentators have always been sceptical that an Aboriginal right to self-government will be found under the framework provided by *Sparrow*. See M. Asch (1992). 'Aboriginal Self-Government and the Construction of Canadian Constitutional Identity', *Alberta Law Review*, XXX: 465, 476–80 and W. I. C. Binnie (1990). 'The Sparrow Doctrine: Beginning of the End or End of the Beginning?', *Queens Law Journal*, 15: 217. For a slightly more optimistic analysis see Asch and Macklem, *supra* note 4, esp. at 506.

21 *R v Sparrow* [1990] 1 S.C.R. 1075, 1094.

22 For example, under the Indian Act 1868. For discussion see Binnie, *supra* note 20, 233 and Borrows, *supra* note 20.

23 *R v Van der Peet* [1996] 2 S.C.R. 507.

scope of s 35 being resolved in favour of Aboriginal peoples.[24] However, from the outset, Lamer CJ also made it clear that because Aboriginal rights were held by Aboriginal peoples precisely because they were Aboriginal, they must in some way be rooted in what it means to be Aboriginal.[25] This demanded, in his view, a necessary degree of specificity in defining the rights in question.[26] When combined with the necessity to 'capture' what is essentially 'Aboriginal' in the right, this resulted in a very restrictive test for the purpose of identifying and establishing Aboriginal rights under s 35.

According to Lamer CJ, the core purpose of s 35 is to protect the distinctive interests of Aboriginal people arising from the fact that they were in occupation of the land living in organized societies with their own practices, customs and traditions prior to the arrival of the Europeans. In his view, the test for establishing Aboriginal rights must therefore be directed at identifying what were the crucial or central elements of those pre-contact societies.[27] Picking up on the language used by the Supreme Court in *Sparrow*, he thus held that in order to be an Aboriginal right, 'an activity must be an element of a practice, custom or tradition *integral to the distinctive culture* of the Aboriginal group claiming the right' (emphasis added).[28] Before this can be determined, however, the applicant's claim must first be characterized correctly. Although Lamer CJ emphasized that the activities in question must be 'considered at a general rather than a specific level' and the court must be sensitive to the fact that the activity may be the contemporary form of a pre-contact practice, custom or tradition, in characterizing the Aboriginal right in question Lamer CJ held that a degree of precision would be required. The courts are thus directed to consider such factors as 'the nature of the action which the applicant is claiming was done pursuant to an Aboriginal right, the nature of the governmental regulation, statute or action being impugned, and the practice, custom or tradition being relied upon to establish the right'.[29] The Aboriginal perspective on characterizing the custom, tradition or practice in question must also be considered,[30] although the Aboriginal right must still remain cognizable to the non-native legal system.[31]

Once the right has been characterized correctly, the court can move on to determine whether the practice, custom or tradition was 'integral to the distinctive culture' of the Aboriginal group. The fact that the claimant can show that the custom, practice or tradition was in existence at the relevant time is not sufficient;

24 Ibid., [24]–[25] (per Lamer CJ); [144] (per L'Heureux-Dube J); [232] (per McLachlin J).

25 Ibid., [20].

26 Ibid., [20].

27 Ibid., [44].

28 Ibid., [46].

29 Ibid., [53].

30 See also, ibid., [145] (per L'Heureux-Dube J).

31 Ibid., [49].

it will be for the claimant to prove that it was a 'central and significant part of the society's distinctive culture'.[32] Lamer CJ expressed the test in several different ways: that the practice, custom or tradition must have been a 'distinguishing' or 'defining feature' of the Aboriginal society or 'one of the things that truly made the society what it was'.[33] It is clear that a custom, practice or tradition that was only 'incidental or occasional' to that society would not be sufficient to meet this criteria.[34] Moreover, although the custom, tradition or practice need not have been distinct in the sense of unique to the culture in question,[35] as an *Aboriginal* right, it must have been something which set the society apart from the European settlers, thus apparently excluding aspects of Aboriginal culture which are common across societies.[36] Lamer CJ also demands a high degree of cultural specificity in proving the factual basis for every claim. Thus it is clear that the existence of Aboriginal rights cannot be determined on a general basis. Every claimed Aboriginal right must be specifically rooted in the cultural practices of the particular Aboriginal community claiming the right. The specific history of each Aboriginal community will therefore need to be examined before it can be determined whether a particular custom, practice or tradition was 'integral to their distinctive culture' – a difficult, time-consuming and hugely expensive process. In practical terms, this means that the 'fact that one group of Aboriginal people has an Aboriginal right to do a particular thing will not be, without something more, sufficient to demonstrate that another Aboriginal community has the same Aboriginal right'.[37]

Timing is also crucially important in satisfying Lamer CJ's 'integral to a distinctive culture' test. Although Lamer CJ emphasized that the practice, custom or tradition, having evolved over time, may be expressed in a contemporary form, the claimant must be able to show that the practice, custom or tradition from which the contemporary right has evolved was integral to the Aboriginal community prior to contact with the European settlers.[38] Continuity between the contemporary practice and its existence pre-contact must thus be established by the claimant. Any practice, tradition or custom which has arisen post-contact or as a result of interaction with non-Aboriginal cultures, will fall outside the scope of s 35.[39] Lamer CJ argues that although this approach roots Aboriginal rights in historical practices, the doctrine of continuity prevents a 'frozen rights' approach.[40]

The majority decision of the Supreme Court in *Van der Peet* laid the foundations for a series of disappointing decisions on Aboriginal rights. The 'integral to a

32 Ibid., [55].
33 Ibid., [55].
34 Ibid., [56]
35 Ibid., [71].
36 Ibid., [56].
37 Ibid., [69].
38 Ibid., [60]–[61].
39 Ibid., [73].
40 Ibid., [64].

distinctive culture' test has proved extremely restrictive for claimants seeking to establish an Aboriginal right under s 35, including the right to self-government.[41] The first problem has been with Lamer CJ's stringent requirement to prove that the relevant customs, practices and traditions existed at the point of first contact. L'Heureux-Dube J argued in her dissent in *Van der Peet* that to restrict s 35 to customs, practices and traditions that existed at the point of contact was contrary to the actual wording of s 35 which makes no mention of any arbitrary 'cut-off' point.[42] Indeed, in her view, by specifically including the Métis peoples within the scope of s 35, the legislature must have specifically contemplated the inclusion of customs, practices and traditions arising post-contact and as a direct result of interaction between Aboriginal and non-Aboriginal cultures.[43] Moreover, although Lamer CJ argued that his approach avoided the problem of 'frozen rights', it is clearly a backward-looking process which privileges Aboriginal cultures as they existed at a somewhat arbitrary point in history.[44] As it was put by L'Heureux-Dube J in her dissent, '[d]efining existing Aboriginal rights by referring to pre-contact or pre-sovereignty practices, traditions and customs implies that Aboriginal culture was also crystallized in some sort of "Aboriginal time" prior to the arrival of Europeans'.[45] It forces the Aboriginal claimant to 'embark upon a search for a pristine Aboriginal society', freezing Aboriginal communities in a 'museum-like' state.[46] Thus, although those traditions, practices and customs existing at the relevant point in history are permitted to develop and evolve, post-contact traditions, customs and practices resulting from normal evolutionary processes, regardless of how significant they may be for the community in question, are denied constitutional recognition.

That said, the much maligned requirement that the custom, tradition or practice supporting the claimed Aboriginal right must have been integral to the distinctive culture of Aboriginal peoples at the point of first contact, is not necessarily fatal to a claim for self-government, including a claim to self-government over child welfare. The Supreme Court in *Van der Peet* again acknowledged that at the point of first contact Aboriginal communities were living in distinct organized societies with their own legal and political structures. It is likely that those structures would have included some mechanism for protecting the community's children. Consequently, whilst those legal and political structures may well have changed dramatically following contact with the European colonial powers, the essential

41 *R v Pamajewon* [1996] 2 S.C.R. 821.

42 This is echoed by McLachlin J in *R v Van der Peet* [1996] 2 S.C.R. 507, [247].

43 [1996] 2 S.C.R. 507, [169].

44 For an excellent critique see J. Borrows (1997). 'The Trickster: Integral to a Distinctive Culture', *Constitutional Forum*, 8: 27, esp. at 28–9. See also R. Barsh and J. Y. Henderson (1997). 'The Supreme Court's Van der Peet Trilogy: Naïve Imperialism and Ropes of Sand', *McGill Law Journal*, 42: 993, 1001–2.

45 [1996] 2 S.C.R. 507, [165].

46 Ibid., [168].

factual basis for a claim to self-government can be traced back to a pre-contact point in history.

Lamer CJ's restrictive approach to the question of how Aboriginal rights are to be characterized and defined has proved much more problematic for a claim to self-government. In order to establish an Aboriginal right, the majority approach in *Van der Peet* requires the court to focus on very specific practices, traditions or customs of the Aboriginal community in question. This approach was again subjected to strong criticism by L'Heureux-Dube J in her dissent. She argued that to separate discrete parts of Aboriginal culture from the general culture of which they form part is a highly artificial process.[47] She therefore advocated a more generic approach that defines Aboriginal rights at a fairly high level of generality and abstraction, protecting 'not a catalogue of individualized practices, traditions or customs' but 'the "distinctive culture" of which Aboriginal activities are manifestations'.[48] McLachlin J, in her dissenting judgment, echoed this concern, arguing that Lamer CJ had focused too narrowly on the specific way in which a right is exercised at a particular point in time, rather than the broader underlying right, the exercise of which may vary considerably over time and place.[49]

L'Heureux-Dube also expressed strong concern about the way in which Lamer CJ's characterization of Aboriginal rights focused too narrowly on aspects of Aboriginal culture which could be said to be 'distinctly Aboriginal'. This has an extremely restrictive effect on the protection afforded to Aboriginal cultures, with Aboriginal cultures being literally defined as 'that which is left over after features of non-Aboriginal cultures have been taken away'.[50] To put it another way, only that which is not 'non-Aboriginal' can be 'Aboriginal'. This clearly poses difficulties for aspects of Aboriginal culture, such as governance structures and mechanisms for protecting vulnerable children, which are shared in general terms with non-Aboriginal societies. It is difficult to conceptualize the right to self-government either generally or more specifically with respect to child welfare as something distinctly Aboriginal, although the way in which self-government or certain aspects of it are implemented within Aboriginal communities may well be (such as the use of the extended family within many Aboriginal communities to protect children). L'Heureux-Dube J contends that a more holistic approach would afford much greater integrity and respect to Aboriginal cultures:

> The practices, traditions and customs protected under s 35(1) should be those that are sufficiently significant and fundamental to the culture and social organization of a particular group of Aboriginal people … Put another way, the Aboriginal practices, traditions and customs which form the core of the lives of native people and which provide them with a way and means of living as

47 See also Barsh and Henderson, *supra* note 44, 1000–1.

48 [1996] 2 S.C.R. 507, [157].

49 Ibid., [238]–[241].

50 Ibid., [154].

> an organized society will fall within the scope of the constitutional protection under s. 35(1).

The right to self-government would clearly sit much more comfortably within this broader more generic approach.

Section 35 and the right to self-government

The more recent decision of the Supreme Court in *R v Sappier; R v Gray* (2006),[51] has softened some of the harsher effects of Lamer CJ's judgement in *Van der Peet*, emphasizing that 'distinctive' does not mean unique,[52] or that it is the single most important defining character of the society,[53] or that the culture would be 'fundamentally altered without it'.[54] Moreover, the courts' focus, according to Bastarache J, should be on the distinctive features of the 'pre-contact way of life of a particular Aboriginal community' rather than on highly specific discrete activities.[55] Nevertheless, despite the Supreme Court's move to a less restrictive interpretation of *Van der Peet*, the integral to a distinctive culture test remains firmly entrenched in Canadian law and has been applied in subsequent cases relating to self-government with predictably disappointing results. The question of whether the inherent right to self-government would be excluded from the scope of s 35 by Lamer CJ's restrictive approach in *Van der Peet* was answered in the case of *R v Pamajewon*.[56] Whilst both *Sparrow* and *Van der Peet* were concerned with fishing rights, *R v Pamajewon* was directly concerned with the right to self-government. The case concerned an attempt by the Shawanaga First Nation and the Eagle Lake First Nation to pass laws purporting to establish a range of gambling activities on the reserve. The appellants were charged with gambling related offences contrary to the Criminal Code. The Shawanga First Nation challenged the convictions asserting an inherent right to self-government. The Eagle Lake First Nation conceptualized the right more narrowly, arguing that they had an inherent right to be self-regulating in their economic activities. The Supreme Court gave relatively short shrift to the claims. Lamer CJ, giving judgment for the majority, held that the issue was to be determined in accordance with the test laid down in *Van der Peet*, the first stage of which was to accurately characterize the right in question. The court could then go on to determine whether that activity was a

51 *R v Sappier*; *R v Gray* [2006] 2 S.C.R. 686.

52 Ibid., [45]. So the fact that another society would have adopted similar methods of survival or governance at that particular time and faced with that particular environment does not preclude a finding of distinctiveness.

53 Ibid., [40].

54 Ibid., [41]. For commentary on this decision see J. McEvoy (2007). 'Aboriginal Activities and Aboriginal Rights: A Comment on *R v Sappier; R v Gray*', *Indigenous Law Journal,* 6: 1, esp. at 14–20.

55 Ibid., [45].

56 [1996] 2 S.C.R. 821.

defining feature of the culture of the Shawanga and Eagle Lakes peoples.[57] The claim to self-government fell at the first hurdle. In characterizing the claim, Lamer CJ held that the Aboriginal right in question was not a right to self-government but the right to participate in, and to regulate, high stakes gambling activities on the reservation.[58] To characterize the claim as a right to self-government was, in Lamer CJ's view, to conceptualize the right at an excessive level of generality.[59] In order to conduct the necessary enquiry into whether the claimed Aboriginal right was integral to the specific history and culture of the group in question, Lamer CJ held that the claim had to be broken down into the specific aspect of self-government being claimed – here, the right to participate in and regulate on-reserve gambling. Generic claims to self-government would not be entertained.[60] Once the right had been characterized in this way, the Supreme Court found it relatively easy to dispose of the matter. Although they accepted the evidence given at trial that, at the point of contact, the Ojibwa participated in informal gaming activities, the Court did not accept that the regulation of large-scale commercial gambling activities, a 'twentieth century phenomena', was ever of central significance to the culture of the Ojibwa people.

The Supreme Court's decision in *Pamajewon* precludes the courts from even entertaining a claim that the Aboriginal peoples of Canada have an inherent right to self-government protected under s 35 of the Constitution.[61] Such claims will simply be dismissed as overly broad and general. It remains possible that individual components of a self-governing regime, such as the right to self-government over child welfare, will be deemed sufficiently particularized to be justiciable under s 35.[62] However, for Aboriginal communities hoping that judicial recognition of the

57 Ibid., [25].

58 Ibid., [26].

59 Ibid., [27].

60 L'Heureux-Dube J, who gave a separate judgment, was prepared to characterize the right more broadly. In her view the correct characterization of the right was the 'right to gamble'. However, despite her more open approach in *Van der Peet*, she agreed with the majority that to characterize the claim as the right to self-government was overly broad. She also agreed with the majority that gambling was not 'connected enough to the self-identity and self-preservation of the appellants' Aboriginal societies to deserve the protection of s 35(1)'. Ibid., [38]–[40].

61 See, for example, *Mississaugas of Scugog Island First Nation v National Automobile, Aerospace, Transportation and General Workers Union of Canada* (2007) ONCA 814, [47].

62 With respect to self-government over child welfare, see discussion below. See also *Mississaugas of Scugog Island First Nation v National Automobile, Aerospace, Transportation and General Workers Union of Canada*, ibid., in which the First Nation failed in its attempt, pursuant to its right of Aboriginal self-government, to 'establish the legal right to enact its own code of labour law to govern collective bargaining in relation to a commercial undertaking'. Having characterized the right in issue as 'the right to regulate labour relations on aboriginal lands', and applying *Pamajewon*, the Ontario Court of Appeal held that there was 'no evidence of an aboriginal practice, custom or tradition that supports

inherent right to self-government would assist in advancing their position at the negotiation table, the Supreme Court seems, at least for now, to have firmly closed that door.[63]

Self-government over child welfare

As noted above, the Supreme Court's disappointing jurisprudence on Aboriginal self-government does not preclude a successful claim being brought on the more specific question of whether self-government over child welfare constitutes an Aboriginal right under s 35. However, the limited case law on this more specific question has in fact been equally disappointing. In 2000, the parents of an Innu child attempted to challenge the constitutionality of the Youth Protection Act P. 34.1 on the grounds that it infringed the inherent right of the Innu Nation to self-government over all matters concerning the protection of Innu youth. However, applying the Supreme Court's decision in *Van der Peet*, the claim was dismissed on technical grounds, the court holding that having 'provided no particulars as to the nature of the Aboriginal right at issue, other than to mention that the Innu had a policy of settling disputes concerning youth protection within the Nation, the community or the extended family', the claim had been pleaded in insufficient detail and at an excessive level of generality.[64] The question arose again before the Saskatchewan Queen's Bench (Family Law Division) in *Re R.T.*[65] In defending the policy of the Saskatchewan Department of Community Resources and Employment (DCRE) not to place Aboriginal children for adoption without the consent of the Band or the NASC agency, the Band and the agency argued that the Aboriginal community had a constitutionally protected right under s 35 to 'speak for the children'. Although this way of conceptualizing the right suggested something akin to legal guardianship over the children, the arguments presented on behalf of the Band made it clear that it amounted, in essence, to a claim to self-government over the placement and adoption of Aboriginal children:

> In this case, the NASC Agency/band argue that Aboriginal "notions of community and kinship" are an integral part of Aboriginal society. First Nations

---

the right to enact a [contemporary, market-based] labour relations code'. The fact the First Nation had traditionally regulated the work activities of its members was dismissed as lacking sufficient particularity, 'the organization of work at that level of generality being a feature of every human society'.

63 In *Delgamuukw v British Columbia* [1997] 3 S.C.R. 1010, the Supreme Court held that errors of fact made by the trial judge and the resultant need for a new trial made it impossible to determine the issue of self-government. Interestingly, the Supreme Court did not reject the claim on the basis it was overly broad and generalized, suggesting perhaps a more open approach where the claim to self-government is tied to a claim to Aboriginal title.

64 *Re Adolescent* [2001] 4 C.N.L.R. 1.

65 *Re R.T., M.T., M.A.T., A.L. and K.A.* (2004) SKQB 503. For the facts of this case see discussion in Chapter 3 at p. 110.

> families and communities share responsibility for the upbringing, training, education and well-being of their children. They submit that the Aboriginal right of self-government includes the legal right and moral obligation to speak for persons who are under a legal disability, such as children. As this "right" has never been extinguished, *The Child and Family Services Act* cannot impair it by placing Aboriginal children for adoption without the band's consent.[66]

Ryan-Froslie J. gave only cursory consideration to the argument, holding that there was insufficient evidence in this case to support the Band's position:

> The only evidence called by the NASC Agency/band was that of Dr. Katz who testified that "kinship" is an Aboriginal "value" and that "community" plays an important role in the raising of Aboriginal children. There was no evidence of what happens to Aboriginal children when no "kinship" or "community" resources are available to care for them. His evidence falls far short of establishing the right asserted by the NASC Agency/band.[67]

Applying the *Van der Peet* test, the court went on to hold that the right was too vague and general, having not been defined with a sufficient degree of specificity, that self-government over child welfare was neither a distinctive nor defining feature of the Band's culture and, even if it could be established that there was such a right, there was no evidence that it existed pre-contact.[68]

Given the importance of the issue of self-government over child welfare for Aboriginal communities, the brevity of the discussion in both of these cases is disappointing. However, the judgments clearly illustrate the difficulties facing Aboriginal communities in satisfying the stringent conditions imposed by the Supreme Court for establishing an Aboriginal right under s 35, particularly with respect to the importance of the way in which the Aboriginal right is conceptualized and the evidence required to establish the 'distinctive culture' and 'pre-contact' tests. There is certainly nothing within either of these cases to suggest that, given the current attitude of the courts towards self-government, attempting to establish a more specific right to Aboriginal self-government over child welfare has any more immediate prospect of success.

The Power of the Sovereign to Extinguish and Infringe Aboriginal Rights

Establishing there is a constitutionally protected right to self-government in the Canadian courts, either generally or more specifically with respect to child welfare, currently looks a remote prospect. However, even assuming an Aboriginal community was able to successfully negotiate the hurdles set down in *Van der*

66 Ibid., [58].
67 Ibid., [60].
68 Ibid., [60].

Peet, the scope and meaning of the right to self-government would still fall to be determined. Unfortunately, there is nothing within the current jurisprudence of the court to suggest that it would deliver a concept of self-government in which Aboriginal sovereignty was afforded any greater recognition and respect. Indeed, a more fundamental challenge to Aboriginal sovereignty remains to be faced: the Supreme Court's unquestioning acceptance of the sovereign right of the Crown to extinguish and, post-constitutional entrenchment in 1982, regulate Aboriginal rights at will. As Michael Asch and Patrick Macklem argue, far from proceeding from an inherent rights approach, this betrays the Court's actual adherence to a contingent rights approach.[69] It entrenches Canadian sovereignty over Aboriginal peoples, vesting overriding power in the Canadian government to confine and limit Aboriginal rights in accordance with its own agenda. Aboriginal rights, including the Aboriginal right to self-government over child welfare, thus remain deeply dependant on the will of the Canadian government.

Extinguishment

It was accepted without question by the Supreme Court in *R v Sparrow* that until 1982 Aboriginal rights could be extinguished at will by the British Crown. Although the threshold for establishing extinguishment was set high, with the Supreme Court holding that the Crown must prove a 'clear and plain intent', prior to 1982 there were no constitutional limits on the Crown (and the federal government as its successor) simply legislating to extinguish any Aboriginal rights it deemed appropriate.[70] Whether or not the federal government had so acted to extinguish the Aboriginal right to self-government is a controversial question.[71] The Supreme Court has yet to rule on the issue. There are, however, strongly differing views discernible at the provincial court level. Those who support the position that any right to self-government was successfully extinguished by the British Crown's unilateral assertion of sovereignty point to the Royal Proclamation of 1763, the treaties entered into between the Crown and the First Nations and the granting of exclusive jurisdiction over 'Indians and Lands reserved for the Indians' to the federal government under s 91(24) of the Constitution Act 1867, as evidence of the clear and plain intent of the Crown.[72] However, in an important judgment of the British Columbia Supreme Court, Williamson J took the contrary view, holding

69 Asch and Macklem, *supra* note 4. See also Asch, *supra* note 20, 476–80.

70 It was however confirmed in *Delgamuukw v British Columbia* [1997] 3 S.C.R. 1010, [173]–[175] that the power to extinguish Aboriginal rights rests exclusively with the federal government. For further discussion see Binnie, *supra* note 20, 227–31.

71 Binnie, ibid., 223.

72 *R v Pamajewon* [1996] 2 S.C.R. 821, [14] and [19] and *Delgamuukw v British Columbia* [1997] 3 S.C.R. 1010, [20], [34] and [45]. Cf. *Delgamuukw v British Columbia* [1997] 3 S.C.R. 1010, [59]–[65]. For discussion, see Asch and Macklem, *supra* note 4, 509–10 and B. Ryder (1991). 'Demise and Rise of the Classical Paradigm in Canadian Federalism: Promoting Autonomy for the Provinces and First Nations', *McGill Law Journal*, 36: 309, 309–20.

that space had remained within the constitutional structure of Canada for a third level of Aboriginal government to survive.[73]

Campbell v British Columbia (2000) concerned a challenge brought by three opposition members of the British Columbia legislative assembly to the constitutionality of the Nisga'a Final Agreement. It was argued that insofar as the Nisga'a Agreement, a landmark modern treaty between the Nisga'a, the federal government and the BC provincial government, purported to bestow legislative powers on Nisga'a government that could prevail over federal and provincial law it was unconstitutional. The basis for this argument was that any Aboriginal right to self-government had been extinguished by the exhaustive division of powers between the federal and provincial governments set down in ss 91 and 92 of the Constitution Act 1867.[74] The British Columbia Supreme Court disagreed. Williamson J held that ss 91 and 92 did not exclude continuing self-government by Aboriginal peoples because all that was distributed between the federal and provincial governments by virtue of those provisions were the powers which until 1867 had been vested in the colonies.[75] Anything outside the powers of the colonies or which the imperial authorities had chosen to leave undisturbed, including Aboriginal rights to self-government, therefore remained outside the powers of the federal and provincial governments: it was a division entirely 'internal' to the Crown.[76] Indeed, the only real effect of s 91(24) on the position of Aboriginal peoples was that exclusive jurisdiction over 'Indians and Lands reserved for Indians' was assigned to the federal government who now stood with respect to Aboriginal peoples in the place of the imperial Crown.[77] The court supported this conclusion by pointing to the continuing existence and recognition within the Canadian courts of Aboriginal legal systems and laws.[78] Williamson J argued that this made it clear that a limited right of self-government, including a degree of legislative power, remained with Aboriginal peoples post-confederation.[79] In the absence of clear and plain extinguishment, the court thus concluded that the Aboriginal right to self-government, including law-making powers, must now be protected under s 35 of the Constitution.

Campbell v British Columbia provides strong support for the argument that Aboriginal rights to self-government have survived express extinguishment. However, even if the approach adopted by Williamson J were to find favour with the Supreme Court, there is a second potential difficulty to be negotiated. Although

---

73 *Campbell v British Columbia (Attorney General)* [2000] 4 C.N.L.R. 1. On the question of whether the Nisga'a are now recognized as constituting a third level of government within Canada's federal structure see Graben, *supra* note 12.

74 *Campbell v British Columbia (Attorney General)*, ibid., [12].

75 Ibid., [76].

76 Ibid., [76] and [81].

77 Ibid., [82].

78 Ibid., [83]–[110].

79 Ibid., [86].

the Supreme Court has yet to rule on whether Aboriginal self-government has been extinguished due to express executive or legislative action by the Canadian government, a minority judgment of the Supreme Court has addressed the question of whether an Aboriginal right to self-government may have been extinguished by virtue of its *necessary incompatibility* with the Crown's assertion of sovereignty.[80] *Mitchell v M.N.R.* (2001) concerned a claim by a member of the Mohawk Nation to be free to engage in unrestricted trade across the US–Canadian border pursuant to an Aboriginal right protected under s 35. In establishing whether an alleged Aboriginal right fell within the protective scope of s 35, Binnie J[81] modified the test set down in *Van der Peet* to introduce the concept of 'sovereign incompatibility'.[82] Whilst it is clear that not all Aboriginal practices, traditions and customs are incompatible with the Crown's assertion of sovereignty, Binnie J held that there are legitimate concerns as to how some Aboriginal customs and traditions, such as engaging in cross-border trade, may be reconciled with contemporary Canadian sovereignty.[83] The claimants argued that although they accepted the fact of Canadian sovereignty, inherent Aboriginal rights, which in their case included the right to cross the international border without restriction or control, originated in Mohawk sovereignty and were an expression of their surviving autonomy as members of the Iroquois Confederacy.[84] Binnie J rejected this argument, holding that one of the 'defining characteristics' of the British Crown's acquisition of sovereignty over Canada was that it acted as a necessary limit on any incompatible Aboriginal rights.[85] Any Aboriginal rights which were necessarily inconsistent with the inherent sovereignty of the Crown were therefore automatically extinguished.[86] Applying this to the facts of the case, Binnie J held that the right to exercise control over its international borders has always been 'a fundamental attribute of sovereignty', such that the alleged Aboriginal right to move and trade freely across the Canadian border would be fundamentally incompatible with the core attributes of Canadian sovereignty. Any such right would therefore have been automatically extinguished, removing the need to prove a 'clear and plain' intent on the part of the Canadian federal government.[87]

80 *Mitchell v M.N.R.* [2001] 1 S.C.R. 911. For commentary, see Borrows, *supra* note 20, 309–10.

81 Giving judgment on behalf of himself and Major J.

82 Having found that the evidence failed to establish that the right to engage in cross-border trade was integral to the distinctive culture of the Mohawk people, the majority held that it was unnecessary to rule on the relevance of the 'sovereign incompatibility' test to establishing rights under s 35.

83 [2001] 1 S.C.R. 911, [67].

84 Ibid., [117]–[118].

85 Ibid., [150].

86 Ibid., [151].

87 Ibid., [160].

Binnie J is careful to make clear that the doctrine of 'sovereign incompatibility' does not 'foreclose' the argument on internal self-government.[88] Indeed, he points out that the sovereign incompatibility argument has not precluded the United States from sanctioning internal forms of self-government which are considered expressions of residual Aboriginal sovereignty.[89] It is, however, clear from his analysis that any Aboriginal right which infringes on the 'external relations' power of the Canadian government will almost inevitably fall foul of this doctrine.[90] He also notes that 'sovereign incompatibility' was accepted as a legitimate limitation on the powers of Aboriginal self-government in the 1993 working report of the Royal Commission on Aboriginal Peoples.[91] This approach therefore raises serious questions as to the scope of any surviving right to Aboriginal self-government in which Aboriginal sovereignty constitutes a core component. It poses a further, potentially significant, obstacle to successfully establishing meaningful sovereignty for Aboriginal peoples under s 35 of the Constitution, including their ultimate right to decide on matters internal to the community without limitation or control by the Canadian state.

Infringement

Post 1982, Aboriginal rights cannot be extinguished. However, it has always been the case and remains so despite the constitutional entrenchment of Aboriginal rights in s 35, that Aboriginal rights can be infringed. This was again unquestioningly accepted by the Supreme Court in *Sparrow* despite the absence of any clear mandate justifying regulatory measures within the language of the constitutional provisions themselves.[92] Nevertheless, the Supreme Court had no difficulty reading the government's regulatory power into s 35, holding that Aboriginal rights are not absolute and the validity of any legislation that purports to infringe Aboriginal rights will simply depend on whether or not it meets the *Sparrow* justificatory test.[93] This justificatory test, according to Dickson CJ, must be informed by the historical fiduciary relationship between Aboriginal peoples and the Crown which places a special 'trust-like' responsibility on the government and restrains any unfettered exercise of sovereign power.[94] This requires that any

88 Ibid., [165].

89 Ibid., [165].

90 Ibid., [167].

91 Ibid., [150].

92 As s 35 falls outside the Charter, it is not subject to the justificatory provisions for permitted infringements of Charter rights contained within s 1. Similarly, it is not subject to the legislative override contained within s 33. See K. McNeil (1988). 'The Constitution Act 1982, Sections 25 and 35', *Canadian Native Law Reporter*, 1: 1, 12; I. Barkin (1990). 'Aboriginal Rights: A Shell without the Filling', *Queen's Law Journal*, 15: 307, 315; G. Christie (2000). 'Justifying Principles of Treaty Interpretation', *Queen's Law Journal*, 26: 143, 58.

93 *R v Sparrow* [1990] 1 S.C.R. 1075, 1109.

94 Ibid., 1108 and 1109.

regulation of Aboriginal rights must: (1) be enacted according to a valid objective; and (2) uphold the honour of the Crown.[95]

Dickson CJ's justificatory test is clearly informed by the perceived need to find an acceptable 'compromise' between the constitutional priority being afforded to Aboriginal rights and the wider interests of Canadian society.[96] He does, however, envisage the justificatory standard in *Sparrow* providing a high level of substantive protection for Aboriginal rights against legislative encroachment:

> The constitutional recognition afforded by the provision therefore gives a measure of control over government conduct and a strong check on legislative power. While it does not promise immunity from government regulation in a society that, in the twentieth century, is increasingly more complex, interdependent and sophisticated, and where exhaustible resources need protection and management, it does hold the Crown to a substantive promise. The government is required to bear the burden of justifying any legislation that has some negative effect on any Aboriginal right protected under s 35(1).[97]

This burden, according to the court, will be a heavy one. Dickson CJ provides some guidance as to what will constitute a valid legislative objective for the justificatory test, specifically referring to: conserving and managing a natural resource; measures preventing harm to the general populace or to Aboriginal peoples themselves; or other 'compelling and substantial' objectives. Importantly, the Court rejects a broad 'public interest' justification, holding that it is 'so vague as to provide no meaningful guidance and so broad as to be unworkable as a test for the justification of a limitation on constitutional rights'.[98]

The justificatory standard set down in *Sparrow* provides important protection for Aboriginal peoples against the absolute sovereignty of the Canadian government. However, the value of that protection has been eroded by subsequent interpretations of the *Sparrow* test which have seen it reduced to little more than the 'public interest' standard explicitly rejected by Dickson CJ as too 'vague' and 'unworkable'.[99] The Supreme Court returned to the question of the justificatory standard for the infringement of Aboriginal rights in *R v Gladstone*,[100] the court concluding that, given the particular circumstances of the case, the *Sparrow* test would need to be 'adapted'. In addressing the question of what may constitute a 'compelling and substantial' objective justifying the Crown's infringement of Aboriginal rights, Lamer CJ was clearly concerned to find some means by which

---

95 Ibid., 1110.

96 Ibid.

97 Ibid.

98 Ibid., 1113.

99 K. McNeil (2004). 'The Vulnerability of Indigenous Land Rights in Australia and Canada', *Osgoode Hall Law Journal*, 42: 271, 290–1.

100 *R v Gladstone* [1996] 2 S.C.R. 723.

the broader interests of Canadian society could be accommodated within the framework of a s 35 analysis. He thus concluded that 'compelling and substantial' objectives would include those that are directed at the 'reconciliation of Aboriginal prior occupation with the assertion of the sovereignty of the Crown'.[101] It transpired that what is meant by 'reconciliation' in this context is that the government will be justified in infringing Aboriginal rights in order to protect the broader interests of Canadian society:

> Because, however, distinctive Aboriginal societies exist within, and are a part of, a broader social, political and economic community, over which the Crown is sovereign, there are circumstances in which, in order to pursue objectives of compelling and substantial importance to that community as a whole (taking into account the fact that Aboriginal societies are a part of that community), some limitation of those rights will be justifiable. Aboriginal rights are a necessary part of the reconciliation of Aboriginal societies with the broader political community of which they are part.[102]

The broad grounds on which the government could potentially be allowed to infringe Aboriginal rights becomes immediately clear as Lamer CJ goes on to comment that objectives such as 'the pursuit of economic and regional fairness' and the 'historical reliance upon, and participation in, the fishery by non-Aboriginal groups' are the type of objectives which will satisfy this standard.[103]

Lamer CJ's expanded justificatory test did not, however, attract the unanimous support of the Supreme Court. Indeed, McLachlin J launched a strong attack on this expansive justificatory test in her dissent in *Van der Peet*, arguing that it was inconsistent with the authorities and 'ultimately more political than legal'.[104] She argued that the objectives suggested by Lamer CJ as potentially justifying infringement were a long way from the 'compelling and substantial objectives' envisaged by Dickson CJ in *Sparrow*. Of particular interest are McLachlin J's comments as to the political nature of the expanded test, her argument being that it appeals more to political expediency than the legal entitlement of Aboriginal peoples. By introducing what amounts to a broad 'public interest' test she argued that the focus of the court's analysis had shifted to the 'social justifiability' of the measure, rather than the right in question. This, in her view, was to turn the purpose of s 35 on its head. Moreover, acutely aware of the wider political context in which these claims were being brought, she argued that it is unnecessary and

101 Ibid., [72].

102 Ibid., [73].

103 For critique see Barsh and Henderson, *supra* note 44, 999.

104 *R v Van der Peet* [1996] 2 S.C.R. 507, [302]. For discussion as to the legitimacy of Lamer CJ's approach to the justificatory test in *Gladstone,* see G. Christie (2002). 'Aboriginal and Normativity, Judicial Justification of Recent Developments in Aboriginal Law', *Canadian Journal of Law and Society*, 17: 41.

inappropriate for the courts to attempt to achieve a 'reconciliation' of Aboriginal and non-Aboriginal interests through the mechanism of s 35. She acknowledged that one of the fundamental purposes of s 35(1) was to achieve a just and lasting settlement for Aboriginal peoples which, of necessity, must involve reconciliation with the larger non-Aboriginal community. However, this goal of reconciliation does not, in her view, require the judiciary to embark upon an exercise which, in effect, authorizes the transfer of constitutionally protected Aboriginal rights to non-Aboriginal interests 'without the consent of the Aboriginal people, without a treaty and without compensation'.[105] Indeed, she argued that such an approach was unconstitutional as it amounted, in essence, to the unilateral extinguishment of Aboriginal rights.[106] In her view, the process of reconciliation was best achieved not in the courts but at the negotiation table, with the role of the courts being to define Aboriginal rights and, where established on the evidence, afford full legal protection to those rights pending negotiations as to how the entitlements of Aboriginal peoples can be accommodated within non-Aboriginal law.[107] This is where the political process must take over and some form of reconciliation found.[108]

Lamer CJ was not convinced by this critique. Indeed, the Chief Justice took the opportunity provided by the subsequent case of *Delgamuukw v British Columbia*[109] to further entrench and even extend yet further his expansive interpretation of the *Sparrow* justificatory standard. As a result of these decisions, the substantive demands being placed on the Canadian government by virtue of s 35 are therefore fairly derisory. Applying *Gladstone* to cases of resource allocation, the government would be expected to demonstrate that the process by which the resource is allocated is fair and that it reflects the prior interest of the Aboriginal community. In concrete terms, Lamer CJ suggests that this might entail accommodating the participation of Aboriginal peoples in the development of the resources of the province or reducing economic barriers to Aboriginal uses of their land.[110] In some cases, nothing more than consultation with the Aboriginal community

105 [1996] 2 S.C.R. 723, [310].

106 Ibid., [315]–[316].

107 For an exceptionally thoughtful example of the BC Supreme Court striving to fulfill this crucial role in the process of reconciliation see, *Tsilhqot'in Nation v British Columbia* (2007) BCSC 1700, esp at [1338]–[1382]. See also Christie, *supra* note 104, 69–70. For a good discussion of the importance of recognizing the equal sovereign rights of Aboriginal peoples and basing Canadian constitutional identity on a model of negotiated settlements and treaties see Asch, *supra* note 20, 487–91 and Asch and Macklem, *supra* note 4.

108 [1996] 2 S.C.R. 723, [313]. McLachlin J, now speaking unanimously for the Supreme Court, maintained this position in *Haida Nation v British Columbia (Ministry of Forests)* [2004] 3 S.C.R. 511. See further discussion below.

109 *Delgamuukw v British Columbia* [1997] 3 S.C.R. 1010.

110 Ibid., [167].

will be required, with the scope and nature of the consultation depending on the significance of the interests at stake:

> In occasional cases, when the breach is less serious or relatively minor, it will be no more than a duty to discuss important decisions that will be taken with respect to lands held pursuant to Aboriginal title. Of course, even in these rare cases when the minimum acceptable standard is consultation, this consultation must be in good faith, and with the intention of substantially addressing the concerns of the Aboriginal peoples whose lands are at issue. In most cases, it will be significantly deeper than mere consultation. Some cases may even require the full consent of an Aboriginal nation, particularly when provinces enact hunting and fishing regulations in relation to Aboriginal lands.[111]

Significantly, in *Haida Nation v British Columbia (Ministry of Forests)*[112] the Supreme Court extended this duty to consult to situations where resolution of the claimed Aboriginal right was still pending. The Supreme Court also addressed the nature of the duty, explaining that it arose as 'part of a process of fair dealing and reconciliation', the exact scope of the duty being determined by what was required to 'maintain the honour of the Crown'.[113] The Supreme Court went on to emphasize the highly variable nature of the duty, holding that, depending on the strength of the Aboriginal claim in question, the 'honour of the Crown' would sometimes demand accommodation of the Aboriginal interest, in other circumstances no more than the provision of information would be required.[114] The Court also emphasized that the duty on the Crown was to consult in good faith, not to reach agreement.[115]

From the Aboriginal perspective, the Supreme Court's subsequent interpretation of the *Sparrow* standard is a further significant blow to their hopes of achieving a just settlement within Canadian society. The broad discretion it affords to the federal government to continue to override even constitutionally protected Aboriginal rights seriously undermines the inherent right theory and the potential of s 35 to deliver real autonomy for Aboriginal peoples. It is important to note that *Gladstone* and *Delgamuukw* were both concerned with resource allocation and how to reconcile Aboriginal claims with the continued availability of the resource for non-native users. An important factor underpinning Lamer CJ's approach was the potentially unlimited nature of some Aboriginal claims over Canadian land and natural resources which, if recognized, would effectively exclude all other users

---

111 Ibid., [168]. For an excellent critique of Lamer CJ's expanded justificatory test see, McNeil, *supra* note 99, 286–97.

112 *Haida Nation v British Columbia (Ministry of Forests)* [2004] 3 S.C.R. 511. See also *Taku River Tlingit First Nation v British Columbia (Project Assessment Director)* [2004] 3 S.C.R. 550.

113 *Haida Nation v British Columbia (Ministry of Forests)*, ibid., [32] and [45].

114 Ibid., [43]–[44].

115 Ibid., [42].

from utilizing the resource. However, it is to be expected that the broad framework of principles established for justifying infringements of Aboriginal rights in these cases will be applied to self-government claims. These potentially 'unlimited' claims to Aboriginal sovereignty raise the spectre of the federal government being permitted to severely limit many aspects of Aboriginal self-government in order to meet the 'compelling' objectives of the 'broader political community of which they are part'. Under this constitutional model, the governance powers of Aboriginal peoples therefore remain firmly subjected to the control of the federal government, with the only substantive protection from the unilateral imposition of federal regulation being the rather hollow duty of consultation set down in *Haida Nation*. The hierarchical relationship this perpetuates between Aboriginal and non-Aboriginal peoples is powerfully expressed by James Youngblood Henderson:

> From my vantage point, the problem with the Court's justified infringement test is that it reinforces a colonial legal consciousness: it fuels that colonial practice of developing a justificatory legal and political regime to disguise the self-aggrandizing, self-originating authority of the colonialists, and it extends their tyranny over Aboriginal peoples.[116]

The unquestionable assumption of sovereignty

The Supreme Court's decisions on extinguishment and infringement reveal the inherent limitations of the non-native legal system determining questions of Aboriginal sovereignty and governance.[117] Underpinning all of the Supreme Court's decisions on Aboriginal rights is one unquestionable assumption that seriously undermines its ability to act as an effective tool of decolonization: the overriding sovereignty of the Canadian government. The vitally important question of how the Crown acquired the sovereign power and authority to extinguish or limit the 'inherent' rights of Aboriginal peoples is never seriously examined.[118] To ask that question would risk bringing into dispute the sovereignty and very legitimacy of the modern Canadian state, including its own constitutional position, and that is something the Supreme Court is simply not prepared to do.[119] This is made clear in unequivocal terms by Dickson CJ in his judgment in *Sparrow*:

> It is worth recalling that while British policy towards the native population was based on respect for their right to occupy their traditional lands, a proposition

116 J. Y. Henderson (2000). 'Constitutional Powers and Treaty Rights', *Saskatchewan Law Review*, 63: 719, 747. See also P. Macklem (1991). 'First Nations, Self-Government and the Borders of the Canadian Legal Imagination', *McGill Law Journal*, 36: 382.

117 For an excellent analysis of both the limitations and possibilities of working within the Canadian legal system see Macklem, ibid.

118 Ibid., 450–1.

119 Other Canadian courts have simply considered the issue to be non-justiciable. See, for example, *R v Francis* 2007 CanLII 8009 (ON S.C.).

> to which the Royal Proclamation of 1763 bears witness, *there was from the outset never any doubt that sovereignty and legislative power, and indeed the underlying title, to such lands vested in the Crown*[120] (emphasis added).

This unquestioned acceptance of Crown sovereignty underpins all of the Supreme Court's subsequent decisions on Aboriginal rights. Thus whilst it is acknowledged that inherent Aboriginal rights must be reconciled with Canadian sovereignty, the very fact of Canadian sovereignty remains incontrovertible. Yet, from an Aboriginal perspective, it is this claim to sovereignty which lies at the very heart of the dispute with non-native Canada. Aboriginal peoples do not simply accept the legitimacy of the Canadian state and its unilateral authority over their people and their lands. Thus, in order for reconciliation to be achieved, it is this fundamental clash over Canadian sovereignty which must first be resolved.

The issue of Canadian sovereignty is touched upon at various points in the judgments of the Supreme Court. L'Heureux-Dube J, in her dissent in *Van der Peet*, referred to the question of how Canadian sovereignty was acquired but made no attempt to resolve the issue, simply observing that 'in the eyes of international law, the settlement thesis is the one rationale which can most plausibly justify European sovereignty over Canadian territory and the native people living on it although there is still debate as to whether the land was indeed free for occupation'.[121] Interestingly, McLachlin J in her dissent began by excluding the settlement thesis as the basis for Canadian sovereignty, arguing instead that the '*Grundnorm*' of settlement in Canada was cession:

> The Aboriginal people could only be deprived of the sustenance they traditionally drew from the land and adjacent waters by solemn treaty with the Crown, on terms that would ensure to them and to their successors a replacement for the livelihood that their lands, forests and streams had since ancestral times provided them.[122]

---

120 *R v Sparrow* [1990] 1 S.C.R. 1075, 1103.

121 [1996] 2 S.C.R. 507, [108]–[109]. The settlement thesis is perhaps the most problematic of the potential legal justifications for the Crown's assertion of sovereignty. See M. Asch (2002). 'From Terra Nullius to Affirmation: Reconciling Aboriginal Rights with the Canadian Constitution', *Canadian Journal of Law and Society*, 17: 23, 24.

122 [1996] 2 S.C.R. 507, [272] (per McLoughlin J). Cession does appear to be the most promising and principled legal route by which the acquisition of Crown sovereignty can be justified. Founded on the principle of consent, cession at least demands that Aboriginal peoples agreed to surrender their sovereignty and their lands to the incoming colonial powers in exchange for certain promises and guarantees. The difficulty is in determining whether this 'free will' surrender did in deed take place. See: Asch and Macklem, *supra* note 4, 573–4 and 513–14; Asch, ibid., 486–7; and J. Borrows (1994). 'Constitutional Law from a First Nation Perspective', *UBC Law Review*, 28: 1.

However, acknowledging the difficulties this creates in British Columbia where treaties were never entered into, she draws back from accepting the potential implications of this for the legitimacy of contemporary Canadian sovereignty, preferring instead to fall back on a less 'desirable' version of the settlement thesis in which the Aboriginal peoples of British Columbia were simply overrun by the greater strength of the non-native settlers.[123]

The question of Canadian sovereignty and how it may exist, if at all, alongside pre-existing Aboriginal sovereignty was given more detailed consideration by the minority judgment of Binnie and Major JJ in *Mitchell v M.N.R.*[124] The doctrine of 'sovereign incompatibility', which the minority held defeated the Aboriginal right in that case, gave rise to the direct question of whether the assertion of Crown sovereignty had necessarily extinguished all claims to any residual Aboriginal sovereignty. The judgment of Binnie J is interesting in that he attempts to shift the focus of the debate away from the extent to which Aboriginal and non-Aboriginal sovereignty are in conflict, to developing a concept of Canadian sovereignty which builds upon and embraces the sovereignty of both Aboriginal and non-Aboriginal peoples. As noted above, it was concluded on the facts of the case that the claimed Aboriginal right to move and trade freely across the Canadian/US border did not survive the Crown's assertion of sovereignty because the right to control its international borders is a fundamental aspect of Canadian sovereignty. However, in reaching this conclusion Binnie J argued that this should not be perceived negatively as a case of Aboriginal sovereignty being overridden and extinguished by non-Aboriginal sovereignty. Rather, it should, in his view, be seen as an example of how shared Aboriginal and non-Aboriginal sovereignty is operating to protect the common interests of both communities.[125] He acknowledged that the Mohawk perception of the relationship between Aboriginal and non-Aboriginal people may fundamentally differ from that of non-Aboriginal people. As he notes, in the Mohawk tradition that relationship is signified by the 'two-row' wampum in which Aboriginal and non-Aboriginal people travel down two separate but parallel paths:

> In one path travels the Aboriginal canoe. In the other path travels the European ship. The two vessels co-exist but they never touch. Each is the sovereign of its own destiny.[126]

However, Binnie J argued that this concept of the 'two-row' wampum cannot have survived as an expression of the modern-day relationship between Aboriginal and

---

123 [1996] 2 S.C.R. 507, [273]. It is argued by Graben that McLachlin CJ takes a more open approach in *Haida Nation*, suggesting that Aboriginal sovereignty remains intact in those nations which have not yet negotiated treaties. See Graben, *supra* note 12, 90.

124 [2001] 1 S.C.R. 911.

125 Ibid., [164].

126 Ibid., [128].

non-Aboriginal people. Adopting the recommendations of the Royal Commission on Aboriginal Peoples, he held that what had subsequently emerged was a 'merged' or 'shared' sovereignty in which '[a]boriginal and non-Aboriginal Canadians *together* form a sovereign entity with a measure of common purpose and united effort'.[127] According to this perspective, Aboriginal peoples should be regarded as full and equal partners with non-Aboriginal peoples in modern-day Canada. Aboriginal peoples do not therefore stand in opposition to, nor are they subjugated by, Canadian sovereignty.[128] They are part of it.[129] To the extent that Canadian sovereignty therefore claims a monopoly over the exercise of certain rights, it does so as the inheritor of both traditions, operating to protect the national common interests of both communities and as an expression of 'collective sovereignty'.[130]

Binnie J's judgment in *Mitchell* has a certain rhetorical appeal. He points to a vision of contemporary Canadian sovereignty which is consensual, based on a willing partnership between Aboriginal and non-Aboriginal peoples and furthers the common interests and goals of both communities. Furthermore, space could be created within this constitutional framework for the exercise of sovereign authority by Aboriginal peoples within their respective spheres of jurisdiction, particularly on matters purely internal to their communities such as child welfare. However, Binnie J again fails to deal in any convincing way with the most fundamental aspect of his argument. Whilst acknowledging the differing Mohawk perspective on the relationship between Aboriginal and non-Aboriginal peoples, notably absent is any explanation of how the 'two canoes' of the 'two-row wampum' became the one unified ship of Canadian sovereignty. It is suggested at one point in his judgment that the sovereign will of the Mohawk people was gradually overborne and destroyed by the reality of European 'dominion'.[131] However, the acquisition of sovereignty by prescription sits uneasily with Binnie J's vision of modern Canadian sovereignty being founded on the core principles of partnership, mutual interest and consent. Yet, nowhere does Binnie J explain how and when the Aboriginal peoples of Canada entered Canadian sovereignty as the willing partners of non-Aboriginal peoples. For Binnie J, the Constitution Act 1982 represents a key pivotal moment at which reconciliation between Aboriginal and non-Aboriginal peoples was achieved.[132] From the perspective of many Aboriginal communities, however, they have yet to be afforded the opportunity to 'negotiate their way into Canada' and it flies in the face of reality to suggest that the Constitution Act 1982 represents any such negotiated solution. Running through Binnie J's judgment is thus an unresolved tension between a vision of modern Canadian sovereignty that is shared, consensual and mutually beneficial,

127 Ibid., [129].
128 Ibid., [135].
129 Ibid., [135].
130 Ibid., [164].
131 Ibid., [113].
132 Ibid., [129].

and one in which the reality of Canadian sovereignty was gradually imposed upon Aboriginal peoples by the greater strength and dominion of non-native society. Clearly, in the absence of consent, those aspects of Aboriginal sovereignty lost to Canadian sovereignty were not, as Binnie J would like to suggest, voluntarily surrendered in a mutually beneficial merger of interests.

The leading Supreme Court decisions on Aboriginal rights therefore fail to establish any convincing foundation for the assertion of Canadian sovereignty over Aboriginal peoples. The tentative nature of the answers suggested and the lack of consensus amongst Canada's leading jurists reveals the fragile and deeply problematic nature of Canadian sovereignty. However, despite these intense difficulties, for the most part the Supreme Court simply refuses to engage with the question. The 'bottom line' for the Canadian Supreme Court is that regardless of the uncertainties surrounding the issue, Canadian sovereignty cannot be questioned in the Canadian courts.[133] The same 'bottom line' has been firmly established in the Australian courts. As it was succinctly expressed by Brennan J giving judgment in *Mabo*, the acquisition of sovereign authority over a territory by a sovereign state is 'an act of State, the validity of which is not justiciable in the municipal courts'.[134] Moreover, given its own dependence on the assumed legitimacy of Australian sovereignty, the Australian High Court has expressly acknowledged the inherent limitations of the Australian legal system in addressing Aboriginal claims, observing that whilst the common law may be modified to bring it into conformity with contemporary notions of justice and human rights, it 'cannot be destroyed'.[135] In other words, the integrity of the Australian legal system must be preserved, precluding any outcome which would 'fracture a skeletal principle' of the institution.

The same pressures and limitations are operating upon the Canadian courts. The Canadian Supreme Court is acutely aware of the need to avoid igniting a constitutional crisis with potentially far-reaching consequences for the political, economic and legal stability of modern-day Canada. To avoid such a crisis, limits must be imposed on Aboriginal rights and that limit is Canadian sovereignty. Only then can the institutional, economic and political integrity of Canada be protected. Canadian sovereignty therefore provides the point beyond which the Supreme Court will not go. However, by avoiding the issue of Canadian sovereignty the Supreme Court risks simply perpetuating the colonial injustice felt by many Aboriginal peoples.

---

133 Macklem, *supra* note 116, 451. See also *Campbell v British Columbia* [2000] 4 C.N.L.R. 1, [124].

134 *Mabo v The State of Queensland (No. 2)* [1991–1992] 175 C.L.R. 1, 31. See also, at 78 (per Deane and Gaudron JJ).

135 Ibid., 30.

Negotiating Canadian and Aboriginal sovereignty

The discomfort of the Canadian Supreme Court when called upon to determine questions of Aboriginal and Canadian sovereignty is clear. However, as clear as the tensions and difficulties surrounding the issue may be, a change in direction is unlikely. As McNeil has observed in the context of disputes over Aboriginal title, the Supreme Court is responding not to the strength or weakness of the legal arguments but to the pressing economic and political considerations to which Aboriginal rights give rise.[136] Given the highly charged context of these disputes, the clear 'message' being sent to Aboriginal communities by the Supreme Court is that the courts are not the appropriate forum in which to try and resolve such explosive issues as the legitimacy of Canadian sovereignty. It has been a constant theme of the Supreme Court's judgments on Aboriginal rights that 'reconciliation' cannot be achieved through the adversarial, win-lose mentality of litigation. Repeated appeals are therefore made for the parties to seek a solution at the negotiating table, not in the courts. As it was put by Lamer CJ in *Delgamuukw*:

> By ordering a new trial, I do not necessarily encourage the parties to proceed to litigation and to settle their dispute through the courts. As was said in *Sparrow* … s. 35(1) "provides a solid constitutional base upon which subsequent negotiations can take place". Those negotiations should also include other aboriginal nations which have a stake in the territory claimed. Moreover, the Crown is under a moral, if not a legal duty to enter into and conduct those negotiations in good faith. Ultimately, it is through negotiated settlements, with good faith and give and take on all sides, reinforced by the judgments of this Court, that we will achieve what I stated in *Van der Peet* … to be a basic purpose of s. 35(1) – "the reconciliation of the pre-existence of aboriginal societies with the sovereignty of the Crown". Let us face it, we are all here to stay.[137]

McLachlin C.J.C. reiterated this position in *Haida Nation*:

> Treaties serve to reconcile pre-existing Aboriginal sovereignty with assumed Crown sovereignty, and to define Aboriginal rights guaranteed by s. 35 of the Constitution Act, 1982. Section 35 represents a promise of rights recognition and "[i]t is always assumed that the Crown intends to fulfil its promises" … This promise is realized and sovereignty claims reconciled through the process of honourable negotiation.[138]

---

136 McNeil, *supra* note 99, 297–301.

137 *Delgamuukw v British Columbia* [1997] 3 S.C.R. 1010, [186]. See also *R v Sparrow* [1990] 1 S.C.R. 1075, 1105 (per Dickson CJ); *Delgamuukw v British Columbia* [1997] 3 S.C.R. 1010, [207] (per La Forest J); *R v Van der Peet* [1996] 2 S.C.R. 507, [313] (per McLachlin J).

138 *Haida Nation v British Columbia (Minister of Forests)* [2004] 3 S.C.R. 511, [20].

Christie suggests that the Supreme Court's decisions on Aboriginal rights have been carefully gauged to push the Canadian government and Aboriginal peoples to the negotiation table.[139] It can be argued, for example, that the Supreme Court took the opportunity provided by s 35 in *Sparrow* to hand Aboriginal peoples 'a strong constitutional hand' with a view to forcing a reluctant government to the table.[140] Similarly, although pulling back from the highpoint of *Sparrow* when Aboriginal rights began to pose a significant threat to non-Aboriginal interests, subsequent decisions such as *Delgamuukw* have created a 'dynamic tension conducive to negotiation'.[141] As Christie argues, by upholding broadly defined Aboriginal rights heavily qualified by the regulatory power of the government, the position is made sufficiently complicated and 'cumbersome' for the Canadian authorities that negotiation to achieve much-needed certainty still represents the best way forward.[142]

Nevertheless, the retreat from *Sparrow* combined with the Supreme Court's emphasis on negotiated solutions has worked to the considerable disadvantage of Aboriginal peoples. The limitations of the Supreme Court's approach are such that litigation under s 35 is not going to deliver a vision of Aboriginal self-government which challenges in any way entrenched Canadian sovereignty. Only negotiations through the political process can therefore deliver real autonomy for Aboriginal peoples. However, the frustrating reality of the political process is that without the strong constitutional foundation for Aboriginal rights promised by Dickson CJ in *Sparrow*, Aboriginal peoples face a difficult, perhaps impossible, struggle in extracting any meaningful degree of internal sovereignty from the federal and provincial governments at the negotiation table, even over matters entirely internal to the community such as child welfare. For Aboriginal peoples, engaging with the institutional power structures of non-native Canada can be an intensely dispiriting experience.

Treaty Negotiations

Current Status of Treaty Negotiations

Aboriginal communities entering into self-government negotiations with the Canadian government are clearly not assisted by the more recent jurisprudence of

139 Christie, *supra* note 104, 62–3. See also Binnie, *supra* note 20, 219–21 and 240–1.

140 Christie, ibid., 62–3.

141 S. Imai (2003). 'Sound Science, Careful Policy Analysis, and Ongoing Relationships: Integrating Litigation and Negotiation in Aboriginal Lands and Resources Disputes', *Osgoode Hall Law Journal*, 41: 587, 600.

142 Christie, *supra* note 104, 62–3. For a good discussion of the relationship between litigation and negotiation and the limitations of the former in the context of Aboriginal rights see Imai, ibid.

the Canadian Supreme Court. However, despite these limitations, recent years have seen some positive developments at the negotiation table. The federal government and Aboriginal communities have been involved in the negotiation of modern treaties since the 1970s. In more recent years, the provincial governments have also become more actively engaged in this process, with self-government negotiations now usually proceeding on a tripartite basis. The last 40 years have therefore seen a number of agreements reached between individual Aboriginal communities and the Canadian government which have, to differing degrees, secured a measure of autonomy and self-government for Aboriginal communities.[143] However, the turning point in the political process came in 1995 with the federal government's official acceptance of the inherent right policy. The federal government's crucial acceptance of the First Nations' inherent right to self-government has meant that, in practice, self-government, including self-government over child welfare, is for many Aboriginal communities in Canada now a very real prospect.[144]

The federal and provincial governments are currently engaged in self-government negotiations with Aboriginal communities all over Canada. The exact form of the negotiations depends on the geographical location of the community, whether or not the community has unsettled land claims, and the historic relationship between the Aboriginal community and the Canadian government, in particular whether there is an existing treaty relationship between them.[145] Under the 1995 Federal Policy Guide, self-government negotiations may be undertaken with Aboriginal communities on a stand-alone basis. However, in many cases, self-government negotiations will be conducted alongside unresolved land or other treaty claims. The federal government has established several different processes for addressing outstanding Aboriginal claims.

In 1973, the federal government established the specific claims process to deal with any outstanding grievances Aboriginal communities may have regarding the Crown's fulfilment of its obligations and responsibilities under the historic treaties or arising from its administration of First Nations land and assets under the Indian Act 1876.[146] The federal government's Policy Guide makes it clear that whilst it will not 're-open, change or displace' historic treaties, it is prepared to negotiate self-government agreements which build upon them. Alongside the specific claims process, the federal government also established the comprehensive land claims process. This process is intended to deal with any outstanding claims to Aboriginal

143 See, for example: the James Bay and Northern Quebec Agreement and the Cree Naskapi (of Quebec) Act 1984; the Sechelt Self-Government Act 1986; and the Yukon Self-Government Agreements.

144 For the current status of the ongoing treaty negotiations see the website of the Department of Indian and Northern Affairs at: www.ainc-inac.gc.ca/pr/agr/index_e.html#Self-Government%20Agreements.

145 For further information see the website of the Department of Indian and Northern Affairs at: www.ainc-inac.gc.ca/al/index-eng.asp.

146 www.ainc-inac.gc.ca/al/ldc/spc/index-eng.asp.

title and natural resources where the issue of Aboriginal title has not been dealt with by treaty or other legal means.[147] The original focus of the lands claim process was on achieving certainty over the ownership, use and management of land. However, the federal government has been prepared to negotiate self-government agreements alongside claims relating to Aboriginal title in a comprehensive claims process. There are now 26 comprehensive claims and self-government agreements in effect, including 11 Yukon First Nations agreements entered into under the Council for Yukon Indians Umbrella Final Agreement.[148] Negotiations are continuing with nearly 20 communities across Canada.

In British Columbia, a separate treaty process has been established under the auspices of the BC Treaty Commission, an independent body established to oversee and facilitate negotiations.[149] Sixty First Nations are currently engaged in negotiations, albeit many are still at an early stage. The first Final Agreement was successfully ratified by the Tsawwassen First Nation in July 2007.[150] There are currently eight First Nations in the final stage of negotiations.

Rights secured under modern treaties are constitutionally protected as treaty rights under s 35.[151] In accordance with the 1995 Federal Policy Guide, this should also now include the core provisions of self-government agreements.[152] The Nisga'a Agreement which took effect in 2000 was the first comprehensive claims agreement to include both constitutionally protected land and self-government provisions.[153] This was followed by the Tlicho Agreement in 2003.[154] The self-government provisions of the Final Agreements resulting from the BC Treaty

147 www.ainc-inac.gc.ca/al/ldc/ccl/index-eng.asp.

148 www.ainc-inac.gc.ca/al/ldc/ccl/ipt/index-eng.asp. For detailed analysis of the Yukon agreements see P. Hogg and M. E. Turpel (1995). 'Implementing Aboriginal Self-Government: Constitutional and Jurisdictional Issues', *Canadian Bar Review*, 74(2): 187.

149 For further information see: www.bctreaty.net.

150 www.bctreaty.net/files/updates.php. The Maa-Nulth First Nations also ratified their Final Agreement in October 2007.

151 Constitution Act 1982, being Schedule B to the Canada Act 1982 (U.K.), 1982, c. 11, s 35.

152 *Supra* note 9.

153 The Nisga'a Agreement covers 2,000 square kilometres in Northern British Columbia, populated by approximately 4,500 people belonging to four Aboriginal communities: Gingolx, Gitwinkshilkw, Lax Galt'sap and New Aiyansh. The Agreement provides for the establishment of Nisga'a Lisims Government and payment to the Nisga'a of $190 million. See, Canada, Department of Indian Affairs and Northern Development (2007). *General Briefing Note on the Comprehensive Land Claims Policy of Canada and the Status of Claims*. Ottawa: Supply and Services. As to its constitutional status see Graben, *supra* note 12, 73–9.

154 The Tlicho Agreement covers 210,000 square kilometres in the North West Territories, populated by approximately 3,500 people belonging to four communities: Rae Edzo, Rae Lakes, Wha Ti and Wekweti. The Agreement provides for the establishment of Tlicho Government and a payment of $152 million as well as a share in royalties from the development of the MacKenzie Valley. See, *General Briefing Note*, ibid., 8–9.

Process also enjoy constitutional protection.[155] Where an agreement was entered into between the federal government and an Aboriginal community before 1995, the self-government provisions, which are contained within a side agreement, do not enjoy constitutional protection. The federal government has, however, indicated it is willing, with the agreement of all parties, to consider re-negotiating the status of these agreements.[156] This includes all the self-government agreements entered into under the Council for Yukon Indians Umbrella Final Agreement which was signed in 1993.[157]

Securing constitutional protection for self-government agreements as treaty rights under s 35 is obviously of crucial importance if they are to be protected against unilateral interference at the will of the Canadian government.[158] However, it should be noted that Aboriginal communities engaging in this process are being asked to pay a considerable price in exchange for constitutional protection of their rights.[159] Before 1995, the federal government, motivated by a strong concern that certainty was achieved with respect to Aboriginal claims over land and resources, insisted on a policy of 'surrender and exchange' whereby any existing Aboriginal rights under s 35 of the Constitution had to be surrendered in exchange for the package of rights secured through the treaty. That policy has since been modified such that Aboriginal rights no longer have to be 'surrendered'. However, important restrictions still apply. Thus the Nisga'a Agreement and the BC Final Agreements provide that the Agreement constitutes 'full and final settlement' of the group's Aboriginal rights and that Aboriginal rights under s 35 continue but only as modified by the treaty.[160] The Tlicho Agreement takes a slightly different approach providing that the Tlicho agree not to assert any Aboriginal rights other than those found within the treaty.[161] With the federal and provincial governments requiring Aboriginal communities to limit their constitutionally protected rights to those specifically provided for within the treaty, there is clearly a considerable amount at stake for First Nations contemplating entering into these agreements. It is, however, important to note the important caveat to this position set down by the Supreme Court of Canada in *Beckman v Little Salmon/Carmacks First Nation*. In dealing with the duty to consult where a modern treaty has been concluded, the Supreme Court of Canada held that whilst the treaty must be given first

155 See, for example, the Tsawwassen Final Agreement, ch. 2, para. 1.

156 *Supra* note 9.

157 Note that Hogg and Turpel argue that the self-government provisions contained within the Yukon Agreements would be constitutionally protected in any event as Aboriginal rights under s 35. See Hogg and Turpel, *supra* note 148, 211–12.

158 As was the case with the historic treaties before 1982. For ways to strengthen self-government agreements which are not constitutionally protected see T. Dickson (2004). 'Self-Government by Side Agreement?', *McGill Law Journal*, 49: 419.

159 Ibid., 447–8.

160 Nisga'a Final Agreement 1999, ch. 2, paras. 22–25 and Tsawwassen First Nations Final Agreement 2006, ch. 2, paras. 12–15.

161 Tlicho Agreement 2003, para. 2.6.

consideration when determining the scope of the parties' respective rights and obligations, constitutional rights and duties continue to persist, thereby denying the treaty the final and exclusive word on the scope of the rights in question.[162] As conceptualized by the Supreme Court, modern treaties are an important part of an ongoing process of reconciliation and constitution building, they are not an 'absolute code' or the final word in defining Aboriginal relations with non-native Canada.

The Federal Government Policy Guide

Individual self-government agreements will differ greatly depending on the particular circumstances of the community. However, the federal government's 1995 Policy Guide provides the general framework within which these individual agreements must be negotiated. The Guide establishes the parameters of the negotiations, setting down certain non-negotiable conditions and outlining what matters may and may not be subject to discussion. Thus the Guide begins by making it clear that self-government will not 'include a right of sovereignty in the international law sense, and will not result in sovereign independent nations'.[163] The intention, according to the federal government, is to consolidate and strengthen the relationship between Aboriginal and non-Aboriginal peoples within Canada. Aboriginal governments and institutions will therefore have to operate within the framework of the Canadian Constitution and jurisdiction will be limited, very broadly, to matters 'internal to the group, integral to its distinct Aboriginal culture, and essential to its operation as a government or institution'.[164] The Guide goes on to provide a more detailed list of those matters which the federal government regards as falling within the core jurisdiction of Aboriginal governments. Adoption, child welfare, social services and the administration/enforcement of Aboriginal laws are all included within this list. For matters falling within the core jurisdiction of Aboriginal governments, the Guide indicates that in some cases Aboriginal law will need to be harmonized with existing federal and provincial law but in other areas it will be sufficient to simply transfer jurisdiction to the Aboriginal community. Beyond matters of a purely internal nature, the Guide indicates that the federal government may be willing to negotiate some measure of Aboriginal control. However, in these areas the Guide makes it clear that primary law-making authority will remain with the federal or provincial governments whose laws will prevail in the event of conflict. Included within this second list is the administration of justice. Finally, the Guide lists a number

162 *Beckman v Little Salmon/Carmacks First Nation* (2010) SCC 53, [10], [52]–[71]. Deschamps J and LeBel J disagreed with the majority, arguing that the treaty must be regarded as a 'complete code' and given 'full effect', resort to the common law only being legitimate when the treaty is completely silent on the issue.

163 *Supra* note 9.

164 Ibid.

of matters over which the federal government is not prepared to enter into negotiations. In these areas the federal government will retain its exclusive law-making authority. These non-negotiable matters are divided into two main groups: (1) powers related to Canadian sovereignty, defence and external relations; and (2) other national interest powers, including management and regulation of the national economy, maintenance of national law, and protection of the health and safety of all Canadians.

The treaty process has obvious attractions to the federal government. By insisting that self-government proceed through political negotiation and agreement, rather than by litigation or the unilateral exercise of the right protected under s 35 of the Constitution, the federal government is able to control the process and avoid jurisprudentially difficult questions about the foundations of Canadian sovereignty. For Aboriginal communities, avoiding the expense and uncertainties of litigation also has a strong attraction, particularly in light of recent Supreme Court decisions. At the very least, the negotiation process holds out the promise of achieving workable self-government arrangements within the short to medium term future. However, if decolonization is to be the yardstick against which the modern treaties are to be evaluated, the limitations of this process are also very clear.[165] By proceeding through negotiated agreements, the framework and substance of which have been determined solely by the federal government, the federal government is able to maintain a strong hold on the scope, form and content of self-government. Through the Federal Policy Guide the federal government is effectively controlling and limiting the right to self-government in accordance with its own priorities and interests, including retaining the power to demand from Aboriginal communities that certain standards and conditions will be met, even within core areas of Aboriginal jurisdiction such as child welfare. The extent to which this undermines the political and cultural autonomy of Aboriginal governments and compromises any claim to internal sovereignty should not be underestimated.[166]

Protecting the Vulnerable – Imposed Limits on Aboriginal Self-Government[167]

The federal government's concern with ensuring certain minimum standards are met by all governments within Canada is understandable. The federal government is naturally anxious that recognition of Aboriginal difference does not fracture the

165 J. Borrows (2001). 'Domesticating Doctrines: Aboriginal Peoples after the Royal Commission', *McGill Law Journal*, 46: 615, 633–6.

166 Ibid., 618–19.

167 An earlier version of the following section has previously been published in S. Harris-Short (2007). 'Self-Government in Canada: A Successful Model for the Decolonisation of Aboriginal Child Welfare?', in S. Tierney (ed.) *Accommodating Cultural Diversity: Contemporary Issues in Theory and Practice*. Aldershot: Ashgate, 99.

normative basis of Canadian society with potentially destabilizing effects.[168] From the federal government's perspective it would be intolerable if implementation of the right to self-government were to result in the creation of Aboriginal enclaves where principles of good governance, as understood by non-native society, were ignored, the basic rights and freedoms of Aboriginal citizens were not respected, and Aboriginal communities were denied the same basic standard of health, education and social services as other Canadian citizens.[169] It is an understandable concern of the federal government that whilst Aboriginal peoples remain part of Canada, the federal government is ultimately responsible for ensuring Aboriginal peoples are not disadvantaged relative to other sectors of Canadian society and that their fundamental rights and interests as Canadian citizens are respected. These obligations and responsibilities of course extend to potentially vulnerable Aboriginal children living within self-governing communities, a point made clear by Ryan-Froslie J in *Re R.T.* in her analysis of the provincial government's obligations to Aboriginal children under section 15 of the Canadian Charter.[170] During the course of self-government negotiations, the federal government has therefore insisted on the inclusion of a number of measures aimed at ensuring the fundamental rights and interests of Aboriginal individuals living within self-governing communities are protected.

Standards of good governance

One important requirement imposed by the federal government on Aboriginal communities has been to make certain basic standards of good democratic governance a precondition of self-government.[171] The Policy Guide makes it clear that self-governing Aboriginal communities must develop and entrench within their internal constitutions adequate systems of political and financial accountability and ensure that their law-making and decision-making procedures are open, transparent and fair.[172] The benchmark against which the suitability of these accountability measures are to be judged 'are those existing for other governments and institutions of similar size' – although the Guide also makes it clear that they need not be identical in all respects.[173] These requirements are

168 K. Wilkins (1999). 'But We Need the Eggs: The Royal Commission, the Charter of Rights and the Inherent Right of Aboriginal Self-government', *University of Toronto Law Journal*, 49: 53, 55–7.

169 Ibid., 82–3.

170 *Re R.T., M.T., M.A.T., A.L., and K.A.* (2004) SKQB 503, [75]–[93].

171 For the purposes of the following analysis, the Nisga'a Final Agreement and the Carcross/Tagish First Nation Self-Government Agreement (entered into under the Yukon Umbrella Agreement) will be used to illustrate the federal government's approach to negotiated settlements. Where relevant, reference will also be made to the more limited Agreement in Principle reached between the Blood Tribe, the federal government and Alberta on the implementation of self-government over child welfare on Blood Tribe lands.

172 *Supra* note 9, 12–14.

173 Ibid.

faithfully incorporated into the various self-government agreements concluded to date. Both the Carcross/Tagish First Nation Self-Government Agreement and the Nisga'a Final Agreement include detailed provisions as to the substantive content of their respective constitutions. The Carcross/Tagish Agreement provides that their Constitution must provide for a citizenship code;[174] the composition, membership, powers, duties and procedures of the governing bodies of the Carcross/Tagish Nations;[175] systems ensuring financial accountability;[176] recognition and protection of the rights and freedoms of Carcross citizens;[177] and procedures for challenging the validity of Carcross/Tagish First Nation laws.[178] The Nisga'a Final Agreement contains even more detailed provisions as to the form and content of the Nisga'a Constitution, providing amongst other things that the Nisga'a Government must be democratically accountable to Nisga'a citizens;[179] that elections for Nisga'a Lisims Government and each Nisga'a Village Government must be held at least every five years;[180] that all Nisga'a citizens must be eligible to vote in Nisga'a elections and to hold office in Nisga'a Government;[181] and that the Constitution must recognize and protect the rights and freedoms of Nisga'a citizens.[182]

The extent to which a very Western democratic system of government has been entrenched in these provisions, at the potential expense of more traditional and culturally appropriate models of Aboriginal governance is concerning. As Borrows argues, the structure of Nisga'a governance adopted in the Agreement 'significantly departs from, and in most respects replaces, the traditional House (wilps) system of government' and 'represent[s] a substantial challenge to Nisga'a attempts to fashion their lives in different economic, social and political terms from those of the majority around them'.[183]

Harmonization with existing federal or provincial standards

A second important mechanism employed by the federal government to ensure certain standards are met by Aboriginal governments and institutions is to insist that when an Aboriginal government is exercising jurisdiction over certain matters, that jurisdiction is exercised in accordance with federal or provincial standards. The Federal Policy Guide provides that even in core areas of Aboriginal jurisdiction 'harmonization of laws' may be required. The Nisga'a Final Agreement thus states that whilst the Nisga'a have jurisdiction over the delivery of child welfare services,

174 Carcross/Tagish First Nation Self-Government Agreement 2005, 10.1.1.
175 Ibid., 10.1.2.
176 Ibid., 10.1.3.
177 Ibid., 10.1.4.
178 Ibid., 10.1.5.
179 Nisga'a Final Agreement 1999, 11.9(k).
180 Ibid., 11.9(k)(i).
181 Ibid., 11.9(k)(ii).
182 Ibid., 11.9(o).
183 Borrows, *supra* note 165, 635–6.

including legislative powers, a precondition of exercising the jurisdiction is that they establish standards that are comparable to provincial standards:

> 11.89. Nisga'a Lisims Government may make laws in respect of child and family services on Nisga'a Lands, provided that those laws include standards comparable to provincial standards intended to ensure the safety and well-being of children and families.

A similar precondition is placed on Nisga'a jurisdiction over adoption. Whilst the Agreement establishes that Nisga'a Government will be able to make laws in respect of the adoption of Nisga'a children, it is prescribed that those laws must meet the provincial standard of making the best interests of the child the paramount consideration – a problematic requirement for many Aboriginal communities who would traditionally take a much more communal or relationship-based approach to child welfare.[184]

The Blood Tribe Governance and Child Welfare Agreement in Principle takes a similar approach. Whilst the Agreement provides that the Blood Tribe Government will have law-making authority over a range of child welfare and child protection matters, the Blood Tribe also acknowledges 'the need for the harmonization of Blood Tribe Law and Alberta laws in respect of Child Welfare matters' and 'the need for the Blood Tribe Government to harmonize its programs and services relating to Child Welfare matters and program and service standards with Alberta, and where necessary, with Canada, to ensure the most efficient and effective use of resources'.[185] More specifically, the Agreement-in-Principle provides that the Blood Tribe will ensure that provincial standards are met in a number of respects including ensuring that the best interests of the child is the paramount consideration in ensuring the safety and protection of children,[186] that facility-based services substantially conform to the design and program standards of provincial facilities elsewhere in Alberta,[187] that programmes and services are delivered by appropriately qualified staff,[188] that a duty to report child welfare concerns is placed on every person in the Blood Tribe Government's jurisdiction,[189] and that a system is developed for the independent audit and service practice review of child welfare standards in accordance with standards agreed between the Blood Tribe Government and the Province.[190]

184 Nisga'a Final Agreement 1999, 11.96.

185 Blood Tribe Governance and Child Welfare Agreement in Principle 2003, 9.17–9.18.

186 Ibid., 5.3(a).

187 Ibid., 5.3(b).

188 Ibid., 5.3(c).

189 Ibid., 5.3(d).

190 Ibid., 5.3(e).

A similar underlying concern with providing for comparable standards of service delivery is evident in the Yukon self-government agreements, albeit the language in the individual agreements is considerably more open than that found in the Nisga'a and Blood Tribe Agreements. As regards the delivery of *devolved* programmes and services, although the Yukon Umbrella Agreement and the Carcross/Tagish Final Agreement state that financial transfer agreements are to be entered into with the intention of specifying 'the obligations of all parties, including minimum program delivery standards',[191] the Final Agreement and the Carcross/Tagish Self-Government Agreement at least make it clear that the formulation of basic common standards are to be the subject of *negotiation* rather than unilateral federal imposition.[192] Moreover, the law-making powers of individual Yukon First Nations, which under the Carcross/Tagish Self-Government Agreement specifically includes the provision of social and welfare services, adoption, and the guardianship, custody, care and placement of Carcross/Tagish First Nation children, would appear to be subject to no express limitations or restrictions.

However, even where the Aboriginal community is afforded relatively unfettered law-making authority in an area such as child welfare, there is a further important potentially assimilatory feature of all these agreements which threatens to undermine the cultural autonomy promised by the Aboriginal community's assumption of jurisdiction: Aboriginal law, at least at the appellate level, will continue to be interpreted, implemented and enforced through the provincial/territorial courts.[193] It is certainly questionable whether, in performing this role, the provincial/territorial court system will be able to set aside their deeply entrenched cultural biases to maintain the cultural integrity of Aboriginal legal systems.

Federal paramountcy

A third mechanism employed by the federal government has been to retain paramount authority over certain specific areas of jurisdiction. As the 1995 policy statement provides:

> The government takes the position that negotiated rules of priority may provide for the paramountcy of Aboriginal laws, but may not deviate from the basic principle that those federal and provincial laws of overriding national or provincial importance will prevail over conflicting Aboriginal laws.[194]

191 Umbrella Final Agreement between the Government of Canada, the Council for Yukon Indians, and the Government of the Yukon 1993, [24.6.1.2] and Carcross/Tagish First Nation Final Agreement 2005, [24.6.1.2].

192 Carcross/Tagish First Nation Final Agreement 2005, [24.6.1.2] and Carcross/Tagish First Nation Self-Government Agreement 2005, [17.3.5].

193 Nisga'a Final Agreement 1999, [12.45–12.48]; Blood Tribe Governance and Child Welfare Agreement in Principle 2003, [6.8]–[6.9]; and Carcross/Tagish First Nation Self-Government Agreement 2005, [13.6.4.2.]. Borrows, *supra* note 165, 636.

194 *Supra* note 9, 11. The Royal Commission supported the existence of this general overriding authority vested in the federal government, arguing that even within the core

The position could be taken that as laws pertaining to the 'protection of the health and safety of all Canadians' constitute matters falling within the 'national interest', this provides the constitutional basis for the federal government to retain overriding jurisdictional authority in an area such as child welfare. This is not, however, the approach that has been adopted to child welfare in the Nisga'a and Blood Tribe Agreements, both of which explicitly provide that Nisga'a or Blood Tribe Law will prevail to the extent of any inconsistency or conflict with federal or provincial law.[195] Less clear is the Carcross/Tagish Self-Government Agreement which provides that Canada and the Carcross/Tagish First Nation shall enter into negotiations to conclude an agreement providing for those areas in which Carcross/Tagish legislation shall prevail over federal laws 'of general application'.[196] However, the requirement that the law must be of 'general application' would seem to preclude the federal government passing overriding legislation in the specific field of Aboriginal or, more specifically, Carcross/Tagish child welfare, as child welfare is a matter generally falling within the jurisdiction of the province.

More worrying is the lack of constitutional status given to the Yukon self-government agreements and, when concluded, that which will be afforded to the Blood Tribe Final Agreement. Despite the federal government's apparent commitment in the 1995 Policy Guide to protecting self-government agreements as treaty rights under s 35, not all agreements are being afforded such protection.[197] This lack of constitutional entrenchment renders them vulnerable to unilateral repudiation by the federal government, albeit this 'sovereign authority' is subject to any constitutionally entrenched requirements of the treaty itself, such as the duty of consultation specified in the Yukon Umbrella Final Agreement.[198] Moreover, even in the case of agreements protected under s 35, such as the Nisga'a Agreement, the federal government is still able to infringe constitutionally protected treaty rights provided the prescribed justificatory standard set down by the Supreme Court in *Sparrow*, *Gladstone* and *Delgamuukw* is met.[199] Given the broader considerations set down by Lamer CJ as potentially justifying an infringement of rights under

---

sphere of Aboriginal jurisdiction, the federal government retains the ultimate power 'in matters of overriding importance to the federal government'. RCAP, *supra* note 1, 214–16.

195 Nisga'a Final Agreement 1999, 11.91. Blood Tribe Governance and Child Welfare Agreement in Principle 2003, [5.5].

196 Carcross/Tagish First Nation Self-Government Agreement, [13.5.2]. It is specifically provided that Carcross/Tagish law will prevail over Yukon law of general application. See [13.5.3].

197 *Supra* note 9. See: Blood Tribe Governance and Child Welfare Agreement in Principle 2003, [9.1] and Umbrella Final Agreement between the Government of Canada, the Council for Yukon Indians and the Government of the Yukon 1993, [24.12.1].

198 Umbrella Final Agreement between the Government of Canada, the Council for Yukon Indians, and the Government of the Yukon 1993, [24.10.1]. See Dickson, *supra* note 158, 421, 430–1 and 450–1.

199 *R v Marshall* [1999] 3 S.C.R. 593, [6] and [24]–[45], confirming *R v Badger* [1996] 1 S.C.R. 771. For commentary on the *Marshall* decisions see, Henderson, *supra*

s 35, it is at least now plausible to argue that infringements of Aboriginal law-making powers could be justified pursuant to the federal government's fiduciary obligations and the broad principles articulated by the Supreme Court to 'protect the Aboriginal peoples from themselves', the 'broader public interest' or 'for the good of the community as a whole'.

Canadian Charter of Rights and Freedoms

The fourth and most controversial weapon of control in the armoury of the federal government is its 'non-negotiable' requirement that all Aboriginal governments be bound by the Canadian Charter of Rights and Freedoms. The Federal Policy Guide provides:

> The Government is committed to the principle that the *Canadian Charter of Rights and Freedoms* should bind all governments in Canada, so that Aboriginal peoples and non-Aboriginal Canadians alike may continue to enjoy equally the rights and freedoms guaranteed by the Charter. Self-government agreements, including treaties, will, therefore, have to provide that the Canadian Charter applies to Aboriginal governments and institutions in relation to all matters within their respective jurisdictions and authorities.[200]

The Royal Commission took exactly the same view, arguing 'all people in Canada are entitled to enjoy the protection of the Charter's general provisions in their relations with governments in Canada no matter where in Canada the people are located or which governments are involved'.[201] As the Charter purportedly represents the embodiment of Canadian society's most fundamental norms and values, its uniform application across all Canadian governments has clearly acquired vital symbolic significance for the federal government.[202] It has also acquired great symbolic importance for those concerned about the potential 'misuse' of power by Aboriginal governments and the resulting vulnerability of the rights and interests of individuals living within self-governing Aboriginal communities.[203] Indeed, the mandatory application of the Charter to all Aboriginal governments has attracted strong support from some Aboriginal women, most notably the Native Women's Association of Canada (NWAC), who argue that the subordination of the individual to the group has no legitimate foundation within contemporary Aboriginal cultures and the Charter therefore constitutes an appropriate and vital source of protection for individual women and children against public, and perhaps even private, abuses

note 116 and Borrows, *supra* note 165, 628–30. On the question of the federal government's right to infringe even constitutionally protected treaties, see Graben, *supra* note 12, 74–5.

200 *Supra* note 9, 4.

201 RCAP, *supra* note 1, 230.

202 Wilkins, *supra* note 168, 80.

203 Ibid., 82–3.

of power.[204] Although the effectiveness of the Charter as a means of advancing the rights of Aboriginal children should not be too readily assumed, the right to life, liberty and security of the person enshrined within section 7 of the Charter does at least have the potential, as is clear from the case of *Re R.T.*,[205] to provide specific protection against inadequate, harmful and perhaps even abusive child welfare policies and practices.[206]

However, the application of the Charter to self-governing Aboriginal communities has proved extremely contentious. It has attracted strong opposition from a range of Aboriginal leaders, including leading Aboriginal scholars, who argue that the norms, values and individual rights embodied in the Charter are fundamentally inconsistent with the values, socio-economic organization and basic cultural norms of traditional Aboriginal communities.[207] The differences are explained by Boldt and Long:

> North American Indian tribes ... did not have the experience of feudalism. Moreover, unlike European states, the foundation of their social order was not based on hierarchical power wielded by a centralized political authority. Power and authority could not be claimed by or delegated to any individual or subset of the tribe; it was vested only in the tribe as a whole. The tribal community performed all governmental functions in an undifferentiated fashion. Although highly organized, the tribes did not undergo the separation of state and church from the community. Social order was based on spiritual solidarity derived from the moral integration that came from acquiescence to tribal customs. By

204 See, e.g., T. Nahanee (1996). 'Dancing with a Gorilla: Aboriginal Women, Justice and the Charter', in *Royal Commission on Aboriginal Peoples, Round Table Discussion on Justice Issues*. Ottawa: Minister of Supply and Services, Canada, 359, 367–77.

205 *Re R.T., M.T., M.A.T., A.L., and K.A.* (2004) SKQB 503.

206 Ibid., [65]–[69]. Note, however, that the Charter has generally failed to make much of an impact on children's rights and family law more generally. See, e.g., S. Toope (1991). 'Riding the Fences: Courts, Charter Rights and Family Law', *Canadian Journal of Family Law*, 9: 57; S. Boyd (2000). 'The Impact of the Charter of Rights and Freedoms on Canadian Family Law', *Canadian Journal of Family Law*, 17: 293; and N. Bala (2000–2001). 'The Charter of Rights and Family Law in Canada: A New Era', *Canadian Family Law Quarterly*, 18: 373. Jennifer Koshan is equally cautious regarding the Charter's effectiveness as a mechanism for protecting the individual rights of Aboriginal women. See J. Koshan (1998), 'Aboriginal Women, Justice and the Charter: Bridging the Divide?', *UBC Law Review*, 32(1): 23.

207 M. E. Turpel (1989–1990). 'Aboriginal Peoples and the Canadian Charter: Interpretative Monopolies, Cultural Differences', *Canadian Human Rights Yearbook*, 6: 3; M. E. Turpel (1992). 'Aboriginal Peoples and the Canadian Charter of Rights and Freedoms: Contradictions and Challenges', in J. Banfield (ed.) *Readings in Law and Society*. Concord: Captus Press; M. Boldt and A. Long (1992). 'Tribal Philosophies and the Canadian Charter of Rights and Freedoms', in J. Banfield (ed.) *Readings in Law and Society*, Concord: Captus Press; and P. Monture-Angus (1999). *Journeying Forward. Dreaming of First Nations Independence*. Halifax, NS: Fernwood Publishing, 135–50.

> unreservedly accepting customary authority as their legitimate guide in living and working together, Indians were freed from the need for coercive personal power, hierarchical authority relationships, and a separate ruling entity to maintain order. Because no state and no rulers existed, individuals had no need for protection from the authority of others. Custom not only offered a well-elaborated system of individual duties and responsibilities, but was designed to protect human dignity. If all members of the tribe obeyed the sacred customs, then as a logical outcome each member would be assured of equality, self-worth, personal autonomy, justice, and fraternity – that is human dignity. Dignity was protected by a system of unwritten, positively stated mutual duties rather than negatively stated individual legal rights. With the exception of his obligation to impersonal custom, the individual was restrained in his autonomy and freedom. Anything not proscribed by custom was "permitted".[208]

To put it in its starkest terms, Mary Ellen Turpel has argued that on one side stands the Charter with its Western liberal tradition of 'individualism, competition and self-interest', on the other stands the Aboriginal philosophy of 'spiritual unity, consistency, co-operation and self-denial'.[209] Whilst in contemporary Canada such a strong dichotomy between the two cultures may now be overstated, it is clear that, given its roots in the particular socio-economic and political experiences of the West and its resulting cultural bias, in the view of many Aboriginal and non-Aboriginal commentators, the application of the Charter to Aboriginal communities poses a serious threat to their identity and survival as distinct cultural communities: that it is, in other words, just another tool of assimilation in the hands of a colonial government.[210]

Some protection against the Charter's potentially assimilatory effects is afforded by s 25 of the Charter which provides: 'the guarantee in this Charter of certain rights and freedoms shall not be construed so as to abrogate or derogate from any Aboriginal, treaty or other rights or freedoms that pertain to the Aboriginal peoples of Canada.' The Federal Policy Guide claims that s 25 ensures that the Charter strikes a 'sensitive balance between individual rights and freedoms, and the unique values and traditions of Aboriginal peoples in Canada'.[211] An Aboriginal self-governing community could thus seek to employ s 25 to try and exempt culturally-based child welfare practices from Charter scrutiny. However, there is considerable uncertainty as to the exact scope of s 25 and its affect on Aboriginal rights, such as the right to self-government. Some commentators argue that on a strict reading of s 25, Aboriginal rights have clear priority over any competing Charter rights, such that, any Charter right which 'abrogates' or 'derogates' from the Aboriginal right to self-government would

208 Cited by Wilkins, *supra* note 168, 88–9.

209 Turpel (1992), *supra* note 207, 243.

210 Boldt and Long, *supra* note 207, 247. See also Wilkins, *supra* note 168, 86–97.

211 *Supra* note 9.

have to give way.[212] This would effectively immunize self-government rights from Charter-based challenges. However, other commentators disagree that s 25 has this protective function, arguing that the intention behind s 25 was to shield distinctive Aboriginal and treaty rights from Charter challenges by non-native groups, such as a challenge brought to the right to self-government under the equality guarantee enshrined in s 15. Its purpose was not to protect Aboriginal governments from alleged violations of the individual rights and interests of their own citizens.[213] This is the approach taken to s 25 by Bastarache J in his minority judgment in the Supreme Court decision of *R v Kapp*.[214] Although supporting an interpretation of s 25 which would afford strong protection to Aboriginal rights from equality challenges brought by non-Aboriginal groups, Bastarache J refused to accept s 25 would operate as a shield against challenges brought by Aboriginal individuals against their own governments – a shield which would render the federal government's insistence that the Charter apply to all self-governing communities entirely futile.[215] Hogg and Turpel suggest a middle ground. They contend that whilst s 25 does not prevent Aboriginal governments from being subjected to Charter challenges, it does provide a clear basis for adopting an interpretation of Charter rights that is 'deferential to Aboriginal culture'.[216] Efforts would thus be made in each case, within the limits of the right, for an interpretation of the Charter to be found which is consistent with the community's cultural traditions and practices, particularly where different standards apply and the difference is integral to a culturally-based policy of the community.[217] Adopting this approach, section 25 would have the capacity to create some, albeit limited, space for Aboriginal difference to emerge. However, even this more modest interpretation of s 25 is controversial. On the one hand it undermines the uniform application of the Charter to all Canadian governments and arguably results in differential protection being afforded to different groups of Canadian citizens.[218] On the other hand, it does not protect Aboriginal communities from substantive scrutiny in non-native courts under a rights-based regime, much of which it claims to be culturally alien and inappropriate.

The Charter has clearly been a divisive issue within many Aboriginal communities. It raises complex questions about how to define and articulate the

212 Wilkins, *supra* note 168, 109–11.

213 Hogg and Turpel, *supra* note 148, 214–15; B. Slattery (1982–1983). 'The Constitutional Guarantee of Aboriginal and Treaty Rights', *Queens Law Journal*, 8: 232, 239–40; and W. Pentney (1987). 'The Rights of the Aboriginal Peoples of Canada and the Constitution Act, 1982. Part I. The Interpretive Prism of Section 25', *UBC Law Review*, 22: 21, 28–9.

214 *R v Kapp* [2008] 2 SCR 483, [76]–[110]. The majority decided the case on different grounds but expressed concern at Bastarache J's approach to s 25.

215 Hogg and Turpel, *supra* note 148, 215.

216 Ibid.

217 Ibid.

218 Wilkins, *supra* note 168, 109.

essential values of a living culture and how marginalized and disempowered groups are to secure a meaningful role within that process. Monture-Angus, for example, is critical of NWAC whose approach, she argues, is not based 'in a cultural understanding of Aboriginal reality' and who are unable, in her view, to give a voice to Aboriginal 'tradition'. She thus argues that whilst NWAC is able to give a voice to those who have experienced the effects of 'urbanization' and 'disenfranchisement', it does not and should not purport to represent the position of all Aboriginal women.[219] There is of course nothing unusual or problematic about the existence of dissent and debate between the different factions of a mature political community. The question of the application of the Charter to Aboriginal governments is, essentially, an issue for each individual community to resolve as an exercise of its right to self-determination. Should a community choose to adopt the Charter as an appropriate reflection of the normative basis of its society, it is clearly free to do so. What is, however, inappropriate if decolonization is to be achieved is for the federal government to impose the Charter on Aboriginal self-governing communities. As Monture-Angus argues:

> [O]ne must conclude that an unconsented to application of the Charter to Indian governments acting in both their traditional capacity and in a traditional way (where gender respect is an absolute requirement) would be an unlawful and unallowable intrusion on the sovereignty of Indian nations. Such an incursion must be seen as a direct threat and a re-entrenchment of colonial patterns of oppression, which many people see as the source of the majority of our present difficulties.[220]

The process of colonization in Canada provides damning evidence of the damage that can be caused to the very fabric of a society when faced with the *imposition* of the culturally rooted norms, mores and practices of another socio-political community. Not only are imposed 'solutions' lacking cultural grounding and a required sense of community acceptance and/or ownership an inappropriate perpetuation of colonialism, they risk further destabilizing Aboriginal communities by undermining traditional governance structures and customary methods of exercising control over potentially powerful groups.[221] In short, such 'solutions' are ultimately likely to fail and may well worsen rather than improve the position of vulnerable individuals. It is therefore deeply unfortunate that this continuing imposition of another's 'worldview' represents the current approach to the implementation of Aboriginal self-government in Canada.

---

219 Monture-Angus, *supra* note 207, 148–9.

220 Ibid., 150.

221 Wilkins, *supra* note 168, 78–9, 90–1 and 96.

Conclusion

The constitutional protection afforded to Aboriginal and treaty rights under s 35 of the Canadian Constitution and the federal government's subsequent acceptance that Aboriginal peoples have an inherent right to self-government constitute hugely significant steps forward in the struggle of Aboriginal peoples. As a result of these developments, self-government, including self-government over child welfare, has become a reality for many Aboriginal people in Canada, promising to deliver to Aboriginal communities at least some measure of autonomy and control over their own social, cultural, political and economic affairs. The substantial progress which has been made in recent years should not be forgotten. However, if Canada's progress on self-government is to provide a potential model for other jurisdictions such as Australia, the serious risks and limitations of this process also need to be addressed.

The federal government's 'non-negotiable' conditions for entering into a self-government agreement with an Aboriginal community make the modern treaty process, as the principal mechanism for achieving self-government, deeply problematic in many respects. It is clearly questionable whether real autonomy is being secured for self-governing Aboriginal communities when the Canadian government is still so clearly defining the 'rules of the game'. As Gordon Christie puts it, '[t]hey begin with the assumption that the state (or dominant society) is there, a given, and then imagine Indigenous peoples coming to this center of power to try to argue (somehow) that they should have a place within the larger system'.[222] By subjecting Aboriginal law-making authority in core areas such as child welfare to existing non-native standards and by reserving to itself substantial overriding control, the federal government has successfully narrowed the constitutional space in which Aboriginal difference can emerge. Borrows shares Christie's concerns, arguing that there is a serious 'imbalance' within the current treaty negotiations such that rather than enhancing the opportunities for Aboriginal peoples to exercise self-determination over their lives, 'the contemporary treaty relationship requires Aboriginal conformity with Canadian practices, customs, traditions and laws'.[223] He continues:

> [T]hese developments may contain as much cause for concern as for celebration. Even though these agreements certainly increase the options available to Aboriginal peoples, they simultaneously limit opportunities to pursue objectives that may differ in significant ways from those of Canada. Perhaps this circumscription is to be expected in any negotiated process where "give and take" is found on both sides of the table. On balance, however, Aboriginal peoples are giving up much more in this process than they are gaining. At

222 G. Christie (2007). 'Culture, Self-Determination and Colonialism: Issues around the Revitalization of Indigenous Legal Traditions', *Indigenous Law Journal*, 6: 13, 16.

223 Borrows, *supra* note 165, 634.

> the same time, Canada seems to be giving up much less with respect to its governmental structure and system of landholding.[224]

The Canadian government's concern to maintain its constitutional integrity based on core liberal values and the protection of its individual citizens is understandable. However, the current approach betrays the right of indigenous peoples to self-determination. With the founding tenets of the Canadian state remaining completely unchallenged, it is certainly questionable whether self-government in Canada has made any significant inroads into the colonial power structures of non-native society. It hardly amounts to successful decolonization when the locus of power remains unchanged:

> Historically, power permeated the relationship between dominant society and Aboriginal nations. For many generations the colonial state has unceasingly directed power to the task of subjugating and controlling Aboriginal nations (and families and individuals). This power continues to be wielded, though now in more subtle, entrapping forms. To move to a post-colonial world this power must be tempered and controlled (to allow, for example, Indigenous legal traditions to be revitalized and integrated into a threefold pluralist world).[225]

It is clear that if self-determination is to be secured for Aboriginal peoples, the Canadian government must be willing to return to Aboriginal communities much greater power and authority over their internal affairs, including child welfare, than has so far been the case. However, the restrictions imposed on self-government by the Canadian government in the ongoing treaty negotiations, and the recent disappointing decisions of the Supreme Court on Aboriginal rights under s 35, make clear that Aboriginal peoples remain fundamentally subordinate to the unchallenged sovereignty of the Canadian state. What Borrows calls the 'domesticating doctrines' employed by the Supreme Court and the Canadian federal government keep Aboriginal peoples effectively trapped under non-native control and authority and simply represent a further stage in the imposition of colonial rule.[226]

Breaking through this colonial mindset is essential if real progress is to be made on achieving internal sovereignty for indigenous peoples. However, the clear and firmly entrenched position of the Canadian authorities, a position which it is safe to assume would be shared by the Australian authorities, suggests that only limited progress on fundamental questions such as Aboriginal 'sovereignty' will be made at the domestic level. It perhaps needs to be faced that at the domestic level there is a certain point beyond which neither the government nor the courts are ever likely to go. That point is the Crown's assumed sovereignty over Aboriginal peoples

224 Ibid.

225 Christie, *supra* note 222, 17.

226 Borrows, *supra* note 165, 618–19 and 661.

and their land. Whilst that assumption of sovereignty continues unchallenged, Aboriginal peoples will always remain subject to the overriding control of the Canadian or the Australian state. The current position of the Canadian federal government may therefore represent the 'high' point of domestic law and policy on the right of Aboriginal peoples to self-government without some form of external pressure being brought to bear upon them. In other words, given the unreceptive nature of the domestic audience, if a way is to be found to break through these barriers to achieving a vision of self-government underpinned by Aboriginal sovereignty it may be necessary to look beyond the constitutional boundaries and colonial mindset of the Canadian state to the rich body of norms and principles on indigenous rights now enshrined in international law. It is thus to the potential of international law to help break through the current impasse and deliver a model of self-government over child welfare in Canada and Australia that remains faithful to the right of indigenous peoples to self-determination whilst protecting the rights and interests of potentially vulnerable children living within self-governing communities that the final two chapters of this book now turn. Can international law deliver effective decolonization for Aboriginal children and their families?

PART IV
Broadening Horizons: Indigenous Peoples, Self-Determination and Protecting Children's Rights under International Law

Chapter 6
Indigenous Peoples, Self-Determination and Self-Government in International Law

Introduction

As with domestic law, there is a certain danger for Aboriginal peoples in engaging with international law. Operating within the constraints of a positivistic framework, modern international law is law made by states, for states. It is a system which first and foremost seeks to protect the vested interests of its constituent members and, at least until recently, has therefore shown very little interest in individuals or sub-state groups, particularly where the interests of the latter are perceived to threaten or destabilize state interests and security. A number of constraining factors would seem to make it an unlikely forum for successfully advancing the claims of indigenous peoples.[1] The positivist foundations of international law with its restricted focus on the rights and duties of states; its exclusion of sub-state groups; its rigid adherence to the principle of state sovereignty; and its strong dependence on the principle of state consent are just some of the more problematic for indigenous peoples. No matter how compelling the moral imperative may be, no norm of international law can become legally binding upon a particular state unless the state freely accepts the obligation or at least does not object to it. This makes international law, particularly in the sphere of international human rights, a somewhat unusual and at times intensely frustrating system. States are being asked to regulate their behaviour by assuming legally binding obligations with respect to their own citizens which are not always consistent with the state's own interests.[2] It is thus no surprise to find that when the key interests and priorities of the state, as it perceives them, are at stake, the state has not always been willing to cooperate. At the very heart of the system is a deep tension – a tension between principle and practice, between justice and self-interest, between the powerless and the powerful. It is a tension that has permeated the relationship between Aboriginal

1 J. Anaya (2004). *Indigenous Peoples in International Law* (2nd edn). New York: Oxford University Press, 19–20. See also H. Patrick Glenn (2011). 'The Three Ironies of the UN Declaration on the Rights of Indigenous Peoples', in S. Allen and A. Xanthaki (eds) *Reflections on the UN Declaration on the Rights of Indigenous Peoples*. Oxford: Hart, 171, esp. at 172–9 and J. Anaya (2007). 'Indigenous Law and Its Contribution to Global Pluralism', *Indigenous Law Journal*, 6: 3, 3–5.

2 C. Tomuschat (1993). 'Self-Determination in a Post-Colonial World', in C. Tomuschat (ed.) *Modern Law of Self-Determination*. Dordrecht: Martinus Nijhoff, 10.

peoples and international law. In a system run by states, for states, the very same obstacles encountered by indigenous peoples at the domestic level would seem to bar the way to progress within the international arena.

The history of the troubled relationship between indigenous peoples and international law makes bleak reading.[3] Given the crucial role played by international law in securing the colonization and subjugation of indigenous peoples, it is difficult to imagine how it could be said to provide a promising forum in which the contemporary claims of indigenous peoples to self-determination and sovereignty could be successfully advanced. However, despite the injustices committed against them, indigenous peoples have never abandoned the struggle for recognition of their rights under international law.[4] Indeed, determined to fight for recognition of their true international status, international law is perceived by many indigenous peoples as the only appropriate forum for advancing their claims which are regarded as 'essentially and fundamentally international in character'.[5] Indigenous peoples have therefore resolutely refused to accept the 'domestic status' to which nineteenth-century positivists abandoned them.[6] In more recent years, this determination to keep pushing at the conscience of the international community has been rewarded, with international law gradually responding more and more positively to the critical situation facing many indigenous peoples around the world. Facilitated by a number of important changes in the conceptual structure of international law, the post-1945 era has witnessed some highly significant developments in the field of indigenous rights.[7] Although the positivist school continues to exert a strong constraining hold over the 'revolutionary' potential of international law, the complex interaction of international law's constituent members with one another and with the IGOs, NGOs and numerous other organizations who together constitute the conscience of the international community, indigenous rights have enjoyed a certain renaissance. Perhaps most importantly, indigenous peoples have once again been able to claim their place as legitimate subjects of international law.[8]

---

3 See Anaya (2004), *supra* note 1, ch. 1 and P. Thornberry (2002). *Indigenous Peoples and Human Rights*. Manchester: Manchester University Press, ch. 3. For a more general analysis of the imperialism of international law see, A. Anghie (2005). *Imperialism, Sovereignty and the Making of International Law*. New York: Cambridge University Press, especially ch. 1.

4 Thornberry, ibid., 82.

5 G. Marks (2000). 'Sovereign States v Peoples: Indigenous Rights and the Origins of International Law', *Australian Indigenous Law Reporter*, 5: 1, 1.

6 Ibid., 5.

7 Indeed, Anaya contends that some of these structural changes are due to the way in which indigenous peoples have engaged with international law, pushing the international legal system to embrace 'a greater pluralism in the global legal and political landscape'. See Anaya (2007), *supra* note 1, 5.

8 Marks, *supra* note 5, 3 and 5.

The second half of the twentieth century saw a number of significant achievements for indigenous peoples. Concern for the situation of indigenous peoples at the international level was in many ways spearheaded by the ILO. The adoption of ILO Conventions No. 107 and No. 169 played a central role in bringing indigenous peoples back into the framework of international law.[9] It was, however, the UN's comprehensive agenda and increasingly high-profile work on indigenous rights that helped transform the legal landscape for indigenous peoples. In recent years, led by the work of the UN Working Group on Indigenous Populations (WGIP) and its associated expert mechanisms,[10] the UN has significantly raised the profile and status of its work in the field of indigenous rights. A Special Rapporteur on the Situation of Human Rights and Fundamental Freedoms of Indigenous Peoples was appointed in 2001,[11] a Permanent Forum on Indigenous Issues was established as a subsidiary organ of the Economic and Social Council in 2000,[12] and in 2007 the Human Rights Council established a new Expert Mechanism on the Rights of Indigenous Peoples as a subsidiary body of the Human Rights Council to replace the now disbanded WGIP.[13] These various mechanisms have all played a crucial role in raising awareness of the critical problems faced by indigenous peoples and have provided an important platform for discussion and debate between indigenous communities and the wider international community. Although many questions pertaining to indigenous rights remain deeply contentious, this has allowed the UN to make enormous strides towards building an international consensus on a number of core indigenous issues.[14] Nowhere is that 'core of common opinion'[15] more evident than in the General Assembly's adoption of the United Nations Declaration on the Rights of Indigenous Peoples in September 2007.[16]

---

9 C107 Convention concerning the Protection and Integration of Indigenous and Other Tribal and Semi-Tribal Populations in Independent Countries. Adopted 26 June 1957. Entered into force 2 June 1959. C169 Convention concerning Indigenous and Tribal Peoples in Independent Countries. Adopted 7 June 1989. Entered into force 5 September 1991. Nineteen states have ratified the Convention. For general commentary see, C. M. Brolmann and M. Y. A. Zieck (1993). 'Indigenous Peoples', in C. M. Brolmann, R. Lefeber and M. Y. A. Zieck (eds) *Peoples and Minorities in International Law*. Dordrecht and London: Martinus Nijhoff, 187, 199–209.

10 Established under ECOSOC Res. 1982/34. The WGIP was disbanded alongside its parent body, the UN Commission on Human Rights, in 2006.

11 Established under CHR Res. 2001/57. The Special Rapporteur's mandate was renewed by the Human Rights Council in 2007. In 2008 Professor James Anaya was appointed as the second Special Rapporteur. See: www2.ohchr.org/english/issues/indigenous/rapporteur.

12 See ECOSOC Res. 2000/22.

13 HRC Res. 6/36.

14 Anaya (2004), *supra* note 1, 64.

15 Ibid.

16 A/Res/61/295.

The Declaration constitutes an important landmark for indigenous relations with the international community. Although not legally binding, the UN Declaration constitutes a fundamentally important statement of the rights of indigenous peoples under international law that is capable of exerting a powerful influence over both international and domestic policy-making in this area.[17] It contains a number of ground-breaking provisions, not only setting down a number of important substantive guarantees as to indigenous rights, but also providing strong recognition of the conceptual basis for the international subjectivity of indigenous peoples. The Declaration's preambular paragraphs are particularly revealing as to the transformation that has occurred in the approach of the international community towards the status of indigenous peoples. Of particular significance is the *unqualified* recognition afforded to all indigenous peoples as peoples 'equal to all other peoples' under international law. Closely allied to this unqualified recognition of indigenous peoples as a 'peoples' is the recognition afforded to their original and continuing subjectivity under international law. The 'historic injustices' suffered by indigenous peoples 'as a result of their colonization and dispossession of their lands, territories and resources' is acknowledged, as is the original nation-to-nation relationship between states and indigenous peoples in the recognition accorded to treaties and other agreements between states and indigenous peoples as matters of 'international concern, interest, responsibility and character'.

The collective nature of the rights of indigenous peoples is a key feature of the Declaration and is again specifically acknowledged within the preamble. Contrary to the traditional state/individual dichotomy entrenched in international law, the Declaration recognizes indigenous peoples as distinct collectives standing between indigenous individuals and the state and holding rights and responsibilities with respect to their own citizens in fields such as governance and citizenship which are akin to the rights and responsibilities international law has long recognized and protected as inhering within states. Overwhelming emphasis is placed on the collective autonomy of indigenous peoples in their political, legal, social and

---

17 C. Charters (2009). 'Indigenous Peoples and International Law and Policy', in B. Richardson, S. Imai and K. McNeil (eds) *Indigenous Peoples and the Law. Comparative and Critical Perspectives*. Portland: Hart Publishing, 175. Opinions as to the status to be accorded to the rights enshrined within the Declaration differ. Some commentators are cautious, arguing that the Declaration should not be 'inflated' in an effort to raise it (inappropriately) to the level of binding international law. According to this view, the Declaration should be accepted in accordance with states' intentions as an aspirational political tool to be utilized at national negotiation tables to add legitimacy to the political claims of indigenous groups. See S. Allen (2011). 'The UN Declaration on the Rights of Indigenous Peoples and the Limits of the International Legal Project', in S. Allen and A. Xanthaki (eds) *Reflections on the UN Declaration on the Rights of Indigenous Peoples*. Oxford: Hart, 225. Other commentators have emphasized the 'legal' nature of the Declaration, either as an expression of customary international law or as an 'interpretative mechanism' through which existing fundamental rights can be understood. Ibid., 227–33.

economic lives, at the heart of which is acknowledged to be the right of indigenous peoples 'to practice and revitalize their cultural traditions and customs'.[18] The right of indigenous peoples to maintain and strengthen 'their distinct political, legal, economic, social and cultural institutions'[19] is thus recognized, alongside their right to promote, develop and maintain their own 'institutional structures and their distinctive customs, spirituality, traditions, procedures, practices and, in cases where they exist, juridical systems or customs'.[20] Closely linked to the right of indigenous peoples to maintain and develop their own 'decision-making institutions'[21] is the right to exercise effective control over their own lands and their own economic and social development.[22] However, the singularly most significant development in the Declaration is the inclusion within its substantive provisions of the unequivocal, unqualified right of indigenous peoples to self-determination. In the words of Article 3:

> Indigenous peoples have the right to self-determination. By virtue of that right they freely determine their political status and freely pursue their economic, social and cultural development.

Underpinning all other measures in the Declaration, the right to self-determination has potentially profound implications for states in terms of their future relationship with indigenous peoples.

In accepting the international standing of indigenous peoples and the possibility of an unqualified right to self-determination, the Declaration represents an extraordinary transformation in the treatment of indigenous peoples under international law. As Thornberry commented with respect to the Declaration when still in draft form, '[t]here is no more "radical" document in the field of international human rights. In the spectrum from reform to revolution, the text reaches towards the upper revolutionary end'.[23] This, of course, makes the Declaration extremely contentious. It is not without significance that the initial attempt to secure the General Assembly's adoption of the Declaration was deferred due to concerns expressed by a number of African countries,[24] and when finally put to a vote in September 2007, Canada, Australia, the United States and New Zealand all voted against (although all four states have subsequently endorsed it).[25]

18 UN Declaration on the Rights of Indigenous Peoples, Article 11.

19 Ibid., Article 5.

20 Ibid., Article 34.

21 Ibid., Article 18.

22 Ibid., Articles 20, 23, 26 and 28.

23 Thornberry, *supra* note 3, 375.

24 GA/SHC/3878.

25 There were 143 votes in favour, four against and 11 abstentions. A/61/PV.107. Australia announced its endorsement of the Declaration on 3 April 2010 (www.un.org/esa/socdev/unpfii/documents/Australia_official_statement_endorsement_UNDRIP.pdf), followed by New Zealand on 20 April 2010 (www.beehive.govt.nz/release/supporting-

Despite the controversy surrounding its adoption, the Declaration's significance in pushing forward the indigenous rights agenda should not be underestimated. The Declaration has already started to play a central role in structuring international relations between indigenous peoples and states under international law.[26] It will increasingly provide the context within which the international debate on the rights of indigenous peoples, including the right to self-determination, will be conducted, and will stand as a benchmark against which the decisions and actions of states will be subjected to critical analysis and evaluation. Both the Special Rapporteur and the Permanent Forum have strongly embraced the Declaration as providing the relevant normative standards for their work with states in the field of indigenous rights. There are early signs that the Treaty bodies are similarly prepared to embrace the Declaration as an important interpretative tool.[27] Despite the strong voices standing out against its legally binding character,[28] the Declaration and its controversial provisions are therefore already strongly entrenched within the normative framework of international law. It will constitute a continuing source of pressure on states to bring their practices and policies on indigenous peoples into line with its provisions.

Indigenous Peoples' Right to Self-Determination under Article 3 of the UN Declaration

Self-determination is central to the aspirations of indigenous peoples. Having witnessed the powerful role played by self-determination in the decolonization of Africa and Asia, it is the promise of self-determination to deliver effective liberation from colonial rule and return sovereign authority and power to indigenous communities that has captured the collective imagination of indigenous peoples around the world. As the international indigenous movement has grown in strength and influence, the right to self-determination has thus become their distinctive rallying cry. Yet, the struggle for recognition is not an easy one. Whilst indigenous peoples perceive the right to self-determination as a potentially powerful liberating force, states perceive it as a potentially destabilizing threat.

---

un-declaration-restores-nz039s-mana), Canada on 12 November 2010 (www.ainc-inac.gc.ca/ap/ia/dcl/stmt-eng.asp) and the United States on 16 December 2010 (www.state.gov/documents/organization/153223.pdf).

26 Charters, *supra* note 17, 175.

27 See, for example, the Committee on the Rights of the Child, General Comment No. 11 (2009), *Indigenous Children and their Rights under the Convention,*CRC/C/GC/11, [10] and Committee on Economic, Social and Cultural Rights, General Comment No. 21, *Right of Everyone to Take Part in Cultural Life (art. 15, para. 1(a), of the International Covenant on Economic, Social and Cultural Rights)*, E/c.12/GC/21, [7].

28 In endorsing the Declaration, the Australian, New Zealand, Canadian and US governments all emphasized its status as a non-legally binding aspirational document. *Supra* note 26.

The right of indigenous peoples to self-determination under international law is thus hugely controversial. This controversy is further complicated by the fact that self-determination is itself a complex and fiercely contested concept.[29] A lack of clarity as to who may claim the right to self-determination and what the substance of that right may entail has, in recent years, exacerbated the difficulty in finding a consensus on the specific question of indigenous peoples and the right to self-determination. This makes the successful inclusion of an unqualified right to self-determination in Article 3 of the UN Declaration all the more remarkable.

It is natural that in the wake of the adoption of the Declaration, discussion has turned to focus on the scope, meaning and significance of the right to self-determination as enshrined in Article 3.[30] The exact meaning of the right remains deeply contested. Debate centres on whether Article 3 is simply intended to recognize and confirm an existing customary law right of indigenous peoples 'as a colonized peoples' to self-determination under international law or marks a new and novel approach to the distinct situation of indigenous peoples trapped within the territorial boundaries of a post-colonial state.[31] With the scope and meaning of Article 3 still to be determined, it is important not to lose sight of the crucial question of whether indigenous peoples have an existing customary law right to self-determination. Not only is any such right already legally binding on states, thus overcoming the non-legally binding nature of the Declaration as a whole, but it is vital that the customary law right should inform current discussion as to the scope and meaning of Article 3, in particular by keeping to the fore of the debate the inextricable link in international law between the right to self-determination, decolonization and sovereignty. Undoubtedly, the content of indigenous peoples' right to self-determination as informed by customary international law will be

---

29 For perhaps the most comprehensive analysis of the scope and meaning of the right to self-determination in contemporary international law see A. Cassese (1995). *Self-determination of Peoples – A Legal Reappraisal.* New York and Cambridge: Cambridge University Press. For an excellent, more recent, summary see A. Xanthaki (2005). 'The Right to Self-Determination: Meaning and Scope', in N. Ghanea and A. Xanthaki (eds), *Minorities, Peoples, and Self-Determination.* Leiden: Martinus Nijhoff.

30 For an excellent discussion of the meaning of Articles 3 and 4 of the Declaration see H. Quane (2011). 'The UN Declaration on the Rights of Indigenous Peoples: New Directions for Self-Determination and Participatory Rights?', in S. Allen and A. Xanthaki (eds) *Reflections on the UN Declaration on the Rights of Indigenous Peoples.* Oxford: Hart, 259.

31 Quane sees the options somewhat differently. Having rejected the argument that Article 3 contains unqualified acceptance of the right to self-determination as traditionally understood in international law, she argues that Article 3 either represents a development of the existing *internal* right to self-determination or a completely new internal right. Both of these alternatives will be rejected in favour of an approach that affirms the right of indigenous peoples to self-determination as traditionally understood, that right being qualified in its application to indigenous peoples by the existing norms of international law. Ibid., 264–9.

stronger and potentially more far-reaching than any 'new' and 'unrestrained' interpretation of a *sui generis* right to self-determination 'created' by the Declaration. The well-trodden debate over the existing right of indigenous peoples to self-determination is not therefore rendered defunct by the Declaration but should be re-ignited by it.

A 'Colonized Peoples' with an Existing Right to Self-Determination under Customary International Law

Are indigenous peoples 'colonized peoples'?

Indigenous peoples have consistently maintained that as the colonized population of a discrete territory, they constitute a 'colonized peoples' within the accepted categories of international law. As a matter of principle, this argument is utterly convincing. Indigenous peoples, as all other peoples subjected to alien subjugation and domination, should therefore have a clear and unfettered right to self-determination as currently entrenched and understood in international law: they are, in other words, entitled to decolonization. However, such is the nature of international law, whilst the arguments may be sound in principle, establishing a solid legal basis for such a conclusion in the opinion and practice of states is a more difficult task.

There is no one formally accepted or 'official' definition of the term 'indigenous peoples' employed within the United Nations.[32] Attempts to include such a definition within the UN Declaration on the Rights of Indigenous Peoples 2007 were strongly opposed by indigenous groups who insisted on their right to self-identify as indigenous.[33] In the absence of a formal definition, the most

32 Commission on Human Rights, *Technical Review of the United Nations Draft Declaration on the Rights of Indigenous Peoples*, E/CN.4/Sub.2/1994/2, 10. *Study on Treaties, Agreements and Other Constructive Arrangements between States and Indigenous Populations. Second Progress Report Submitted by Mr. Miguel Alfonso Martinez*, Special Rapporteur, E/CN.4/Sub.2/1995/27, 63. As to the contentious issues arising from the competing definitions of indigenous peoples see B. Kingsbury (1998). '"Indigenous Peoples" in International Law: A Constructivist Approach to the Asian Controversy', *American Journal of International Law*, 92: 414.

33 Economic and Social Council, *Report of the Working Group Established in Accordance with Commission on Human Rights Resolution 1995/32 of 3 March 1995*, E/CN.4/1996/84, [30]. See also Economic and Social Council, *Report of the Working Group on Indigenous Populations on its Fourteenth Session*, E/CN.4/Sub.2/1996/21, [32]–[33] and Economic and Social Council, *Report of the Working Group on Indigenous Populations on its Fifteenth Session*, E/CN.4/Sub.2/1997/14, [6]. For the differing views of governments on the question of definition see: Economic and Social Council, *Report of the Working Group on Indigenous Populations on its Fifteenth Session*, E/CN.4/Sub.2/1997/14, [28]. See also Economic and Social Council, *Report of the Working Group on Indigenous Populations on its Thirteenth Session*, E/CN.4/Sub.2/1995/24, [41]–[51] and Economic and Social Council, *Report of the Working Group on Indigenous Populations on its Fourteenth Session*, E/CN.4/Sub.2/1996/21, [27]–[45].

authoritative guidance as to what is meant by the expression 'indigenous peoples' is the definition contained within Article 1 of ILO Convention No. 169 and the working definition set down by Martinez Cobo in his Study of the Problem of Discrimination against Indigenous Populations back in 1986.[34] These somewhat tentative definitions provide a useful starting point in determining whether or not indigenous peoples can be said to share the key characteristics and experiences of a colonized peoples.

A distinctive feature of both definitions is the fundamental connection drawn between indigenous peoples and a particular territorial base. The Cobo definition of indigenous peoples refers to their 'historical continuity with pre-invasion and pre-colonial societies that developed on their territories' and the determination of indigenous peoples 'to preserve, develop and transmit to future generations their ancestral territories'. The ILO definition similarly refers to the descent of indigenous peoples 'from the populations which inhabited the country, or a geographical region to which the country belongs'. For indigenous peoples, their special relationship with the land has always been a defining feature of their cultures. As it was put before the WGIP:

> Many indigenous representatives emphasized that land was at the core of their existence and that the relationship with their land was of spiritual, cultural, and material significance. Besides the question of self-determination, access to and control over lands, territories and natural resources were central for indigenous peoples throughout the world. Indigenous peoples depended on their land for their material and cultural survival and in order to survive they needed to be able to own, use, conserve and organise their own lands, territories and resources. The relationship to land of indigenous peoples was based on a unique philosophy of life and culture and a cosmic vision which evolved from the earth. Several indigenous representatives stated indigenous peoples were the caretakers of the land and that the land took care of them in return. Never before had indigenous communities been in such danger of extinction.[35]

The emphasis placed on indigenous peoples and their special relationship with the land is not, however, to ignore the fact that many indigenous peoples now find themselves permanently separated from their traditional territories.[36] Indeed, from

---

34 Commission on Human Rights, *Technical Review of the United Nations Draft Declaration on the Rights of Indigenous Peoples*, E/CN.4/Sub.2/1994/2, [note by secretariat].

35 Economic and Social Council, *Report of the Working Group on Indigenous Populations on its Seventeenth Session*, E/CN.4/Sub.2/1999/19, [84].

36 For the current numbers of indigenous peoples living in non-indigenous urban centres in New Zealand, the United States, Australia and Canada, see S. Imai (2009). 'Indigenous Self-Determination and the State', in B. Richardson, S. Imai and K. McNeil (eds) *Indigenous Peoples and the Law. Comparative and Critical Perspectives*. Portland: Hart Publishing, 300.

the perception of indigenous peoples, the fact that many indigenous groups have been dispossessed of their land through the forces of conquest or colonization is a vital part of their identity. Both definitions recognize this crucial factor in understanding the contemporary position of indigenous peoples. Cobo refers to indigenous peoples' historical continuity with 'pre-invasion and pre-colonial' societies living on their territories. The ILO Convention refers to occupation of the territory by indigenous peoples 'at the time of conquest or colonisation'. It is these experiences of 'conquest and colonisation' and the resulting alienation of indigenous peoples from their traditional lands that stand indigenous peoples apart from all other minority or sub-state groups.[37]

Many indigenous peoples clearly perceive themselves to be the victims of colonialism, arguing that they have been subjected to a form of alien domination depriving them not only of their land and resources but sovereignty over their own economic, social, cultural and political affairs. In May 2001, an Indigenous Peoples' Millennium Conference was held in Panama in preparation for the World Conference Against Racism to be held in Durban, South Africa, later that year. The agreed statement produced at that Conference clearly emphasizes the colonial context in which indigenous issues must be considered. The preamble sections are particularly striking:

> We note particularly the Declaration of Indigenous Peoples of the Americas and its finding that racial discrimination, xenophobia and related forms of intolerance are characteristics of dominant Western ideology and are reflected in the relationship Western society has maintained with the Indigenous Peoples of the world, constituting a historical problem with deep roots in colonialism and the enslavement of entire peoples, a problem that continues to this very day, denying Indigenous Peoples their right of self-determination … We recognise that colonialism in all its expressions continues to rob us of our ancestral knowledge, cultural and spiritual practices, of our economies and way of life of our Peoples, as well as our cultural and intellectual heritage which forms a part of our spirituality. It is the cause of the loss and ruination of our sacred places, the loss of our traditional health practices and traditional knowledge, and even now extends to the loss of our plant, animal and human genetic resources.[38]

The preamble goes on to adopt language commonly employed by the UN with respect to the decolonization of colonial territories in the post-Second World War

37 J. Anaya (2004). 'International Human Rights and Indigenous Peoples: The Move Toward the Multicultural State', *Ariz. J. Int'l & Comp. L.*, 21: 13, 13.

38 Economic and Social Council, World Conference Against Racism, Racial Discrimination, Xenophobia and Related Intolerance, *Information Received from Indigenous Organisations, Statement on the World Conference Against Racism of the Indigenous Peoples' Millennium Conference, Panama City, Panama, 7–11 May 2001*, E/CN.4/Sub.2/AC.4/2001/8.

period, calling upon states to 'comply with their sacred trust and to guarantee the right of decolonization and self-determination to all Indigenous Peoples in non-self-governing territories'.[39]

The close link between indigenous peoples and experiences of colonial domination is also emphasized by Miguel Martinez in his final report as UN Special Rapporteur on treaties, agreements and other constructive arrangements between states and indigenous populations. Martinez takes the position that there is a need to draw a clear distinction between indigenous peoples and minorities, arguing that it is the European powers' organized colonization of other continents on which indigenous peoples had lived since time immemorial that stands indigenous peoples apart from any other ethnic minority group.[40] Martinez's attempt to tie the concept of indigenous peoples so closely to patterns of colonial expansion is controversial.[41] However, it has the clear advantage that as a culturally discrete, formerly sovereign group with a marked territorial base from which they have commonly been permanently dispossessed through experiences of conquest and/or colonization, indigenous peoples have a tolerably clear and distinct identity under international law.[42] The crucial question is whether these distinctive characteristics are sufficient to establish indigenous peoples as a 'peoples' under international law.

International law has yet to provide us with any comprehensive definition of a 'peoples'. There is thus no one accepted set of objective criteria by which a claim to 'people-hood' may be determined. International law has preferred to proceed on a pragmatic basis taking each 'contender group' on an individual basis. The status of certain categories of peoples under international law has now been established with a fair degree of certainty. It is thus clear that the whole population of a state constitute a 'peoples' under international law,[43] as do the population of an overseas colonial territory.[44] Both of these groups have a right to self-determination and are

---

39 Ibid.

40 *Study on Treaties, Agreements and Other Constructive Arrangements between States and Indigenous Populations. Final Report by Miguel Alfonso Martínez, Special Rapporteur*, E/CN.4/Sub.2/1999/20, [73].

41 See, especially, Kingsbury, *supra* note 32.

42 Ibid., 419 and 448.

43 R. Higgins (1993). 'Postmodern Tribalism and the Right to Secession – Comments by R. Higgins', in C. Brolmann, R. Lefeber and M. Zieck (eds) *Peoples and Minorities in International Law*. Dordrecht and London: Martinus Nijhoff, 29, 29 and H. Quane (1998). 'The United Nations and the Evolving Right to Self-Determination', *International and Comparative Law Quarterly*, 47: 537, 541–7.

44 GA Res. 1514 (XV), *Declaration on the granting of independence to colonial countries and peoples*; GA Resolution 2625 (XXV), *Declaration on Principles of International Law concerning Friendly Relations and Co-operation among States in accordance with the Charter of the United Nations*; and *Legal Consequences for States of the Continued Presence of South Africa in Namibia (South West Africa) Notwithstanding*

entitled to exercise that right in both its external and internal dimensions.[45] It is equally clear under international law that minorities do not constitute a 'peoples' and, consequently, do not have a right to self-determination, howsoever defined.[46] The question is where, if anywhere, indigenous peoples fit within this framework.

The strong relationship between indigenous peoples and a discrete territorial base, alongside their experiences of dispossession and living under alien rule and domination, provides a strong foundation for the argument that indigenous peoples are a colonized peoples falling within the scope of GA Res. 1514 (XV) on the granting of independence to colonial countries and peoples and GA Res. 2625 (XXV) on principles of international law concerning friendly relations and co-operation among states in accordance with the Charter of the United Nations. However, one immediate difficulty with this argument lies in the concept of colonialism contained within GA Res. 1541 (XV) on the *Principles Which Should Guide Members in Determining Whether or Not an Obligation Exists to Transmit the Information called for under Article 73e of the Charter*. Principle IV of GA Res. 1541 (XV) has given rise to what has commonly been described as the 'salt-water' thesis. In guiding states as to whether or not they have an obligation to transmit information under Article 73(e) of the UN Charter on Non-Self-Governing Territories, Principle IV provides:

Security Council Resolution 276 (1970), ICJ Reports 1971, 16 [52]. See also Quane, ibid., esp. at 558.

45 Self-determination as enshrined within Articles 1(2) and 55 of the UN Charter and applied between states means the equal right of states to respect for their sovereign authority over their own territory and non-interference in their domestic affairs. See Higgins, *supra* note 43, 29.

46 Higgins, ibid., 33; Quane, *supra* note 43, 570–1; J. Crawford (1998). 'State Practice and International Law in Relation to Secession', *British Yearbook of International Law*, 69: 85; and P. Thornberry (1989). 'Self-determination, Minorities, Human Rights: A Review of International Instruments', *International and Comparative Law Quarterly*, 38: 867, 887–8. It can be argued that GA Res. 2625 (XXV) supports the right of minorities to secede from their 'host' state when their internal right to self-determination is being denied: that the state is not 'possessed of a government representing the whole people belonging to the territory without distinction as to race, creed or colour'. The argument is noted but not ruled upon by the Supreme Court of Canada in the *Reference re Secession of Quebec* (1998) 37 I.L.M. 1340, [134]–[138]. However, the contention that GA Res. 2625 (XXV) would afford a right of self-determination and unilateral secession to minorities is largely unsupported by state practice and by the most authoritative academic commentators (see Higgins and Crawford above). It is therefore highly unlikely to constitute an accepted norm of general international law. Similarly, commentators generally agree that minorities do not constitute a 'peoples' for the purposes of the right to self-determination enshrined in the common Article 1 of the International Covenants. See T. Franck (1993). 'Postmodern Tribalism and the Right to Secession', in C. Brolmann, R. Lefeber and M. Zieck (eds) *Peoples and Minorities in International Law*. Dordrecht and London: Martinus Nijhoff, 3, 17 and Quane, *supra* note 43, 561–2.

> Prima facie there is an obligation to transmit information in respect of a territory which is *geographically separate* and is distinct ethnically and/or culturally from the country administering it (emphasis added).

The idea that the colonial territory must be 'geographically separate' from the country administering it has generally been interpreted to mean that the two territories must not be contiguous. Whilst indigenous peoples would therefore have qualified as a colonial peoples when the colonies of the New World were administered from Europe, the process of incorporating the traditional territories of the indigenous peoples within the territorial boundaries of the 'post-colonial' state, making them in effect colonial enclaves, would seem to exclude them from this particular definition. The unsatisfactory nature of this approach to colonialism is illustrated by the arbitrary distinctions to which it gives rise. A slightly different approach to identifying colonial territories is, however, suggested in Principle V of Res. 1541 (XV), focusing not so much on the 'separateness' of the territory, as its 'distinctiveness':

> Once it has been established that such a prima facie case of *geographical and ethnical or cultural distinctness* of a territory exists, other elements may then be brought into consideration. These additional elements may be inter alia, of an administrative, political, juridical, economic or historical nature (emphasis added).

This idea of territorial *distinctiveness* would allow for a more nuanced approach to the complex reality of the legacy of colonialism. Moreover, it would be perfectly consistent with the much broader concept of colonialism contained within GA Res. 1514 (XV) and GA Res. 2625 (XXV).

GA Resolution 1514 (XV) contextualizes the right to self-determination by providing that, 'the subjection of peoples to *alien subjugation, domination and exploitation* constitutes a denial of fundamental human rights' (emphasis added).[47] The Resolution goes on to make it clear that this right is not restricted to those territories which have been officially designated as either trust or non-self-governing but extends to 'all other territories which have not yet attained independence'.[48] The wording of GA Res. 2625 (XXV) is similarly susceptible to a more inclusive interpretation, providing in general terms that every state has the duty to promote the self-determination of peoples, 'to bring a speedy end to colonialism, having due regard to the freely expressed will of the peoples concerned; and bearing in mind that subjection of peoples to *alien subjugation, domination and exploitation* constitutes a violation of the principle, as well as a denial of fundamental human rights' (emphasis added). Thus, rather than focusing

47 GA Resolution 1514 (XV). *Declaration on the granting of independence to colonial countries and peoples*, para. 1.

48 Ibid., para. 5.

on the geographical separation of the colonized territories, at the heart of the concept of colonialism enshrined in GA Resolutions 1514 (XV) and 2625 (XXV) is the notion of a peoples who are or have been subjected to some form of alien subjugation, domination and exploitation.

The argument that peoples with a discrete territorial base who are subjected to sustained political, economic and cultural oppression can be appropriately described as a 'colonized peoples' has found some support from Thomas Franck, albeit he terms the position one of 'neo-colonialism'.[49] As thus conceived, indigenous peoples have a strong argument that having first been subjected to 'alien' rule by the European colonizers from the seat of the imperial power itself and then by the equally 'alien' government of the post-colonial state, they fall squarely within the concept of colonialism. The formal severing of links between the European powers and the settler communities clearly did not alter the colonial reality for the indigenous population. Disenfranchised and highly marginalized by the settler population, the geographic location of the seat of 'European' power did not alter its fundamental economic, social, political and cultural distance from the indigenous population. That is not to say, however, that territorial distinctiveness is not important. The existence of a territorial base remains closely tied to the concept of a 'colonized peoples' within the two resolutions. The emphasis in Resolution 2625 (XXV) is, however, somewhat different, with the General Assembly focusing not on the fact of *geographical separation* but on the continuing *status* of the territory as 'distinct and separate' from that of the administering power:

> The territory of the colony or other Non-Self-Governing Territory has, under the Charter, a *status separate and distinct* from the territory of the State administering it; and such *separate and distinct status* under the Charter shall exist until the people of the colony or Non-Self-Governing Territory have exercised their right of self-determination in accordance with the Charter (emphasis added).

There is certainly no reason in principle why a colonial enclave cannot have a separate and distinct status from that of the surrounding territory, even if sustaining a case of *geographical separation* is more difficult.

Support for the 'people-hood' of indigenous peoples at the international level

Historically, states have demonstrated a clear reluctance to accept the use of the term 'peoples' when dealing with the rights of indigenous peoples at the international level. Although ILO Convention No. 169 does employ the term, its importance is substantively undermined by the heavy qualification contained within Article 1(3) that, 'the use of the term peoples within this Convention shall not be construed as having any implications as regards the rights which may attach to the term under international law'. The UN's approach has

49 Franck, *supra* note 46, 13–14. Crawford also provides some support for this approach in his analysis of the case of Bangladesh. See Crawford, *supra* note 46, 96.

been deliberately cautious. The Working Group of the Sub-Commission on Prevention and Discrimination and the Protection of Minorities (the WGIP) used the language of 'populations'; the Special Rapporteur on the situation of human rights and fundamental freedoms uses the term 'people'; and the Permanent Forum effectively avoids the issue by calling itself the 'Permanent Forum on Indigenous Issues'. There was also considerable disappointment at the position adopted in the *Durban Declaration and Programme of Action* following the World Conference against Racism, Racial Discrimination, Xenophobia and Related Intolerance (2001). Preceding the Durban Conference there had been strong support from the WGIP for indigenous peoples to be recognized as 'peoples', 'thereby ending the discriminatory practice of using terms such as indigenous populations or indigenous people when such peoples are referred to collectively'.[50] However, although the problems faced by indigenous peoples are referred to quite extensively throughout the Declaration, indigenous peoples were fiercely critical of the final text for the inclusion of an express disclaimer in paragraph 24 that the use of the term indigenous peoples 'cannot be construed as having any applications as to rights under international law'.[51]

At the institutional level there have, however, in recent years been significant signs of a change in approach. The UN website, for example, makes consistent use of the term 'indigenous peoples'. In a more formal setting, UN documentation on indigenous peoples, such as the various reports of the WGIP and the Special Rapporteur, make constant reference to indigenous peoples as 'peoples'.[52] The term 'indigenous peoples' was also used without qualification in the Johannesburg Declaration on Sustainable Development (2002).[53] The strongest support at the level of the UN for the 'people-hood' of indigenous peoples, has come, however, from the work of the UN Human Rights Committee. The Committee has refused to hear arguments relating to the right to self-determination contained within Article 1 of the Covenant under the individual complaints procedure.[54] It has,

50 Economic and Social Council, *Report of the Working Group on Indigenous Populations on its Eighteenth Session*, E/CN.4/Sub.2/2000/24, [214].

51 World Conference against Racism, Racial Discrimination, Xenophobia and Related Intolerance, *Declaration*, para. 24.

52 See, e.g., Human Rights Council, *Report of the Working Group on Indigenous Populations on its Twenty-fourth Session*, A/HRC/Sub.1/58/22 and *Report of the Special Rapporteur on the Situation of Human Rights and Fundamental Freedoms of Indigenous People, Rodolfo Stavenhagen*, A/HRC/6/15.

53 World Summit on Sustainable Development, *Johannesburg Declaration*, para. 25. This point was appealed to by indigenous peoples at the HRC Working Group in support of their argument that the term 'peoples' should be used without qualification in the Declaration. See Economic and Social Council, *Report of the Working Group Established in Accordance with Commission on Human Rights Resolution 1995/32*, E/CN.4/2003/92, [23].

54 *Lubicon Lake Band v. Canada*, Communication No. 167/1984 (26 March 1990), (A/45/40) (1990).

however, provided clear guidance on the question of the status of indigenous peoples through the State Party reporting procedure. The Committee's Concluding Observations with respect to Canada's fourth periodic report were unequivocal in this regard, with the Committee making it clear that as indigenous peoples are a 'peoples' under international law with a right to self-determination under common Article 1 of the International Covenants, Canada must report under this provision on issues relating to Aboriginal self-government and Aboriginal access to land and resources.[55]

Although the views of the Human Rights Committee are not binding on states, they constitute authoritative confirmation at the international level of the 'peoplehood' of indigenous peoples. The Committee had clearly been moving towards this position for some time, with their comments on states such as Norway and Australia also making it clear that issues pertaining to indigenous peoples, whilst relevant to Article 27, should also be considered as falling within the ambit of Article 1. As Mr Scheinin of the Committee explained to the Australian delegation appearing before the Committee on the examination of Australia's third and fourth periodic report:

> [T]he delegation had not given much support to the idea that the situation of indigenous peoples should be seen as an issue under article 1 of the Covenant. The Committee had on many occasions dealt with article 1 issues together with article 27 issues where indigenous peoples were concerned. Its case law repeatedly emphasised that for State parties to comply with article 27, it was essential that they should ensure the sustainability of the way of life of indigenous people and also secure their effective participation. He would suggest that strengthening the protection of indigenous peoples under article 1 would give depth and substance to Australia's implementation of other provisions of the Covenant.[56]

The Committee then goes on to reiterate this point in its Concluding Observations by dealing with questions relating to Aboriginal autonomy and control over their traditional lands and resources under Article 1 of the Covenant.[57] A similar approach is taken with respect to Norway, the Committee stating in its

55 Human Rights Committee, *Concluding Observations of the Human Rights Committee: Canada. 07/04/99,* CCPR/C/79/Add.105, [7]–[8]. See also, Human Rights Committee, *Consideration of Reports submitted by States Parties under Article 40 of the Covenant, Concluding Observations of the Human Rights Committee, Canada*, CCPR/C/CAN/CO/5, [8]–[9].

56 Human Rights Committee, *Summary Record of the 1856th meeting: Australia 28/07/2000 (Summary Record)*, CCPR/C/SR.1856, [67]. The Committee raised the question of Australia's policy on the right of Aboriginal peoples to self-determination under Article 1 of the Covenant in its list of issues: Human Rights Committee, *List of Issues: Australia. 25/04/2000*, CCPR/C/69/L/AUS, [4].

57 Human Rights Committee, *Concluding Observations of the Human Rights Committee: Australia 24/07/2000*, A/55/40, [506]–[507].

concluding observations that, 'as the Government and Parliament of Norway have addressed the situation of the Sami in the framework of the right to self-determination, the Committee expects Norway to report on the Sami people's right to self-determination under Article 1 of the Covenant, including paragraph 2 of that article'.[58]

The position now being increasingly adopted by the institutions of the UN and, most importantly, by the Human Rights Committee, places significant pressure on states, particularly those who are parties to the Covenant, to accept the 'peoplehood' of indigenous peoples under international law. In recent years there have therefore been some important concessions by key states such as Canada, Australia and the United States. The Canadian government, whilst remaining cautious on the issue of self-determination, has accepted at the international level that indigenous peoples are not just members of an 'ethnic group' but have a 'unique' status and 'unique entitlements'. It thus included within both its 1993 and 2001 Reports (the latter worded in slightly stronger terms than the former) to the UN Committee on the Elimination of Racial Discrimination, the important proviso that:

> While the Convention does not specifically refer to indigenous people, this report continues the practice of covering aspects of the situation of the Aboriginal peoples of Canada that are relevant to the Convention. It must be emphasised, however, that the Aboriginal peoples of Canada are not considered to be members of an "ethnic group" by either Aboriginal people themselves or the federal government. Emphasis is accorded the unique situation of Aboriginal peoples as Canada's original inhabitants and affirms their special relationship with the State, based on unique entitlements.[59]

Canada's position on the use of the term 'peoples' remains ambivalent. There are, however, signs of an increasing willingness amongst Canadian delegates appearing at the UN to adopt the language of 'peoples' rather than 'people' or 'population'. For example, the representative of Canada appearing before CERD at the examination of Canada's thirteenth and fourteenth state periodic reports stated that 'Canada recognised both indigenous and non-indigenous collectivities who qualified as "peoples" under international law had a right of self-determination'.[60] The United States has recently signalled a similar change

58 Human Rights Committee, *Concluding Observations of the Human Rights Committee: Norway. 01/11/99*, CCPR/C/79/Add.112, [17].

59 CERD, *Fourteenth Periodic Reports of States Parties due in 1997: Canada. 12/10/2001*, CERD/C/320/Add.5, [3]. See also, CERD, *Twelfth Periodic Reports of States Parties due in 1993: Canada. 18/07/94*, CERD/C/240/Add.1, [3]. The latter is slightly more cautious in its terms.

60 CERD, *Summary Record of the 1526th meeting: Canada. 09/08/2002*, CERD/C/SR.1526, [14].

of policy to allow the use of the term 'peoples' by its delegates appearing before a range of international fora.[61]

Most significantly, however, these positive signs of a growing willingness amongst states to accept the use of the term 'peoples' at the international level has been translated into a concrete endorsement of their 'people-hood' in the UN Declaration on the Rights of Indigenous Peoples. The question of whether or not indigenous peoples should be referred to as a 'peoples' was a thorny issue throughout negotiations on the Declaration. The position of indigenous peoples was put before the Working Group established by the Commission on Human Rights to draft the UN Declaration on Indigenous Peoples (HRC Working Group) in forceful terms. An explanatory note circulated by the indigenous representatives at the Working Group in 2001 put their case clearly:

> Since the establishment of the Working Group on Indigenous Populations in 1982, indigenous representatives have consistently asserted the critical importance of accurately identifying peoples as "peoples" in the work of the United Nations. There can be no doubt that we are peoples with distinct historical, political and cultural identities and will remain so. We are united by our histories as distinct societies, as well as by our languages, laws and traditions … Clearly, States are obliged to refrain from any action which undermines or violates the Charter of the United Nations. In regard to recognition of our status as "peoples" and our right to self-determination, we call upon the Commission on Human Rights and all States present at this session of the working group unequivocally to resist any attempts by individual States to contravene the purposes and principles of the Charter by proposing a distinction based on race or other prohibited grounds. In particular, by proposing to square bracket the term indigenous peoples, some States are seeking to open the door to developing double standards that are clearly discriminatory.[62]

61 Economic and Social Council, *Indigenous Peoples and their Relationship to Land, Final Working Paper Prepared by the Special Rapporteur, Mrs Erica-Irene A. Daes*, E/CN.4/Sub.2/2001/21, [116]. As to the US position on the internal right to self-determination, see Economic and Social Council, *Report of the Working Group Established in Accordance with Commission on Human Rights Resolution 1995/32 of 3 March 1995*, E/CN.4/2000/84, [49].

62 Economic and Social Council, *Report of the Working Group Established in Accordance with Commission on Human Rights Resolution 1995/32 of 3 March 1995*, E/CN.4/2001/85, Annex II. See also the comments of the indigenous representative speaking on behalf of the Indian Law Resource Centre, the Assembly of First Nations, the International Treaty Four Secretariat, the Navajo Nation, Haudenosaunee, the International Organisation of Indigenous Resource Development, Nakoa Ikaika, the American Indian Law Alliance and the Grand Council of the Crees, at [23]. The concerns of indigenous peoples had previously been expressed in equally forceful terms before the WGIP. See Economic and Social Council, *Report of the Working Group on Indigenous Populations on its Eleventh Session*, E/CN.4/Sub.2/1993/29, [65]–[66].

The fears of some states were, however, expressed equally clearly both at the HRC Working Group and at the WGIP. The representative of Brazil, for example, made his concerns clear to the WGIP, pointing out that:

> [T]he use of the word "peoples", in the plural, would allow interpretation to the effect that indigenous people would be beneficiaries of the right to self-determination. That interpretation would make indigenous peoples the subject of international law, which was inconsistent with existing national constitutional and international law.[63]

Brazil was clearly not alone in its fears as regards the legal consequences of accepting the status of indigenous peoples as 'peoples'.[64] Such was the sensitivity of the issue that the reports of the HRC Working Group all contained an early disclaimer as regards the terminology employed in the report:

> This report is solely a record of the debate and does not imply acceptance of the usage of either the expression "indigenous peoples" or "indigenous people". In this report both are used without prejudice to the positions of particular delegations, where divergences of approach remain.[65]

That disclaimer was accompanied in later reports (as of 2000 onwards) by an explanatory note explaining in more detail:

---

63 Economic and Social Council, *Report of the Working Group on Indigenous Populations on its Twelfth Session*, E/CN.4/Sub.2/1994/30, [37].

64 See, Economic and Social Council, *Report of the Working Group Established in Accordance with Commission on Human Rights Resolution 1995/32 of 3 March 1995*, E/CN.4/2001/85, [93] (per Argentina) and Economic and Social Council, *Report of the Working Group on Indigenous Populations on its Eleventh Session*, E/CN.4/Sub.2/1993/29 (per Sweden). Both suggest that if the term peoples is to be used it must be qualified by a similar clause to that contained within Article 1(3) of ILO Convention No. 169.

65 See, Economic and Social Council, *Report of the Working Group Established in Accordance with Commission on Human Rights Resolution 1995/32 of 3 March 1995*, E/CN.4/1997/102, [3]; Economic and Social Council, *Report of the Working Group Established in Accordance with Commission on Human Rights Resolution 1995/32 of 3 March 1995*, E/CN.4/1998/106, [4]; Economic and Social Council, *Report of the Working Group Established in Accordance with Commission on Human Rights Resolution 1995/32 of 3 March 1995*, E/CN.4/2000/84, [4]; Economic and Social Council, *Report of the Working Group Established in Accordance with Commission on Human Rights Resolution 1995/32 of 3 March 1995*, E/CN.4/2001/85, [4]; Economic and Social Council, *Report of the Working Group Established in Accordance with Commission on Human Rights Resolution 1995/32 of 3 March 1995*, E/CN.4/2002/98, [4]; and Economic and Social Council, *Report of the Working Group Established in Accordance with Commission on Human Rights Resolution 1995/32 of 3 March 1995*, E/CN.4/2003/92, [4].

> There is no consensus on the use of the term "indigenous peoples" in the working group, in part because of the implications this term may have in international law, including with respect to self-determination and individual and collective rights. Some delegations have suggested using other terms in the declaration such as "indigenous individuals", "persons belonging to an indigenous group" or "persons belonging to indigenous peoples". In addition, the terms used in individual articles may vary, depending on the context. Hence, the bracketed use of the term "indigenous peoples" in the draft declaration is without prejudice to an eventual agreement on terminology.[66]

In the final stages of the drafting process there were, however, important signs that state opinion at the working group was beginning to swing in favour of accepting the status of indigenous peoples as a 'peoples'. From 2000 onwards, the early disclaimer over the use of terminology was followed immediately by a separate paragraph noting the view of indigenous representatives that 'all indigenous representatives and *some* Governments could accept the expression "indigenous peoples" as used in the current text of the draft declaration'.[67] It is perhaps telling that in the 2002 report the wording of the paragraph was changed to state that '*many* Governments' could now accept the expression 'indigenous peoples'.[68] The reports of the HRC Working Group record that key states with indigenous populations such as Bolivia,[69] Chile,[70] Finland[71] and Australia[72] were all willing to accept the term 'peoples', subject to important qualifications concerning the right to self-determination.[73]

The clear consensus which emerged from the HRC Working Group on the use of the term 'indigenous peoples' is strongly reflected in the final text of

66 Economic and Social Council, *Report of the Working Group Established in Accordance with Commission on Human Rights Resolution 1995/32 of 3 March 1995*, E/CN.4/2000/84, Annex I.

67 Ibid., [5].

68 Economic and Social Council, *Report of the Working Group Established in Accordance with Commission on Human Rights Resolution 1995/32 of 3 March 1995*, E/CN.4/2002/98, [5].

69 Economic and Social Council, *Report of the Working Group Established in Accordance with Commission on Human Rights Resolution 1995/32 of 3 March 1995*, E/CN.4/1997/102, [42].

70 Ibid.

71 Ibid., [45] and Economic and Social Council, *Report of the Working Group Established in Accordance with Commission on Human Rights Resolution 1995/32 of 3 March 1995*, E/CN.4/2001/85, [76].

72 Economic and Social Council, *Report of the Working Group Established in Accordance with Commission on Human Rights Resolution 1995/32 of 3 March 1995*, E/CN.4/1997/102, [111].

73 Norway has expressed a similar acceptance of the term before the WGIP. See, Economic and Social Council, *Report of the Working Group on Indigenous Populations on its Eleventh Session*, E/CN.4/Sub.2/1993/29, [64].

the Declaration where it is used throughout without qualification or restriction. Indeed, the preambular paragraph affirms in clear and unequivocal terms that 'indigenous peoples are equals to all other peoples, while recognizing the right of all peoples to be different, to consider themselves different, and to be respected as such'. It is significant that at neither the debate preceding the decision of the third committee of the General Assembly in November 2006 to defer consideration of the Declaration nor the subsequent debate at the plenary session of the General Assembly in September 2007 at which the Declaration was finally adopted, did states express any opposition to this key aspect of the final text.[74]

Colonized peoples and the scope and meaning of the right to self-determination

We have thus reached the point, culminating in the adoption of the UN Declaration, where there is sufficiently strong and consistent state practice to support the position that indigenous peoples are entitled to recognition of their 'people-hood' under international law. Such recognition is of *potentially* enormous significance. In the case of the classic decolonization process of the 1960s and 1970s, once the population of a colonized territory had been recognized as a 'peoples' under international law, the right to self-determination followed. Clearly in principle, as a 'colonized peoples', indigenous peoples should be entitled to the same right to self-determination in terms of its scope and meaning, the manner of its exercise and any limitations or restrictions placed upon it, as the right enjoyed by any other colonized peoples under international law. Any other conclusion would be to treat indigenous peoples less favourably than all other peoples, opening up the international community to accusations of discrimination and hypocrisy. As the argument was put by indigenous representatives to the HRC Working Group:

> All peoples must be treated on an equal footing. It would be discriminatory to proclaim self-determination as a right of all peoples, and at the same time to limit its application with respect to indigenous peoples. Self-determination and non-discrimination are pre-emptory norms of international law from which no derogation is permitted. The working group was not mandated to dilute the existing principles.[75]

---

74 General Assembly, Sixty-first session, Third Committee, 53rd Meeting, 28 November 2006, A/61/448 and General Assembly, Sixty-first session, 107th plenary meeting, 13 September 2007, A/61/PV.107.

75 Economic and Social Council, *Report of the Working Group Established in Accordance with Commission on Human Rights Resolution 1995/32 of 3 March 1995*, E/CN.4/2001/85, [71]. See also, Economic and Social Council, *Report of the Working Group Established in Accordance with Commission on Human Rights Resolution 1995/32 of 3 March 1995*, E/CN.4/2000/84, [57] (International Indian Treaty Council), [58], [60], [84] (Saami Council), [76] (representative of the International Work Group for Indigenous Affairs) and [79] (National Aboriginal and Islanders Legal Services Secretariat); Economic and Social Council, *Report of the Working Group Established in Accordance with Commission on Human Rights Resolution 1995/32 of 3 March 1995*, E/CN.4/2001/85, [39]

The meaning of the right to self-determination when applied within the colonial context is relatively uncontroversial.[76] General Assembly Res. 1514 (XV) very firmly links the right to self-determination with decolonization, asserting that with a view to 'bringing to a speedy and unconditional end colonialism in all its forms and manifestations':

> 2. All peoples have the right to self-determination; by virtue of that right they freely determine their political status and freely pursue their economic, social and cultural development.

It is now beyond doubt that, as is the case with the right to self-determination when applied between states, the right of a colonized peoples to 'freely determine their political status' may have external dimensions.[77] Colonized peoples thus have the right, should they so choose, to restoration of their sovereign authority achieved by means of independence and secession from the colonizing power. The manner in which the right to self-determination is to be exercised is touched upon in GA Res. 2625 (XXV). It is clear that the exercise of the right has a number of possible outcomes. However, Res. 2625 identifies three specific methods of implementing the right: 'establishment of a sovereign and independent State, the free association or integration with an independent State, or the emergence into any other political status freely determined by a people'.[78] It should be emphasized that this list is not exhaustive of how the right to self-determination may be exercised: it may need to be implemented flexibly and creatively to deal with the challenging and diverse problems raised by the complex legacy of colonialism.

This understanding of the right to self-determination should constitute the essential meaning of the right to self-determination when applied to indigenous peoples. However, there are important differences between the current situation

---

and [40] (Indian Law Resource Centre, the Assembly of First Nations, the International Treaty Four Secretariat and the Grand Council of the Crees), [66] (Rights and Democracy), [73] (Indian Law Resource Centre), [74] (International Indian Treaty Council) and [87] (Indian Law Resource Centre, Assembly of First Nations, the International Treaty Four Secretariat and the Grand Council of the Crees); Economic and Social Council, *Report of the Working Group Established in Accordance with Commission on Human Rights Resolution 1995/32 of 3 March 1995*, E/CN.4/2003/92, [24].

76 Self-determination as enshrined within Articles 1(2) and 55 of the UN Charter and applied between states means the equal right of states to respect for their sovereign authority over their own territory and non-interference in their domestic affairs. See Higgins, *supra* note 43, 29.

77 For summary see Quane, *supra* note 30, 260–1.

78 Although the wording is slightly less restrictive, this in essence follows Principle VI of GA Res. 1541 which provides that a non-self-governing territory can be said to have achieved a 'full measure of self-government' by (a) emerging into a sovereign independent state; (b) freely associating with an independent state; or (c) integrating with an independent state.

of indigenous peoples living within post-colonial states and the situation that was faced by the populations of the former colonies in Africa and Asia. These differences are clearly relevant to the exercise of the right under contemporary conditions and should help assuage any concerns states may have in accepting Article 3 as unqualified confirmation of the customary law right.

International law has shown some support for the application of the right to self-determination in post-colonial states where it is acknowledged that the decolonization process has failed or is in some way incomplete. Bangladesh provides one example of what could be described as the right to self-determination being employed to deal with unfinished colonial business.[79] However, particularly within the post-colonial context, self-determination, as McCorquodale points out, is not 'an absolute right' without external limits.[80] As a norm of international law, the right to self-determination must be construed within the international legal system as a whole.[81] At the heart of the international legal system is the maintenance of international peace and security, central to which is the principle of territorial integrity.[82] Consequently, McCorquodale argues that, as both GA Res. 1514 (XV) and GA Res. 2626 (XXV) make clear, the right of a state to territorial integrity will constitute a specific limitation on the right to self-determination.[83] The way in which these two potentially 'competing' rights will be accommodated under international law will depend on the individual circumstances of each particular case. In some instances, to deny the right to self-determination in its external manifestation will constitute a much greater threat to international peace and security than will the disruption caused to the territorial integrity of a state.[84] This would be one possible interpretation of why the right to self-determination was typically exercised in the way that it was in the classic decolonization context. In light of the potential instability caused by the continuing presence of the European powers in the colonial territories and the relatively low risk of sparking endless secessionist claims, particularly given the existence of a discrete and separate territorial entity the 'natural' boundaries for which, applying the *uti possidetis* principle, could be settled with a fair degree of finality, the self-determination principle carried much the greater weight in this particular context. In other situations, the principle of territorial integrity will be of much greater importance. The right of a state to territorial integrity, although frequently criticized as a self-serving instrument of the state, clearly serves an important

79 For analysis of the case of Bangladesh, see Crawford, *supra* note 46.

80 R. McCorquodale (1994). 'Self-Determination: A Human Rights Approach', *International and Comparative Law Quarterly*, 43: 856, 875–6.

81 Ibid., 878–9.

82 See also C. E. Foster (2001). 'Articulating Self-determination in the Draft Declaration on the Rights of Indigenous Peoples', *European Journal of International Law*, 12: 141, 145.

83 McCorquodale, *supra* note 80, 879–80.

84 Ibid., 880.

purpose. The disintegration of a stable society of states would be disastrous. The endless multiplication of ethnic 'enclaves' claiming rights over a territorial base to which other minorities and the 'parent' state are likely to assert strong competing claims, would constitute a grave threat to international peace and security. These arguments are clearly pertinent to the claims of indigenous peoples.

The legitimate concerns of the international community over the territorial integrity of states strongly suggests that in the case of indigenous peoples living within the well-established boundaries of a post-colonial state, the balancing of interests will usually be very different from that which was conducted in the context of the decolonization process of the 1960s and 1970s. The physical proximity of the traditional territories of indigenous peoples to the territorial base of the 'colonizing' power makes their apparent integration into the state's territorial boundaries that much more complete. There are, in essence, two distinct 'peoples' with overlapping and competing rights to the same territorial base and, unlike the classic colonial situation in Africa and Asia, there is no distant Empire to which the administering powers in states such as Canada and Australia can simply return. In many cases, indigenous peoples have been permanently alienated from their traditional lands such that there now exists a complex web of competing third party rights and interests in relation to their traditional territories. For an indigenous group to seek to exercise the right to self-determination in its external dimensions therefore poses a much more visible and destabilizing threat to the territorial integrity of the 'host' state than the classic decolonization process. It risks fracturing the territorial integrity of the state at its very heart and quite possibly sparking a flood of similar secessionist claims. In such circumstances, an internal solution must first be explored.[85] That is not to say indigenous peoples have no ultimate right of secession. Even though the territorial integrity of the state constitutes a legitimate qualification on the right to self-determination, if the rights of indigenous peoples are being systematically abused and the state refuses to negotiate over the right to self-determination in good faith, the state cannot be said to be 'conducting [itself] in compliance with the principle of equal rights and self-determination' and thus its right to territorial integrity will give way.[86] However, when understood in this way, the threat posed by self-determination to the territorial integrity of states can be greatly overstated.[87]

In terms of re-structuring relations between indigenous peoples and the state, the traditional right to self-determination thus remains a powerful tool. Although

---

85 The internal dimensions of the right to self-determination will be explored in detail below at pp. 231–40. See generally, Foster, *supra* note 82.

86 This reflects the interpretation of GA Res. 2625 (XXV) usually advanced in favour of the right of minorities to secede as recognised by the Canadian Supreme Court in *Supreme Court of Canada: Reference Re Secession of Quebec* (1998) 37 I.L.M. 1340, [134]–[138]. See fn 42 above.

87 This point is emphasized by a number of commentators. See Xanthaki, *supra* note 29, 23 and Foster, *supra* note 82, 145.

qualified by the state's right to territorial integrity, the essence of the right to self-determination remains unchanged. It is the manner of its exercise which is limited, and limited only by the principle of territorial integrity. The starting point from which this 'internal' right to self-determination is reached is crucially important. Any 'internal' right to self-determination thus understood still proceeds from the position that self-determination promises decolonization in accordance with the freely expressed will of the people. Furthermore, if the internal right to self-determination remains true to its origins as a means of liberating peoples from 'alien subjugation, domination and exploitation' and respects the right of indigenous peoples to 'freely determine their political status and freely pursue their economic, social and cultural development', the internal right to self-determination could deliver innovative models of shared sovereignty and an effective re-structuring of governmental relations within the state. As it is expressed in GA Res. 1541 (XV), the right to self-determination gives indigenous peoples the right to demand that 'immediate steps' are taken 'to transfer all powers to the peoples of those territories, *without any conditions or reservations* in accordance with their freely expressed will and desire' (emphasis added).[88] States such as Australia and Canada would therefore have no legitimate basis on which to simply dictate the 'rules of the game' when embarking on self-government negotiations. The right to self-determination would thus empower indigenous peoples at the domestic level, allowing them to push for more creative solutions to their decolonization claims than states have previously been willing to concede. In particular, the right to self-determination would provide a strong foundation for recognition of indigenous peoples' absolute sovereignty over their internal affairs.

State Practice on Article 3 of the UN Declaration

Standing testament to the extent to which indigenous peoples' right to self-determination is now accepted in international law is Article 3 of the UN Declaration which reproduces in exact terms the *unqualified* right to self-determination as found in GA Res. 1514 (XV) and common Article 1 of the International Covenants:

> Indigenous peoples have the right to self-determination. By virtue of that right they freely determine their political status and freely pursue their economic, social and cultural development.

As Quane points out, this unqualified use of almost identical language to that found in pre-existing texts on the right to self-determination lends support to the position that Article 3 simply recognizes and confirms existing customary

88 GA Resolution 1514 (XV), *Declaration on the granting of independence to colonial countries and peoples*, para. 5.

international law.[89] The drafting history of the Declaration reveals, however, a much more complex reality.

Leading up to the adoption of the UN Declaration there was a clear change in attitude by many states regarding the right of indigenous peoples to self-determination. A minority of states clearly remain hostile to indigenous peoples holding any such right. Australia proved a consistent opponent of Article 3 in the HRC Working Group.[90] In voting against the Declaration at its adoption in 2007, Australia made its firm opposition clear:

> The Australian Government had long expressed its dissatisfaction with the references to self-determination in the declaration. Self-determination applies to situations of decolonization and the break-up of States into smaller States with clearly defined population groups. It also applies where a particular group within a defined territory is disenfranchised and is denied political or civil rights. It is not a right that attaches to an undefined subgroup of a population seeking to obtain political independence. The Government of Australia supports and encourages the full and free engagement of indigenous peoples in the democratic decision-making processes in their country, but it does not support a concept that could be construed as encouraging action that would impair, even in part, the territorial and political integrity of a State with a system of democratic representative Government.[91]

The majority of states have, however, reconciled themselves to the fact that if indigenous peoples are a 'peoples' under international law they will be entitled

89 Quane, *supra* note 30, 265.

90 Economic and Social Council, *Report of the Working Group Established in Accordance with Commission on Human Rights Resolution 1995/32 of 3 March 1995*, E/CN.4/2000/84, [62]. See also, Economic and Social Council, *Report of the Working Group Established in Accordance with Commission on Human Rights Resolution 1995/32 of 3 March 1995*, E/CN.4/2001/85, [89]. Australia has reiterated its opposition to the inclusion of a specific right of indigenous peoples to self-determination before the Human Rights Committee. At the examination of Australia's third and fourth periodic reports, the Australian delegation argued that such a right was unacceptable because it would have implications of separate nations and laws. They emphasized that indigenous peoples could exercise meaningful control over their affairs through 'self-management' and the usual democratic processes. See Human Rights Committee, *Summary Record of the 1856th Meeting: Australia. 28/07/2000*, CCPR/C/SR.1856, [19] and [22].

91 General Assembly, Sixty-first session, 107th plenary meeting, 13 September 2007, A/61/PV.107, Agenda item 68. The USA also expressed concern about the right to self-determination in its explanation for voting against the Declaration. For Canada's explanation as to its opposition to the self-determination provisions in the Declaration see, *Canada's Position: United Nations Draft Declaration on the Rights of Indigenous Peoples – June 29, 2006*, available at: www.ainc-inac.gc.ca/ap/ia/pubs/ddr/ddr-eng.asp.

to the right to self-determination.[92] Indeed, at the HRC Working Group, Costa Rica, Cuba, Denmark, Ecuador, Finland, Norway, Peru, Guatemala and Mexico all aligned themselves with indigenous peoples and expressed support for the inclusion of an unqualified right to self-determination as enshrined in Article 3.[93] This position was argued with some force by Cuba:

> [T]he right of self-determination was well developed in the 1970 Declaration on Principles of International Law concerning Friendly Relations and Cooperation among States in Accordance with the Charter of the United Nations. Cuba considered the concerns of some States with respect to self-determination as unfounded, given that it is clearly expressed in this declaration that nothing in it shall be construed as authorising or encouraging any action which would dismember or impair, totally or in part, the territorial integrity or political unity of sovereign and independent States. He affirmed that the Cuban delegation could not form part of an eventual consensus that would seek to modify or reduce in an arbitrary manner a principle of international law.[94]

However, whilst willing to adopt the language of self-determination, the majority of states made it clear that self-determination as applied to indigenous peoples would mean something very different from the traditional meaning of self-determination as applied to the decolonization claims of the population of an overseas colonized territory. In particular, states showed a clear determination to ensure that the right of indigenous peoples to self-determination could not be interpreted so as to

92 See, e.g., Economic and Social Council, *Report of the Working Group Established in Accordance with Commission on Human Rights Resolution 1995/32 of 3 March 1995*, E/CN.4/1997/102, [45]; Economic and Social Council, *Report of the Working Group Established in Accordance with Commission on Human Rights Resolution 1995/32 of 3 March 1995*, E/CN.4/2001/85, [62] (France); and Economic and Social Council, *Report of the Working Group Established in Accordance with Commission on Human Rights Resolution 1995/32 of 3 March 1995*, E/CN.4/2003/92, [13] (Cuba).

93 Economic and Social Council, *Report of the Working Group Established in Accordance with Commission on Human Rights Resolution 1995/32 of 3 March 1995*, E/CN.4/2003/92, [20].

94 Economic and Social Council, *Report of the Working Group Established in Accordance with Commission on Human Rights Resolution 1995/32 of 3 March 1995*, E/CN.4/2001/85, [70]. See also, Economic and Social Council, *Report of the Working Group Established in Accordance with Commission on Human Rights Resolution 1995/32 of 3 March 1995*, E/CN.4/1998/106, [44](b) and (c); Economic and Social Council, *Report of the Working Group Established in Accordance with Commission on Human Rights Resolution 1995/32 of 3 March 1995*, E/CN.4/2000/84, [67] (Pakistan); Economic and Social Council, *Report of the Working Group Established in Accordance with Commission on Human Rights Resolution 1995/32 of 3 March 1995*, E/CN.4/2001/85, [92] (Denmark); Economic and Social Council, *Report of the Working Group Established in Accordance with Commission on Human Rights resolution 1995/32 of 3 March 1995*, E/CN.4/2003/92, [11] (Guatemala).

violate or jeopardize the territorial and sovereign integrity of the state.[95] This non-negotiable condition for recognition of the right to self-determination was very clear from the discussions at the HRC Working Group:

> [I]t was not so much the right itself but its contents and the consequences of its exercise that caused certain concerns. In this respect, many Governments approached the issue from the point of view that a balance was needed between the right to self-determination of indigenous peoples and the territorial unity and integrity of States. In this regard, certain Governments took the position that the right of self-determination as referred to in article 3 needed to be qualified, or elaborated in a way which preserves the territorial integrity of States and their constitutional frameworks where these meet current human rights standards. Some Governments were not yet ready to propose what form a qualification should take while others referred to instruments such as the International Labour Organisation Convention No. 169 and the 1970 Declaration on principles of International law concerning Friendly Relations and Cooperation among States in Accordance with the Charter of the United Nations which both contain provisions guaranteeing the territorial and political unity and integrity of States.[96]

Clear protection for the territorial and political integrity of states with indigenous populations was finally enshrined in Article 46 of the UN Declaration. Again in terms very similar to those found within GA Res. 1514 (XV) and GA Res. 2625 (XXV), Article 46 of the Declaration provides:

> Nothing in this Declaration may be interpreted as implying for any State, people, group or person any right to engage in any activity or to perform any act contrary to the Charter of the United Nations or construed as authorizing or encouraging

95 Although again it should be noted that this fracturing of territorial integrity would be very unlikely even if it were to be accepted that indigenous peoples enjoyed the same right to self-determination as all other colonized peoples.

96 Economic and Social Council, *Report of the Working Group Established in Accordance with Commission on Human Rights Resolution 1995/32 of 3 March 1995*, E/CN.4/1996/84, [45]–[46]; Economic and Social Council, *Report of the Working Group Established in Accordance with Commission on Human Rights Resolution 1995/32 of 3 March 1995*, E/CN.4/1997/102, [42]. See also, Economic and Social Council, *Report of the Working Group Established in Accordance with Commission on Human Rights Resolution 1995/32 of 3 March 1995*, E/CN.4/1998/106, [44](f); Economic and Social Council, *Report of the Working Group Established in Accordance with Commission on Human Rights Resolution 1995/32 of 3 March 1995*, E/CN.4/2000/84, [53] (Brazil), [54] (Columbia), [56] (Ecuador), [61] (Russian federation), [73] (Guatemala), [74] (Mexico), [78] (New Zealand), [80] (Venezuela) and [81] (Norway); E/CN.4/2001/85 at [64] (Mexico), [82] (Norway), [83] (Spain); and Economic and Social Council, *Report of the Working Group Established in Accordance with Commission on Human Rights Resolution 1995/32 of 3 March 1995*, E/CN.4/2001/85, [109] (New Zealand).

> any action which would dismember or impair, totally or in part, the territorial integrity or political unity of sovereign and independent States.

The effect of Article 46 in protecting the territorial integrity of the state against the right to self-determination was reiterated by nearly every state delegate who spoke at the adoption of the Declaration. In the words of the Japanese delegate:

> The revised version of article 46 correctly clarified that the right to self-determination did not give indigenous peoples the right to be separate and independent from their countries of residence, and that that right should not be invoked for the purpose of impairing the sovereignty of a State, its national and political unity, or territorial integrity.[97]

This position was reiterated in unequivocal terms by Australia and the United States when endorsing the Convention.[98]

It is clear from the debates on self-determination during the drafting and adoption of the Declaration that from the perspective of the participating states the absolute requirement to protect the territorial integrity of the state meant that the right of indigenous peoples to self-determination could be a limited internal right only. To underline this point within the Declaration, the view emerged within the working group that the unqualified right to self-determination in Article 3 should be contextualized by placing Article 4 dealing specifically with the internal dimensions of the right immediately thereafter.[99] This comprehensive or 'package-deal' approach to self-determination attracted widespread support.[100] Perhaps somewhat surprisingly this included support from indigenous groups.

During the drafting process many indigenous groups expressed their willingness to accept the restrictions imposed on the right to self-determination by Article 46. From the perspective of indigenous peoples, Article 46 did no more than GA Res. 1514 (XV) and GA Res. 2625 (XXV) in imposing limits on the right to self-determination in accordance with existing international law. Moreover, the great majority of indigenous peoples expressed no desire for independent statehood or secession. As was made clear by indigenous peoples before the HRC Working Group, states have nothing to fear from indigenous peoples as regards their basic territorial integrity: most indigenous groups do not

97 See also the statements of Argentina, Jordan, Mexico, Sweden, Brazil, Suriname, Iran, India, Myanmar, Paraguay, Turkey, Philippines and Egypt. General Assembly, Sixty-first session, 107th plenary meeting, 13 September 2007, A/61/PV.107.

98 Australia statement of support, *supra* note 25, Part III.1.

99 Economic and Social Council, *Report of the Working Group Established in Accordance with Commission on Human Rights Resolution 1995/32 of 3 March 1995*, E/CN.4/2006/79, [20]. For the text of Article 4 see below at p. 240.

100 Economic and Social Council, *Report of the Working Group Established in Accordance with Commission on Human Rights Resolution 1995/32 of 3 March 1995*, E/CN.4/2005/89, [40]–[46].

seek independence from the state but some form of internal sovereignty within its existing territorial boundaries.[101] As a representative of Lumad Mindanaw Peoples Federation explained, 'self-determination for his people meant self-governance of their territory within the sovereignty of the nation-State'.[102] A representative of the Indian Movement 'Tupaj Amaru' similarly stressed that 'self-determination and autonomy in local affairs was a condition for the survival of indigenous identity and did not imply any intention to create States within States'.[103] Indeed, in an attempt to persuade participating states that they had nothing to fear from the right of indigenous peoples to self-determination, some indigenous representatives tried to distance themselves from the position that self-determination must have the predetermined outcome of independent statehood that its role in the decolonization of Africa and Asia might suggest and emphasized instead that self-determination is an 'ongoing process' with 'a broad scope of possible outcomes suited to specific situations'.[104]

There would thus appear to be an emerging consensus between states and indigenous peoples as to the more limited internal scope of the right to self-determination as applied to indigenous peoples. The vital question which remains to be determined is what this 'internal right' to self-determination will mean in practice. An interpretation which starts from the customary law right of indigenous peoples and remains true to its essential tenets can deliver the effective decolonization of indigenous peoples whilst protecting the territorial integrity of the state. Moreover, it would respect the rights of indigenous peoples as 'a colonized peoples' under international law. An interpretation of the internal

---

101 Economic and Social Council, *Report of the Working Group Established in Accordance with Commission on Human Rights Resolution 1995/32 of 3 March 1995*, E/CN.4/1996/84, [47]. Economic and Social Council, *Report of the Working Group Established in Accordance with Commission on Human Rights Resolution 1995/32 of 3 March 1995*, E/CN.4/1998/106, [44](g); Economic and Social Council, *Report of the Working Group Established in Accordance with Commission on Human Rights Resolution 1995/32 of 3 March 1995*, E/CN.4/2000/84, [83]–[85]; Economic and Social Council, *Report of the Working Group Established in Accordance with Commission on Human Rights Resolution 1995/32 of 3 March 1995*, E/CN.4/2001/85, [91].

102 Economic and Social Council, *Report of the Working Group Established in Accordance with Commission on Human Rights Resolution 1995/32 of 3 March 1995*, E/CN.4/2000/84, [69].

103 Economic and Social Council, *Report of the Working Group Established in Accordance with Commission on Human Rights Resolution 1995/32 of 3 March 1995*, E/CN.4/2001/85, [86].

104 Economic and Social Council, *Report of the Working Group Established in Accordance with Commission on Human Rights Resolution 1995/32 of 3 March 1995*, E/CN.4/2000/84, [71]. See also Economic and Social Council, *Report of the Working Group Established in Accordance with Commission on Human Rights Resolution 1995/32 of 3 March 1995*, E/CN.4/1996/84, [47]; Economic and Social Council, *Report of the Working Group Established in Accordance with Commission on Human Rights Resolution 1995/32 of 3 March 1995*, E/CN.4/2001/85, [91].

right which abandons the previously accepted meaning of self-determination in international law, attempting instead to craft a new and distinctive right for indigenous peoples, is likely to prove a much more ambivalent offering.

The Scope and Meaning of an 'Internal Right' to Self-Determination

Leading authorities on indigenous rights have expressed very real concern about the meaning to be attributed to any more limited internal right to self-determination. Martinez, for example, in his study on treaties, agreements and other constructive arrangements between states and indigenous populations expresses strong concern about the value of this 'internal' concept of self-determination, questioning whether internal restructuring alone will free indigenous peoples from the dictates of the state: in essence, whether it is capable of delivering effective decolonization. The questions raised by Martinez are critical. If internal self-determination is to mean no more than ensuring more effective methods of securing indigenous peoples a voice in 'certain aspects of the non-indigenous political order', Martinez questions 'just how much of a real impact this type of measure will have in the enormous effort required to achieve more just relations between both sectors of these societies'.[105] Even assuming that internal self-determination will deliver some form of separate autonomous political authority for indigenous peoples within the state, Martinez has substantial doubts as to its effectiveness:

> The Special Rapporteur notes, however, that recognition of "autonomy" for indigenous peoples within the State (whatever powers or restrictions thereto are established), most probably will neither automatically end States' aspirations to exert eventually the fullest authority possible (including integrating and assimilating those peoples) nor nullify whatever inalienable rights these people may have as such.[106]

These concerns extend to the modern treaty process currently being pursued in Canada. Martinez is highly sceptical as to the effectiveness of such agreements if indigenous peoples are forced to negotiate on terms dictated by 'one-sided government policies' and such agreements are to be implemented and enforced exclusively at the domestic level.[107] Martinez therefore advises indigenous peoples to give such autonomy arrangements very careful consideration before committing

105 *Study on Treaties, Agreements and Other Constructive Arrangements between States and Indigenous Populations, Third Progress Report Submitted by Mr Miguel Alfonso Martinez, Special Rapporteur*, E/CN.4/Sub.2/1996/23, [226].

106 *Study on Treaties, Agreements and Other Constructive Arrangements between States and Indigenous Populations. Final Report by Miguel Alfonso Martínez, Special Rapporteur*, E/CN.4/Sub.2/1999/20, [135].

107 Ibid., [138]–[146]. One of the 'non-negotiables' which has caused particular concern at the international level is the policy of extinguishment. See p. 182 above.

to them.[108] If the internal right to self-determination is to provide better protection for indigenous peoples in their relationships with national governments, it is clear that strong guidance is needed from states at the international level.

Discussions between states and indigenous peoples at the HRC Working Group failed to produce any clear consensus as to the substantive meaning to be attributed to the emerging internal right to self-determination. In fact, the views of the participating states as to what the right would mean in practice were often expressed in very vague and general terms. The United Kingdom was the only state to argue at the General Assembly debate on the Declaration that the right of indigenous peoples to self-determination was a new and distinct right and thus 'separate and different from the existing right of all peoples to self-determination in international law'.[109] If the Declaration does not mark the creation of a 'new' international right, the fundamental tenets of the right to self-determination under existing international law should thus inform its essential meaning when exercised internally. However, the conservatism of some governments in terms of the degree of autonomy they would be prepared to concede to indigenous groups was clear in the HRC Working Group:

> Some Governments stated that they could not accept separate political, legal, economic and social systems for indigenous peoples since this would be discriminatory towards the rest of the population of the State and infringe upon the right to equal treatment. Other Governments stated that the rights contained in Part V would have to be carried out within the framework of existing democratic State structures and could not infringe upon constitutional provisions that regulate the election of governmental representatives and the passing of legislation. With regard to the latter aspect, it was stated that in a democratic society all people have equal rights to participation and decision-making.[110]

A number of states tried to equate indigenous peoples' right to internal self-determination with the Human Rights Committee's popular exposition of the internal dimensions of the right to self-determination as contained within common Article 1 of the two International Covenants.[111] In accordance with what Franck has

108 Ibid., [302]–[303].

109 General Assembly, Sixty-first session, 107th plenary meeting, 13 September 2007, A/61/PV.107. The United States subsequently adopted this position, their statement of support reading: 'The Declaration's call is to promote the development of a concept of self-determination for indigenous peoples that is different from the existing right of self-determination in international law. The purpose of the Declaration was not to change or define the existing right of self-determination under international law.' *Supra* note 25.

110 Economic and Social Council, *Report of the Working Group Established in Accordance with Commission on Human Rights Resolution 1995/32 of 3 March 1995*, E/CN.4/1996/ 84, [80].

111 Quane suggests that this is one possible meaning to be attributed to the internal right in the Declaration, albeit she argues that the right would need to be expanded and

argued to be the re-conceptualization of the right to self-determination as a right to 'democratic governance', indigenous peoples' right to self-determination has thus been suggested to amount to little more than the right of an individual citizen to effective participation in the democratic bodies of the state.[112] This interpretation of the right to self-determination differs quite markedly from what had been the prevailing understanding of the right within the decolonization context. The close association between the right to self-determination and the decolonization movement suggested that the right to self-determination was a right which could be exercised once and once only by the peoples of a territory. As Franck points out, self-determination was thus a unique event encapsulated by the phrase: 'one man, one vote, one time'.[113] There was no perception during the classic decolonization period that self-determination could have an ongoing significance in empowering the 'peoples' of a territory once the decolonization process was complete and, as was typically the case, a sovereign state had been established. Indeed, as Franck argues, decolonization was often followed by the creation of a dictatorship or some other form of authoritarian rule.[114] HRC General Comment No. 12, however, suggests the right to self-determination demands something quite different. In discussing the reporting obligations of states under Article 40 of the Covenant, the Committee notes that all states parties have an obligation to report under Article 1 but 'many of them completely ignore [it], provide inadequate information in regard to it or confine themselves to a reference to election laws'.[115] The Committee goes on to explain that, 'with regard to paragraph 1 of article 1, states parties should describe the constitutional and political processes which in practice allow the exercise of this right'.[116] The Committee thus points to an important 'internal' dimension of the right which focuses not upon the 'external' status of a peoples but, in the words of McCorquodale, upon the continuing right of the 'peoples within a State to choose their political status, the extent of their political participation and the form of their government'.[117] It is, in other words, concerned with the internal structuring of the relationship between the government of the state and its peoples

developed to make it meaningful. Quane, *supra* note 30, 267. On the internal right as understood in international law, see Office of the High Commissioner for Human Rights, *The Right to Self-determination of Peoples (Art. 1): 13/03/84. CCPR General Comment 12. (General Comments) 1984,* [2]–[4]. For commentary, see McCorquodale, *supra* note 80, 864; Higgins, *supra* note 43, 31–2; and Cassese, *supra* note 29, 46–53. Foster suggests something similar arguing that at the core of indigenous peoples' right to self-determination should be the right to 'representative government'. See Foster, *supra* note 82.

112 Cited by Higgins, ibid., 32 (fn 4). See also Franck, *supra* note 46, 20–1.

113 Franck, ibid., 10.

114 Ibid.,10.

115 Office of the High Commissioner for Human Rights, *The Right to Self-determination of Peoples (Art. 1): 13/03/84. CCPR General Comment 12. (General Comments) 1984*, [2].

116 Ibid., [4].

117 McCorquodale, *supra* note 80, 864.

with a view to ensuring that the right of peoples to 'determine their own political and economic and social destiny' is effectively secured.[118]

In order to achieve self-determination as thus understood, a strong link is forged between Article 1 and an individual's civil and political rights as protected under the Covenant, such that Article 1 can be accurately described as the overall 'manifestation of the totality of rights embodied in the Covenant'.[119] By ensuring the right of an individual to freedom of expression, freedom of assembly, the right to vote and so forth, it is argued that the right of the population to freely determine its political, economic and social status will be effectively guaranteed. Violations of these rights, on the other hand, will constitute an infringement of the right of the population to internal self-determination. Pursuant to the Committee's approach, the internal constitutional workings of the state have thus become, under the ambit of Article 1, a common item for consideration in State Party Reports.[120] Indeed, Higgins states that the Committee now addresses the right to self-determination in the course of its dialogue with virtually every state who appears before it.[121]

The Committee's shifting focus towards the 'internal' dimensions of the right to self-determination is important.[122] The international community has embarked upon a process whereby the right to self-determination is, in effect, being 're-conceptualized'. Although the Human Rights Committee has been complicit in this process, the move to transform the right to self-determination into what is effectively a 'right to democracy' was initiated by Western states; thus explaining their concern during the drafting of Article 1 of the International Covenants to make sure that the right to self-determination applied not just to peoples under colonial rule but to 'all peoples' including peoples living in post-colonial and socialist states. As Cassese explains:

> Only after the socialist and Third World countries had made inroads in the battle against colonialism did the Western States take the offensive. At that point, they began emphasising that the principle ought to be interpreted as the right of the peoples of every State freely to choose a system of government that fully meets

118 Higgins, *supra* note 43, 32.

119 Cassese, *supra* note 29, 53.

120 See, for example, HRC, *Consideration of Reports Submitted by States Parties under Article 40 of the Covenant, Concluding Observations of the Human Rights Committee, Georgia*, CCPR/C/GEO/CO/3, [6]; HRC, *Consideration of Reports Submitted by States Parties under Article 40 of the Covenant, Concluding Observations of the Human Rights Committee, Sudan*, CCPR/C/SDN/CO/3, [7]; HRC, *Consideration of Reports Submitted by States Parties under Article 40 of the Covenant, Concluding Observations of the Human Rights Committee, Brazil*, CCPR/C/BRA/CO/2, [5].

121 Higgins, *supra* note 43, 31.

122 Cassese reports that the Committee is increasingly turning its attention to internal self-determination and that Committee members and States 'tend to lay greater emphasis on the importance of internal self-determination as a truly democratic decision-making process'. Cassese, *supra* note 29, 46–7.

> the aspirations of the people. According to the Western States, the principle of self-determination enshrined in the UN Charter contemplated (1) *internal* self-determination and (2) *universality* of application. The Western States also linked the principle to human rights but in a different sense than that advocated by the socialist countries. For the West, self-determination was the quintessence of democratic freedom or, in other words, the synthesis of the civil and political rights of every people. In brief, the principle was conceived as the fundamental criterion for the democratic legitimisation of governments.[123]

Western democratic states have thus enthusiastically embraced the 'internal' dimensions to the right to self-determination, with many key states voicing strong support for the Committee's approach. The UK government has been chief amongst them, explaining in a statement to the General Assembly that:

> Self-determination is not a one off exercise. It cannot be achieved for any people by one revolution or one election. It is a continuous process. It requires that peoples be given continuing opportunities to choose their governments and social systems and to change them when they so choose ... many peoples today are deprived of their right of self-determination by elites of their own countrymen.[124]

The HRC's central focus on the internal aspects of self-determination can be understood as not so much a re-conceptualization of the right to self-determination as a return to its original Wilsonian foundations in the democratic ideals of 'popular sovereignty' and securing the 'consent of the governed'.[125] These democratic ideals have always been present to some degree in the international community's understanding of how the right to self-determination is to be realized. It was emphasized most notably in the ICJ's decision in *Western Sahara* with the Court reiterating 'that the application of the right of self-determination requires a free and genuine expression of the will of the peoples concerned'.[126] Indeed, Justice Dillard in his separate opinion, encapsulated the importance of securing a free voice for the whole population in determining how the right to self-determination should be exercised with his now infamous assertion that 'it is for the people to determine the destiny of the territory and not the territory the destiny of the people'.[127]

However, important as the internal dimensions of the right to self-determination clearly are, the direction in which some commentators would like to see the right to self-determination 'evolve' under international law, such that the right of a peoples

123 Ibid., 46–7.

124 Cited ibid., 302.

125 Ibid., 19.

126 *Western Sahara, Advisory Opinion*, ICJ Reports 1975, 12, [55] and [59].

127 Ibid., 12, 122.

to 'freely express their will' is being transformed from an important means of securing its effective exercise into the *sole* content of the right, is problematic if the importance of the external dimensions of self-determination are thereby forgotten or ignored. Self-determination still has an important role to play in the ongoing decolonization project. It has not run its course or exhausted its purpose. There is, however, a growing determination amongst some in the international community to see self-determination as an instrument in determining the external status of a 'peoples' consigned to the archives of history and the right to self-determination reborn, to use the words of Franck, as a 'right to democratic governance'.[128] Once perceived as a 'revolutionary' liberating principle with the capacity to 'tear at the legacies of empire',[129] the right to self-determination is being tamed. The arguments of Franck in this regard are revealing:

> The probable redefinition of self-determination does recognise an international legal right, but it is not to secession but to democracy. In the transition from colonial to post-colonial contexts, the right is being reinterpreted in the practice of States to take on new vigor as the instrument for regional and global enforcement of minimal standards of governmental legitimacy. This is rooted both in developing human rights law and in the evolution of the international community's thinking about the causes of war ... In that as yet imperfect but emerging consensus self-determination is being redefined and given a new life.[130]

International law has, however, yet to reach this point. Whilst the external right of peoples to self-determination is recognized and respected at the international level, international concern has naturally turned to focus on the internal dimensions of the right: the right to representative government secured through the totality of rights enshrined within the ICCPR. To suggest, however, that the internal aspects of the right to self-determination can somehow be divorced from the external dimensions of the right, such that one can exist without the other, is fundamentally misconceived. As the indigenous organizations from Australia argued before HRC Working Group:

> [T]he distinction between internal and external self-determination suggested by some States was unhelpful. The equating of external self-determination with secession was artificial as it restricted the right and restricted choices. The right of self-determination required States to recognise human rights internally, within the territories, and also at the international level.[131]

---

128 Cited by Higgins, *supra* note 43, 32 (fn 4).

129 Anaya (2004), *supra* note 1, 98.

130 Franck, *supra* note 46, 20–1.

131 Economic and Social Council, *Report of the Working Group Established in*

An indigenous representative from the Indian Council of South America made a similar point, arguing:

> [T]he division of self-determination into internal and external manifestations is a way of diverting the discussion. Internal self-determination is a multiple manifestation of individual rights and freedom of association, which States claim to grant to indigenous peoples in the same way as to other citizens. Linking external self-determination to the disintegration of States was a means of bringing non-indigenous peoples into opposition with indigenous peoples.[132]

The inextricable link between the two dimensions of the right to self-determination was made clear in the 1975 *Helsinki Final Act*, in which the European states meeting under the auspices of the Conference on Security and Co-operation in Europe explicitly drew together both its external and internal aspects, declaring:

> By virtue of the principle of equal rights and self-determination of peoples, all peoples have the right in full freedom, to determine, when and as they wish, their internal and external political status, without external interference and to pursue as they wish their political, economic, social and cultural development.[133]

Whilst placing great emphasis on the internal right to self-determination, the UN Committee on the Elimination of Racial Discrimination has similarly stressed the continuing relevance and importance of the external dimensions of the right in liberating peoples from alien subjugation and control:

> In respect of the self-determination of peoples two aspects have to be distinguished. The right to self-determination of peoples has an internal aspect, that is to say, the rights of all peoples to pursue freely their economic, social and cultural development without outside interference. In that respect there exists a link with the right of every citizen to take part in the conduct of public affairs at any level, as referred to in article 5(c) of the International Convention on the Elimination of All Forms of Racial Discrimination. In consequence, Governments are to represent the whole population without distinction as to race, colour, descent or national or ethnic origin. The external aspect of self-

---

Accordance with Commission on Human Rights Resolution 1995/32 of 3 March 1995 on its Seventh Session, E/CN.4/2001/85, [78].

132 Economic and Social Council, *Report of the Working Group Established in Accordance with Commission on Human Rights Resolution 1995/32 of 3 March 1995 on its Seventh Session*, E/CN.4/2001/85, [84].

133 Organization for Security and Co-operation in Europe, *Conference on Co-operation and Security in Europe, Final Act, Helsinki 1975*, Declaration on Principles Guiding Relations between Participating States, Principle VIII. Equal Rights and Self-determination of Peoples.

> determination implies that all peoples have the right to determine freely their political status and their place in the international community based upon the principle of equal rights and exemplified by the liberation of peoples from colonialism and by the prohibition to subject peoples to alien subjugation, domination and exploitation.[134]

The emerging right to 'democratic governance' is thus a right belonging to 'peoples' who continue to hold an attendant right to external self-determination; a right which *may* be exercised through their international personality as a sovereign state. The external right has not therefore ceased to exist or ceased to be of relevance and importance. Its exercise may, however, be limited in its application to indigenous peoples given the particular constraints of their territorial position.

Although misconceived, Canada has at times adopted the particularly restrictive approach to the 'internal right to self-determination' advanced by Franck, arguing before the HRC Working Group that '[a]lthough, traditionally, the right to self-determination was understood to apply in the colonial context and was equated essentially with a right of Statehood, that view had evolved and was now seen by many as a right which could continue to be enjoyed in a functioning democracy in which citizens participated in the political system and had the opportunity to have input in the political processes that affected them'.[135] Sweden has similarly focused on the democratic aspects of the internal right to self-determination, suggesting that the right to self-determination will be largely realized through the imposition on the state of a clear 'duty to consult and cooperate' and ensuring indigenous peoples effective participation in democratic systems.[136] If this approach were to prevail it would be difficult to discern how the collective right of indigenous peoples to self-determination differed from the right to 'democratic governance' enjoyed by all individuals, minorities and sub-state groups pursuant to the right of the whole peoples of a state to internal self-determination. The right of indigenous peoples to self-determination must, however, mean something. It must promise more than that which is already guaranteed to indigenous individuals by virtue of their citizenship of the state.

A number of states have acknowledged this reality before the HRC Working Group. Despite the conservative position adopted by such influential states as Canada and Sweden, there was some quite considerable support for a more progressive and far-reaching understanding of indigenous peoples' right to self-determination. In the early stages of the drafting process the right was expressed

134 CERD, *Right to Self-determination: 23/08/96 CERD General Recommendation 21 (General Comments)*, [4]–[5].

135 Economic and Social Council, *Report of the Working Group Established in Accordance with Commission on Human Rights Resolution 1995/32 of 3 March 1995*, E/CN.4/2000/84, [50].

136 General Assembly, Sixty-first session, 107th plenary meeting, 13 September 2007, A/61/PV.107 (per Sweden).

by some governments as involving 'various types of power-sharing'[137] and 'the right of distinct peoples within a State to make decisions on their own affairs'.[138] Norway similarly expressed the right as including 'the right of indigenous peoples to participate at all levels of decision-making in legislative and administrative matters and in the maintenance and development of their political and economic systems'.[139] Spain suggested that the right would involve 'a process of political, territorial and administrative decentralisation that would permit indigenous peoples to participate in all decision-making that affected them, but that would in no case threaten State sovereignty or the territorial integrity of democratic States'.[140] A more detailed explanation of the right in question was attempted by Guatemala, who described it in the following terms:

> The exercise of self-determination allowed peoples and national groups to define, within States, their political condition through processes of decentralisation and autonomy, allowing them to participate effectively in setting policies of economic, social and cultural development. If there was belief in the democratic system, denying or limiting the right to self-determination was contradictory, for inside a pluralistic and participatory democracy in which human rights and fundamental freedoms were respected, the fulfilment of the right to self-determination would come about by defining or redefining the political legal order, structuring the adequate levels of decentralisation and autonomy.[141]

Russia took one of the more progressive positions before the HRC Working Group, arguing that 'the relevant articles of the draft declaration have to be formulated in such a way as to reflect the internal aspect of the right of self-determination which meant for his Government wide autonomy within existing States'.[142] At times Canada also adopted a more encouraging position, drawing a clear link between the internal right of indigenous peoples to self-determination and their overriding

137 Economic and Social Council, *Report of the Working Group Established in Accordance with Commission on Human Rights Resolution 1995/32 of 3 March 1995*, E/CN.4/1996/84, [88].

138 Ibid., [43].

139 Economic and Social Council, *Report of the Working Group Established in Accordance with Commission on Human Rights Resolution 1995/32 of 3 March 1995*, E/CN.4/2000/84, [81].

140 Economic and Social Council, *Report of the Working Group Established in Accordance with Commission on Human Rights Resolution 1995/32 of 3 March 1995*, E/CN.4/2001/85, [83].

141 Economic and Social Council, *Report of the Working Group Established in Accordance with Commission on Human Rights Resolution 1995/32 of 3 March 1995*, E/CN.4/2003/92, [11].

142 Economic and Social Council, *Report of the Working Group Established in Accordance with Commission on Human Rights Resolution 1995/32 of 3 March 1995*, E/CN.4/2001/85, [90].

goal of decolonization through the restoration of pre-colonial independence and sovereign decision-making powers. Indeed, Canada has argued before the Human Rights Committee that 'in the context of Canadian history, the right of self-determination meant restoring independent governance and the decision-making powers which those peoples had enjoyed prior to colonialism'.[143] The United States has also leant some support to this position, stating that the Declaration's concept of self-determination is consistent with the United States' existing recognition of federally recognized tribes as 'political entities that have inherent sovereign powers of self-governance'.[144] This recognition of the relationship between self-determination and the inherent sovereignty of indigenous peoples is crucially important.

Article 4 of the Declaration provides some further guidance as to the intended substance of the right:

> Indigenous peoples, in exercising their right to self-determination, have the right to autonomy or self-government in matters relating to their internal and local affairs, as well as ways and means for financing their autonomous functions.

Of course much will turn on the meaning attributed to the phrase 'autonomy or self-government in matters relating to their internal and local affairs'.[145] Earlier drafts of this provision had included a more detailed, non-exhaustive list, of those matters over which indigenous peoples could exercise autonomy. The list included 'culture, religion, education, information, media, health, housing, employment, social welfare, economic activities, land and resources management, environment and entry by non-members'.[146] Although not included within the final text of the Declaration, this provides a good indication of the range of matters falling within the jurisdiction of indigenous communities. It attracted quite strong support from indigenous peoples at the HRC Working Group and little opposition from states.[147]

---

143 Human Rights Committee, *Summary Record of the 1738th meeting: Canada. 07/03/99*, CCPR/C/SR.1738, [3].

144 US statement of support, *supra* note 25.

145 For a an excellent discussion of the relationship between the internal right to self-determination and the Declaration's various 'rights to participate in public life', see Quane, *supra* note 30, 269–84.

146 Draft Article 31 of the United Nations Declaration on the Rights of Indigenous Peoples. As to the views of states about this provision see Economic and Social Council, *Report of the Working Group Established in Accordance with Commission on Human Rights Resolution 1995/32 of 3 March 1995*, E/CN.4/1996/84, [88]; Economic and Social Council, *Report of the Working Group Established in Accordance with Commission on Human Rights Resolution 1995/32 of 3 March 1995*, E/CN.4/2000/84, [70] (Finland).

147 Economic and Social Council, *Report of the Working Group Established in Accordance with Commission on Human Rights Resolution 1995/32 of 3 March 1995*, E/CN.4/1996/84, [88].

Conclusion

The inclusion of an unqualified right to self-determination in Article 3 of the UN Declaration on the Rights of Indigenous Peoples constitutes a hugely significant step forward for indigenous peoples. In recent years, attention has naturally focused on the drafting of the Declaration and whether an unqualified right to self-determination would survive the political tensions surrounding it. In light of the successful adoption of the Declaration in 2007, attention must now turn to resolving the many outstanding questions as to the substantive meaning of this apparently unqualified right and the myriad of ways in which it may be exercised. It is only once these questions have been answered that the true extent of the gains made by indigenous peoples in the Declaration can be properly evaluated.

Whilst it is to be expected that debates over the right of indigenous peoples to self-determination will now be framed within the terms of Articles 3 and 4 of the UN Declaration, it is important that the arguments supporting the right of indigenous peoples to self-determination under existing customary international law are not forgotten. Indeed, as the international community engages in the crucial task of interpreting and applying the right to self-determination enshrined in Article 3, it is particularly timely to revisit the purported right of indigenous peoples as 'a colonized peoples' to an existing right to self-determination under international law. It has been argued in this chapter that indigenous peoples are indeed 'a colonized peoples' with unresolved colonial business – who await, in other words, decolonization. As colonized peoples they have the unqualified right to self-determination which may, in certain circumstances, be exercised in its external dimensions. However, given the strong protection afforded by international law to the territorial integrity of states and the physical geographical positioning of most indigenous peoples within the well-established borders of post-colonial states (the 'colonial enclave' problem), it will only be in the most exceptional circumstances that the external exercise of the right could be justified. Internal solutions to the exercise of indigenous peoples' right to self-determination must thus be found but they are solutions which must remain faithful to the key tenets of self-determination as a tool of decolonization, delivering liberation from alien subjugation and oppression. Understood in this way, true independence and autonomy from the colonizing power and restoration of indigenous sovereignty remain at the heart of the right albeit realized in this particular context through a re-structuring of indigenous–state relations at the national rather than the international level.[148] It is this rich understanding of the right to self-determination which should inform the meaning of the right as now enshrined in Article 3 of the UN Declaration. It is an understanding that can meet the interests and concerns of both indigenous peoples and states.

---

148 Although this doesn't preclude some external forms of exercising the right. See Xanthaki, *supra* note 29, 25–6.

The starting point for interpreting the right to self-determination in Article 3 of the UN Declaration is of fundamental importance. Decolonization provides that starting point. Any 'new' and 'distinct' concept of an internal right which seeks to distance itself from self-determination's strong routes in the decolonization project of international law must be resisted. Self-determination cannot be equated with the right to 'democratic governance' that has come to dominate the jurisprudence of the HRC on the common Article 1 of the International Covenants. Indigenous peoples, as a colonized peoples, are entitled to much more. In accordance with existing international law, Article 3 must be understood as intended to unravel, so far as it is now possible to do so, the devastating consequences of colonialism for indigenous peoples. Whilst it has largely been accepted that indigenous peoples' right to self-determination must be exercised within the existing territorial boundaries of the post-colonial state, any further limitations on the sovereignty and autonomy of indigenous peoples must be strictly construed. Self-determination as thus understood promises to deliver a radical re-structuring of state–indigenous relations far beyond that which has so far been conceded domestically by states such as Canada and Australia.

Whilst the final scope and meaning of indigenous peoples' right to self-determination as enshrined in Article 3 of the UN Declaration remains to be determined, there is therefore much within the current understanding of the right in international law that is encouraging. A number of states during the drafting of the Declaration suggested a strong substantive content to the internal exercise of the right and provided support, in varying degrees, for the right of indigenous peoples to establish separate, autonomous, perhaps even sovereign, political, legal and economic systems, including very importantly a measure of control over their traditional territories and resources. If future interpretations of Articles 3 and 4 can remain faithful to these essential tenets of self-determination as a tool of liberation, there is much about which indigenous peoples can be optimistic.

Chapter 7
Protecting the Vulnerable within the Framework of Self-Determination

Introduction

A concept of internal self-determination which is informed by the colonial experiences of indigenous peoples and remains focused on achieving the overriding goal of liberating Aboriginal lands and communities from the alien governments that surround them, can do much to meet the core concerns of indigenous peoples. However, it remains to be asked whether international law can deliver the same promising future for potentially vulnerable Aboriginal individuals living within autonomous self-governing communities. If international law is to embrace a concept of self-determination which promises to vest 'sovereign' powers in Aboriginal governments, protecting the basic human rights of individuals living within those communities will be an issue of fundamental importance for the international community. Indeed, international law may seem able to provide a ready answer to this crucial question in the protection provided to all individuals by the international law of human rights, regardless of their socio-economic background or the government under which they live. However, such easy answers rarely exist to complex problems such as that of indigenous peoples.

Striking an appropriate balance between securing effective protection for the rights of indigenous children whilst upholding and respecting the right of indigenous peoples to self-determination will not be easy. Difficult questions arise: can international human rights law provide adequate and appropriate protection to the rights and interests of potentially vulnerable indigenous children, without compromising the basic cultural integrity of indigenous communities? If the arguments as to cultural legitimacy can be overcome, who will be responsible for protecting the rights of indigenous individuals within self-governing communities: indigenous governments or the state? And if indigenous communities are to be responsible for protecting the rights of indigenous individuals, who will be answerable to the international community for any violations of those rights? It is unlikely that the answers to these questions will be found within the orthodox doctrines of international law. The international community is seeking to fashion a tailored response to the self-determination claims of indigenous peoples. A similarly tailored response is required to the protection of indigenous individuals. If progress is to be made on these issues, new and perhaps innovative approaches to the relationship between indigenous individuals, indigenous peoples, the state and, ultimately, the international community, will need to be explored.

Indigenous Peoples and Human Rights

Part of the concern of both states and commentators over affording recognition to the collective rights of indigenous peoples, including their right to self-determination, has been rooted in the common perception that some aspects of indigenous cultures are simply 'incommensurable' with the existing body of international human rights norms. This raises the spectre of a direct conflict developing within international human rights law between the right of the collective to self-determination and the rights of indigenous individuals. If the right of indigenous peoples to self-determination is given its most literal interpretation it confers a right on indigenous peoples to determine for themselves the social, cultural and political system under which they wish to live and a free choice as to the values by which their collective lives as a community should be governed.[1] Applying this principle of self-determination, there is no guarantee, or perhaps even likelihood, that in exercising this right to determine their own internal systems of governance, the community will choose a liberal democratic model of government that slips neatly and tidily into the existing framework of international law. Indeed, the fear of commentators is that indigenous peoples will choose to endorse a range of deeply entrenched socio-political traditions and practices that do not sit easily with the concept of human rights, at least as conceived and understood in the West. Concerns about traditional punishments, the treatment of women and other vulnerable family members, and the 'undemocratic' nature of indigenous tribal governments are prominent amongst the anticipated difficulties.[2]

1 D. Makinson (1988). 'Rights of Peoples: A Logician's Point of View', in J. Crawford (ed.) *The Rights of Peoples.* Oxford: Clarendon, 69, 85.

2 See, for example, D. Sanders (1993). 'Self-Determination and Indigenous Peoples', in C. Tomuschat (ed.) *Modern Law of Self-determination.* Dordrecht and London: Martinus Nijhoff Publishers, 70; Makinson, ibid., 85; G. Triggs (1988). 'The Rights of Peoples and Individual Rights: Conflict or Harmony?' in J. Crawford (ed.) *The Rights of Peoples.* Oxford: Clarendon, 143; Australian Law Reform Commission (ALRC) (1986). *The Recognition of Aboriginal Customary Laws*, No. 31, Vol. 1. Canberra: Australian Government Publishing Service, 8. For a more recent analysis of the potential clash between the cultures of indigenous peoples and women's rights see A. Xanthaki (2010). 'Multiculturalism and International Law: Discussing Universal Standards', *Human Rights Quarterly*, 32: 21 and A. Xanthaki (2011). 'The UN Declaration on the Rights of Indigenous Peoples and Collective Rights: What's the Future for Indigenous Women?', in S. Allen and A. Xanthaki (eds) *Reflections on the UN Declaration on the Rights of Indigenous Peoples*. Oxford: Hart, 413.

Reconciling Indigenous Peoples' Right to Cultural Integrity and Individual Human Rights

Clashing rights: the debate surrounding the accommodation of group rights

The potential clash between Aboriginal cultures and the individual rights of Aboriginal people has generally been conceptualized as an inconsistency between two competing human rights which the state must find a way to reconcile within the existing framework of international human rights law. The right of a peoples to the protection of their cultural values and practices constitutes an essential part of the broader right to self-determination and is now well-established within the body of mainstream human rights norms.[3] The rights of minorities, albeit conceptualized as individual rather than group rights, are recognized under Article 27 of the International Covenant on Civil and Political Rights (ICCPR).[4] The subsequent work of the Human Rights Committee has led to the development of a substantial body of jurisprudence on the cultural rights of minority groups, including the cultural rights of indigenous peoples.[5] The collective right of indigenous peoples to the protection of their cultural identity has been afforded strong protection under ILO Convention No. 169 and the UN Declaration on the Rights of Indigenous Peoples, with a number of articles emphasizing the right of indigenous peoples to respect for their cultural values, practices, traditions and customs.[6] The Committee on Economic, Social and Cultural Rights has recently embraced this more controversial approach, holding that the right of everyone to take part in cultural life as protected under Article 15 of the Covenant on Economic, Social and Cultural Rights (CESCR) can be a collective right inhering in the community or group.[7] However, whilst generally supportive of widening the scope

3 For an excellent discussion of current protections for cultural rights in international law, see Xanthaki (2010), ibid.

4 Article 27 provides: 'In those States in which ethnic, religious, or linguistic minorities exist, persons belonging to such minorities shall not be denied the right, in community with the other members of their group, to enjoy their own culture, to profess and practise their own religion, or to use their own language.'

5 See, for example, Human Rights Committee, *The Rights of Minorities (Art. 27): 08/04/94. CCPR General Comment 23. (General Comments)*, CCPR/C/21/Rev.1/Add.5. See also, *Sandra Lovelace v. Canada*, Communication No. R.6/24, (A/36/40) (1981), 166; *Ivan Kitok v. Sweden*, Communication No. 197/1985, CCPR/C/33/D/197/1985 (1988); *Lubicon Lake Band v. Canada*, Communication No. 167/1984 (26 March 1990), (A/45/40) (1990); *Lansman v Finland, Communication No 671/1995: Finland. 22/11/96*, CCPR/C/58/D/671/1995. Individual committee members have also championed the need to protect and secure traditional Aboriginal cultures and economies through the State Party reporting procedures. See, for example, the comments of Scheinin when considering Australia's 3rd and 4th periodic reports: Human Rights Committee, *Summary Record of the 1856th Meeting: Australia 28/07/2000 (Summary Record)*, CCPR/C/SR.1856, [65].

6 See, for example, Articles 2 and 5 of ILO Convention No. 169.

7 Committee on Economic, Social and Cultural Rights, *General Comment No. 21,*

of international human rights law to embrace the concept of collective rights to cultural integrity, the weight of academic literature has traditionally taken a fairly uncompromising stance on the overriding importance of individual rights where a conflict between the rights of an individual and the rights and interests of the group cannot be avoided and some form of compromise must be found.[8] Indeed, the view of many commentators is that collective rights, where recognized, must not be allowed to prejudice the protection of individual interests: individual human rights must take priority. Consequently, where accommodation is needed between the culture and traditions of the collective and the human rights of its individual members, it is the culture and traditions of the group that must give way.

Brownlie is one of the strongest proponents of this view. Attacking what he describes as the 'low quality debate in this field', he argues that commentators who raise the issue of incompatibility between indigenous customs and traditions and existing human rights standards are wrongly dismissed with accusations of paternalism.[9] In his view, the real paternalists are those commentators who assume that indigenous populations cannot adapt to international human rights standards. For Brownlie, the applicability of international human rights standards to indigenous peoples is simply non-negotiable and communal interests must not be allowed to take priority over human rights values.[10] Adopting this rather hard-line approach, if indigenous cultures have to change and adapt to meet existing standards then so be it. Rich takes a very similar position. He argues that there must exist a rough hierarchy among the subjects of human rights law and 'that the individual as the ultimate beneficiary of all human rights has primacy'.[11] Consequently, in Rich's view there can be no human rights, including group rights, which detract from the rights of the individual.[12] The rights of the individual must prevail. This position is also reflected in the writings of Kamenka, who argues in similar terms that whilst claims to collective 'third-generation rights' can be valid and protected by the international law of human rights, they are valid only insofar as they support and strengthen core civil and political rights, rather than destroy them.[13]

Right of Everyone to Take Part in Cultural Life (art. 15, para. 1(a), of the International Covenant on Economic, Social and Cultural Rights), E/c.12/GC/21, [9].

8 For more recent approaches which are more deferential to the cultural rights of the group see J. Anaya (2004). 'International Human Rights and Indigenous Peoples: The Move Toward the Multicultural State', *Ariz. J. Int'l & Comp. L.*, 21: 13 and Xanthaki (2010) and Xanthaki (2011), *supra* note 2.

9 I. Brownlie (1988). 'The Rights of Peoples in Modern International Law', in J. Crawford (ed.) *The Rights of Peoples*. Oxford: Clarendon, 1, 15.

10 Ibid., 90 and 99.

11 R. Rich (1988). 'The Right to Development: A Right of Peoples', in J. Crawford (ed.) *The Rights of Peoples*. Oxford: Clarendon, 39, 43.

12 Ibid.

13 E. Kamenka (1988). 'Human Rights, Peoples' Rights', in J. Crawford (ed.) *The Rights of Peoples*. Oxford: Clarendon, 127, 139.

Whilst keen to protect the rights of individuals from being unduly undermined by the interests of the group, commentators have, however, also stressed that the rights and interests of the individual and the rights and interests of the group are often supportive and complementary, with the survival of the group recognized as an essential factor in promoting the interests of the individual.[14] Cultural, religious and linguistic rights are frequently cited as classic examples of individual rights that can only be exercised in any meaningful way in community with other members of the group. In this context, the protection and survival of the group is accepted as essential to the realization of these individual entitlements, leading commentators to concede that measures to protect the group may be justified even if it means some immediate interference with the rights of its individual members. In resolving this potential clash of rights, commentators have emphasized the need for flexibility if the rights of the individual are not to be fundamentally undermined in the longer term.[15] International human rights law has always allowed for flexibility in interpreting and implementing normative human rights standards, allowing for compromises and accommodation between two existing and apparently conflicting rights when necessary. The same principles of flexibility and accommodation can be applied whether or not the rights in question are two individual rights or an individual and a collective right.[16]

Xanthaki has become a strong proponent of this view, affording considerably more weight to the cultural integrity of the group and its *intrinsic* value than has traditionally been the case.[17] She argues that invoking 'a pre-determined hierarchy of individual rights above cultural rights is a simplistic solution'.[18] In her view, a system that recognizes and respects cultural rights only up until the point that those rights come into conflict with the dominant individualistic rights-based framework of the West 'rings of cultural imperialism'.[19] Greater accommodation by the dominant legal framework to the cultural worldview of indigenous peoples is therefore needed, with adjustments to the 'universal' standards of the West, 'tailored to the particular circumstances of each context'.[20] A flexible approach is called for; one that does not approach conflict between the group and individual

14 This line of argument is based on the theoretical work of liberal scholars such as Kymlicka and Taylor. See, for example W. Kymlicka (1991). *Liberalism, Community and Culture*. Oxford: Clarendon Press and C. Taylor (1992). 'Multiculturalism and the "Politics of Recognition": An Essay', in A. Gutmann (ed.) *Multiculturalism*. Princeton: Princeton University Press.

15 This balancing exercise can thus be conceptualized both as between two individual rights and as between the rights of the individual and the group, although the latter is ultimately for the protection of its individual members.

16 See, for example, Triggs, *supra* note 2, 143.

17 This is different from seeing the value of the group only in instrumental terms, that is, for the role it plays in ultimately advancing the rights of the individual.

18 Xanthaki (2010), *supra* note 2, 44.

19 Ibid., 44.

20 Ibid.

with a predetermined hierarchy of norms but where 'conflicts between rights, principles, and norms are generally solved on an ad hoc basis, after taking into account various considerations'.[21] The outcome of this balancing process will be highly fact- and context-specific, depending on the relative importance of the rights and interests at stake and the degree of interference that is contemplated. Adopting this model of conflict resolution, in some cases the rights of the group will take precedence, in others the rights of the individual will prevail.

In developing her approach, Xanthaki draws on the work of Anaya. Both of these leading commentators, whilst generally sympathetic to the cultural claims of indigenous peoples, accept there must be limits to the level of 'adjustment' that can be expected of international human rights law.[22] Xanthaki is clear in her view that the accommodation of group rights cannot be permitted to fracture the very 'foundations' of the international human rights system.[23] Her endorsement of indigenous peoples' cultural integrity is thus heavily qualified. Whilst willing to accept that cultural practices may restrict human rights at the margins, she does not believe that cultural practices that 'violate the core of these rights can be tolerated in the name of cultural diversity'.[24] The 'core' or the 'essence' of existing human rights law is thus protected, Xanthaki concluding: '[i]n my view, no cultural practices and beliefs can violate these values and no real adjustment can be initiated to these rights.'[25] The greater respect shown to the cultural integrity of indigenous peoples in Xanthaki's approach is to be welcomed. However, the extent to which this qualified approach can really address the legitimate concerns of indigenous peoples as to the ethnocentric nature of international human rights law will depend on the level of adjustment and accommodation that is tolerated in the name of cultural difference. It also depends on whether the 'core' or 'essence' of the human rights system can successfully defend itself against the same accusations of cultural imperialism which undoubtedly exist around the margins.[26]

Reconciling the group and the individual in international law

As the views of leading commentators have changed towards greater accommodation of group interests within the framework of international human rights law, so have the UN treaty bodies proved themselves increasingly willing and able to protect the communal interests of the group, even where the individual rights of community members are at stake. The Human Rights Committee has been at the forefront of these developments. Its willingness to protect the communal interests of the group under the auspices of Article 27 was made clear in its General Comment on the rights of minorities:

21 Ibid.

22 Anaya, *supra* note 8, 25.

23 Xanthaki (2010), *supra* note 2, 45.

24 Ibid., 46.

25 Ibid., 45.

26 See further discussion below.

> Although the rights protected under article 27 are individual rights, they depend in turn on the ability of the minority group to maintain its culture, language or religion. Accordingly, positive measures by States may also be necessary to protect the identity of a minority and the rights of its members to enjoy and develop their culture and language to practise their religion, in community with the other members of the group.[27]

In its jurisprudence under the Optional Protocol, the Human Rights Committee has also proved itself willing to undertake a balancing of group and individual rights, even where this balancing of interests may compromise the absolute protection traditionally afforded to the individual. The decision of the Human Rights Committee in the case of *Kitok v Sweden*[28] provides a good example of the ability of the international community to carry out this balancing exercise under Article 27 of the ICCPR within the framework of international human rights law. The complainant in *Kitok* was a member of a Sami family who had been active in reindeer husbandry for over a century. The author had been denied membership of a Sami Village and he contended that this constituted a violation of his rights under Article 27 of the ICCPR. Under Swedish legislation, membership of a Sami village brought with it certain important rights to engage in reindeer husbandry, as well as a range of other hunting and fishing rights. Although the initial decision as to membership was made by the Sami community, an appeal could be made to the Swedish courts. In light of this, the Swedish government tried to argue that this was not in fact a dispute between Mr Kitok and the state but between Mr Kitok and the Sami community. The Committee rejected this argument, pointing out that it was Swedish legislation that was responsible for dividing the Sami into members and non-members of a Sami village and restricting the rights of the latter. However, the Committee was more sympathetic to the argument that the restrictions imposed on non-Village members were necessary for the protection of reindeer husbandry and thereby the Sami culture. The Swedish government argued:

> As in every society where conflict occurs, a choice had to be made between what is considered to be in the general interest on the one hand and the interests of the individual on the other. A special circumstance here is that reindeer husbandry is so closely connected to the Sami culture that it must be considered part of the Sami culture itself. In this case the legislation can be said to favour the Sami community in order to make reindeer husbandry economically viable now and in the future.[29]

27 Human Rights Committee, *The Rights of Minorities (Art 27): 08/04/94. CCPR General Comment 23 (General Comments)*, CCPR/C/21/Rev.1/Add.5, [6.2].

28 *Ivan Kitok v. Sweden*, Communication No. 197/1985, CCPR/C/33/D/197/1985 (1988).

29 Ibid., [4.3].

The Committee therefore concluded that restrictions on the rights of an individual were permissible provided that it could be shown that the restrictions had a reasonable and objective justification and were necessary for the continued viability and welfare of the minority as a whole.[30] Applying that principle to Kitok's case, the Committee concluded that there had been no violation of Article 27, noting in particular that Mr Kitok had been permitted by the Sami community to graze and farm reindeer and engage in hunting and fishing.[31]

Decisions such as *Kitok* reflect the increasing importance afforded to cultural integrity when carrying out the required balancing of rights within the framework of international human rights law. However, whilst UN treaty bodies, such as the Human Rights Committee, have been prepared to further the communal interests of the group, even where the individual rights of community members are at stake, there is a clear limit as to how far this accommodation of the group will go. Thornberry reports that whilst the UN treaty bodies are generally sympathetic to indigenous peoples and the need to protect their cultural values, practices and traditions,[32] where the right of the individual engaged is perceived as of fundamental importance, UN bodies, such as the Human Rights Committee, have been much less accommodating. For example, the Human Rights Committee have taken an uncompromising position on the need for the Australian government to secure the abolition of traditional Aboriginal punishments such as 'spearing the thigh', which, in the Committee's view, amount to cruel, inhuman and degrading treatment or punishment contrary to Article 7 of the ICCPR.[33] The Committee on Economic, Social and Cultural Right's General Comment on the right of everyone to take part in cultural life reflects this uncompromising stance where the culture or traditions of the group are deemed harmful to the rights of individuals:

> The Committee wishes to recall that, while account must be taken of national and regional particularities and various historical, cultural and religious backgrounds, it is the duty of States, regardless of their political, economic or cultural systems, to promote and protect all human rights and fundamental freedoms. Thus, no-one may invoke cultural diversity to infringe upon human rights guaranteed by international law, nor to limit their scope.[34]

---

30 Ibid., [9.7]–[9.8].

31 Ibid., [9.8].

32 On the sensitivity of UN treaty bodies to Aboriginal cultures, see generally P. Thornberry (2002). *Indigenous Peoples and Human Rights*. Manchester: Manchester University Press, esp. at pp. 190–1, 194–7 (Committee on Economic, Social and Cultural Rights); p. 224 (Committee on the Elimination of Racial Discrimination); and pp. 225–41 (UN Committee on the Rights of the Child).

33 Ibid., 136–8.

34 *General Comment No. 21*, *supra* note 7, [18].

Importantly, however, the Committee sets down a structured framework within which any limitations or restrictions on the cultural integrity of the group must be justified.[35] Thus the burden will fall on the state to demonstrate that any purported limitation on the cultural integrity of the group pursues a legitimate aim, is compatible with the nature of the right of everyone to take part in cultural life and is strictly necessary for the promotion of general welfare in a democratic society. In short, any such limitations or restrictions must be proportionate: the least restrictive measure possible to achieve the effective protection of the competing right.[36]

The key human rights instruments dealing specifically with indigenous peoples have tried to draw a similar balance between the protection of indigenous cultures and the individual rights of the members of the group. Where the international community has chosen to afford specific recognition to the collective rights of indigenous peoples, those rights have thus been heavily qualified by core human rights guarantees. In many ways, ILO Convention No. 169 marked a turning point in attitudes towards indigenous peoples by affording clear recognition to their collective social, economic and cultural rights and their right to 'respect for their social and cultural identity, their customs and traditions and their institutions'.[37] The protection to be afforded to the cultural integrity of indigenous peoples is, however, unequivocally qualified in the Convention by the need for compliance with both national and international human rights standards. The unacceptability of any discrimination on the grounds of sex is made clear in Article 3 of the Convention,[38] whilst both Articles 8 and 9 explicitly subject the practice of indigenous customs and traditions to their compatibility with national and international human rights standards. Thus Article 8 provides that indigenous peoples 'have the right to retain their own customs and institutions' but only insofar as 'these are not incompatible with fundamental rights defined by the national legal system and with internationally recognized human rights'. Article 9 similarly provides that 'the methods customarily practised by the peoples concerned for dealing with offences committed by their members shall be respected' but only 'to the extent compatible with the national legal system and internationally recognized human rights'.

The inclusion of core human rights guarantees within the UN Declaration proved much more contentious. In general terms, the Declaration places by far the greater emphasis on indigenous peoples' collective rights. Thus, whilst the

---

35 Ibid., [19]

36 Xanthaki (2010), *supra* note 2, 46; Xanthaki (2011), *supra* note 2, 430–1.

37 ILO Convention No. 169, Article 2. See also, Article 5.

38 Article 3 of ILO Convention No. 169 provides: 'Indigenous and tribal peoples shall enjoy the full measure of human rights and fundamental freedoms without hindrance or discrimination. The provisions of the Convention shall be applied without discrimination to male and female members of these peoples.'

rights of indigenous people as individuals have not been entirely neglected,[39] the treatment of the individual is often rather unsatisfactory. During the drafting process, this gave rise to strong concern that the Declaration as a whole did not provide sufficient protection for indigenous individuals. In the final stages of the drafting process there was therefore a concerted effort by a number of states to try and redress the balance between the group and the individual and bring down the Declaration much more firmly in favour of the individual. These efforts met with mixed results.

At the HRC Working Group even the very idea of protecting collective rights within the framework of the Declaration did not escape challenge. Indeed, the idea of enshrining collective rights within the international law of human rights continued to attract considerable state opposition. The disquiet expressed by many Western states is understandable. At a fundamental level, to afford recognition and protection to the collective interests of the group seems to run counter to the very purpose of the international human rights system. Human rights, as traditionally conceived, are intended to protect the individual from the potential abuses of the group. To afford rights and protection to the group under the rubric of international human rights law is thus, in the opinion of some, an anathema. Several states, including influential states such as France, the United States and Japan, adopted this particularly uncompromising position before the HRC Working Group; the representative of France expressing in unequivocal terms the view of the French government that collective rights simply did not exist in international human rights law.[40] The UK maintained this position before the General Assembly,

39 The majority of provisions in the UN Declaration on the Rights of Indigenous Peoples are in fact primarily concerned with indigenous peoples' collective rights. Only Article 2 (non-discrimination), Article 6 (the right to a nationality), Article 7 (life, mental integrity, liberty and security of person), Article 8 (ethnocide and cultural genocide), Article 9 (right to belong to an indigenous community in accordance with the traditions and customs of the community), Article 14 (education), Article 17 (labour protection), Article 21 (economic and social conditions), Article 22 (protection of the vulnerable), Article 24 (health) and Article 33 (national citizenship) explicitly refer to the rights of indigenous peoples as individuals.

40 Economic and Social Council, *Report of the Working Group Established in Accordance with Commission on Human Rights Resolution 1995/32 of 3 March 1995*, E/CN.4/1997/102, [108]. See also, Economic and Social Council, *Report of the Working Group Established in Accordance with Commission on Human Rights Resolution 1995/32 of 3 March 1995*, E/CN.4/1997/102, [112] (Japan) and [113] (Sweden); Economic and Social Council, *Report of the Working Group Established in Accordance with Commission on Human Rights Resolution 1995/32 of 3 March 1995*, E/CN.4/2001/85, [65] (Japan). The opposition of these states may have become less vociferous in recent years as the Report from the 2002 Working Group records the view of the Chairperson-Rapporteur that during the debate on the issue, 'he had not heard any intervention that could be interpreted as denying the existence of collective rights as such'. See, Economic and Social Council, *Report of the Working Group Established in Accordance with Commission on Human Rights Resolution 1995/32 of 3 March 1995*, E/CN.4/2002/98, [37]. However, concern

stating during the debate on the adoption of the Declaration that the UK 'did not accept that some groups in society should benefit from human rights that were not available to others' and 'did not accept the concept of collective human rights in international law'.[41] In line with these more hard-line views, some governments continued to object to the use of the collective term 'peoples' in the Declaration on the basis that it may lead to a denial of the rights of individuals in favour of collective rights.[42]

Amongst those states willing to concede the inclusion of collective rights within the Declaration, a number took an equally uncompromising stance on the relationship between the individual and the group, maintaining that collective rights must only be seen as a 'reinforcement for the enjoyment of individual rights' and that their exercise must not be allowed to interfere with or violate the rights of individuals.[43] Sweden explicitly adopted this position before the General Assembly, arguing that whilst it was willing to accept collective rights outside the framework of international law, 'it was of the firm opinion that individual human rights prevailed over the collective rights mentioned in the Declaration'.[44] In accordance with the usual principles of norm creation in the international sphere, states could not accept the inclusion of new collective rights within the Declaration that were perceived as contradicting, impinging upon or weakening their existing and chronologically prior human rights duties under international law.

Over the course of the drafting process, states pressed for the inclusion of a number of provisions and amendments which would guarantee much stronger protection for the rights of indigenous individuals, particularly those of women and children.[45] In later sessions of the Working Group, a general consensus developed amongst participating states as to the desirability of drafting, with

---

among these states about the relationship between collective and individual rights clearly remains. See, for example, Economic and Social Council, *Report of the Working Group Established in Accordance with Commission on Human Rights Resolution 1995/32 of 3 March 1995*, E/CN.4/2003/92, [67] (US, UK and France).

41 General Assembly, Sixty-first session, 107th plenary meeting, 13 September 2007, A/61/PV.107.

42 Economic and Social Council, *Report of the Working Group Established in Accordance with Commission on Human Rights Resolution 1995/32 of 3 March 1995*, E/CN.4/1996/84, [38].

43 Economic and Social Council, *Report of the Working Group Established in Accordance with Commission on Human Rights Resolution 1995/32 of 3 March 1995*, E/CN.4/1996/84, [50].

44 General Assembly, Sixty-first session, 107th plenary meeting, 13 September 2007, A/61/PV.107.

45 Economic and Social Council, *Report of the Working Group Established in Accordance with Commission on Human Rights Resolution 1995/32 of 3 March 1995*, E/CN.4/1996/84, [40] and [56]; Economic and Social Council, *Report of the Working Group Established in Accordance with Commission on Human Rights Resolution 1995/32 of 3 March 1995*, E/CN.4/2001/85, [121].

particular reference to the United Nation Convention on the Rights of the Child (UNCRC), a new additional article on the rights of indigenous children.[46] States such as Sweden, the Netherlands, France and Switzerland led the calls for a much stronger all-embracing 'safeguard' clause which would make it clear that exercising rights under the Declaration would not be allowed to prejudice or interfere with the rights of individuals as protected under existing international human rights law.[47] The Working Group also considered a number of proposals to include within more of the individual paragraphs an explicit reference to the need for indigenous peoples to conform with international human rights standards. Where the Declaration confers specific protection on particular cultural practices and traditions (see, for example, Articles 11 and 12 of the Declaration[48]), it was thus suggested at an early session of the Working Group that their compatibility with existing international human rights standards should first be established.[49]

Indigenous representatives at the Working Group were strongly opposed to these attempts to secure a greater level of protection for the rights of individuals within the Declaration, arguing that such explicit reference to international human rights standards was unnecessary and jeopardized one of the primary objectives of the Declaration. Indigenous groups emphasized that within Aboriginal cultures, the community and the individual are mutually supportive and complementary, reinforcing rather than undermining one another. They therefore argued that recognition of collective rights simply could not 'lead to a denial of the rights of individuals'.[50] In the face of this opposition, states did not get everything they

46 Economic and Social Council, *Report of the Working Group Established in Accordance with Commission on Human Rights Resolution 1995/32 of 3 March 1995*, E/CN.4/2002/98, [65].

47 Economic and Social Council, *Report of the Working Group Established in Accordance with Commission on Human Rights Resolution 1995/32 of 3 March 1995*, E/CN.4/1997/102, [109].

48 Article 11 provides: 'Indigenous peoples have the right to practise and revitalize their cultural traditions and customs. This includes the right to maintain, protect and develop the past, present and future manifestations of their cultures, such as archaeological and historical sites, artefacts, designs, ceremonies, technologies and visual and performing arts and literature.' Article 12 provides: 'Indigenous peoples have the right to manifest, practise, develop and teach their spiritual and religious traditions, customs and ceremonies; the right to maintain, protect and have access in privacy to their religious and cultural sites; the right to the use and control of their ceremonial objects; and the right to repatriation of their human remains.'

49 Economic and Social Council, *Report of the Working Group Established in Accordance with Commission on Human Rights Resolution 1995/32 of 3 March 1995*, E/CN.4/1997/102, [76] and [78]. Note, however, that states agreed at a later session of the Working Group that in some instances such a reference was unnecessary. See, Economic and Social Council, *Report of the Working Group Established in Accordance with Commission on Human Rights Resolution 1995/32 of 3 March 1995*, E/CN.4/2002/98, [67].

50 Economic and Social Council, *Report of the Working Group Established in Accordance with Commission on Human Rights Resolution 1995/32 of 3 March 1995*, E/

wanted and many of the proposals failed to find their way into the final text. The result of this strained negotiating process was a somewhat unhappy compromise. The rights of indigenous peoples 'as peoples' now sit uncomfortably within the Declaration next to the rights of indigenous people 'as individuals' as if they were one and the same thing and the relationship between the two straightforward and unproblematic.[51]

There is some limited guidance as to how any potential conflict between the rights of the group and the rights of indigenous individuals is to be resolved, with some fundamental human rights principles firmly entrenched within the final text. Thus, despite the emphasis on collective rights, the individual has been accorded precedence in a number of instances. In line with the approach taken in ILO Convention No. 169, some provisions are explicitly qualified by human rights guarantees. Article 34, for example, provides that indigenous cultural traditions and values will only be protected insofar as they are consistent with core human rights standards:

> Indigenous peoples have the right to promote, develop and maintain their institutional structures and their distinctive customs, spirituality, traditions, procedures, practices and, in the cases where they exist, juridical systems or customs, in accordance with international human rights standards.

This is, however, the only substantive provision in which indigenous cultures are specifically required to comply with the standards enshrined in international human rights law.

In recognition of the frequent concerns raised about gender inequalities within indigenous communities, a specific non-discrimination clause has been included. Article 44 thus provides:

> All the rights and freedoms recognized herein are equally guaranteed to male and female indigenous individuals.

The importance of protecting against gender discrimination in the context of community membership is further reinforced by Article 9 which unequivocally states that whilst indigenous peoples and individuals have the right to belong to an indigenous community or nation in accordance with their particular traditions and customs, 'no discrimination of any kind may arise from the exercise of such

---

CN.4/1996/84, [39]. See also, Economic and Social Council, *Report of the Working Group Established in Accordance with Commission on Human Rights Resolution 1995/32 of 3 March 1995*, E/CN.4/1997/102, [62].

51 Article 1, for example, provides: 'Indigenous peoples have the right to the full enjoyment, as a collective or as individuals, of all human rights and fundamental freedoms as recognized in the Charter of the United Nations, the Universal Declaration of Human Rights and international human rights law.'

a right'. This particular concern with the potential vulnerability of both women and children is carried through into Article 22 of the Declaration which places an obligation on states, in conjunction with indigenous peoples, to 'ensure that indigenous women and children enjoy the full protection and guarantees against all forms of violence and discrimination'.

The strong concern amongst states that the rights of indigenous children may be jeopardized by placing too much emphasis on the collective rights of indigenous groups was also clearly evident in the debate over the legitimacy of removing indigenous children from their communities. Article 7.2 of the Declaration now provides:

> Indigenous peoples have the collective right to live in freedom, peace and security as distinct peoples and shall not be subjected to any act of genocide or any other act of violence, including forcibly removing children of the group to another group.

The language prohibiting the forcible removal of children is considerably more restrictive than earlier drafts which prohibited in general terms 'the removal of indigenous children from their families and communities under any pretext'. States were strongly opposed to the suggestion within this earlier draft that removing indigenous children from their families and communities could never be justified even if the child was being subjected to grave physical and emotional abuse. States therefore maintained the firm position, now reflected in the final wording of Article 7, that in such circumstances it may be in 'the child's interests to be removed from their families and communities, whether the child [is] indigenous or non-indigenous ... and that in those circumstances indigenous people and communities should not receive preferential treatment'.[52]

In addition to these specific protections for indigenous individuals, the Declaration contains a more general safeguard clause in the form of Article 46 which provides a sweeping guarantee qualifying all of the Declaration's substantive provisions with basic human rights protections. Article 46 is drafted in very broad and general terms, providing:

> 2. In the exercise of the rights enunciated in the present Declaration, human rights and fundamental freedoms of all shall be respected. The exercise of the

52 Economic and Social Council, *Report of the Working Group Established in Accordance with Commission on Human Rights Resolution 1995/32 of 3 March 1995*, E/CN.4/1996/84, [61]. See also, Economic and Social Council, *Report of the Working Group Established in Accordance with Commission on Human Rights Resolution 1995/32 of 3 March 1995*, E/CN.4/2002/98, [56]. Similar concerns have been raised regarding the question of community membership and discrimination: Economic and Social Council, *Report of the Working Group Established in Accordance with Commission on Human Rights Resolution 1995/32 of 3 March 1995*, E/CN.4/1996/84, [67]–[68].

> rights set forth in this Declaration shall be subject only to such limitations as are determined by law and in accordance with international human rights obligations. Any such limitations shall be non-discriminatory and strictly necessary solely for the purpose of securing due recognition and respect for the rights and freedoms of others and for meeting the just and most compelling requirements of a democratic society.
>
> 3. The provisions set forth in this Declaration shall be interpreted in accordance with the principles of justice, democracy, respect for human rights, equality, non-discrimination, good governance and good faith.

In line with the approach adopted by the UN treaty bodies, Article 46.2 imposes strict conditions of proportionality and necessity on any provisions, whether national or international, which purport to limit or restrict indigenous peoples' cultural rights. Individual human rights cannot therefore automatically trump the cultural integrity of the group but neither can the group automatically trump the individual. A balance is required.[53]

The final text of Article 46 should go some way to assuage concerns about the potential vulnerability of disempowered groups, such as women and children, within self-governing indigenous communities. However, the potentially problematic impact of late additions to the text, from the perspective of indigenous peoples, should be noted. Until the very final stages of the drafting process it was clear that the human rights standards to which indigenous peoples would be expected to adhere were those enshrined within international law. Suggestions that indigenous peoples should be subjected to domestic law raised clear objections not just from indigenous peoples but from state delegations who generally appeared to agree that the appropriate standards by which indigenous peoples should be bound were the 'universal standards' enshrined in international human rights law and not the potentially more restrictive standards enshrined in the municipal law of states.[54] This approach was welcomed as a significant improvement on ILO Convention No. 169 which explicitly subjects the rights of indigenous peoples to national legislation. However, the late insertion of the caveat in Article 46.2 that the rights of indigenous peoples may be subject to such limitations 'as are determined by law' creates an ambiguity, suggesting that indigenous peoples' rights may be subjected to national as well as international law. This interpretation found some favour with states addressing the General Assembly during the debate

53 Xanthaki (2010), *supra* note 2, 46; Xanthaki (2011), *supra* note 2, 430–1.

54 Economic and Social Council, *Report of the Working Group Established in Accordance with Commission on Human Rights Resolution 1995/32 of 3 March 1995*, E/CN.4/2002/98, [51] and [53]. See also, Economic and Social Council, *Report of the Working Group Established in Accordance with Commission on Human Rights Resolution 1995/32 of 3 March 1995*, E/CN.4/2001/85, [153].

on the adoption of the Declaration.[55] However, such a broad interpretation of Article 46.2 is deeply problematic. It would run counter to the whole tenor of the Declaration, represent a considerable challenge to indigenous legal and political autonomy, once again 'domesticate' the indigenous problem to the will of states and fundamentally undermine the right to self-determination. It therefore needs to be resisted.

Self-Determination and Human Rights

International human rights law provides a clear and fairly consistent answer to commentators who are concerned about the rights and interests of vulnerable individuals living within indigenous communities. Whilst international human rights law is increasingly sympathetic to the importance of collective rights, such rights, even within the Declaration, will only be protected insofar as they can be shown to be consistent with existing international human rights standards. This balancing approach to reconciling the collective and individual rights of indigenous peoples is closely modelled on the approach which the international community has adopted with respect to the collective rights and interests of ethnic, religious and linguistic minorities. However, indigenous peoples' right to self-determination as enshrined in Article 3 of the Declaration adds an important additional dimension to the debate.

The prevailing approach of the international community to the individual and collective rights of indigenous peoples is based upon certain core assumptions about the structuring of relationships between indigenous individuals, indigenous communities and the state. These assumptions fail to give sufficient recognition to the distinctive status of indigenous peoples and the fundamentally different nature of the right to self-determination when compared to all other collective rights which may be held by minority groups. Self-determination is qualitatively different. It promises to confer on indigenous peoples not just a right to cultural integrity but a right to exercise 'sovereign' powers over their own internal affairs. Autonomous indigenous groups exercising a right to self-determination are therefore in a fundamentally different position from a minority group: they have a sovereign authority to determine for themselves the social, cultural and political values by which they wish to live. They have a right, in other words, to determine their own legal and political systems. It is therefore strongly questionable whether the application of international human rights standards to this new autonomous political body can really be that simple. It is certainly arguable that the right to self-determination, as a peremptory norm of international law, takes priority over all other international standards, thereby giving indigenous peoples the right to

55 General Assembly, Sixty-first session, 107th plenary meeting, 13 September 2007, A/61/PV.107 (per Mexico and Namibia).

accept or reject any existing international human rights norms they regard as inconsistent with their own distinctive value systems.[56]

International law can, however, provide an answer to this dilemma. The fact that indigenous peoples have a right to self-determination does not absolve them of the responsibility of upholding and protecting the rights and interests of indigenous individuals living within their respective territories – in fact quite the opposite.[57] The right of indigenous peoples to self-determination may well be a peremptory norm of international law. There are, however, others, including the right of individuals to be protected from the systematic violation of their basic human rights. There is nothing within the doctrines of international law to suggest one peremptory norm should trump the other.

There is, moreover, much that can be said at the level of principle in favour of the general proposition that indigenous peoples should not be exempted or absolved from compliance with existing international human rights standards. At stake for indigenous peoples is the fundamental question of how they see their future role within the international community. In short, indigenous peoples must ask themselves whether they want to be part of this world, or stand apart from it. Indigenous peoples have fought hard for recognition of their international personality: to be accepted as subjects of international law. To be accepted as legitimate actors on the international stage is not however a cost-free exercise. If indigenous peoples want to be accepted under international law as quasi-sovereign entities exercising autonomous power over their own people, they will be expected to accept the duties and responsibilities which are now accepted as an integral part of holding such a status. This is not to reject the argument that before there can be meaningful interaction with the international community indigenous peoples must first be able to re-establish their own integrity as 'independent' autonomous nations. However, if political, economic, social and cultural autonomy can be delivered by self-determination, the future relationship between indigenous peoples and the wider international community will need to be addressed.

The right to self-determination dictates that the duty to protect the basic fundamental rights and interests of Aboriginal individuals properly rests, in the first instance, with indigenous governments exercising sovereign powers and acting in accordance with their own cultural values and traditions. Although not engaging with the language of self-determination, Anaya comes close to this position, arguing that '[i]n any assessment of whether a particular cultural practice is prohibited rather than protected, the cultural group concerned should be accorded a certain deference for its own interpretive and decision-making processes in the application of human rights norms, just as states are accorded such

56 W. Kymlicka (1999). 'Review: Theorizing Indigenous Rights', *The University of Toronto Law Journal*, 49: 281, 292.

57 See generally, R. McCorquodale (1994). 'Self-Determination: A Human Rights Approach', *International and Comparative Law Quarterly*, 43: 856.

deference'.[58] It is, however, clear that even according such deference to Aboriginal governments, the international community will not abandon its concern for potentially vulnerable individuals living within self-governing communities. In today's increasingly global society where the discourse of international human rights has become firmly entrenched within the legal and political mores of even the most powerful states, 'sovereignty' is no longer regarded as absolute.[59] It is a relative concept, qualified most notably by human rights considerations. Even the world's most powerful states have accepted the requirement to surrender absolute control over their internal affairs, agreeing to subject the way in which they treat their own citizens to the scrutiny of other states in accordance with internationally recognized minimum standards. The question must be asked why Aboriginal governments exercising autonomous political powers and seeking to take their rightful place on the domestic and/or international stage should be treated any differently. International law's constantly evolving understanding of the right to self-determination accords with this approach.

Self-Determination and the Protection of Individual Rights under International Law

The 'external' right to self-determination as traditionally understood and applied in the context of states and former colonies had little to say about the protection of individual human rights once the right to self-determination had been exercised and the independence of the state established. International law's apparent indifference to the potentially precarious situation of vulnerable individuals, such as women and children, within self-determining communities, has been the subject of persuasive academic critique.[60] As Charlesworth and Chinkin point out, 'apparently successful claims to self-determination typically fail to deliver the same level of personal freedom and autonomy for women as for men'. Indeed, they contend that 'in many cases it emerges that achievement of national self-determination has led to a regression in the position of women'.[61] However, state practice on the modern law of self-determination indicates an important change in emphasis, with much greater interest now being shown in the internal dimensions of the right being exercised.

---

58 Anaya, *supra* note 8, 26. Xanthaki suggests a similar approach, arguing that responsibility for decisions regarding the re-evaluation of potentially harmful traditions must rest with the community themselves. See Xanthaki (2011), *supra* note 2, 431.

59 See Statement of the former UN Secretary-General, Boutros Boutros-Ghali, quoted in R. McCorquodale and R. Pangalangan (2001). 'Pushing Back the Limitations of Territorial Boundaries', *European Journal of International Law*, 12: 867, 880.

60 H. Charlesworth and C. Chinkin (2000). *The Boundaries of International Law. A Feminist Analysis*. Manchester: Manchester University Press.

61 Ibid., 154–5.

A close link has developed in recent years between the external and internal dimensions of the right to self-determination, with international attention increasingly focusing on the internal dimensions of self-determination as a continuing right. Championed by both the UN Human Rights Committee (HRC) and the UN Committee on the Elimination of Racial Discrimination (CERD), the right to internal self-determination has, as noted in the previous chapter, firmly established itself, in Franck's words, as a right to 'democratic governance'.[62] As Cassese explains, if the right to internal self-determination is to have any meaning, individuals must be able to exercise those rights and freedoms which make the expression of a free and popular will possible.[63] In its General Comment No. 12 on the right to self-determination, the HRC emphasizes the interdependency between the right to self-determination as enshrined in Article 1 of the ICCPR and the body of human rights norms contained within the remainder of the Covenant:

> The right of self-determination is of particular importance because its realisation is an essential condition for the effective guarantee and observance of individual human rights and for the promotion and strengthening of those rights ... The article [article 1] imposes on all States parties corresponding obligations. This right and the corresponding obligations concerning its implementation are interrelated with other provisions of the Covenant and rules of international law ... With regard to paragraph 1 of article 1, States should describe the constitutional and political processes which in practice allow the exercise of this right.[64]

Central to the concept of internal self-determination and the emerging right to democratic governance is thus the need to protect the whole spectrum of civil and political rights as enshrined in core international human rights texts such as the ICCPR.[65] In other words, self-determination as now understood demands of governments that they are able to effectively guarantee the basic human rights of all their citizens.[66]

---

62 Cited by R. Higgins (1993). 'Postmodern Tribalism and the Right to Secession – Comments by R. Higgins', in C. Brolmann, R. Lefeber and M. Zieck (eds) *Peoples and Minorities in International Law*. Dordrecht and London: Martinus Nijhoff, 29, 32 (fn 4). See also T. Franck (1993). 'Postmodern Tribalism and the Right to Secession', in C. Brolmann, R. Lefeber and M. Zieck (eds) *Peoples and Minorities in International Law*. Dordrecht and London: Martinus Nijhoff, 3, 20–1.

63 A. Cassese (1995). *Self-determination of Peoples – A Legal Reappraisal*. New York and Cambridge: Cambridge University Press, 53.

64 Human Rights Committee, *The Right to Self-determination of Peoples (Art. 1): 13/03/84. CCPR General Comment 12. (General Comments) 1984*, HRI/GEN/1/Rev.1, 12 (1994), [1]–[4].

65 Cassese, *supra* note 63, 53.

66 See, for example, *Algiers Declaration on the Rights of Peoples*, 1976, discussed in Cassese, ibid., 298.

The close link that has developed between the right to self-determination and the protection of fundamental civil and political rights has had wider implications for the way in which the right to self-determination is generally conceptualized. Self-determination was traditionally conceived as a collective right: as a right of peoples to be exercised against other states. This collective right remains important. However, as attention has come to focus on the internal dimensions of the right and the language of self-determination has become entrenched within the daily parlance of international human rights discourse, the right to self-determination has gradually found itself located not just within a 'peoples' but within the people's individual constituent members: it has become a human right.

This now widely accepted understanding of the relationship between self-determination and human rights provides strong guidance as to the likely attitude of the international community towards indigenous peoples, their right to self-determination and the protection of vulnerable individuals living within self-governing communities. As Kamenka has argued:

> Peoples are above all people, members of the human race. As such, they are entitled to dignity, respect and the recognition that they are fully members of the human race. They are not entitled to immunity from outside or internal criticism of their dominant customs, practices and traditions in so far as these are themselves destructive of respect for persons, of moral compassion and of the recognition of the moral equality of all people and the destructive character of pain, suffering and deprivation as regular features of social life. They do not have a moral right, in the name of collective self-determination, to deal as they wish with their own people, any more than we now believe that governments and nation States have such a moral right. The rights of peoples can become rights against one's own people. They regularly do. They should not.[67]

Thornberry takes a similarly strong approach. Commenting on the objections raised by indigenous peoples to the inclusion of provisions aimed at securing the protection of individual rights and interests within the UN Declaration, he calls on indigenous peoples to engage constructively with the international community on these issues:

> Reasons to resist general human rights references based on self-determination do not carry far. Self-determination is not a vehicle for the destruction of individual rights. Rather, accepting a general human rights reference demonstrates to governments that the indigenous do not intend to trample on rights. In assessing the relationship between the priorities of the collective and those of the individual, international bodies use the vocabulary of necessity and proportionality, equity and balance of rights. Indigenous peoples can also trade in that currency.[68]

67 Kamenka, *supra* note 13, 133.

68 Thornberry, *supra* note 32, 381.

Indigenous Peoples' Right to Self-Determination and Human Rights – Restructuring the Legal Relationship

Indigenous peoples' right to self-determination does not therefore, in and of itself, affect the applicability of international human rights standards to self-governing communities. Indeed, the right to self-determination reaffirms the overriding human rights guarantees found within Article 46 of the UN Declaration. There is, however, a further level of complexity in understanding the relationship between indigenous peoples' right to self-determination, the rights of indigenous individuals and the state. It is clear that the right of indigenous peoples to self-determination is a right that is claimed and exercised against the 'host state' within the state's territorial boundaries and within the overriding framework of international human rights law. This has important implications for the manner in which self-determination can be exercised, for not only are 'host states' such as Canada and Australia under a legal obligation to respect the collective right of indigenous peoples to self-determination, they also remain responsible, as made clear in Article 22.2 of the UN Declaration,[69] for ensuring that the fundamental rights of *all* individuals within their jurisdiction are protected, including all Aboriginal individuals living within the territorial boundaries of the state. These individuals do not lose their human rights entitlements because the group has a simultaneous right to self-determination.[70] The state is thus faced with a web of rights-based claims from both groups and individuals. This complexity in the state's obligations means that the collective right of indigenous peoples to self-determination will not be absolute.[71] Where indigenous peoples' right to self-determination comes into conflict with individual rights recognized and protected under international law some kind of reconciliation or balance must be found.[72]

International law usually affords considerable discretion to the state in seeking to strike an acceptable balance between conflicting rights and interests.[73] The state would, for example, have considerable freedom to regulate or restrict the right of a religious minority to carry out certain practices on children in accordance with their traditions and beliefs if the state deemed such practices to be harmful and in contravention of the child's basic rights. However, it is here that the qualitatively different nature of the right to self-determination matters: the very nature of a 'people's' right to self-determination logically demands a different and more

69 Article 22.2 provides: 'States shall take measures, in conjunction with indigenous peoples, to ensure that indigenous women and children enjoy the full protection and guarantees against all forms of violence and discrimination.'

70 McCorquodale, *supra* note 57, 874–5.

71 Ibid., 875–6.

72 As several commentators have pointed out, the need to find a balance between the potentially conflicting rights of the group and its individual members does not raise a new or particularly difficult challenge for international human rights law.

73 McCorquodale, *supra* note 57, 875, 878 and 885.

complex relationship between the individual, the group and the state. The core scope and meaning of indigenous peoples' right to self-determination limits the state's usual discretion to balance the competing rights and interests of Aboriginal peoples (held both as collectives and as individuals) in accordance with the state's own core values and priorities. Self-determination, whilst not conferring a right to statehood, does recognize the right of indigenous peoples to establish themselves as quasi-sovereign autonomous polities, not just with claims against the state but with governmental powers, duties and responsibilities owed directly to its own citizens. The core effect of the right to self-determination is thus to vest principal responsibility over all matters internal to the self-determining community, including responsibility for protecting the various rights and interests of its own members, in the Aboriginal community itself, not in the state.[74] It is this fact that fundamentally changes the way in which the protection of indigenous individuals should be approached.

If indigenous peoples' right to self-determination is to be respected, the primary responsibility for protecting vulnerable individuals within indigenous communities must lie, at least in the first instance, with autonomous indigenous governments. One can understand the concern to which this may give rise amongst states who have indigenous populations living within their territorial borders. Under current international law, indigenous peoples lack the international personality to become parties to the main human rights treaties or their monitoring mechanisms.[75] It is the state, and not the indigenous community, who is responsible for ensuring compliance throughout its territory with all international human rights norms by which, whether under customary international law or treaty law, the state is bound. As Anaya has pointed out, 'on the international plane, a State is judged as a unitary actor, notwithstanding a division of powers that may exist among the branches of the State's government or as a result of confederation'.[76] The obligation on the state as a 'unitary actor' to secure compliance with its international obligations regardless of the constitutional division of powers and responsibilities within its borders is clear[77] and has proved particularly problematic for federal states such as Canada and Australia. Indeed, the difficulties experienced by federal states in compelling different branches of government to comply with the state's international obligations has been the subject of much comment and criticism by the treaty monitoring bodies, with committees such as the UN Committee on the Rights of the Child (CROC) observing that it may lead to situations where

74 Anaya conceptualizes this more weakly outside the framework of self-determination as the need to accord 'deference' to the decision-making processes of the group. Anaya, *supra* note 8, 26.

75 Although if the state parties were minded to do so the treaty could be amended to allow indigenous peoples to become parties if they so desired.

76 Anaya, *supra* note 8, 132.

77 See, e.g., Article 50 of the International Covenant on Civil and Political Rights.

the minimum standards of the Convention are not applied to all children.[78] To add a further level of complexity to this system by the creation of autonomous indigenous governments who may well be hostile to the core liberal values of the state and, indeed, the very concept of individual human rights, is understandably a matter of legitimate concern for the state. However, to confer that responsibility on indigenous peoples is what self-determination demands and provided the self-determining community is acting in accordance with international standards – it is effectively protecting the recognized rights and interests of its individual citizens or, alternatively, drawing an acceptable balance between competing claims within the margin of discretion international law accords to states – the host state will have no basis on which to intervene. If it does, it will be violating the right of the indigenous group to self-determination and to govern itself in accordance with its own culturally grounded political, legal, economic and social systems.

The role of the state with respect to autonomous indigenous communities should therefore be a strictly limited one derived entirely from the obligations it owes to indigenous individuals under international law. Only if the community is failing to comply with international human rights standards or acting outside the state's margin of appreciation, thereby rendering the state in breach of its international obligations, as determined ultimately by the relevant international body, will the state have any legitimate basis for intervention.[79] The appropriate standards with which self-governing indigenous communities must therefore comply are international standards and not those imposed by the state; although the state retains residual authority to intervene should those international standards be breached.

A model of how this relationship between the state, indigenous peoples and the individual would work in practice is provided by the Anishnaabe Government Final Agreement.[80] Paragraphs 169–174 of the Agreement deal with Canada's international legal obligations and the responsibilities of the United Anishnaabeg Council and First Nations. The United Anishnaabeg Council and First Nations undertake to ensure that their respective laws and governmental actions shall not cause Canada to be unable to perform its international obligations and that they will take such steps as are necessary to remedy any such breach when identified by either Canada or an international tribunal.[81] In return, Canada agrees to consult with the United Anishnaabeg Council whenever a law or action of the United Anishnaabeg Council or First Nations gives rise to an issue before an international tribunal regarding Canada's compliance with its international

78 Committee on the Rights of the Child, Thirty-fourth session, *Consideration of Reports Submitted by States Parties under Article 44 of the Convention, Concluding Observations: Canada*, CRC/C/15/Add.215, [8]–[9].

79 In such a situation the strict conditions for limiting or restricting Aboriginal rights under Article 46 of the UN Declaration would be met.

80 Anishnaabe Government Agreement (2004). On file with author.

81 Ibid., paras. 169, 171 and 174.

legal obligations.[82] In the context of Aboriginal child welfare, this division of responsibilities would work as follows. An Aboriginal child welfare agency may decide to place a child who has been abused by her mother with an extended family member on the reserve. The agency takes the view that, despite the fact that the child may have some continuing contact with her mother, it is better both for the development of the child's identity and for the future viability of the community as a whole that the child remain living with his or her family on the reserve. The non-Aboriginal government and its agencies may disagree with how that balancing of the various interests has been carried out. It may have given greater weight to the right of the child to be protected from abuse than the weight afforded by the Aboriginal community to the child's right to cultural identity, and it may well have disregarded the interests of the Aboriginal community altogether. However, provided the community's balancing of interests falls within the margin of discretion that international law would accord the state, thereby ensuring the community's actions are in accordance with the child's various rights under the UNCRC (see in particular Article 8.1, 19.1, 20.3 and 30), there will be no breach of the child's rights under international human rights law as determined by the Committee on the Rights of the Child, no international obligation on the Canadian state to act, and therefore no basis for the state to intervene and impose its own particular standards on the indigenous community involved. The child may be treated differently from her non-indigenous neighbour but such plurality of child protection policies and practices is perfectly acceptable within the overriding parameters of international human rights law.

International Human Rights Law: Culturally Appropriate or Culturally Imperialist?

The response of an international lawyer to concerns about the protection of potentially vulnerable indigenous individuals living within self-governing communities is therefore a positive one: self-governing indigenous communities will be bound to comply with existing international human rights standards. Moreover, in the context of protecting children's rights, international law, through the UNCRC, is able to provide a detailed comprehensive body of rights protection devoted to the particular needs and interests of potentially vulnerable children: a tool for advancing children's rights unparalleled in the domestic law of either Canada or Australia. The more difficult question is whether indigenous communities *should* be bound by these *existing* human rights standards. Given the cultural differences that exist between indigenous communities and much of the developed world, the imposition of the existing human rights paradigm on indigenous peoples raises very real issues as to the 'cultural legitimacy' of those standards. As Kymlicka has succinctly put it: 'is it a form of cultural imperialism

82 Ibid., para. 173.

to expect indigenous communities to abide by "Euro-centric" principles of individual civil and political rights?'[83]

If the effective decolonization of Aboriginal peoples is the ultimate goal, there must be strong concerns that such an objective is fundamentally undermined by the imposition of existing international human rights standards: a body of law which has itself been criticized for its imperialist tendencies.[84] As Kymlicka goes on to observe, this potential clash between indigenous cultures and international human rights law is somewhat ironic. In his words, 'the popular reason or basis for singling out indigenous peoples is not their history of mistreatment but their cultural "Otherness" – in particular, their isolation from, and repudiation of, modern ways of life'.[85] Yet, as he points out, it is somewhat incongruous having sought to justify the right of indigenous peoples to self-determination in order to protect the distinctive cultures of indigenous peoples from the assimilating tendency of culturally alien governments, to then insist that the right to cultural integrity and autonomy only holds force insofar as the cultural values and traditions they promote conform to Western notions of democracy and human rights.[86] This raises difficult questions. Is it acceptable in the name of human rights to 'violate' the integrity of indigenous cultures? Should we demand that indigenous governments with centuries-old traditions of non-democratic governance be democratic?[87] What attitude should the international community adopt to child-rearing practices such as customary adoption that have deep roots within indigenous cultures and traditions but may conflict with norms now entrenched within the UNCRC?[88] The final part of this chapter will attempt to address these difficult but fundamentally important questions.

Reconciling International Human Rights to Aboriginal Cultural Values

The question of whether or not the imposition of international human rights law on indigenous peoples amounts to a subtle form of cultural imperialism depends on whether existing international standards can be reconciled with Aboriginal cultures and worldviews. If indigenous peoples are able to embrace international human rights as compatible with their own cultural values, the problem of whether or not indigenous peoples can be expected to comply with international human rights law, to a large extent, falls away. Given the resistance Canadian Aboriginal

83 Kymlicka, *supra* note 53, 291.

84 M. Mutua (2001). 'Savages, Victims and Saviors: The Metaphor of Human Rights', *Harvard International Law Journal*, 42: 201 and S. Harris-Short (2003). 'International Human Rights Law – Imperialist, Inept and Ineffective? Cultural Relativism and the United Nations Convention on the Rights of the Child', *Human Rights Quarterly*, 25: 130.

85 Kymlicka, *supra* note 56, 290.

86 Ibid., 292.

87 Ibid.

88 Ibid.

communities have shown to the imposition of the Canadian Charter on Aboriginal governments, a positive endorsement of international human rights law may seem unlikely. At least on the face of it, if indigenous peoples are unable to accept the Canadian Charter because of its individualistic, rights-based focus, there is little reason to suppose that indigenous peoples will be able to embrace the existing body of international human rights law any more enthusiastically.

With more detailed analysis, there are, however, grounds for thinking that indigenous peoples will be able to respond more positively to the imposition of international human rights law than they have with respect to the imposition of the Canadian Charter. As opposed to the Euro-centric cultural foundations of the Canadian state, the UN and the various human rights bodies that fall within its ambit represent a plurality of different cultures, traditions and faiths. The UN is now, if it has not always been, a truly international forum in which the challenges of cultural diversity have to be faced. The international community is clearly aware that if the international human rights paradigm is to be universally effective, it has to speak in a way that has meaning not just for states in the West but for all of the world's cultures, including indigenous peoples. The highly abstract nature of international human rights law allows considerable scope for the development of a culturally sensitive interpretative framework whereby individual norms can be situated within and mediated through an individual community's own particular cultural framework.[89] As it has been expressed by the Committee on Economic, Social and Cultural Rights, human rights must be culturally appropriate. They must be interpreted and implemented in a way that is 'pertinent and suitable to a given cultural modality or context, that is, respectful of the culture and cultural rights of individuals and communities'.[90] Given the growing commitment of the international community to the accommodation of cultural difference, international human rights standards can thus be drafted, interpreted and implemented in such a way that they can respond effectively to cultural difference, more particularly indigenous cultural difference. If international human rights law is able to meet this challenge we can be cautiously optimistic that Aboriginal communities will be able to recognize and accept international human rights standards as 'their own': that is, as an accepted and integral part of their own cultures, rather than rejecting them as a foreign, inappropriate and irrelevant imposition.

The Accommodation of Cultural Difference in the UN Convention on the Rights of the Child

There is clearly a great deal of work that still has to be done to move international human rights law away from its very Western liberal foundations. However, as

89 See J. Tilley (2000). 'Cultural Relativism', *Human Rights Quarterly*, 22: 501, 514 and 520 and E. Brems (1997). 'Enemies or Allies? Feminism and Cultural Relativism as Dissident Voices in Human Rights Discourse', *Human Rights Quarterly*, 19: 136, 158.

90 *General Comment No. 21*, *supra* note 7, [16(e)].

regards the protection of indigenous children, it is promising that the UNCRC represents the high point of efforts to date to find the kind of cross-cultural legitimacy that may open the way for indigenous leaders to be able to accept the standards it espouses as their own. The extent to which the UNCRC is responsive, in general terms, to cultural differences in child-rearing practices and traditions has been widely debated in the academic literature. Scholars such as Philip Alston have applauded the UNCRC for its cultural inclusiveness, arguing that near-universal ratification stands as a testimony to its universal reach.[91] Thus whilst recognizing that the Convention is by no means a perfect model of cultural legitimacy, Alston takes the view that the final text 'is probably more sensitive to different approaches and perspectives than most of the principal human rights treaties adopted earlier'.[92] In his recent work on indigenous peoples and human rights, Thornberry considers in some depth the extent to which the text of the UNCRC can be said to be inclusive of indigenous cultures. In his concluding comments, albeit with some important caveats, he is similarly positive as to the cultural sensitivity of the Convention's text and the work of the monitoring committee.[93]

The drafting of the UNCRC was, in many respects, encouraging as a model of open and inclusive norm creation.[94] Although the process had a number of flaws, with state participation being far from fully inclusive, the determined and constructive contributions of a small number of states from the developing world, in addition to a strong Islamic presence in the final stages of the drafting process, ensured that non-Western states, with varying degrees of success, were able to implant their particular cultural mark on the final text.[95] Other than through NGOs, indigenous peoples were not, of course, afforded the opportunity to make a direct contribution to the drafting process. However, the more inclusive the international community is of non-Western cultures and traditions, particularly cultures from the developing world subjected to similar pressures from colonization and globalization, the more open and responsive the international community is likely to be to indigenous cultures.

There are a number of the Convention's substantive provisions that one can point to as generally supportive of cultural diversity and demonstrating considerable sensitivity to the importance of situating children's rights within local cultures and traditions. In emphasizing the Convention's capacity for culturally sensitive application, Alston, amongst others, has pointed in particular to the best

91 See P. Alston (1994). 'The Best Interests Principle: Towards a Reconciliation of Culture and Human Rights', in P. Alston (ed.) *The Best Interests of the Child: Reconciling Culture and Human Rights*. Oxford: Clarendon Press.

92 Ibid., 321–32.

93 Thornberry, *supra* note 32, 225–41, esp. at 240.

94 S. Harris-Short (2001). 'Listening to "the Other"? The Convention on the Rights of the Child', *Melbourne Journal of International Law*, 2: 304, 350.

95 Ibid., 322–32.

interests principle as enshrined within Article 3.[96] The indeterminacy of the best interests principle can of course be exploited as a tool of cultural imperialism and assimilation.[97] However, the indeterminacy of the best interests principle can also be more positively employed to ensure that in all actions concerning children, the child's cultural identity and environment is taken into account. As Alston notes, the best interests principle is 'inextricably linked to the cultural context in which it is invoked'.[98] Thornberry agrees, commenting that 'such a principle appears eminently capable of cultural contextualisation'.[99] Clearly, the best interests of the child will mean different things to different people located within different cultures. It is thus only when the principle is applied to a particular child within a particular cultural context that its substantive meaning can be properly determined. Given the wide reach of the best interests principle and its central role within the Convention as a general interpretative provision, the cultural sensitivity it allows to indigenous peoples should prove a crucial factor in determining the ability of indigenous communities to embrace the Convention's standards. Indeed, Alston is optimistic that it is the ability of abstract norms such as the best interests principle to accommodate a diverse range of cultural perspectives that allows communities to act in accordance with their particular cultural imperatives whilst remaining committed to the implementation of internationally recognized standards.[100]

There are, nevertheless, important limits as to how far the indeterminacy of the best interests principle can be used to advance cultural rights. Whilst in theory the best interests principle, as interpreted at the local level, could be used to justify a diverse range of practices considered harmful or prejudicial to the child's best interests, the meaning to be attributed to the child's best interests cannot be entirely culturally determined. As Alston argues, the body of rights contained within the Convention provide a normative framework standing apart from any one particular cultural context to inform and guide its interpretation and application. In his words, the Convention as a whole 'give[s] a greater degree of certainty to the content of the best interests principle ... provid[ing] a number of signposts capable of guiding those seeking to identify what is in the best interests of the child, and excludes from the equation, by implication, various other elements'.[101]

Within these broad parameters, the best interests of the child, if interpreted in an informed and sensitive manner, still has the potential to play a central role in mediating between the 'universal' standards enshrined within the Convention

96 Article 3 provides: 'In all actions concerning children, whether undertaken by public or private social welfare institutions, courts of law, administrative authorities or legislative bodies, the best interests of the child shall be a primary consideration.' The best interests principle is also expressly referred to as the guiding principle in Articles 9.1, 18 and 21, again allowing for cultural sensitivity within those particular contexts.

97 See Chapter 3, esp at pp. 57–62.

98 Alston, *supra* note 91, 5.

99 Thornberry, *supra* note 32, 226.

100 Alston, *supra* note 91, 22.

101 Ibid., 19.

and the particularity of the child's cultural environment. This was borne out to a significant degree by CROC's General Comment No. 11 on indigenous children.[102] Of particular significance is the Committee's apparent willingness to conceptualize the best interests principle as both a collective and an individual right, emphasizing that the best interests of indigenous children cannot be considered in isolation from the collective interests of the group.[103] Thus, although making clear that the best interests of the child 'cannot be neglected or violated in preference for the best interests of the group', the Committee holds that the collective cultural rights of the child must form an inherent part of determining the child's best interests.[104] This represents a marked departure from the highly individualistic conceptualization of the best interests principle that has prevailed in Canada and Australia.

The Convention also includes more specific recognition of the importance of protecting and supporting the child within the context of his/her particular cultural environment. As the preamble states, in elucidating the rights enshrined within the Convention the international community have 'tak[en] due account of the importance of the traditions and cultural values of each people for the protection and harmonious development of the child'. In particular, in seeking to support the child within his or her cultural environment, the Convention recognizes the crucial role to be played by the child's family and immediate community. The text acknowledges that it is primarily the family and the community who can provide cultural meaning and context to the Convention's otherwise abstract principles. As Article 5 provides:

> States Parties shall respect the responsibilities, rights and duties of parents or, where applicable, the members of the extended family or community as provided for by local custom, legal guardians or other persons legally responsible for the child, to provide, in a manner consistent with the evolving capacities of the child, appropriate direction and guidance in the exercise by the child of the rights recognized in the present Convention.[105]

This clearly identifies the child with his or her parents, extended family and local cultural community, conferring primary responsibility upon this extended group for providing direction and guidance as to the interpretation and implementation of the child's rights. CROC has endorsed the centrality of the extended family to

---

102 Committee on the Rights of the Child, General Comment No. 11, *Indigenous Children and their Rights under the Convention*, CRC/C/GC/11.

103 Ibid., [30]–[31].

104 Ibid., [32].

105 As regards the Convention's support for the family, the Preamble provides that: 'the family, as the fundamental group of society and the natural environment for the growth and well-being of all its members and particularly children, should be afforded the necessary protection and assistance so that it can fully assume its responsibilities within the community.'

protecting the rights and interests of indigenous children, urging States Parties in its General Comment on indigenous children to 'ensure effective measures are implemented to safeguard the integrity of indigenous families and communities by assisting them in their child-rearing responsibilities'.[106] Moreover, not only does Article 5 emphasize the importance of the child's family and local community in translating the Convention into a meaningful reality for the child, but it has been applauded for its sensitivity to cultural differences in family structure and formation. Article 5's inclusion of the extended family has been particularly welcomed; the extended family being a concept prevalent within many tribal and indigenous cultures by which grandparents, siblings, aunts and uncles, even wider community members, are all embraced as holding shared responsibility for the care of the child.[107] As Barsh correctly points out, this departure from the traditional Western notion of the nuclear household has not been sustained throughout the Convention with several Articles making reference only to the child's parents or legal guardians (see, for example, Articles 9, 14.2, 18, 29.1(c) and 40.2(b)(iii)). In light of this inconsistency, Barsh argues that the concept of 'family' enshrined within the UNCRC remains inherently 'euro-centric'.[108] However, Article 5's role as a general interpretative principle of the Convention makes recognition of the extended family within Article 5 of greater significance than Barsh would suggest.[109] Article 5 dictates that whenever the Convention makes reference to the child's family or to those who have responsibility for the child (see the Preamble, Articles 3.2, 8.1, 21(a), 27.2) the concept of 'family' should be interpreted in a culturally sensitive manner and, more particularly, in a manner which has meaning for indigenous communities.[110]

The UNCRC has clearly gone some way towards recognizing that supporting the child within the context of his/her cultural community and striving to ensure that the Convention is supportive rather than destructive of local traditions and values is of fundamental importance to securing the long-term interests of the child. Unlike other UN human rights treaties with a clear individualistic ethos, the child is not conceptualized within the UNCRC as a self-reliant, de-contextualized and atomized individual, but as an individual who is deeply dependent for his or her survival and well-being on a complex web of family and community relations. More specifically, the Convention acknowledges that a secure cultural environment is essential to the child's developing sense of cultural identity. Indeed,

106 *Supra* note 102, [46].

107 Harris-Short, *supra* note 94, 324.

108 R. Barsh (1989). 'The Convention on the Rights of the Child: A Re-Assessment of the Final Text', *New York Law School Journal of Human Rights*, 7: 142, 146–7.

109 See the comments of the US delegate when first introducing the article to the drafting group for consideration: Economic and Social Council, *Question of a Convention on the Rights of the Child: Report of the Working Group on a Draft Convention on the Rights of the Child*, E/CN.4/1987/25 (1987), [101].

110 Harris-Short, *supra* note 94, 326.

the importance of supporting the child's sense of place within a particular culture, as well as respecting cultural differences in others, is given strong recognition in Article 29 which provides that the child's education must be directed to 'the development of respect for the child's parents, his or her own cultural identity, language and values, for the national values of the country in which the child is living, the country from which he or she may originate, and for civilizations different from his or her own'.[111] The Convention's generally positive approach to cultural life and its importance to the child's healthy development is further reflected in the detailed provisions of Article 31 which seek to foster and support the child's developing sense of cultural identity by facilitating the child's free and active participation in various cultural activities.[112] Similarly, the damage that can be caused by removing the child from the security of his/her immediate cultural environment is also expressly recognized, with Article 20 providing that where the child must be placed in alternative care, 'due regard shall be paid to the desirability of continuity in a child's upbringing and to the child's ethnic, religious, cultural and linguistic background'.[113] Recognition of the crucial role played by the child's family and community in helping to foster the child's developing sense of cultural identity is thus strongly entrenched within the Convention.

The Convention also promotes, in more general terms, a strong positive view of indigenous cultures. As recognized by the Committee in its General Comment on indigenous children, as the child's best interests are inextricably bound up with the interests of his or her immediate community, providing support and protection for indigenous children will necessarily imply providing support and protection for indigenous communities and cultures.[114] Whilst the Convention does not confer direct protection on the right of indigenous peoples to cultural integrity, it acknowledges indigenous cultures to be of distinct significance, distinguishing their values and practices from both the dominant culture of the state and from other ethnic, national and religious minorities.[115] Indeed, as Thornberry notes,

111 See, UNCRC, Article 29.1(c).

112 Article 31 of the UNCRC provides: '1. State Parties recognise the right of the child to rest and leisure, to engage in play and recreational activities appropriate to the age of the child and to participate freely in cultural life and the arts. 2. State Parties shall respect and promote the right of the child to participate fully in cultural and artistic life and shall encourage the provision of appropriate and equal opportunities for cultural, artistic, recreational and leisure activity.'

113 UNCRC, Article 20.3.

114 *Supra* note 102, [30]–[32].

115 See Article 29(d) of the UNCRC which provides: 'States Parties agree that the education of the child shall be directed to the preparation of the child for responsible life in a free society, in the spirit of understanding, peace, tolerance, equality of sexes, and friendship among all peoples, ethnic, national and religious groups and persons of indigenous origin.' For short commentary on the drafting of this provision see Thornberry, *supra* note 32, 232. See also Article 17(d) which deals with the child's right of access to a wide variety of information from both national and international sources and includes a positive reference

the Convention is notable as the first international human rights treaty to include specific recognition of the importance of indigenous cultures. Article 30, which is thus of particular significance, provides:

> In those States in which ethnic, religious or linguistic minorities or persons of indigenous origin exist, a child belonging to such a minority or who is indigenous shall not be denied the right, in community with other members of his or her group, to enjoy his or her own culture, to profess and practise his or her own religion, or to use his or her own language.

Article 30 constitutes a positive endorsement of indigenous cultures and the right of the child to be able to enjoy the advantages of participating in the cultural life of his or her community. The Convention thus demands that when dealing with issues pertaining to Aboriginal children, the state and the international community should start from a position of respect for indigenous cultures. Indeed, this position is closely reflected in the Statement of Understanding entered by Canada upon its ratification of the Convention:

> It is the understanding of the Government of Canada that, in matters relating to Aboriginal peoples of Canada, the fulfilment of its responsibilities under article 4 of the Convention must take into account the provisions of article 30. In particular, in assessing what measures are appropriate to implement the rights recognized in the Convention for Aboriginal children, due regard must be paid to not denying their right, in community with other members of their group, to enjoy their own culture, to profess and practice their own religion and to use their own language.

As with Article 3, there are again limits as to the respect which will be accorded to indigenous cultures. As Thornberry points out, the specific wording of Article 30 closely reflects the wording of Article 27 of the ICCPR, albeit with the inclusion of specific reference to children of indigenous origin.[116] Although the Committee has signalled an important departure from the orthodox position under Article 27 by conceptualizing the right under Article 30 as 'being both individual and collective',[117] it is nevertheless clear that in the event of a serious conflict between the child and the group, the rights of the individual child must prevail. Article 30 thus contains important limitations on the extent to which the child can be subordinated to the wider cultural interests of the group. When the child's continued participation in his or her culture jeopardizes the child's other core interests, such

---

to the importance of supporting indigenous children's linguistic needs. The preservation of indigenous languages is generally regarded as of fundamental importance to the survival of indigenous cultures.

116 Thornberry, ibid., 234.

117 *Supra* note 102, [16].

as the right to physical integrity, it is the group's cultural rights which will have to yield.[118] This specific qualification on the right of the child to 'enjoy his/her culture' is reiterated in express terms by Article 24(3) of the Convention which provides that: 'States Parties shall take all effective and appropriate measures with a view to abolishing traditional practices prejudicial to the health of children.' The Committee strongly endorsed this position in its General Comment on indigenous children:

> The Committee underlines that cultural practices provided by article 30 of the Convention must be exercised in accordance with other provisions of the Convention and under no circumstances may be justified if deemed prejudicial to the child's dignity, health and development. Should harmful practices be present, inter alia early marriages and female genital mutilation, the State party should work together with indigenous communities to ensure their eradication.[119]

Whilst a number of the Convention's provisions therefore purport to support a diverse range of cultural practices and traditions, that sensitivity to cultural difference is always subject to a baseline of protection: such traditions must not be harmful to the child.

Despite these limits, it is fair to conclude that many of the Convention's substantive provisions are capable of supporting a respectful and inclusive approach to indigenous cultures. This is not to suggest that the Convention is without difficulties for indigenous groups. There are several provisions which raise questions as to their compatibility or otherwise with Aboriginal traditions and practices. For example, difficulties may arise with respect to Articles requiring a degree of formality in decision-making that is foreign to many indigenous cultures; such formalities being more closely associated with notions of due judicial process as entrenched within many Western cultures.[120] Indeed, such difficulties have already materialized with respect to customary adoption as practised within many indigenous communities, prompting Canada to enter a reservation to Article 21 of the Convention following consultation with Aboriginal leaders.[121] In an attempt to protect this form of adoption from challenge by the international community, Canada's reservation provides:

---

118 Alston, *supra* note 91, 22.

119 *Supra* note 102, [22].

120 See, for example, UNCRC, Articles 9.1, 21 and 40.2.

121 See: Committee on the Rights of the Child, *Initial Reports of States Parties due in 1994: Canada. 28/07/94, (State Party Report)*, CRC/C/11/Add.3, [160]; Committee on the Rights of the Child, *Summary Record of the 214th meeting: Canada. 30/05/95 (Summary Record)*, CRC/C/SR.214, [59]; and Committee on the Rights of the Child, *Consideration of Reports Submitted by State Parties under Article 44 of the Convention, Concluding Observations of the Committee on the Rights of the Child: Canada*, CRC/C/15/Add.37, [10] and [18].

> With respect to ensuring full respect for the purposes and intent of article 20(3) and article 30 of the Convention, the Government of Canada reserves the right not to apply the provisions of article 21 to the extent that they may be inconsistent with customary forms of care among Aboriginal peoples in Canada.

Such reservations to individual Convention standards are, however, commonplace and, when strictly targeted and defined, give little grounds for concern. More problematic is the possibility that indigenous peoples may remain deeply resistant to the whole of the Convention on strongly entrenched philosophical grounds.

At the heart of the issue is whether indigenous peoples are able to conceptualize the child as an individual holder of rights and interests distinct from and indeed enforceable against the community to which he or she belongs. Thornberry suggests that this is likely to be indigenous peoples' essential difficulty with the Convention:

> The end problem for the Convention is not that this or that specific concept or principle may be difficult to fit into an indigenous or other world-view, but that the essential principle of the Convention – the child as subject of rights – may not. On the whole, the CRC appears to address culture as instrumental – as a means to deliver up rights of the child. The problem arises where culture is a thicker, more encompassing concept that reaches out to frame and condition notions of individual and collective identity, social respect, religion, aesthetics and moral value in ways which do not easily cohere with the Convention's prescriptions.[122]

The philosophy of the Convention is clear. The child is to be recognized as of intrinsic value: as an individual whose rights and interests as a *child* as well as a *potential adult* are to be taken seriously and respected.[123] Traditional paternalistic/welfare-orientated approaches to the child whilst still evident in the Convention's protective provisions are essentially rejected; as are approaches which conceptualize the child primarily in instrumental terms, either as 'a community asset' or as a future holder of rights whose needs and interests as a child can be legitimately sacrificed in order to maximize welfare in adulthood. It is this underlying philosophical premise of the Convention as regards the child and the child's position as an individual rights-holder within the community which may prove irreconcilable with more communally orientated indigenous cultures. Of course, should indigenous peoples find the philosophical premise of the Convention difficult to reconcile with their particular cultural worldview, they are by no means alone in having to work through these conceptual difficulties. The Convention has proved difficult for many, if not all cultures, with several groups, including

122 Thornberry, *supra* note 32, 241.

123 See generally, T. Campbell (1992). 'The Rights of Minors: As Person, As Child, As Juvenile, As Future Adult', *International Journal of Law and the Family*, 6: 1.

some who adhere to a strong Western liberal tradition, struggling to accept the Convention's conceptualization of the child as an autonomous individual with a range of empowering participatory rights. Indeed, some of the fiercest opposition to the Convention has come from the United States where the perception that the Convention confers rights on the child to independence and autonomy has been the source of strong criticism and concern.[124]

However, whilst conceptualization of the child as a holder of individual rights is exceptionally difficult for many cultures, the UNCRC is in many respects more conducive to achieving a successful reconciliation with communally based cultures than other international human rights instruments. The clear recognition it affords not just to the individuality of the child but to the child's inter-dependence with family and community and its marked sensitivity to the importance of communal interests do much to improve its cultural reach. The Convention promotes a view of childhood that recognizes the centrality of family and community but refuses to allow the child to become a mere instrument of culture and tradition. In other words, the child remains a subject of immediate individual value and concern. Particularly when mediated through their own cultural framework, it is perhaps not unduly optimistic to presume that this is a view of childhood to which indigenous peoples can positively relate.

Whilst not underestimating the difficulties to be overcome, the UNCRC therefore provides, at the very least, a promising starting point for conducting a genuine and constructive cross-cultural dialogue between indigenous peoples, the state and the international community as to the rights, interests and needs of indigenous children. Certainly indigenous peoples may feel more comfortable in beginning that dialogue on the basis of the standards enshrined within the UNCRC than they do with respect to many domestically imposed human rights laws.

The Committee on the Rights of the Child

Key to the success of the UNCRC as a means of reconciling Aboriginal cultural traditions with international human rights standards will be the Convention's monitoring Committee and how it responds to the challenge of indigenous difference. It is disappointing to note that the Committee has not always responded sensitively to claims of cultural difference or paid sufficient regard to the cultural context in which the Convention's standards are to be interpreted and implemented. This tension between the Convention's *potential* for cultural inclusiveness and the actual practice of the Committee has been particularly evident in its consideration of State Party Reports from the developing world

124 See generally, B. Hafen and J. Hafen (1996). 'Abandoning Children to their Autonomy: The United Nations Convention on the Rights of the Child', *Harvard International Law Journal*, 37: 449. Cf. S. Kilbourne (1998). 'The Wayward Americans – Why the USA Has Not Ratified the UN Convention on the Rights of the Child', *Child and Family Law Quarterly*, 10: 243.

where an uncompromising and particularly Western perspective has been adopted on a number of traditional practices. Clearly this does not bode well for an inclusive approach to traditional indigenous cultures.[125] The Committee has so far failed to grapple with the potential clash between some indigenous cultures and the Convention's standards, the Committee being more concerned with the myriad of serious socio-economic problems faced by indigenous children and their families in many parts of the world.[126] However, the issue of cultural difference will at some point have to be faced.

To date there have been only limited indications outside the General Comment on indigenous children of how the Committee is likely to respond to claims of indigenous difference. One opportunity for the Committee to take a clear position on the issue arose with respect to traditional Aboriginal adoption practices and Canada's reservation to Article 21. The issue of Canada's reservation to Article 21 was first raised by the Committee when considering Canada's Initial State Party Report in 1995. It was raised again at its consideration of Canada's Second Periodic Report in 2003. On both occasions the Committee expressed concern at the reservation and requested that the State Party review the reservation and consider the possibility of withdrawing it.[127] Canada, in response, attempted to defend the reservation explaining that the reservation had been entered because of a concern that the requirement under Article 21 that adoption should be authorized only by competent authorities might prevent custom adoption as practised in some Aboriginal communities.[128] The Committee did not accept this explanation, urging

125 For detailed analysis see, Harris-Short, *supra* note 94, 332–49.

126 See, for example, Committee on the Rights of the Child, *Consideration of Reports Submitted by State Parties under Article 44 of the Convention, Concluding Observations of the Committee on the Rights of the Child: Canada*, CRC/C/15/Add.37, [17] and [26]; Committee on the Rights of the Child, *List of Issues: Canada 10/02/95*, CRC.C.9/WP.1, [5], [26] and [30]. Committee on the Rights of the Child, *Consideration of Reports Submitted by States Parties under Article 44 of the Convention, Concluding Observations: Canada*, CRC/C/15/Add.215, [59]. Committee on the Rights of the Child, *Consideration of Reports Submitted by States Parties under Article 44 of the Convention, Concluding Observations of the Committee on the Rights of the Child: Australia: 10/10/97*, CRC/C/15/Add.79, [22] and [32]. Mrs Karp of the Committee did however raise the issue of Aboriginal attitudes towards incest when considering Canada's initial State Party Report: Committee on the Rights of the Child, *Summary Record of the 214th Meeting: Canada. 30/05/95 (Summary Record)*, CRC/C/SR.214, [71].

127 Committee on the Rights of the Child, *Consideration of Reports Submitted by State Parties under Article 44 of the Convention, Concluding Observations of the Committee on the Rights of the Child: Canada*, CRC/C/15/Add.37, [18] and [26]; Committee on the Rights of the Child, *Consideration of Reports Submitted by States Parties under Article 44 of the Convention, Concluding Observations: Canada*, CRC/C/15/Add.215, [6].

128 Committee on the Rights of the Child, *Summary Record of the 214th Meeting: Canada. 30/05/95 (Summary Record)*, CRC/C/SR.214, [59].

the Canadian government to continue consultations with Aboriginal representatives with a view to the reservation being withdrawn.[129]

More encouraging are some of the Committee's comments, albeit limited, regarding the importance of showing sensitivity to indigenous cultures in its Concluding Observations on Canada's second periodic report and Australia's combined second and third periodic report. With respect to Canada, the Committee applauded the government's efforts to 'promote and protect cultural diversity' and welcomed the establishment of First Nations Child and Family Services who can provide 'culturally sensitive services to Aboriginal children and families within their communities'.[130] Similarly, with respect to child welfare provision for Australia's Aboriginal children, the Committee called on the Australian government to reduce the number of Aboriginal children placed in out-of-home care by improving its support for indigenous families, fully implementing the Indigenous Child Placement Principle, and intensifying its cooperation with indigenous communities to find suitable placements for children in need of alternative care.[131] The Australian government was also 'encouraged' to strengthen its efforts to secure full implementation of HREOC's recommendations in the *Bringing Them Home* report and, in particular, 'to ensure full respect for the rights of Aboriginal and Torres Strait Islander children to their identity, name, culture, language and family relationships'.[132] The importance of a child's Aboriginal identity and the centrality of a child's family relationships to his or her well-being were thus expressly acknowledged. Beyond these specific references to the child's Aboriginal heritage, the Committee was clearly deeply concerned as to the persisting vulnerability of Aboriginal children across the entire social spectrum: a fact which dominated its Concluding Observations on Australia.[133]

There are thus some positive signs in the work of the Committee that it can respond sensitively to the cultural needs of Aboriginal children. Undoubtedly, that sensitivity would be improved by the introduction of a number of fairly modest changes to the Committee's procedures. Apart from the obvious disadvantage of lengthening yet further the voluminous reports of federal states such as Canada and Australia, it would, for example, be entirely appropriate, particularly as more and more Aboriginal communities become self-governing, for information regarding implementation of the Convention's standards in indigenous communities to be separated out and contained within its own section of the report, as indeed is

129 Committee on the Rights of the Child, *Consideration of Reports Submitted by States Parties under Article 44 of the Convention, Concluding Observations: Canada*, CRC/C/15/Add.215, [7].

130 Ibid., [21], [22] and [30].

131 Committee on the Rights of the Child, *Consideration of Reports Submitted by States Parties under Article 44 of the Convention, Concluding Observations: Australia*, CRC/C/15/Add.268, [39].

132 Ibid., [32].

133 Ibid., [5], [24], [47], [48], [51], [55], [57], [59], [72], [74], [75]–[77].

the current practice for the individual provinces, states and territories. It would also represent a major step forward if indigenous peoples were to be afforded the opportunity to speak directly to international monitoring bodies such as CROC concerning questions of compliance. The people best placed to speak about the challenges of implementing international human rights standards within autonomous indigenous communities are indigenous leaders. At the time Canada's second periodic report was being considered by CROC, the Committee was holding a general day of discussion on the rights of indigenous children in Geneva. Yet, as was pointed out by indigenous leaders at the general day of discussion, not one of the 20 Canadian delegates appearing before the Committee was indigenous. Moreover, as it turned out, the inclusion of an indigenous representative on the Canadian delegation would have been particularly valuable as it faced several difficult questions from the Committee regarding its reservation to Article 21. It would undoubtedly have been better for the Committee to have had the opportunity to raise their concerns directly with indigenous leaders rather than mediate through the state. The Committee would then have had the benefit of a direct dialogue with indigenous peoples, giving indigenous peoples the opportunity to explain to the Committee the cultural context in which customary adoptions are practised and why they are therefore considered by the communities involved to safeguard the best interests of the child. In turn, the Committee would have been able to explore with indigenous leaders why it considers the procedural safeguards enshrined within Article 21 to be essential for the protection of the child's interests, regardless of the cultural context in which the adoption is taking place. The extent to which indigenous leaders are accorded a direct voice in forums such as the UN treaty bodies is therefore a key issue which could usefully be reviewed by both the Committees and States Parties and appropriate steps taken within a relatively short timeframe.

Conclusion

The protection of individual rights now constitutes a core part of modern international law. With just one or two notable exceptions, even the most powerful states have accepted that the way in which they treat their own citizens is a matter of international concern. Both in law and principle, indigenous peoples do not stand in any different position. International law dictates that those exercising a right to self-determination must do so within a framework of respect for individual human rights. Indigenous peoples' right to self-determination will not therefore be at the expense of the human rights entitlements of individual citizens. This clear position under international law is faithfully reflected in the UN Declaration on the Rights of Indigenous Peoples, with the rights of potentially vulnerable groups, such as women and children, given particular attention.

However, if indigenous peoples' right to self-determination is to be respected, two important points must follow. First, the appropriate human rights standards to which indigenous peoples are to be expected to adhere are those enshrined in international law and not the municipal law of states. Second, the principal responsibility for ensuring the rights of indigenous individuals are effectively protected must rest, not with the state, but with autonomous indigenous governments. This means that the state's mandate to intervene within self-governing Aboriginal communities must be strictly limited to situations where the fundamental rights of indigenous individuals, as protected under international law, are being routinely violated, thereby rendering the state in breach of its own international obligations. International law thus strikes a fundamentally different but more principled balance between indigenous peoples' right to self-determination and the protection of indigenous individuals than that which is currently struck within the municipal law of states.

Does that mean international law provides the answer to concerns about the protection of potentially vulnerable children living within autonomous self-governing communities? International law provides *an* answer; whether that answer is acceptable to indigenous communities is yet to be explored with the communities themselves. Underlying issues as to the cultural legitimacy of international human rights law will not be easily resolved. Little is achieved if the colonizing legal norms of domestic law are replaced by international standards with similar assimilatory tendencies. However, international human rights law must now respond effectively to the rich variety of cultures within the international community if it is to retain any credible claim to universal legitimacy. Responding to these pressures, the UNCRC, whilst not a perfect model of culturally inclusive norm creation, clearly speaks in a more meaningful way to non-Western cultures than previous human rights instruments in both international and domestic law. It certainly provides a more culturally appropriate starting point for entering into dialogue with indigenous peoples as to the rights of indigenous children living within their communities. It is therefore hoped that within the framework of modern international law, indigenous peoples can find the space and freedom they have historically been denied to develop their own culturally grounded mechanisms of protection and accountability; space and freedom which is currently not possible when working within the suffocating constraints of the 'legal and political imagination' of the Canadian and Australian states.

PART V
Conclusions

Chapter 8
Conclusion

Colonialism has left a terrible legacy in many parts of the world. However, one of the least known yet most appalling legacies of the colonial era is the devastating impact European settlement wrought on the indigenous peoples of the 'New World'. Violence, disease and dispossession marked the early relationship between the European colonizers and the original inhabitants of the land. But worse was to come. The horrific accounts of Aboriginal children being torn from their families and communities and the abuse to which they were subsequently subjected are deeply shocking. The missions and residential schools in Canada and Australia stand as one of the most potent symbols of the totally misconceived iniquity of European imperialism. And yet, whilst the residential schools may have closed, for Aboriginal peoples in Canada and Australia, colonialism cannot be consigned to the annals of history: it remains a current reality.

Aboriginal communities across Canada and Australia continue to fight for the decolonization of their communities. Most remain dispossessed of their traditional lands and resources and subjected to the sovereign will of alien governments. Aboriginal communities are often highly marginalized, with many crippled by severe social and economic problems. These difficulties are exacerbated by the intense pressure placed on indigenous cultures and their social and political systems by the assimilating forces of the non-native communities that surround them. In short, colonialism continues to penetrate into every aspect of contemporary Aboriginal lives. Aboriginal child welfare is no exception.

Continuing problems in the field of Aboriginal child welfare need to be understood within the context of both the past and present colonial experiences of Aboriginal communities. The economic, social and political consequences of the colonial legacy in Canada and Australia has created one of the most challenging environments in which to safeguard Aboriginal children from abuse. The removal of large numbers of Aboriginal children from their families and communities has intensified these difficulties by causing a serious dislocation in Aboriginal cultural norms and practices, including most significantly Aboriginal patterns of child rearing. In the now familiar phrase, the removal of Aboriginal children initiated a 'circle of abuse' which continues to have a profound impact on contemporary Aboriginal family life. Levels of physical, emotional and sexual abuse within Aboriginal communities are worryingly high. Non-native authorities have responded to this phenomenon with repeat patterns of removals. And so the circle has become entrenched.

The continuing disproportionate removal of Aboriginal children from their families can to some extent be convincingly explained. No matter how sympathetic one may be to the position of Aboriginal peoples, it is difficult to countenance leaving children in situations of known risk, whatever the underlying cause of those risks may be. Poverty and social dislocation are known contributing factors to high levels of child abuse and neglect. Thus, it is to be expected that until the grave social and economic problems facing Aboriginal communities are addressed, disproportionate numbers of Aboriginal children will continue to be removed into state care. The picture with respect to Aboriginal children is, however, more complex. As Kline argues, the continuing removal of Aboriginal children from their families is rooted not only in the social and economic consequences of colonialism, but in the colonial underpinnings of the child protection system itself. Aboriginal peoples have been excluded from that system, with Aboriginal cultures being misunderstood, devalued or simply ignored by the law and the people who are responsible for its application. As Kline points out, the apparently neutral façade of non-native child protection legislation has obscured the extent to which Western cultural bias is entrenched within the system and has allowed the imperialist attitudes of both non-native social workers and the judiciary towards Aboriginal families and their communities to go largely unchecked.

Unravelling the complexities of colonialism is a difficult task. There are no easy answers. In recent years, tremendous goodwill has been demonstrated by Aboriginal communities and all those involved in the governance and delivery of Aboriginal child welfare services to address the worst failings of the non-native child protection system. Concerted efforts have been made in both Canada and Australia to accommodate Aboriginal cultural perspectives within the governing legislation and to ensure that decision-makers are responsive at every stage of the process to the importance of Aboriginal culture in promoting the welfare of Aboriginal children. Aboriginal child welfare agencies exercising delegated provincial powers are now commonplace in Canada and play a crucial role in helping to sensitize provincial services to the cultural needs of Aboriginal communities. The capacity of the provincial system to provide a culturally appropriate service to Aboriginal communities is being further strengthened in Canada by the creation of Aboriginal administrative authorities such as that now in operation in Manitoba. And yet, despite the efforts of recent years, Aboriginal children continue to be removed from their families in both Canada and Australia in wholly disproportionate numbers.

The disappointing results of recent reforms to the non-native child welfare system exemplify the inherent limitations of trying to work within what is still, at its core, a culturally alien system. The very foundations of that system must be fundamentally transformed. The only long-term solution to the crisis still facing many Aboriginal families and communities is decolonization. That means self-government. It is widely accepted by academic commentators that only Aboriginal self-government over child welfare can reverse the devastating effects of the non-native child welfare system on Aboriginal communities. Problems with Aboriginal child welfare cannot, however, be looked at in isolation. The economic, social, cultural and legal obstacles to keeping Aboriginal children safe within their families and communities are inextricably linked. At the root of all these problems is colonization. Aboriginal peoples need to be freed from colonial rule and have restored to them the land and resources and legal and political authority required to rebuild their devastated communities. Self-government underpinned by a secure economic base promises to rejuvenate the political, social and cultural lives of Aboriginal communities. Aboriginal children and future generations of children to come will be the main beneficiaries of this process. It is only within the context of healthy, flourishing communities that long-term solutions to Aboriginal child welfare can be found.

For many readers of this book, particularly in Australia, to talk of self-government as a solution to the current crisis over Aboriginal child welfare is to enter the realm of the impossible and to engage in the worst kind of mere academic speculation. Political opposition to self-government remains firmly entrenched and such are the intractable nature of the problems facing Aboriginal communities that self-government, even to the most sympathetic of observers, seems neither feasible nor desirable. Whilst communities struggle to deal with such immediate concerns as the lack of suitable housing, sanitation, ineffective leadership, alcohol and drug abuse, violence and, within some communities, the rampant sexual abuse of children, academic debate as to the meaning of decolonization and self-government in national and international law can seem very far removed from the pressing realities of their lives. That reality is fully acknowledged, as are the challenges and risks it poses for successful self-government. Aboriginal children such as Lester Desjarlais need to be protected. Self-government in the hands of damaged communities can seem a dangerous distraction from that most basic need. However, whilst much more must clearly be done within the existing system to help and support Aboriginal communities to keep their children safe, it is also important when faced with what sometimes seem to be the impossible hurdles of everyday life, to retain a focus on the principal goal. The non-native child welfare system will not provide a long-term solution for Aboriginal families. Despite the problems, efforts to find a workable framework for self-government, including self-government over child welfare, must continue.

If the promise of self-government is to be realized, it must deliver on two core objectives. It must secure decolonization for Aboriginal communities whilst ensuring the fundamental rights and interests of Aboriginal children are satisfactorily protected. Decolonization for Aboriginal peoples means not only restoration of their land and resources but the restoration of Aboriginal sovereignty over all their internal affairs. The concept of sovereignty is key. It means that on matters lying within their sole jurisdiction, such as child welfare, Aboriginal communities are subjected to no higher constitutional authority. The controlling hand of the federal government must be removed and their sovereign right to govern restored without provisos or conditions. This in turn means that responsibility for the protection of the fundamental rights of Aboriginal children must lie with Aboriginal peoples and not the state. It is for each self-governing community to determine, in accordance with its own particular cultural, social and political norms, how the most vulnerable within its society will be protected from both public and private abuses of power.

In recent years, Canada has made enormous strides towards the implementation of Aboriginal self-government. As a result of the federal government's acceptance of the inherent rights policy in 1995, self-government, through the modern treaty process, has become a reality for many Aboriginal communities. Where self-government has been successfully negotiated, control over Aboriginal child welfare and other family law matters has formed a core part of the powers conferred on Aboriginal governments. For states such as Australia, where self-government remains a much more distant prospect, the failures and successes of Aboriginal self-government in Canada hold important lessons. The successes can be built upon and the mistakes avoided. Again, the somewhat pessimistic conclusions reached on the current model of self-government in Canada should not detract from the enormous effort and goodwill which has been put into the treaty process by both Aboriginal and Canadian leaders. However, when measured against the two core objectives for successful self-government, the Canadian model falls worryingly short. The successful decolonization of Aboriginal peoples cannot be achieved whilst the Canadian government so selfishly guards its own sovereign power and authority. Its unilateral imposition of conditions and standards on Aboriginal governance, even within core areas of Aboriginal jurisdiction such as child welfare, betrays its rigid adherence to a hierarchical relationship between the Canadian government and Aboriginal peoples based on sovereign and subject, not equal partnership. Aboriginal peoples are not being given the constitutional space to determine their own legal and political futures. Ultimate sovereignty remains firmly entrenched in the Canadian government. Nowhere is that more evident than in the federal government's non-negotiable requirement that, despite the strong opposition of many Aboriginal leaders, the Canadian Charter of Rights and Freedoms must apply to all Aboriginal governments. Whilst purporting to enshrine the core democratic values of Canadian society, many Aboriginal communities wholly reject the Charter as a culturally alien, assimilatory tool of the West. Yet, without consultation or compromise, Aboriginal governments are required to comply. To expect the Canadian Charter to provide an effective safeguard for Aboriginal children when imposed on a hostile community is quite simply misconceived.

For Aboriginal communities engaging in self-government negotiations or seeking to push forward a self-government agenda, there is a huge amount at stake. Agreements reached within the framework of the modern treaty process are likely to define the relationship between the government and Aboriginal peoples for generations to come. It is therefore vital that the framework for negotiations is right. Decolonization must remain at the heart of the process, with the sovereignty of Aboriginal peoples over their lands and their communities at the foundation of the new relationship. However, within the boundaries of what the Canadian government have been willing to concede, the core tenets of decolonization have not been met. And without the Canadian government being subjected to strong legal or political pressure at the domestic level to do more, there is little reason to suppose that this position will change. It is to these limitations in domestic law and politics, that international law may provide an answer.

International law must be approached with a fair degree of caution. A law made by states for states is likely to be inherently problematic for sub-state groups such as indigenous peoples. Despite recent significant advances in the field of indigenous rights, there is clearly no international forum to which indigenous peoples can turn for a quick and effective remedy. However, that is not to say that the 'soft' pressure which characterizes international law cannot be effective. Moreover, even in the absence of hard remedies, international law now contains a rich body of legal principles on which indigenous and non-indigenous leaders could draw at the national negotiation table to provide a way out of the current domestic impasse on self-government. The emerging international consensus on indigenous peoples' internal right to self-determination, as embodied in Articles 3 and 4 of the UN Declaration, holds much of promise for indigenous communities. The internal right to self-determination is clearly limited in important ways. However, with its roots firmly planted in the right of colonized peoples to decolonization, it has the potential, if interpreted faithfully within this context, to liberate Aboriginal peoples from the hold of 'alien' colonial governments, at least in their internal matters. Self-determination as thus understood embraces a vision of shared horizontal sovereignty between governments and indigenous communities in their respective jurisdictions that differs markedly from municipal law's rigid adherence to the overriding 'vertical' sovereignty of the state. It needs, however, to be emphasized that legal recognition of the internal sovereignty of indigenous peoples is not the dangerous threat it is often perceived to be by states. Under international law, the territorial integrity and external sovereignty of the state is firmly protected. Indigenous peoples may be sovereign but that sovereignty can be exercised only on internal matters and within established territorial borders. Indigenous peoples have no right to secede from their host-state and their subjectivity in international law continues to be mediated through the state.

International law thus enshrines a concept of self-determination that both promises decolonization and internal sovereignty for indigenous peoples, whilst meeting the key objections and concerns of states. That includes the clear concern of states regarding the protection of the fundamental rights and interests of indigenous individuals living within self-governing communities. It is clear as a matter of international law that self-determination has no effect on the entitlement of indigenous individuals to the protection of their basic human rights. However, the relevant legal standards by which indigenous individuals are protected are those enshrined in international law and not the domestic law of states. It is also clear under international law that pursuant to indigenous peoples' right to self-determination, responsibility for the protection of the fundamental rights and interests of indigenous individuals should fall, in the first instance, on self-governing indigenous communities. Otherwise, the right to self-determination will be compromised. However, the structuring of relationships between indigenous peoples and the state under international law is such that the state retains a residual role as 'guardian of those rights'. Whilst indigenous communities are afforded a margin of discretion and may interpret and implement international standards differently from their non-native counterparts, they cannot act in ways which would be unlawful for the state. If indigenous communities do not comply with international standards as determined in dialogue with states or ultimately by the relevant international body, the state, which remains ultimately accountable under international law for the treatment of indigenous individuals within its jurisdiction, will have the right to intervene.

The question when examined as one of principle is more difficult. Concerns about the unilateral imposition of the Canadian Charter on indigenous communities centre on its Euro-centric bias and assimilating tendencies. Is the international law of human rights really any different? Should indigenous peoples be expected to comply with international standards that are in many ways culturally specific to the West? If the cultural integrity of indigenous peoples is to be respected and protected, it is incongruous to impose upon them a culturally alien and potentially destructive set of legal norms. However, whilst international human rights law is by no means an exemplary model of cultural inclusiveness and accommodation, it is immeasurably better than the often mono-cultural standards of the state. International human rights law strives to talk in a meaningful way to many different peoples situated within very different socio-economic and cultural contexts. Formulated at a highly abstract level, its general principles can be given meaning only when interpreted and understood within those concrete cultural contexts. International human rights law thus permits of considerable sensitivity to cultural difference. Its commitment to achieving truly universal standards is reflected in the final text of the UNCRC. Whilst it would be disingenuous to suggest that indigenous communities will not find any of its provisions problematic, the Convention is distinctive for its accommodation of a wide range of cultural perspectives and for its sensitivity to the importance of culture and community in advancing the welfare of the individual child. By situating the child so firmly within its family, community and culture, there are strong grounds for optimism that there is much within the Convention with which indigenous communities can agree. It provides at least a more inclusive starting point in the search for culturally appropriate standards to protect the fundamental rights and interests of vulnerable individual children living within self-governing communities.

Simple solutions to complex problems such as Aboriginal child welfare in Canada and Australia do not exist. It would be naïve to think that they did. However, HREOC were clearly right in concluding that decolonization is the only long-term solution to the problems facing Aboriginal communities, including problems over child welfare. Decolonization means self-determination, which means Aboriginal sovereignty over all internal matters such as child welfare must be restored. The risks of self-government cannot, however, be ignored. Self-government would be a hollow victory if it came at the expense of more vulnerable children such as Lester Desjarlais. In moving forward with self-government a balance must be found – a balance between Aboriginal sovereignty and the protection of individual Aboriginal children. Canada has failed to get that balance right. It has failed both to respect the decolonization of Aboriginal peoples whilst securing effective protection for vulnerable Aboriginal children. International law provides an alternative way forward. It is certainly not suggested here that it provides a perfect answer. It does, however, provide an answer that ensures a comprehensive culturally inclusive framework of protection for indigenous children's rights whilst holding true to the fundamental tenets of self-determination as a process of decolonization.

Aboriginal peoples have a right to self-determination and effective decolonization. Aboriginal children have a right to be safe, healthy and secure. It is hoped that the arguments presented here can help towards the realization of these most basic entitlements of Aboriginal peoples, families and their children.

Bibliography

Aboriginal Child Sexual Assault Taskforce (2006). *Breaking the Silence: Creating the Future – Addressing Child Sexual Assault in Aboriginal Communities in NSW*. Attorney General's Department, NSW.

Aboriginal Justice Inquiry of Manitoba (1991). *Report of the Aboriginal Justice Inquiry of Manitoba: The Justice System and Aboriginal People*, vol. 1. Winnipeg: Manitoba.

Aboriginal Justice Inquiry – Child Welfare Initiative (2001). *Promise of Hope: Commitment to Change*. Available at: www.aji-cwi.mb.ca/pdfs/promiseofhope.pdf.

Alberta Children's Services, *2006–07 Annual Report*. Available at: www.child.alberta.ca/home/documents/rpt_06-07_annual.pdf.

Alberta Children's Services (2008). *Children and Youth Services Business Plan 2008–11*. Available at: www.finance.alberta.ca/publications/budget/budget2008/child.pdf.

Allen, S. (2011). 'The UN Declaration on the Rights of Indigenous Peoples and the Limits of the International Legal Project', in S. Allen and A. Xanthaki (eds) *Reflections on the UN Declaration on the Rights of Indigenous Peoples*. Oxford: Hart, 225.

Alston, P. (1994). 'The Best Interests Principle: Towards a Reconciliation of Culture and Human Rights', in P. Alston (ed.) *The Best Interests of the Child: Reconciling Culture and Human Rights*. Oxford: Clarendon Press, 1.

An-Na'im, A. (1992). 'Introduction', in A. An-Na'im (ed.) *Human Rights in Cross-cultural Perspectives – A Quest for Consensus*. Philadelphia: University of Pennsylvania Press, 1.

An-Na'im, A. (1992). 'Toward a Cross-Cultural Approach to Defining International Standards of Human Rights', in A. An-Na'im (ed.) *Human Rights in Cross-cultural Perspectives – A Quest for Consensus*. Philadelphia: University of Pennsylvania Press, 19.

An-Na'im, A. (1994). 'Cultural Transformation and Normative Consensus on the Best Interests of the Child', in P. Alston (ed.) *The Best Interests of the Child: Reconciling Culture and Human Rights*. Oxford: Clarendon Press, 62.

Anaya, J. (2004). *Indigenous Peoples in International Law* (2nd edn). New York: Oxford University Press.

Anaya, J. (2004). 'International Human Rights and Indigenous Peoples: The Move Toward the Multicultural State', *Ariz. J. Int'l & Comp. L.*, 21: 13.

Anaya, J. (2007). 'Indigenous Law and Its Contribution to Global Pluralism', *Indigenous Law Journal*, 6: 3.

Anghie, A. (2005). *Imperialism, Sovereignty and the Making of International Law*. New York: Cambridge University Press.

Asch, M. (1992). 'Aboriginal Self-Government and the Construction of Canadian Constitutional Identity', *Alberta Law Review*, XXX: 465.

Asch, M. (2002). 'From Terra Nullius to Affirmation: Reconciling Aboriginal Rights with the Canadian Constitution', *Canadian Journal of Law and Society*, 17: 23.

Asch, M. and Macklem, P. (1991). 'Aboriginal Rights and Canadian Sovereignty: An Essay on *R v Sparrow*', *Constitutional Studies*, XXIX: 498.

Ashcroft, B., Griffiths, G. and Tiffin, H. (eds) (1995). *The Post-Colonial Studies Reader*. London: Routledge.

Australia. Law Reform Commission (1986). *The Recognition of Aboriginal Customary Laws*, No. 31, Vol. 1. Canberra: Australian Government Publishing Service.

Australian Institute of Health and Welfare (2011). *Child Protection Australia 2009–10*. AIHW Cat no. CWS 39. Canberra: AIHW (Child Welfare Series No. 51).

Australian Museum Online (2004). *Indigenous Australia: Family*. Available at: http://australianmuseum.net.au/Indigenous-Australia-Family.

Bala, N. (2000–2001). 'The Charter of Rights and Family Law in Canada: A New Era', *Canadian Family Law Quarterly*, 18: 373.

Barkin, I. (1990). 'Aboriginal Rights: A Shell without the Filling', *Queen's Law Journal*, 15: 307.

Barsh, R. (1989). 'The Convention on the Rights of the Child: A Re-Assessment of the Final Text', *New York Law School Journal of Human Rights*, 7: 142.

Barsh, R. (1996). 'Indigenous Peoples and the UN Commission on Human Rights: A Case of the Immovable Object and the Irresistible Force', *Human Rights Quarterly*, 18: 782.

Barsh, R. and Henderson J. Y. (1997). 'The Supreme Court's Van der Peet Trilogy: Naïve Imperialism and Ropes of Sand', *McGill Law Journal*, 42: 993.

Binnie, W. I. C. (1990). 'The Sparrow Doctrine: Beginning of the End or End of the Beginning?', *Queens Law Journal*, 15: 217.

Blackstock, C. (2007). 'Residential Schools: Did They Really Close or Just Morph into Child Welfare?', *Indigenous Law Journal*, 6: 71.

Boldt, M. (1993). *Surviving as Indians. The Challenge of Self-Government*. Toronto: University of Toronto Press.

Boldt, M. and Long, A. (1992). 'Tribal Philosophies and the Canadian Charter of Rights and Freedoms', in J. Banfield (ed.) *Readings in Law and Society*. Concord: Captus Press, 212.

Borrows, J. (1994). 'Constitutional Law from a First Nation Perspective', *UBC Law Review*, 28: 1.

Borrows, J. (1994). 'Contemporary Traditional Equality: The Effect of the Charter on First Nations Politics', *University of New Brunswick Law Journal*, 43: 19.

Borrows, J. (1997). 'The Trickster: Integral to a Distinctive Culture', *Constitutional Forum*, 8: 27.

Borrows, J. (2001). 'Domesticating Doctrines: Aboriginal Peoples after the Royal Commission', *McGill Law Journal*, 46: 615.

Borrows, J. (2002). *Recovering Canada. The Resurgence of Indigenous Law*. Toronto: University of Toronto Press.

Borrows, J. (2005). 'Creating an Indigenous Legal Community', *McGill Law Journal*, 50: 153.

Borrows, J. (2005). 'Tracking Trajectories: Aboriginal Governance as an Aboriginal Right', *UBC Law Review*, 38: 285.

Bourassa, C. (2010). *Summary Review of the Manitoba Child Welfare System for the Saskatchewan Child Welfare Review Report*. Available at: http://saskchildwelfarereview.ca/Review-Manitoba-Child-Welfare-System-CBourassa.pdf.

Boyd, S. (2000). 'The Impact of the Charter of Rights and Freedoms on Canadian Family Law', *Canadian Journal of Family Law*, 17: 293.

Brems, E. (1997). 'Enemies or Allies? Feminism and Cultural Relativism as Dissident Voices in Human Rights Discourse', *Human Rights Quarterly*, 19: 136.

British Columbia Ministry of Children and Family Development (2002). *Aboriginal Governance Discussion Paper*. On file with author.

British Columbia Ministry of Children and Family Development (2007). *2006/07 Annual Service Plan Report*. Available at: www.bcbudget.gov.bc.ca/Annual_Reports/2006_2007/cfd/cfd.pdf.

British Columbia Royal Commission on Family and Children's Law (1975). *Native Families and the Law: Tenth Report of the Royal Commission on Family and Children's Law*. Vancouver: The Commission.

Brolmann, C. M. and Zieck, M. Y. A. (1993). 'Indigenous Peoples', in C. M. Brolmann, R. Lefeber and M. Y. A. Zieck (eds), *Peoples and Minorities in International Law*. Dordrecht and London: Martinus Nijhoff, 187.

Brownlie, I. (1988). 'The Rights of Peoples in Modern International Law', in J. Crawford (ed.) *The Rights of Peoples*, Oxford: Clarendon, 1.

Brownlie, I. (1992). *Treaties and Indigenous Peoples*. Oxford: Clarendon Press.

Brunton, R. (1998). *Betraying the Victims*. Melbourne: Institute of Public Affairs.

Bull, S. (1989). 'The Special Case of the Native Indian Child', *Advocate*, 47: 523.

Campbell, T. (1992). 'The Rights of Minors: As Person, As Child, As Juvenile, As Future Adult', *International Journal of Law and the Family*, 6: 1.

Canada, Department of Indian Affairs and Northern Development (1995). *Federal Policy Guide for Aboriginal Self-Government. The Government of Canada's Approach to Implementation of the Inherent Right and the Negotiation of Aboriginal Self-Government*. Ottawa: Supply and Services.

Canada, Department of Indian Affairs and Northern Development (2007). *General Briefing Note on the Comprehensive Land Claims Policy of Canada and the Status of Claims*. Ottawa: Supply and Services.

Carasco, E. (1986). 'Canadian Native Children: Have Child Welfare Laws Broken the Circle?', *Canadian Journal of Family Law*, 5: 111.

Cassese, A. (1995). *Self-determination of Peoples – A Legal Reappraisal*. New York and Cambridge: Cambridge University Press.

Cassidy, F. (ed.) (1991). *Aboriginal Self-Determination*. Lantzville: Oolichan Books.

Cassidy, F. and Bish, R. (1991). *Indian Government: Its Meaning in Practice*. Lantzville: Oolichan Books.

Cerna, C. (1994). 'Universality of Human Rights and Cultural Diversity: Implementation of Human Rights in Different Socio-Cultural Context', *Human Rights Quarterly*, 6: 740.

Charlesworth, H. and Chinkin, C. (2000). *The Boundaries of International Law. A Feminist Analysis*. Manchester: Manchester University Press.

Charters, C. (2009). 'Indigenous Peoples and International Law and Policy', in B. Richardson, S. Imai and K. McNeil (eds) *Indigenous Peoples and the Law. Comparative and Critical Perspectives*. Portland: Hart Publishing, 161.

Christie, G. (2000). 'Justifying Principles of Treaty Interpretation', *Queen's Law Journal*, 26: 143.

Christie, G. (2002). 'Aboriginal and Normativity, Judicial Justification of Recent Developments in Aboriginal Law', *Canadian Journal of Law and Society*, 17: 41.

Christie, G. (2007). 'Culture, Self-Determination and Colonialism: Issues Around the Revitalization of Indigenous Legal Traditions', *Indigenous Law Journal*, 6: 13.

Clark, S. (1992). 'Crime and Community Issues and Directions in Aboriginal Justice', *Canadian Journal of Criminology*, 34: 513.

Commission on Human Rights, *Report of the Special Rapporteur on the Situation of Human Rights and Fundamental Freedoms of Indigenous People*. E/CN.4/2002/97.

Commission on Human Rights, *Report of the Special Rapporteur on the Situation of Human Rights and Fundamental Freedoms of Indigenous People*. E/CN.4/2003/90.

Commission on Human Rights, *Report of the Special Rapporteur on the Situation of Human Rights and Fundamental Freedoms of Indigenous People*. E/CN.4/2004/80.

Commission on Human Rights, *Report of the Special Rapporteur on the Situation of Human Rights and Fundamental Freedoms of Indigenous People*. E/CN.2005/88.

Commission on Human Rights, *Technical Review of the United Nations Draft Declaration on the Rights of Indigenous Peoples*. E/CN.4/Sub.2/1994/2.

Committee on Economic, Social and Cultural Rights, *General Comment No 21, Right of Everyone to Take Part in Cultural Life (art. 15, para. 1(a), of the International Covenant on Economic, Social and Cultural Rights)*. E/C.12/GC/21.

Committee on the Elimination of Racial Discrimination, *Fourteenth Periodic Reports of States Parties due in 1997: Canada. 12/10/2001*. CERD/C/320/Add.5.

Committee on the Elimination of Racial Discrimination, *Right to Self-determination: 23/08/96 CERD General Recommendation 21 (General Comments)*. A/51/18.

Committee on the Elimination of Racial Discrimination, *Summary Record of the 1526th Meeting: Canada. 09/08/2002*. CERD/C/SR.1526.

Committee on the Elimination of Racial Discrimination, *Twelfth Periodic Reports of States Parties due in 1993: Canada. 18/07/94*. CERD/C/240/Add.1.

Committee on the Rights of the Child, *Consideration of Reports Submitted by States Parties under Article 44 of the Convention, Concluding Observations of the Committee on the Rights of the Child: Australia: 10/10/97*. CRC/C/15/Add.79.

Committee on the Rights of the Child, *Consideration of Reports Submitted by States Parties under Article 44 of the Convention, Concluding Observations: Australia*. CRC/C/15/Add.268.

Committee on the Rights of the Child, *Consideration of Reports Submitted by States Parties under Article 44 of the Convention, Concluding Observations of the Committee on the Rights of the Child: Canada*. CRC/C/15/Add.37.

Committee on the Rights of the Child, *Consideration of Reports Submitted by States Parties under Article 44 of the Convention, Concluding Observations: Canada*. CRC/C/15/Add.215.

Committee on the Rights of the Child, *Initial Reports of States Parties due in 1994: Canada. 28/07/94 (State Party Report)*. CRC/C/11/Add.3.

Committee on the Rights of the Child, *List of Issues: Canada 10/02/95*. CRC.C.9/WP.1.

Committee on the Rights of the Child, General Comment No. 11 (2009). *Indigenous Children and their Rights under the Convention*. CRC/C/GC/11.

Committee on the Rights of the Child, *Summary Record of the 214th meeting: Canada. 30/05/95 (Summary Record)*. CRC/C/SR.214.

Committee on the Rights of the Child, *Summary Record of the 89th Meeting: Sudan*. CRC/C/SR.89 (1994).

Committee on the Rights of the Child, 34th session, 3 October 2003, *Day of General Discussion on the Rights of Indigenous Children, Recommendations*. Available at: www2.ohchr.org/english/bodies/crc/docs/discussion/indigenouschildren.pdf.

Crawford, J. (1998). 'State Practice and International Law in Relation to Secession', *British Yearbook of International Law*, 69: 85.

Cunneen, C. (1998). 'Reforming Juvenile Justice and Creating the Space for Indigenous Self-Determination', *UNSW Law Journal*, 21(1) (Forum 4, No 3): 241.

Cunneen, C. and Libesman, T. (2002). 'Removed and Discarded: The Contemporary Legacy of the Stolen Generations', *Australia Indigenous Law Reporter*, 55; 7(4).

Daes, Erica-Irene, Special Rapporteur, *Economic and Social Council, Protection of the Heritage of Indigenous Peoples – Final Report of the Special Rapporteur, Mrs Erica-Irene Daes, in Conformity with Subcommission Resolution 1993/44 and Decision 1994/105 of the Commission on Human Rights*. E/CN.4/Sub.2/1995/26.

Daes, Erica-Irene, *Indigenous Peoples and their Relationship to Land – Preliminary Working Paper*. E/CN.4/Sub.2/1997/17.

Daes, Erica-Irene, *Indigenous Peoples and their Relationship to Land, Final Working Paper Prepared by the Special Rapporteur, Mrs Erica-Irene A. Daes*. E/CN.4/Sub.2/2001/21.

Daes, Erica-Irene, *Indigenous Peoples' Permanent Sovereignty over Natural Resources – Final Report of the Special Rapporteur, Erica-Irene A. Daes*. E/CN.4/Sub.2/2004/30.

Department of Community Services (NSW) (1999). *Aboriginal Policy Directions – The Right to Better Service*. On file with author.

Dewar, J. (1997). 'Indigenous Children and Family Law', *Adelaide Law Review*, 19: 217.

Dickson, T. (2004). 'Self-Government by Side Agreement?', *McGill Law Journal*, 49: 419.

Donnelly, J. (2003). *Universal Human Rights in Theory and Practice* (2nd edn). New York: Cornell University Press.

Durbach, A. (2001). 'Welcome Address', in *Moving Forward – Achieving Reparations for the Stolen Generations: Conference Papers, 15th – 16th August 2001, University of New South Wales, Sydney*. Sydney: Human Rights and Equal Opportunity Commission.

Durst, D. (1999). 'The Wellness of Aboriginal Children: Seeking Solutions through Self-government', in J. Hylton (ed.) *Aboriginal Self-Government in Canada: Current Trends and Issues*. Saskatoon: Purich Pub, 187.

Economic and Social Council, *Question of a Convention on the Rights of the Child: Report of the Working Group on a Draft Convention on the Rights of the Child*. E/CN.4/1987/25 (1987).

Economic and Social Council, *Report of the Open-ended Inter-sessional Ad Hoc Working Group on a Permanent Forum for Indigenous People in the United Nations System*. E/CN.4/1999/83.

Economic and Social Council, *Report of the Open-ended Inter-sessional Ad Hoc Working Group on a Permanent Forum for Indigenous People*. E/CN.4/2000/86.

Economic and Social Council, *Report of the Second Workshop on a Permanent Forum for Indigenous People within the United Nations System Held in Accordance with Commission on Human Rights Resolution 1997/30*. E/CN.4/1998/11.

Economic and Social Council, *Report of the Sub-Commission on Prevention of Discrimination and Protection of Minorities, Note verbale dated 18 January 1995 from the Permanent Mission of Denmark to the United Nations Office at Geneva addressed to the United Nations Centre for Human Rights*. E/CN.4.1995/141.

Economic and Social Council, *Report of the Working Group Established in Accordance with Commission on Human Rights Resolution 1995/32 of 3 March 1995*. E/CN.4/1996/84.

Economic and Social Council, *Report of the Working Group Established in Accordance with Commission on Human Rights Resolution 1995/32 of 3 March 1995*. E/CN.4/1997/102.

Economic and Social Council, *Report of the Working Group Established in Accordance with Commission on Human Rights Resolution 1995/32 of 3 March 1995*. E/CN.4/1998/106.

Economic and Social Council, *Report of the Working Group Established in Accordance with Commission on Human Rights Resolution 1995/32 of 3 March 1995*. E/CN.4/2000/84.

Economic and Social Council, *Report of the Working Group Established in Accordance with Commission on Human Rights Resolution 1995/32 of 3 March 1995*. E/CN.4/2001/85.

Economic and Social Council, *Report of the Working Group Established in Accordance with Commission on Human Rights Resolution 1995/32 of 3 March 1995*. E/CN.4/2002/98.

Economic and Social Council, *Report of the Working Group Established in Accordance with Commission on Human Rights Resolution 1995/32 of 3 March 1995*. E/CN.4/2003/92.

Economic and Social Council, *Report of the Working Group Established in Accordance with Commission on Human Rights Resolution 1995/32 of 3 March 1995*. E/CN.4/2005/89.

Economic and Social Council, *Report of the Working Group Established in Accordance with Commission on Human Rights Resolution 1995/32 of 3 March 1995*. E/CN.4/2006/79.

Economic and Social Council, *Report of the Working Group on Indigenous Populations on its Eleventh Session*. E/CN.4/Sub.2/1993/29.

Economic and Social Council, *Report of the Working Group on Indigenous Populations on its Twelfth Session*. E/CN.4/Sub.2/1994/30.

Economic and Social Council, *Report of the Working Group on Indigenous Populations on its Thirteenth Session*. E/CN.4/Sub.2/1995/24.

Economic and Social Council, *Report of the Working Group on Indigenous Populations on its Fourteenth Session*. E/CN.4/Sub.2/1996/21.

Economic and Social Council, *Report of the Working Group on Indigenous Populations on its Fifteenth Session*. E/CN.4/Sub.2/1997/14.

Economic and Social Council, *Report of the Working Group on Indigenous Populations on its Seventeenth Session*. E/CN.4/Sub.2/1999/19.

Economic and Social Council, *Report of the Working Group on Indigenous Populations on its Eighteenth Session*. E/CN.4/Sub.2/2000/24.

Economic and Social Council, World Conference Against Racism, Racial Discrimination, Xenophobia and Related Intolerance, *Information Received from Indigenous Organisations, Statement on the World Conference Against Racism of the Indigenous Peoples' Millennium Conference, Panama City, Panama, 7–11 May 2001*. E/CN.4/Sub.2/AC.4/2001/8.

Englelstad, D. and Bird, J. (eds) (1992). *Nation to Nation: Aboriginal Sovereignty and the Future of Canada*. Concord, Ontario: Anasi Press.

Falk, R. (1992). 'Cultural Foundations', in A. An-Na'im (ed.) *Human Rights in Cross-cultural Perspectives – A Quest for Consensus*. Philadelphia: University of Pennsylvania Press, 44.

Family Law Council (Australia) (2004). *Recognition of Traditional Aboriginal and Torres Strait Islander Child-rearing Practices. Response to Recommendation 22: Pathways Report, Out of the Maze*. Commonwealth of Australia.

Family Law Pathways Advisory Group (Australia) (2001). *Out of the Maze. Pathways to the Future for Families Experiencing Separation. Report of the Family Law Pathways Advisory Group*. Commonwealth of Australia.

Finkler, H. (1992). 'Community Participation in Socio-Legal Control: The Northern Context', *Canadian Journal of Criminology*, 34: 503.

Fossett, R. (1989–1991). *Aboriginal Child Welfare in Canada: Literature Review and Selected Bibliography*. Public Inquiry into the Administration of Justice and Aboriginal People, Paper No. 15, vol. 4. Manitoba: The Inquiry.

Foster, C. E. (2001). 'Articulating Self-determination in the Draft Declaration on the Rights of Indigenous Peoples', *European Journal of International Law*, 12: 141.

Franck, T. (1993). 'Postmodern Tribalism and the Right to Secession', in C. Brolmann, R. Lefeber and M. Zieck (eds) *Peoples and Minorities in International Law*. Dordrecht and London: Martinus Nijhoff, 3.

Freeman, M. (1998). 'Human Rights and Real Cultures: Towards a Dialogue on "Asian Values"', *Netherlands Quarterly of Human Rights*, 16: 25.

Gough, P. (2006). 'Manitoba's Child Welfare System', Centre of Excellence for Child Welfare. Available at: www.cecw-cepb.ca/sites/default/files/publications/en/ManitobaChildWelfareSystem34E.pdf.

Gove Inquiry into Child Protection (1995). *Report of the Gove Inquiry into Child Protection in British Columbia: Matthew's Legacy, Volume 1*. Vancouver: The Inquiry.

Graben, S. (2007). 'The Nisga'a Final Agreement: Negotiating Federalism', *Indigenous Law Journal*, 6: 63.

Greschner, D. (1992). 'Aboriginal Women, the Constitution, and Criminal Justice', *U.B.C. Law Rev.*, Aboriginal Justice Special Edition, 338.

Hafen, B. and Hafen, J. (1996). 'Abandoning Children to their Autonomy: The United Nations Convention on the Rights of the Child', *Harvard International Law Journal*, 37: 449.

Hallett, B. (2006). *Aboriginal People in Manitoba*. Queen's Printer Canada.

Hammersmith, B. (1992). 'Aboriginal Women and Self-Government', in D. Engelstadt and J. Bird (eds) *Nation to Nation: Aboriginal Sovereignty and the Future in Canada*. Don Mills, Ontario: Anansi Press, 53.

Harris-Short, S. (2001). 'Listening to "the Other"? The Convention on the Rights of the Child', *Melbourne Journal of International Law*, 2: 304.

Harris-Short, S. (2003). 'International Human Rights Law – Imperialist, Inept and Ineffective? Cultural Relativism and the United Nations Convention on the Rights of the Child', *Human Rights Quarterly*, 25: 130.

Harris-Short, S. (2007). 'Self-Government in Canada: A Successful Model for the Decolonisation of Aboriginal Child Welfare?', in S. Tierney (ed.) *Accommodating Cultural Diversity: Contemporary Issues in Theory and Practice*. Aldershot: Ashgate, 99.

Henderson, J. Y. (2000). 'Constitutional Powers and Treaty Rights', *Saskatchewan Law Review*, 63: 719.

Henderson, J. Y. (2006). 'First Nations Jurisprudence and Aboriginal Rights: Defining the Just Society'. Canada: Native Law Centre.

Higgins, R. (1993). 'Postmodern Tribalism and the Right to Secession – Comments by R. Higgins', in C. Brolmann, R. Lefeber and M. Zieck (eds) *Peoples and Minorities in International Law*. Dordrecht and London: Martinus Nijhoff, 29.

Hogg, P. and Turpel, M. E. (1995). 'Implementing Aboriginal Self-Government: Constitutional and Jurisdictional Issues', *Canadian Bar Review*, 74(2): 187.

Holder, C. and Corntassel, J. (2002). 'Indigenous Peoples and Multicultural Citizenship: Bridging Collective and Individual Rights', *Human Rights Quarterly*, 24: 126.

Howard, R. (1993). 'Cultural Absolutism and the Nostalgia for Community', *Human Rights Quarterly*, 15: 315.

Howard, R. and Donnelly, J. (1989). 'Human Dignity, Human Rights and Political Regimes', in J. Donnelly (ed.) *Universal Human Rights in Theory and Practice*. Ithaca and London: Cornell University Press, 66.

Hughes, E. N. (2006). *BC Children and Youth Review: An Independent Review of BC's Child Protection System*. Available at: www.mcf.gov.bc.ca/bcchildprotection/pdf/BC_Children_and_Youth_Review_Report_FINAL_April_4.pdf.

Human Rights and Equal Opportunity Commission (1997). *Report of the National Inquiry Into the Separation of Aboriginal and Torres Strait Islander Children from their Families*. Commonwealth of Australia.

Human Rights and Equal Opportunity Commission (1998). *Bringing Them Home: Implementation Progress Report*. Reproduced at (1999) *Australian Indigenous Law Reporter*, 4.

Human Rights and Equal Opportunity Commission (2006). *A Statistical Overview of Aboriginal and Torres Strait Islander Peoples in Australia*. Available at: www.humanrights.gov.au/social_justice/statistics/index.html.

Human Rights Committee, *Concluding Observations of the Human Rights Committee: Australia. 24/07/2000*. A/55/40.

Human Rights Committee, *Concluding Observations of the Human Rights Committee: Canada. 07/04/99*. CCPR/C/79/Add.105.

Human Rights Committee, *Concluding Observations of the Human Rights Committee: Norway. 01/11/99*. CCPR/C/79/Add.112.

Human Rights Committee, *Consideration of Reports Submitted by States Parties under Article 40 of the Covenant, Concluding Observations of the Human Rights Committee, Canada*. CCPR/C/CAN/CO/5.

Human Rights Committee, *Consideration of Reports Submitted by States Parties under Article 40 of the Covenant, Concluding Observations of the Human Rights Committee, Georgia*. CCPR/C/GEO/CO/3.

Human Rights Committee, *Consideration of Reports Submitted by States Parties under Article 40 of the Covenant, Concluding Observations of the Human Rights Committee, Sudan*. CCPR/C/SDN/CO/3.

Human Rights Committee, *List of Issues: Australia. 25/04/2000*. CCPR/C/69/L/AUS.

Human Rights Committee, *Summary Record of the 1856th Meeting: Australia 28/07/2000 (Summary Record)*. CCPR/C/SR.1856.

Human Rights Committee, *Summary Record of the 1738th meeting: Canada. 07/03/99 (Summary Record)*. CCPR/C/SR.1738.

Human Rights Committee, *The Rights of Minorities (Art. 27): 08/04/94. CCPR General Comment 23. (General Comments)*. CCPR/C/21/Rev.1/Add.5.

Human Rights Committee, *The Right to Self-determination of Peoples (Art. 1): 13/03/84. CCPR General Comment 12. (General Comments) 1984*. HRI/GEN/1/Rev.1, 12 (1994).

Human Rights Council, *Report of the Special Rapporteur on the Situation of Human Rights and Fundamental Freedoms of Indigenous People*. A/HRC/6/15.

Human Rights Council, *Report of the Working Group on Indigenous Populations on its Twenty-fourth Session*. A/HRC/Sub.1/58/22.

Hudson, P. and McKenzie, B. (2003). 'Extending Aboriginal Control Over Child Welfare Services – The Manitoba Child Welfare Initiative', *Canadian Review of Social Policy*, 51: 49.

Hylton, J. (ed.) (1994). *Aboriginal Self-government in Canada: Current Trends and Issues*. Saskatoon: Purich Publishing.

Ibhawoh, B. (2000). 'Between Culture and Constitution: Evaluating the Cultural Legitimacy of Human Rights in the African State', *Human Rights Quarterly*, 22: 838.

Ibhawoh, B. (2001). 'Cultural Relativism and Human Rights: Reconsidering the Africanist Discourse', *Netherlands Quarterly of Human Rights*, 19: 43.

Imai, S. (2003). 'Sound Science, Careful Policy Analysis, and Ongoing Relationships: Integrating Litigation and Negotiation in Aboriginal Lands and Resources Disputes', *Osgoode Hall Law Journal*, 41: 587.

Imai, S. (2009). 'Indigenous Self-Determination and the State', in B. Richardson, S. Imai and K. McNeil (eds) *Indigenous Peoples and the Law. Comparative and Critical Perspectives*. Portland: Hart Publishing, 285.

Inquiry into Response by Government Agencies to Complaints of Family Violence and Child Abuse in Aboriginal Communities (2002). *Putting the Picture Together*. State Law Publisher, Western Australia.

Jackson, M. (1988). *Locking Up Natives in Canada: Report to the Canadian Bar Association Committee on Imprisonment and Release*. Ottawa: Canadian Bar Association.

Kamenka, E. (1988). 'Human Rights, Peoples' Rights', in J. Crawford (ed.) *The Rights of Peoples*. Oxford: Clarendon, 127.

Kilbourne, S. (1998). 'The Wayward Americans – Why the USA Has Not Ratified the UN Convention on the Rights of the Child', *Child and Family Law Quarterly*, 10: 243.

Kimelman, E. (1985). *Manitoba Review Committee on Indian and Metis Adoptions and Placements, No Quiet Place, The Final Report to the Hon. Muriel Smith, Minister of Community Services*. Winnipeg: Manitoba Community Services.

Kingsbury, B. (1998). '"Indigenous Peoples" in International Law: A Constructivist Approach to the Asian Controversy', *American Journal of International Law*, 92: 414.

Kline, M. (1992). 'Child Welfare Law, "Best Interests of the Child" Ideology and First Nations', *Osgoode Hall Law Journal*, 30: 375.

Kline, M. (1995). 'Complicating the Ideology of Motherhood: Child Welfare Law and First Nations Women', in M. Fineman and I. Karpin (eds) *Mothers in Law: Feminist Theory and the Legal Regulation of Motherhood*. New York: Columbia University Press, 118.

Koshan, J. (1998). 'Aboriginal Women, Justice and the Charter: Bridging the Divide?', *UBC Law Review*, 32(1): 23.

Krosenbrink-Gelissen, L. E. (1991). *Sexual Equality as an Aboriginal Right. The Native Women's Association of Canada and the Constitutional Process on Aboriginal Matters 1982–1987*. Nijmeegs Instituut voor Comparatieve Cultuur – en Ontwikkelingsstudies.

Kuptana, R. (1991). *No More Secrets: Acknowledging the Problem of Child Sexual Abuse in Inuit Communities: The First Step Towards Healing*. Ottawa: Pauktuuit.

Kymlicka, W. (1991). *Liberalism, Community and Culture*. Oxford: Clarendon Press.

Kymlicka, W. (1999). 'Review: Theorizing Indigenous Rights', *University of Toronto Law Journal*, 49: 281.

LaPrairie, C. (1988). 'The Young Offenders Act and Aboriginal Youth', in J. Hudson, J. Hornick and B. Burrows (eds) *Justice and the Young Offender in Canada*. Toronto: Wall and Thompson, 159.

LaPrairie, C. (1992). 'Aboriginal Crime and Justice. Explaining the Present, Exploring the Future', *Canadian Journal of Criminology*, 34: 281.

LaPrairie, C. (1995). 'Conferencing in Aboriginal Communities in Canada: Finding Middle Ground in Criminal Justice', *Criminal Law Forum*, 6: 576.

Luther, E. (2010). 'Whose "'Distinctive Culture"? Aboriginal Feminism and *R. v. Van der Peet*', *Indigenous Law Journal*, 8: 27.

Lynch, P. (2001). 'Keeping them Home: The Best Interests of Indigenous Children and Communities in Canada and Australia', *Sydney Law Review*, 23: 501.

MacDonald, J. (1983). 'The Spallumcheen Indian By-Law and Its Potential Impact on Native Indian Child Welfare Policy in British Columbia', *Canadian Journal of Family Law*, 1: 75.

MacDonald, J. (1985). 'Child Welfare and the Native Indian Peoples of Canada', *Windsor Yearbook of Access to Justice*, 5: 284.

Mackenzie Valley Pipeline Inquiry (1977). *Northern Frontier, Northern Homeland. The Report of the Mackenzie Valley Pipeline Inquiry*. Toronto: James Lorimer; Ottawa: Supply and Services Canada.

Macklem, P. (1991). 'First Nations, Self-Government and the Borders of the Canadian Legal Imagination', *McGill Law Journal*, 36: 382.

Macklem, P. (1996). 'Normative Dimensions on the Right of Aboriginal Self-Government', in Royal Commission on Aboriginal Peoples, *Aboriginal Self-government. Legal and Constitutional Issues*. Ottawa: Ministry of Supply and Services, Canada.

Makinson, D. (1988). 'Rights of Peoples: A Logician's Point of View', in J. Crawford (ed.) *The Rights of Peoples*. Oxford: Clarendon, 69.

Manitoba Family Services and Housing (2007). *Annual Report 2006–07*. Available at: www.gov.mb.ca/fs/about/annual_reports/2006-07/annual_2006-07.pdf.

Marks, G. (2000). 'Sovereign States v Peoples: Indigenous Rights and the Origins of International Law', *Australian Indigenous Law Reporter*, 5: 1.

Martinez, Miguel, Special Rapporteur, *Study on Treaties, Agreements and Other Constructive Arrangements between States and Indigenous Populations. Second Progress Report Submitted by Mr. Miguel Alfonso Martinez, Special Rapporteur*. E/CN.4/Sub.2/1995/27.

Martinez, Miguel, Special Rapporteur, Economic and Social Council, *Study on Treaties, Agreements and Other Constructive Arrangements between States and Indigenous Populations, Third Progress Report Submitted by Mr Miguel Alfonso Martinez, Special Rapporteur*. E/CN.4/Sub.2/1996/23.

Martinez, Miguel, Special Rapporteur, *Study on Treaties, Agreements and Other Constructive Arrangements between States and Indigenous Populations. Final Report by Miguel Alfonso Martínez, Special Rapporteur*. E/CN.4/Sub.2/1999/20.

McCaskill, D. (1985). *Patterns of Criminality and Correction Among Native Young Offenders in Manitoba: A Longitudinal Analysis*. Ottawa: Correctional Services of Canada.

McCorquodale, R. (1994). 'Self-Determination: A Human Rights Approach', *International and Comparative Law Quarterly*, 43: 856.

McCorquodale, R. and Pangalangan, R. (2001). 'Pushing Back the Limitations of Territorial Boundaries', *European Journal of International Law*, 12: 867.

McEvoy, J. (2007). 'Aboriginal Activities and Aboriginal Rights: A Comment on *R v Sappier; R v Gray*', *Indigenous Law Journal*, 6: 1.

McGillivray, A. (1985). 'Transracial Adoption and the Status Indian Child', *Canadian Journal of Family Law*, 4: 437.

McGillivray, A. (1997). 'Therapies of Freedom: The Colonization of Aboriginal Childhood', in A. McGillivray (ed.) *Governing Childhood*. Aldershot: Dartmouth, 135.

McGillivray, A. and Comaskey, B. (1999). *Black Eyes All of the Time. Intimate Violence, Aboriginal Women and the Justice System*. Toronto: University of Toronto Press.

McKenzie, B. and Hudson, P. (1985). 'Native Children, Child Welfare and the Colonization of Native People' in K. L. Levitt and B. Wharf (eds) *The Challenge of Child Welfare*. Vancouver: University of British Columbia, 125.

McNeil, K. (1988). 'The Constitution Act 1982, Sections 25 and 35', *Canadian Native Law Reporter*, 1: 1.

McNeil, K. (2000). 'Aboriginal Title and Section 88 of the Indian Act'. *UBC Law Review*, 34: 159.

McNeil, K. (2004). 'The Vulnerability of Indigenous Land Rights in Australia and Canada', *Osgoode Hall Law Journal*, 42: 271.

Miller, J. R. (1996). *Shingwauk's Vision – A History of Native Residential Schools*. Toronto: University of Toronto Press.

Milloy, J. S. (1999). *'A National Crime' – The Canadian Government and the Residential School System, 1879 to 1986*. Winnipeg: The University of Manitoba Press.

Ministry of Aboriginal Affairs (2005). *Ontario's New Approach to Aboriginal Affairs*. Queen's Printer for Ontario.

Monture, P. (1989). 'A Vicious Circle: Child Welfare and the First Nations', *Canadian Journal of Women and the Law*, 3: 1.

Monture-Angus, P. (1999). *Journeying Forward. Dreaming of First Nations Independence*. Halifax, NS: Fernwood Publishing.

Morse, B. (1980). 'Indian and Innuit Family Law and the Canadian Legal System', *American Indian Law Review*, 8: 199.

Moss, W. (1990). 'Indigenous Self-government and Sexual Equality under the Indian Act', *Queen's L.J.*, 15: 279.

Mutua, M. (1996). 'The Ideology of Human Rights', *Virginia Journal of International Law*, 36: 589.

Mutua, M. (2001). 'Savages, Victims and Saviors: The Metaphor of Human Rights', *Harvard International Law Journal*, 42: 201.

Nahanee, T. (1996). 'Dancing with a Gorilla: Aboriginal Women, Justice and the Charter', in *Royal Commission on Aboriginal Peoples, Round Table Discussion on Justice Issues*. Ottawa: Minister of Supply and Services, Canada, 359.

Northern Territory Government (2007). *Board of Inquiry into the Protection of Aboriginal Children from Sexual Abuse*. Darwin, NT: Government Printer.

NWT Health and Social Services (2004). *Annual Report of the Director of Child and Family Services – 2001/02*.

Obata, K. and Lee, J. (2010). 'Languages of Aboriginal and Torres Strait Islander Peoples – A Uniquely Australian Heritage', *Year Book of Australia 2009–10*, Australian Bureau of Statistics. Available at: www.abs.gov.au/ausstats/abs@.nsf/Latestproducts/1301.0Feature%20Article42009–10?opendocument&tabname=Summary&prodno=1301.0&issue=2009–10&num=&view=.

Office of the Chief Medical Examiner (1992). *The Fatalities Inquiries Act – Respecting the Death of Lester Norman Desjarlais*. Brandon: Ministry of Social Services and Housing.

Office of the High Commissioner for Human Rights (2001). *Leaflet 1: Indigenous Peoples and the UN System: An Overview*. Available at: www.ohchr.org/Documents/Publications/GuideIPleaflet1en.pdf.

Ontario Ministry of Aboriginal Affairs (2005). *Ontario's New Approach to Aboriginal Affairs*. Queen's Printer for Ontario. Available at: www.aboriginalaffairs.gov.on.ca/english/policy/newapproach/newapproach.pdf.

Organization for Security and Co-operation in Europe, *Conference on Co-operation and Security in Europe, Final Act, Helsinki 1975*. Available at: www.osce.org/mc/39501.

Patrick Glenn, H. (2011). 'The Three Ironies of the UN Declaration on the Rights of Indigenous Peoples', in S. Allen and A. Xanthaki (eds) *Reflections on the UN Declaration on the Rights of Indigenous Peoples*. Oxford: Hart, 171.

Pentney, W. (1987). 'The Rights of the Aboriginal Peoples of Canada and the Constitution Act, 1982. Part I. The Interpretive Prism of Section 25', *UBC Law Review*, 22: 21.

Pentney, W. (1987). 'The Rights of the Aboriginal Peoples of Canada in the Constitution Act, 1982. Part II. Section 35: the Substantive Guarantee', *UBC Law Review*, 22: 207.

Perry, M. (1997). 'Are Human Rights Universal? The Relativist Challenge and Related Matters', *Human Rights Quarterly*, 19: 461.

Pollis, A. (1998). 'Towards a New Universalism: Reconstruction and Dialogue', *Netherlands Quarterly of Human Rights*, 16: 5.

Pollis, A. and Schwab, P. (1979). 'Human Rights: A Western Construct with Limited Applicability', in A. Pollis and P. Schwab (eds) *Human Rights: Cultural and Ideological Perspectives*. New York: Praeger Publishers, 1.

Quane, H. (1998). 'The United Nations and the Evolving Right to Self-Determination', *International and Comparative Law Quarterly*, 47: 537.

Quane, H. (2011). 'The UN Declaration on the Rights of Indigenous Peoples: New Directions for Self-Determination and Participatory Rights?', in S. Allen and A. Xanthaki (eds) *Reflections on the UN Declaration on the Rights of Indigenous Peoples*. Oxford: Hart, 259.

Rae, J. (2009). 'Program Delivery Devolution: A Stepping Stone or Quagmire for First Nations?', *Indigenous Law Journal*, 7: 1.

Ralph, S. (1998). 'The Best Interests of the Aboriginal Child', *Australian Journal of Family Law*, 12: 140.

Rich, R. (1988). 'The Right to Development: A Right of Peoples', in J. Crawford (ed.) *The Rights of Peoples*. Oxford: Clarendon, 39.

Royal Commission into Aboriginal Deaths in Custody (c. 1991). *National Report*, Vol. 2. Canberra: Australian Govt. Pub. Service.

Royal Commission into Aboriginal Deaths in Custody (c. 1991). *National Report*, Vol. 4. Canberra: Australian Govt. Pub. Service.

Royal Commission on Aboriginal Peoples (1992). *The Right of Aboriginal Self-Government and the Constitution: A Commentary*. Ottawa: Minister of Supply and Services.

Royal Commission on Aboriginal Peoples (1996). *Bridging the Cultural Divide. A Report on Aboriginal People and Criminal Justice in Canada*. Ottawa: Minister of Supply and Services, Canada.

Royal Commission on Aboriginal Peoples (1996). *Report of the Royal Commission on Aboriginal Peoples. Looking Forward Looking Back*. Part One, Vol. 1. Ottawa: Minister of Supply and Services, Canada.

Royal Commission on Aboriginal Peoples (1996). *Report of the Royal Commission on Aboriginal Peoples. Restructuring the Relationship*. Part One, Vol. 2. Ottawa: Minister of Supply and Services, Canada.

Royal Commission on Aboriginal Peoples (1996). *Report of the Royal Commission on Aboriginal Peoples. Gathering Strength*. Part One, Vol. 3. Ottawa: Minister of Supply and Services, Canada.

Royal Commission on Aboriginal Peoples (1996). *Report of the Royal Commission on Aboriginal Peoples. Perspectives and Realities*. Part One, Vol. 4. Ottawa: Minister of Supply and Services, Canada.

Ryder, B. (1991). 'Demise and Rise of the Classical Paradigm in Canadian Federalism: Promoting Autonomy for the Provinces and First Nations', *McGill Law Journal*, 36: 309.

Samuels, H. (1999). 'Hong Kong on Women, Asian Values and the Law', *Human Rights Quarterly*, 21: 707.

Sanders, D. (1993). 'Self-Determination and Indigenous Peoples', in C. Tomuschat (ed.) *Modern Law of Self-determination*. Dordrecht and London: Martinus Nijhoff Publishers, 55.

Saskatchewan Department of Community Resources (2007). *2007–08, Saskatchewan Provincial Budget – Performance Plan. Saskatchewan Community Resources*. Available at: www.socialservices.gov.sk.ca/cr-performance07-08.pdf.

Sinclair, M., Philips, D. and Bala, N. (1991). 'Aboriginal Child Welfare in Canada', in N. Bala, J. Hornick and R. Vogl (eds) *Canadian Child Welfare – Children, Families and the State*. Toronto: Thompson Educational Publications, 171.

Slattery, B. (1982–1983). 'The Constitutional Guarantee of Aboriginal and Treaty Rights', *Queens Law Journal*, 8: 232.

Slattery, B. (1992). 'First Nations and the Constitution: A Question of Trust', *Canadian Bar Review*, 71: 261.

Smith, M. (1995). *Our Home or Native Land? What Government's Aboriginal Policy is doing to Canada*. Victoria, BC: Crown Western.

Sommerlad, E. (1977). 'Aboriginal Children in the Aboriginal Community: Changing Practices in Adoption', *Australian Journal of Social Issues*, 12.

Stavenhagen, Rodolfo, *Report of the Special Rapporteur on the Situation of Human Rights and Fundamental Freedoms of Indigenous People, Mr Rodolfo Stavenhagen, Submitted Pursuant to Commission Resolution 2001/57*. E/CN.4/2002/97.

Stuart, C. (1982/1983). 'Cross-cultural Treatment for Native Children: A Point from which to Begin', *Journal of Child Law*, 1.

Taylor, C. (1992). 'Multiculturalism and the "Politics of Recognition": An Essay', in A. Gutmann (ed.) *Multiculturalism*. Princeton: Princeton University Press.

Teson, F. (1985). 'International Human Rights and Cultural Relativism', *Virginia Journal of International Law*, 25: 869.

Thornberry, P. (1989). 'Self-determination, Minorities, Human Rights: A Review of International Instruments', *International and Comparative Law Quarterly*, 38: 867.

Thornberry, P. (2002). *Indigenous Peoples and Human Rights*. Manchester: Manchester University Press.

Tiffin, H. (1995). 'Post-Colonial Literature and Counter-Discourse', in B. Ashcroft, G. Griffiths and H. Tiffin (eds) *The Post-Colonial Studies Reader*. London: Routledge, 95.

Tilley, J. (2000). 'Cultural Relativism', *Human Rights Quarterly*, 22: 501.

Tomuschat, C. (1993). 'Self-Determination in a Post-Colonial World', in C. Tomuschat (ed.) *Modern Law of Self-Determination*. Dordrecht: Martinus Nijhoff, 1.

Toope, S. (1991). 'Riding the Fences: Courts, Charter Rights and Family Law', *Canadian Journal of Family Law*, 9: 57.

Triggs, G. (1988). 'The Rights of Peoples and Individual Rights: Conflict or Harmony?', in J. Crawford (ed.) *The Rights of Peoples*. Oxford: Clarendon, 141.

Turpel, M. E. (1989–1990). 'Aboriginal Peoples and the Canadian Charter: Interpretative Monopolies, Cultural Differences', *Canadian Human Rights Yearbook*, 6: 3.

Turpel, M. E. (1992). 'Aboriginal Peoples and the Canadian Charter of Rights and Freedoms: Contradictions and Challenges', in J. Banfield (ed.) *Readings in Law and Society*. Concord: Captus Press.

Vienna Declaration and Programme of Action. A/CONF.157/23.

Victorian Indigenous Family Violence Task Force (2003), *Final Report*. Available at: www.cyf.vic.gov.au/__data/assets/pdf_file/0006/16782/vic-indigenous-family-violence-task-force-report-2003-main.pdf.

Voyiakis, E. (2011). 'Voting in the General Assembly as Evidence of Customary International Law', in S. Allen and A. Xanthaki (eds) *Reflections on the UN Declaration on the Rights of Indigenous Peoples*. Oxford: Hart, 209.

White, L. and Jacobs, E. (1992). *Liberating Our Children Liberating Our Nations, Report of the Aboriginal Committee, Community Panel Child Protection Legislation Review in British Columbia*. British Columbia: Queen's Printer.

Wilkins, K. (1999). 'But We Need the Eggs: The Royal Commission, the Charter of Rights and the Inherent Right of Aboriginal Self-government', *University of Toronto Law Journal*, 49: 53.

World Conference against Racism, Racial Discrimination, Xenophobia and Related Intolerance, *Declaration*. Available at: www.un.org/WCAR/durban.pdf.

World Summit on Sustainable Development, *Johannesburg Declaration*, 2–4 September 2002. Available at: www.un.org/esa/sustdev/documents/WSSD_POI_PD/English/POI_PD.htm.

Wright, S. (2001). *International Human Rights, Decolonisation and Globalisation. Becoming Human*. London: Routledge.

Xanthaki, A. (2005). 'The Right to Self-Determination: Meaning and Scope', in N. Ghanea and A. Xanthaki (eds) *Minorities, Peoples, and Self-Determination*. Leiden: Martinus Nijhoff, 15.

Xanthaki, A. (2007). *Indigenous Rights and United Nations Standards: Self-Determination, Culture and Land*. Cambridge: Cambridge University Press.

Xanthaki, A. (2010). 'Multiculturalism and International Law: Discussing Universal Standards', *Human Rights Quarterly*, 32: 21.

Xanthaki, A. (2011). 'The UN Declaration on the Rights of Indigenous Peoples and Collective Rights: What's the Future for Indigenous Women?', in S. Allen and A. Xanthaki (eds) *Reflections on the UN Declaration on the Rights of Indigenous Peoples*. Oxford: Hart, 413.

Index

For Product Safety Concerns and Information please contact our EU representative GPSR@taylorandfrancis.com
Taylor & Francis Verlag GmbH, Kaufingerstraße 24, 80331 München, Germany

www.ingramcontent.com/pod-product-compliance
Ingram Content Group UK Ltd.
Pitfield, Milton Keynes, MK11 3LW, UK
UKHW022009180926
475701UK00003B/275
9781138261082